LONGER PLAYS

BY MODERN AUTHORS

(AMERICAN)

EDITED BY

HELEN LOUISE COHEN, Ph.D.

Chairman of the Department of English in the
Washington Irving High School in the
City of New York

Editor of "One-Act Plays by Modern Authors"

NEW YORK
HARCOURT, BRACE AND COMPANY

22-8426

PS
634
C6

PRINTED IN THE U. S. A. BY
THE QUINN & BODEN COMPANY
RAHWAY, N. J

To
M. S. S.

ACKNOWLEDGMENTS

That part of the Introduction which deals with the history of dramatic literature in the United States obviously owes much to the original studies of Brander Matthews, Professor of Dramatic Literature in Columbia University, and Member of the American Academy of Arts and Letters; to the research of Arthur Hobson Quinn, Dean of the College, University of Pennsylvania; and to the writings of Montrose J. Moses.

Besides referring gratefully to these authorities, the editor takes pleasure in thanking warmly Augustus Thomas, George S. Kaufman, Marc Connolly, and Booth Tarkington, whose plays are included in this volume. To the courtesy of Messrs. G. P. Putnam's Sons and Messrs. Little, Brown and Company respectively, the editor owes permission to use *Dulcy* and *Beau Brummell.* *The Copperhead* is here printed for the first time. *The Intimate Strangers,* just published in *Harper's Magazine,* has never appeared in book form before.

The editor is again indebted to Helen Hopkins Crandell for her faithful work on the proofs of this book.

CONTENTS

PREFACE

Longer Plays by Modern Authors (*American*) is a companion volume to the same editor's *One-Act Plays by Modern Authors*. Both collections have been undertaken with the aim of furnishing material for the study of modern drama in the class room. The value of such study is now so generally recognized that the latest reading list of the College Entrance Examination Board actually includes two modern plays. This requirement, if properly satisfied, will prepare students who are going on to college to enjoy the opportunities open to them for enlarging their acquaintance with the best writing of contemporary dramatists. But it seems to many progressive teachers of English even more important to give to that larger group whose formal education will come to an end with their years in high school, such familiarity with the modern theatre as will lead the young worker to find both in the printed and in the acted play diversion, solace, and inspiration.

The introductory material in this volume is confined to a brief historical survey of the annals of drama in America. The four plays included are provided also with biographical and critical commentary. For material on the new art of the theatre, the theatres of to-day, dramatic technique, and playwriting, teachers and students are referred to the introduction of *One-Act Plays by Modern Authors*.

The work of American playwrights only is included in this volume because by means of this anthology of longer modern plays, probably the first to be made for use in high schools, it is hoped that the cause of American drama may be well served. This result cannot fail to be secured if the plays in this book are used by the instructor for the purpose of training discriminating audiences and of stimulating in the youth of America a patriotic concern for the welfare of the native drama.

H. L. C.

Washington Irving High School,
New York, 1 March, 1922.

DRAMA IN AMERICA

AN INTRODUCTION

The four plays in this volume have, with one exception, been written and produced since 1918. *Beau Brummell* alone has attained the dignity of years. And yet, because it lacks what is commonly called "structure," Clyde Fitch's comedy of over three decades ago is astonishingly modern in method. Its subject marks it as belonging to the succession of romantic plays that has been unbroken since the eighteenth century. *The Copperhead,* though of more recent date than *Beau Brummell,* somewhat resembles in workmanship the Civil War melodramas of the eighties and nineties of the last century. In theme, *The Copperhead* is aligned with plays on kindred subjects that began to be written during the conflict between the Colonies and England and followed the trail of American history through the difficulties with the Barbary States, the War of 1812, the Mexican War and the Civil War. *Dulcy,* with its penetrating study of American business men and its deadly characterization of a droll feminine type, and *The Intimate Strangers,* with its wise and humorous reflections on the youngest generation, are in a sense similar in motive to the social satires which, beginning with *The Contrast,* have appeared from time to time on our stage.

Though the acted play can be exhaustively studied only in New York, now admittedly the center of theatrical activity in the United States, the vogue of the printed play shows how general and how extended is an intelligent interest in the theatre. A collection like the present one is made in the interests of a widely distributed reading public. The growth of this public is more or less coincident with a dramatic revival that took place in England and in America about forty years ago. As Brander Matthews has recently observed: "The drama of our language . . . underwent an eclipse in the midyears of the nineteenth century. There was then a divorce between literature and the drama so complete that the plays that were actable were unreadable and the plays which were readable were unactable. But a little more than forty years ago there were signs of a reconciliation. The theatre began to regain its old popularity, and plays once more were published in the hope that the verdict of the stage might be confirmed by the judgment of the study."

It has been said more than once by competent critics that there was no American drama till it was founded in 1890 by Clyde Fitch. But Bronson Howard came before Clyde Fitch, and plays have been written and acted in the United States ever since the years following the close of the French and Indian Wars. *The Prince of Parthia,* a romantic tragedy in blank verse, was performed in 1767 in Philadelphia. This was the first American play to be acted by professionals. It was composed by a young poet, Thomas Godfrey. He had been a pupil of William Smith, Provost of the College of Philadelphia, later the University of Pennsylvania, the scene in the mid-eighteenth century of sundry masques, dialogues and entertainments of a quasi-dramatic character. These academic exercises, together with the presence of a company of professional actors in Philadelphia, are supposed to have quickened Godfrey's impulse to write his tragedy.

The scene of his play is laid in Parthia about 200 B.C. The plot suggests, in the pairing off of its characters, the artificial symmetry of classical French tragedy as popularized by various English dramatists of the seventeenth and eighteenth centuries, and, in its machinery of murders and supernatural horrors, the familiar mechanisms of the Elizabethan tragedy of blood. The lines,

> "E'en the pale dead, affrighted at the hour,
> As tho' unsafe, start from their marble goals,
> And howling thro' the streets are seeking shelter,"

call up the familiar lines to a similar effect in *Julius Cæsar,*

> "And graves have yawned and yielded up their dead;
> And ghosts did shriek and squeal about the streets."

A fair sample of the quality of Godfrey's play is to be found in the lines of Lysias, spoken as a soliloquy within the precincts of a prison:

> "The Sun sets frowning, and refreshing Eve
> Lost all its sweets, obscur'd in double gloom.

> This night shall sleep be stranger to these eyes,
> Peace dwells not here, and slumber flies the shock;
> My spirits, like the elements, are warring,
> And mock the tempest with a kindred rage—
> I, who can joy in nothing, but revenge,
> Know not those boasted ties of Love and Friendship;
> *Vardanes* I regard, but as he give me
> Some hopes of vengeance on the Prince *Arsaces*—
> 'Tis to my wish, thus would I form designs,
> Horror should breed beneath the veil of horror,
> And darkness and conspiracies—"

This passage is hardly distinguishable in intent, at any rate, from many similar speeches in the sixteenth century tragedy of revenge, a type transcendently represented by *Hamlet*.

Twenty years elapsed before Royall Tyler's comedy of manners, *The Contrast,* was acted in New York by a group of professionals who called themselves the " Old American Company." This period was something of an interregnum for American playwrights. The lull in dramatic activity was partly the result of a recommendation, passed by the Continental Congress in its Articles of Association, that the Colonists " discountenance and discourage all horse racing and all kinds of gaming, cock fighting, exhibitions of shows, plays and other expensive diversions and entertainments." [1] But the British officers quartered in the Colonies during the Revolutionary War seem to have been devoted to theatricals. They are in no small measure responsible for keeping alive the interest in the theatre during the years between Lexington and Yorktown. General Burgoyne's staff presented a succession of English plays at Faneuil Hall in Boston. A farce, called *The Blockade of Boston,* that may well have been written by Burgoyne himself, was among the pieces attempted in the historic hall. When it was produced on January 8, 1776, its performance was interrupted and the theatre emptied by the news of the attack on Bunker Hill. Major André also, the tragedy of whose life was soon to be the subject of a number of early American plays, was notable as a moving spirit in army theatricals, first in New York and later in Boston. He supplemented his activities as playwright and manager by painting sets of scenes, one of which was in existence till 1821 when the Southwark Theatre in Philadelphia was burned. In Percy

[1] Arthur Hobson Quinn, *The Early Drama,* 1756-1860, *Cambridge History of American Literature,* New York, 1917, Vol. 1, p. 217.

MacKaye's ballad play, *Washington the Man Who Made Us*, acted in 1920 by Walter Hampden, the foremost Shakespearian actor of the present day in America, an engaging picture of Major André's activities in the theatre is given.

Two years before the British finally took their leave, in spite of the recommendations of the Continental Congress there was a revival of theatrical activity of a professional character in the playhouses of Baltimore, Annapolis, and New York. The first American comedy to be acted by a professional company in the post-Revolutionary period was *The Contrast* by Royall Tyler (1757-1826), shown at the John Street Theatre in New York in 1787. Tyler, a New Englander, came to New York as an aide to Major-General Benjamin Lincoln, to help put down Shay's Rebellion. While in the city he visited a theatre for the first time and saw Sheridan's *The School for Scandal*. Two days later he began his own comedy of manners and finished it in a few weeks. When the play was published in 1790 by the actor Thomas Wignell, who created the part of Jonathan, and to whom Tyler had turned over the copyright, the first name on the list of subscribers was George Washington's.[1]

The theme of the play is not unlike the central idea of a recent comedy, Tarkington and Wilson's *The Man from Home*. There is, of course, no similarity at all in the plot or characters. In both plays, however, the "contrast" between a certain fine native dignity and an artificiality conventionally associated with foreigners and foreign importations is played up. The most important character in *The Contrast* from the viewpoint of dramatic history is the servant, Jonathan, who is the first of a long line of stage Yankees.

There is an undoubtedly autobiographical flavor in the dialogue which takes place between Tyler's Jonathan and a fellow servant, in which the Yankee's reaction to his first play-going experience is embodied:

"JENNY.   So, Mr. Jonathan, I hear you were at the play last night.
JONATHAN.   At the play! why, did you think I went to the devil's drawing-room!
JENNY.   The devil's drawing-room!

[1] See *The Contrast*. A Comedy in Five Acts, by Royall Tyler, with a history of George Washington's copy by James Benjamin Wilbur. Boston and New York, 1921.

JONATHAN. Yes; why an't cards and dice the devil's device, and the play-house the shop where the devil hangs out the vanities of the world upon the tenter-hooks of temptation. I believe you have not heard how they were acting the old boy, one night, and the wicked one came among them sure enough, and went right off in a storm, and carried one quarter of the play-house with him. Oh! no, no, no! You won't catch me at a play-house, I warrant you.

.   .   .   .   .   .

JONATHAN. So I went right in, and they showed me away, clean up to the garret, just like meeting house gallery. And so I saw a power of topping folks, all sitting around in little cabins, 'just like father's corn-cribs'; and then there was such a squeaking with the fiddles, and such a tarnal blaze with the lights, my head was near turned."

William Dunlap (1766-1839) is called for reasons hereafter to be catalogued the Father of the American Theatre. He is believed to have been incited to dramatic composition by the success of his slightly older contemporary, Royall Tyler. Dunlap is credited with writing sixty-five plays, some of them adaptations from French and German originals. His connection with the theatre was not confined to play writing: he was for nine years a manager, and toward the end of his life he wrote his *History of the American Theatre*. His tragedy, *André*, performed in New York in 1798, was the first play acted in the United States during Washington's lifetime in which the latter figured as a character. André himself proved to be a favorite character in early American plays. In Dunlap's *André*, Washington is introduced simply as General. His righteous indignation is restrained by the mild-mannered blank verse in which the play is written:

" Think'st thou thy country would not curse the man,
Who, by a clemency ill-tim'd, ill-judg'd,
Encourag'd treason? That *pride* encourag'd,
Which, by denying us the rights of nations,
Hath caused those ills which thou hast now pourtray'd?
Our prisoners, brave and generous peasantry,
As rebels have been treated, not as man.
'Tis mine, brave yeomen, to assert your rights;
'Tis mine to teach the foe, that, though array'd
In rude simplicity, ye yet are men,
And rank among the foremost. Oft their scouts,
The very refuse of the English arms,
Unquestion'd have our countrymen consign'd
To death, when captured, mocking their agonies."

Dunlap is also remembered by students of American literature as the friend and biographer of the novelist Charles Brockden Brown.

The connection of Washington Irving, another one of our first men of letters, with early American drama is quite direct. He is known to have collaborated with John Howard Payne (1791-1852), author of " Home, Sweet Home," in more than one play. *Charles II,* first performed in London in 1824, was their joint venture. " In *The Life and Letters of Washington Irving,* by Pierre Irving (1883), an account is given of Irving's sending the manuscript to Payne in November, 1823, after having revised it and added to it some new ideas. The idea of ' Captain Copp ' constantly trying to sing a song and never being able to complete it, was conceived by Irving to meet the English taste for broad fun. In the introduction by Payne in the edition of 1824 he refers to the literary friend to whom he is ' indebted for invaluable touches.' " [1]

The subjects treated by American playwrights up to the end of the nineteenth century fall for the most part into six categories: the Indians and frontier life; our wars; idiosyncrasies of American character; New York life; American society satirically treated; and the romance of other lands or other times or both. For thirty years or more, American plays have, owing to new European influences and native genius, become so diversified in theme and treatment that the fallacy of describing American drama as a continuous development becomes plain. The topics enumerated continue nevertheless to be popular in our theatre.

Indian plays began to be written for our stage in 1794. Pocahontas herself figured often in these dramatic versions of the ideal Indian, the noble red man of Cooper's imaginings. It is interesting to compare the simplicity of characterization in James W. Barker's (1784-1858) *The Indian Princess* (1808) with the characterization based on intimate observation in Mary Austin's *The Arrow Maker* (1910). In the Indian plays of the early nineteenth century, of which Barker's is typical, there is practically no attempt to present the customs, folk lore or psychology of the American Indian. Bar-

[1] Arthur Hobson Quinn, *Representative American Plays,* New York, 1917, p. 144.

ker's Indian princess, to turn to matters of form, speaks in prose, unrhythmic and unimaginative. At a moment, when with Captain John Smith's head actually inclined to the block, her words might be surcharged with emotion, she delivers herself as follows:

"Oh, do not, warriors, do not! Father, incline your heart to mercy; he will win your battles, he will vanquish your enemies! [*First Signal*] Brother, speak! save your brother! Warriors, are you brave? preserve the brave man! [*Second Signal*] Miami, priest, sing the song of peace; ah! strike not, hold! mercy!"

The blank verse of Barker's English characters hardly lifts the play above the level of this prose.[1]

The most popular of the early Indian plays was *Metamora or the Last of the Wampanoags* (1829), by John Augustus Stone, only an unprinted fragment of which survives in manuscript. This play had a career which lasted for ten years. The duration of its popularity is attributed to the distinguished acting of Edwin Forrest in the title rôle. Barker's *The Indian Princess* and Stone's *Metamora* are for our purpose sufficiently representative of the stage treatment of the literary Indian, which persisted well into the middle of the nineteenth century.

Collections of American plays made within the last few years as source books for the study of dramatic art contain only comparatively late examples of the frontier drama so closely allied in subject with plays about Indians. The first of these frontier dramas in point of time is *The Lion of the West* (1831), by James K. Spaulding, which introduced the famous character of Colonel Nimrod Wildfire, a prototype of several generations of backwoods heroes. Augustin Daly, one of the foremost American managers of the last generation, produced, in 1871, another outstanding play of this character called *Horizon,* which ran for two months. Frank Murdock's *Davy Crockett* (1873), also a study of frontier life, was pronounced by Laurence Hutton in 1891 to be "almost

[1] Barker's play, *Superstition* (1824), resumes the seventeenth century English fashion of using witchcraft as material for drama. Here again there is opportunity for comparison between the early nineteenth century treatment of the theme and Percy MacKaye's *The Scarecrow* (1910).

the best American play ever written. A pure sylvan love-story, told in a healthful, dramatic way, it is a poem in four acts; not perfect in form, open to criticism with faults of construction, failings of plots, slight improbabilities, sensational situations, and literary shortcomings, but so simple and so touching and so pure that it is worthy to rank with any of the creations of the modern stage in any language. The character of Davy Crockett, the central figure, is beautifully and artistically drawn: a strong brave young hunter of the Far West; bold but unassuming; gentle but with a strong will; skilled in woodcraft but wholly ignorant of the ways of the civilized world he had never seen; capable of great love and of great sacrifice for his love's sake; shy, sensitive and proud; unable to read or to write; utterly unconscious of his own physical beauty and of his own heroism; faithful, honest, truthful—in short a natural gentleman." [1] Such later plays as Augustus Thomas's *Arizona* (1899) and *In Mizzoura* (1893) and David Belasco's *The Girl of the Golden West* (1905) may also be thought of as belonging to the category of frontier drama. William Vaughn Moody's *The Great Divide* (1906) represents the highest achievement of the native dramatist in the treatment of this theme. Plays of frontier life continue to be popular on the boards. One of the popular successes of the New York theatrical season of 1920-21 was Porter Emerson Brown's *The Bad Man,* the scene of which is laid on a cattle ranch near the Mexican border in Arizona.

Dunlap's *André,* already mentioned, is one of a number of plays that employed events of the Revolutionary War as their setting and their subject. New testimony to the persistent popularity of André's name is found in the revival in New York in February, 1922, of John Jay Chapman's *The Treason and Death of Benedict Arnold*. Summing up this aspect of American drama, Quinn writes: " Practically every great event from the Boston Tea Party to the Battle of Yorktown was dramatized. The treason of Arnold and André's capture was a favorite theme and it is to our credit that André usually is a heroic figure. Marion and Franklin were also favorites, but

[1] Laurence Hutton, *Curiosities of the American Stage,* New York, 1891, pp. 30-31.

everyone else runs a bad second to Washington so far as the stage is concerned." [1]

Though the list of characters includes no historic names, a representative play of the War of 1812 is *The Triumph at Plattsburg* (1830), by Richard Penn Smith (1799-1859). In two acts a conventional story is told with some humor of the marriage of an American girl to a British officer, and the complications arising therefrom. The dialect of a migrated Scotchman decks out the play with comic touches. How dependent the drama of English-speaking peoples has been since the days of Shakespeare's *Henry V* on the laughter produced by the dialectic difficulties of the Welshman, Frenchman, German, Scotchman, or Irishman, as the case may be!

Plays with a Civil War background or with the actual events of that struggle constituting an integral part of their plot have been common since the eighties of the last century. The leading motive in most of them has been the temporarily thwarted love of war-crossed couples whom fate and the dramatist have assigned to opposite sides of the Mason and Dixon line. Bronson Howard's *Shenandoah* (1889) marks the progress American playwrights were making in learning their craft. The contrast between the almost childish work of Richard Penn Smith, with its wandering story, and the neatly jointed plot of Howard's war drama is striking. The dialogue, too, of the American war play had grown in impressiveness. In Richard Harding Davis's [2] charming and delicate fiction, *The Princess Aline* (1896), we have the hero, to further his own suit, referring appreciatively to the situation embodied in these lines from *Shenandoah*:

"GERTRUDE. Your wound!

KERCHIVAL. Wound! I have no wound. You do love me! [*Seizing her hand.*]

GERTRUDE. Let me call the Surgeon, Kerchival.

KERCHIVAL. You can be of more service to me than he can. [*Detaining her. Very heavy sounds of the battle; she starts, listening.*] Never mind that! It's only a battle. You love me!"

[1] Arthur Hobson Quinn, *The Early Drama, 1756-1860, Cambridge History of American Literature*, New York, 1917, Vol. 1, p. 225.

[2] Richard Harding Davis himself belongs to the history of American drama; a list of his plays would include *The Galloper, The Dictator, The Yankee Consul,* and *Miss Civilization.*

Other popular plays written about Civil War incidents or consequences, to mention but a few, are William Gillette's *Held by the Enemy* (1886) and *Secret Service* (1896), Augustus Thomas's *Alabama* (1891), David Belasco's *The Heart of Maryland* (1895), James A. Herne's *Griffith Davenport* (1899), and Clyde Fitch's *Barbara Frietchie* of the same year. The effect of the Great War upon American drama cannot yet be calculated. The plays on the subject by native writers remembered by the average playgoer are *The Crowded Hour* (1918), by Edgar Selwyn and Channing Pollock, in which a scene at a telephone switchboard behind the lines invites comparison with the telegraph office scene in Gillette's *Secret Service;* James Forbes's *The Famous Mrs. Fair* (1919), which presents a not uncommon type of modern woman in the light of her reactions to war conditions; Booth Tarkington's *Clarence* (1919), the comedy in which arises from the dryly humorous response of the scientific temperament to army life and post-war employment conditions; and Gilbert Emery's *The Hero* (1921), in which the tragedy springs from irreconcilable conflicts in the character of the " hero."

At the present time there are comparatively few plays being written for the purpose of presenting the peculiarities of the typical American. The nearest approach in our current theatrical output to the character play popular in the early and middle years of the nineteenth century are productions like Alice Brown's *Children of Earth* (1915), Augustus Thomas's *Palmy Days* (1919), and Winchell Smith and Frank Bacon's *Lightnin'* (1918). The earliest Jonathan in Tyler's *The Contrast* had many successors, one of the best known being Jonathan Plowboy in *The Forest Rose* (1825), a " pastoral opera " by Samuel Woodworth, author of " The Old Oaken Bucket." Woodworth's Jonathan Plowboy " speaks a dialect that was then supposed to prevail among the less enlightened inhabitants of New England and especially of Connecticut. Jonathan, like all his kin, never supposes or thinks; he ' calculates ' or ' guesses.' Instead of asking he ' axes.' He finds ' an't ' more economical than ' is not.' He declares that ' he wouldn't sarve a negro so.' His favorite expletive is ' darn,' or for variety ' darnation ' used both as a noun and an adjective. His speech is full of homely comparisons pertaining to cows, pigs, etc. . . . His part in the plot . . . is not vital, his function being chiefly to provide comic realism." [1]

The part of Uncle Nat in *Shore Acres* (1892), written and acted by James A. Herne, continued the tradition of the American countryman with such added touches of artistry as lifted conventional characterization into the realm of realism. Herne's American portraits were the delight of the playgoers of a generation ago. Henry George, the eminent economist and publicist, expressed his enthusiasm for Uncle Nat in a well-known letter to Herne. " I cannot too much congratulate you," he wrote, " upon your success. You have done what you sought to do—made a play pure and noble that people will come to hear. You have taken the strength of realism and added to it the strength that comes from the wider truth that realism fails to see; and in the simple portrayal of homely life, touched a *universal* chord." [2]

Herne's plays have none of them appeared in print. Our knowledge of many other productions significant in the history of the stage in America comes to us also from the reminiscences of contemporaries or the records of descendants. These productions live in our records, because they offered rare opportunities to the character actors of their day. Solon Shingle, a Massachusetts type from *The People's Lawyer* (1839), by J. S. Jones; Judge Bardwell Slote, the low politician from *The Mighty Dollar* (1875), by Benjamin Woolf; Colonel Mulberry Sellers, the Southerner from the dramatization of Mark Twain and Charles Dudley Warner's *The Gilded Age* (1874); and Joshua Whitcomb from *The Old Homestead* (1885), are remembered because created severally by Charles Burke, W. J. Florence, John T. Raymond, and Denman Thompson, actors of charmed memory. Even the present generation knows that most popular of all American stage characters, Rip Van Winkle, from the play of the same name. Washington Irving's story was first dramatized in 1829. The version made famous in recent years by Joseph Jefferson (1829-

[1] Oral Sumner Coad: *The Plays of Samuel Woodworth, The Sewanee Review*, Sewanee, 1919, Vol. 27, p. 168.

[2] Quoted by Barrett H. Clark in *The British and American Drama of To-day*, New York, 1915, p. 232.

1905) is the cumulative work of many hands, including Jefferson's own.

To the fifth class of subjects that have been enumerated as most popular on the American stage belong the plays about New York life. Perhaps their nature can best be understood if we think of them as paralleling the topical interest of a contemporary play like Augustus Thomas's dramatization of the Chimmie Fadden stories of Edward W. Townsend, or the sentimental appeal of a piece such as Rida Johnson Young's *Little Old New York* (1920). It will be recalled by those who saw *Little Old New York,* which professed to reproduce the social life of the city a century ago, that the Volunteer Fire Department played an important part in accelerating the interest. In 1848, a play called *A Glance at New York,* the first of a numerous family of New York character plays that held the stage for the next thirty years, ran for twelve weeks in the city the life of which it described. It is said to have been a mere hodge-podge with no artistic merit of any kind, but it proved a success because of the acting of a certain F. S. Chanfrau who took the part of Mose, a " B'hoy " or tough of that day who ran with the fire wagons. " He wore," according to Laurence Hutton's description, " the soap locks of the period, the 'plug hat,' with a narrow black band, the red shirt, the trousers turned up—without which the genus was never seen—and he had a peculiarly sardonic curve of the lip. . . . Mr. Chanfrau's Mose hit the popular fancy at once, and retained it until the Volunteer Fire Department was disbanded."

Another development of the play concerned with the rough and tumble elements of the city is found in the productions of Edward Harrigan and Tony Hart that began in 1876. Their plays, the names of two of the best known of which are *Old Lavender* (1877) and *The Mulligan Guards' Ball* (1870), were a lightly cohering succession of characters and incidents peculiar to New York, the comedians of the company impersonating local Irish, Negro, or German types. Charles Hoyt's farces of twenty years later use the peculiarities of the New York scene for their effects. Walter Pritchard Eaton sees in these burlesques of Harrigan and Hart and in the Hoyt farces the direct antecedents of the plays of those contemporary humorists, George Ade and George Cohan, whose work, as it

appears on the stage to-day, is being closely followed by those
who are interested in the history of drama in America.

Tyler wrote *The Contrast,* as we have seen, after a visit to
The School for Scandal. Satirical studies of American
manners have since been frequent in the theatre. Often
they have been studies of society life in New York or in resorts
or suburbs whither the characteristic social life has been trans-
ferred. One of the best known of American social satires,
Fashion, by Anna Cora Mowatt Ritchie, dramatist and actress,
was produced in New York in 1845. It was, it is interesting
to note, reviewed by Edgar Allan Poe in the *Broadway Journal*
of March 29 of that year. In this play the juxtaposition of
Americans, Europeans, and Americans who have lived abroad
reminds one of the persons to be met with in the novels of
Henry James. Mrs. Mowatt, as she was when she wrote
Fashion, evidently knew her Molière well, for there are scenes
in the play that show plainly the influence of situations in *Les
Femmes Savantes* and *Le Bourgeois Gentilhomme.* Snobbishness
and title-mongering are the particular objects of Mrs. Mowatt's
attack. Bronson Howard's *Saratoga* (1870) is a play of the
same type as *Fashion.* It seems even less indigenous than Mrs.
Mowatt's play. The several scenes laid in the old Academy
of Design in New York and at Congress Springs in Saratoga
provide local color in a diluted form. The *locale* was American even though the maneuvers of the New York society folk
who people the play were manipulated after the English and
French models popular in the American theatre of the day.

The same Clyde Fitch who could turn out romantic period
plays like *Beau Brummell* and *Captain Jinks of the Horse
Marines* was even more emphatically master of the play used
for purposes of social satire. *The Climbers* (1901) is second
only perhaps to Langdon Mitchell's *The New York Idea*
(1906), which, according to the authoritative judgment of
Arthur Hobson Quinn, "represents American social comedy at
its best." In 1918 a satirical social comedy, *Why Marry?* by
Jesse Lynch Williams, won the Pulitzer prize at Columbia
University for the best play of the year, that same prize which
has since been carried off by two strictly realistic plays of
small town or rural American life, Eugene O'Neill's *Beyond
the Horizon* and Zona Gale's *Miss Lulu Bett,* both unrelenting
and unrelieved presentations of actualities.

The romantic play continues to perpetuate itself in our stage history. As romantic poetic drama, *The Prince of Parthia* was the forerunner of such later plays as Robert Montgomery Bird's *The Broker of Bogota* (1834), Nathaniel Parker Willis's *Tortesa the Usurer* (1839), Henry Wadsworth Longfellow's *The Spanish Student* (1843), George Henry Boker's *Francesca da Rimini* (1855), and the verse dramas of Thomas Bailey Aldrich, Josephine Preston Peabody, Cale Young Rice, Percy MacKaye, and Olive Tilford Dargan.

Boker's treatment of the Francesca story is more skillful dramatically than Stephen Phillips' handling of the same material. The English poet's *Paolo and Francesca* was written after Tennyson had shown the possibilities of new and lovelier cadences in English blank verse, yet the lines of Boker's here reprinted are representative of many other passages of real poetry in the American play:

> "PAOLO. . . . And now for the romance. Where left we off?
>
> FRANCESCA. Where Launcelot and Queen Guenevra strayed
> Along the forest, in the Youth of May.
> You marked the figure of the birds that sang
> Their melancholy farewell to the sun—
> Rich in his loss, their sorrow glorified—
> Like gentle mourners o'er a great man's grave.
> Was it not there? No, no; 'twas when they sat
> Down on the bank, by one impulsive wish
> That neither uttered."

Francesca da Rimini was successfully revived, with Otis Skinner in the young lover's part, as lately as 1901.

Kenneth Macgowan, analyzing critically the tendencies that are showing themselves in contemporary drama, in his challenging, brilliant, and sophisticated book, *The Theatre of Tomorrow,* predicts a revival of interest in the poetic drama of romance, and suggests that Sidney Howard's *Swords,* produced in New York in 1921, and Percy MacKaye's *A Thousand Years Ago* (1913) hint at the possibility that free verse and blank verse may be so manipulated, so alternated, as to become less mannered and more expressive for the purpose of the drama. "There may be," he has written, "verse in the future drama, plenty of it; but it will not be limited to a single measure. It will fit the emotion of the scenes and change as the emotion changes."

As illustrative of the responsiveness to varying moods of Percy MacKaye's verse two passages have been chosen from his version of the Turandot legend, *A Thousand Years Ago*. The first is a speech of the strolling actor Capocomico:

> "Precisely, my bully-boy!
> What would you?—At home, half the world is dyspeptic
> With pills of reformers and critics and realists.
> Fun for its own sake?—Pho, it's old-fashioned!
> Art with a mask on?—Unnaturalistic,
> They warn you, and scowl, and wag their sad periwigs.—
> So *we*—the unmatched, immortal, Olympian
> Maskers of Antic,—we, troop of the tragical,
> Symbolical, comical, melodramatical
> *Commedia dell'Arte*—we, once who by thousands
> Enchanted to laughter the children of Europe—
> Behold us now, packed out of town by the critics
> To wander the world, hobble-heel, tatter-elbowed,
> Abegging our way—four vagabond-players,
> And one master director—me, Capocomico!"

But MacKaye's meter provides other music for the lover Calaf's words:

> "Forget?
> Forget that night? That night I died indeed,
> And rose from out the river's chilly death
> Into strange paradise: A garden, walled
> With roses round: A moon, that zoned with pearl
> A spirit there: a lady, garbed in gold
> And her more golden smile! Wrapt in disguise—
> A beggar's cloak, which you had hid me in,
> The river's ooze still staining me with slime—
> On me—*me,* outcast and destroyed, she smiled,
> And tossed for alms the white rose from her hair!—
> [*Taking from his bosom a withered rose, he looks on it rapturously.*]
> My deathless rose!"

The romantic play in prose is more frequent in the course of American drama than the romantic play in verse and has ordinarily been more successful on the stage. The style of acting common in the seventies encouraged the composition of melodramas characterized by rank romantic extravagances. Examples of a progressively more restrained manner in romantic prose plays are Steele MacKaye's *Hazel Kirke* (1880) and *Paul Kauvar, or Anarchy* (1887), *Madame Butterfly* (1900), by John Luther Long and David Belasco, *The Scare-*

crow (1910), by Percy MacKaye, *Kismet* (1911), by Edward Knoblock, and *Romance* (1913), by Edward Sheldon. *The Emperor Jones* (1920), by Eugene O'Neill, dramatizing in all their strangeness and beauty negro folk superstitions against a tangled jungle background, is one of the latest and most impressive of the romantic plays. Imaginative phantasies like Eleanor Gates's *The Poor Little Rich Girl* (1913) and George Hazelton and J. H. Benrimo's *The Yellow Jacket* (1912), have plainly no precedent in the earlier history of our drama.

Likewise new to the tradition of the American stage are such plays as Clyde Fitch's *The Truth* (1906), Eugene Walter's *The Easiest Way* (1909), Charles Kenyon's *Kindling* (1911), Edward Sheldon's *Salvation Nell* (1908), *The Nigger* (1909), and *The Boss* (1911), Rachel Crothers's *He and She* (1911), Joseph Medill Patterson's *Rebellion* (1911), Louis K. Anspacher's *The Unchastened Woman* (1915), a comedy of which William Lyon Phelps has said that it " would be a credit to any dramatist in the world," Frank Craven's *The First Year* (1920), Arthur Richman's *Ambush* (1921), and Eugene O'Neill's *Anna Christie* (1921).

The contribution of Bronson Howard, whose work has several times been mentioned in passing, should certainly be singled out for special comment even in so brief a treatment of the subject as the present one. At a time when American managers were afraid to label plays as native products, Howard forced A. M. Palmer, the manager, to advertise *The Banker's Daughter* as an American comedy, thus establishing a precedent for American plays that were not mere adaptations. In an address delivered at Harvard, 1886, Howard enumerated the following as important considerations in the construction of a play:

" I. The actual strength of the main incident of a play.

II. Relative strength of the main incident, in reference to the importance of the subject; and also the length of the play.

III. Adequacy of the story in relation to the importance and dignity of the main incident and of the subject.

IV. Adequacy of the original motives on which the rest of the play depends.

V. Logical sequence of events by which the main incident is reached.

VI. Logical results of the story after the main incident is passed.

VII. The choice of the characters by which the sequence of events is determined.

VIII. Logical, otherwise natural, use of motives in these particular characters, in leading from one incident to another.

IX. The use of such human emotions and passions as are universally recognized as true, without those special explanations which belong to general fiction and not to the stage.

X. The relation of the story and incidents to the sympathies of the audience as a collection of human beings.

XI. The relation of the story and incidents to the sympathies of the particular audience for which the play is written; to its knowledge and ignorance; its views of life; its social customs; and to its political institutions, so far as they may modify its social views, as in the case of a democracy or an autocracy.

Minor matters—such as the use of comic relief, the relation of dialog to action, the proper use of superfluous characters to prevent an appearance of artificiality in the treatment, and a thousand other details belonging to the constructive side of a play—must also be within the critic's view." [1]

Howard's theories taken in conjunction with his seventeen plays influenced profoundly the development of native American drama.

No survey of American actors has been attempted in this sketch. It is obvious, however, that one cannot really appreciate the circumstances under which American plays have been written unless one is familiar with the art of Edwin Forrest, Charlotte Cushman, the Jeffersons, the Wallacks, Edwin Booth, John McCullough, John T. Raymond, Mary Anderson, the Hacketts, the Drews, the Barrymores, Richard Mansfield, the Sotherns, Otis Skinner, Julia Marlowe, Margaret Anglin, Minnie Maddern Fiske, Augustin Daly's stock company of the eighties,[2] and Daniel Frohman's Lyceum Stock Company of the nineties. These do not exhaust the names that glorify the history of our stage, or begin to suggest the ramifications of

---

[1] *The Autobiography of a Play,* by Bronson Howard, with an Introduction by Augustus Thomas, Dramatic Museum of Columbia University, New York, 1914.

[2] Charles Pike Sawyer, writing of the halcyon days, in a recent newspaper article, refers to "that great revival by Daly of *The Taming of the Shrew,* in its entirety, in October, 1887, when William Gilbert gave that delightful performance of Christopher Sly in the induction. And such a cast there was: Charles Fisher, Otis Skinner, John Drew, George Clarke, Charles Leclercq, Joseph Holland, James Lewis, Frederick Bond, Ada Rehan, Virginia Dreher, Jean Gordon, and Mrs. G. H. Gilbert, to say nothing of Master Willie Collier, employed as call-boy and playing small parts."

the star system to which the stock companies gave place in the organization of the theatre.

Nor has any space been given to the history of theatrical management and methods of production, though, of course, it is generally understood " that the dramatic art of a period made up not alone of the plays that are presented, but of the entire institution of the theatre of the time, comprising its actors, its producers, its managers, its agents, its many artists and workers as well as its writers. The drama of the time is the whole institution of the stage of the time." [1] The fact that in his day Augustin Daly leaned toward German adaptations, that A. M. Palmer in turn gave the preference to French plays, that David Belasco worked at literally realistic stage settings and revolutionized stage lighting, that Charles and Daniel Frohman wisely brought Arthur W. Pinero, James M. Barrie, Henry Arthur Jones, and other English playwrights to the attention of the American public, and that Arthur Hopkins assembled and coördinated the various arts of the theatre in making his productions, is plainly significant. The pooling of theatrical interests by 1896, the fight against the " Theatrical Trust " carried on by certain actors, the recent break-up of the monster combination—all these circumstances have had an obvious and vital bearing on American drama. Experimental producers like the Theatre Guild and the Provincetown Players, both in New York, have made every effort to encourage the American playwright. The plays of Susan Glaspell and of Eugene O'Neill have provided more than one bill for the second of these groups.

Such exponents of the new art of the theatre as Robert Edmond Jones, Norman-bel Geddes, Lee Simonson, and Rollo Peters, designers of interpretive scenery, are helping at this minute to determine what the American drama of the future is to be like. Out of the development of a device like the Clavilux, or color organ, of Thomas Wilfred may come an art of mobile color suitable as the background or the accompaniment of drama, that will suggest the creation of new dramatic forms.

The actors, the managers, and the artists have their place and importance in the scheme of the theatre, but the controlling

[1] T. H. Dickinson, *The Case of American Drama,* Boston and New York, 1915, p. 183.

force in the development of the drama will always be the play-wright. At the moment the commanding figure among the younger generation of American dramatists is Eugene O'Neill. His early contact with the stage through his father James O'Neill, the colorful adventures of his young manhood, a period of serious ill health, and a desultory though amazing education, culminating in study at Harvard in the dramatic workshop of George Pierce Baker, are, all of them, experiences vitally influencing the molds in which his ideas are cast. The subjects that seem most to interest him are the sea, the jungle, the human being warped physically or morally, and the grosser inequalities of society. O'Neill has been writing for nine years. In that time his sense of artistry has caused him to destroy eighteen out of the forty-one plays that he has completed. His vigor and expressiveness, his strength and imagination, and his experiments with a new and original dramatic technique combine to secure for him a conspicuous position among contemporary American playwrights. He represents nothing like a new school in American drama, but his work illustrates forces that are abroad in the theatre to-day.

BEAU BRUMMELL *

By

CLYDE FITCH

Clyde Fitch, author of *Beau Brummell* and of fifty other plays, some of them adaptations,[1] was born May 2, 1865, at Elmira, New York. Part of his childhood was passed at Schenectady; and William Lyon Phelps speaks of having been a schoolmate of Fitch's at Hartford, Connecticut. His college days were spent at Amherst from which he was graduated in 1886. Active as an undergraduate in theatricals, his impersonation of that sentimental heroine, Lydia Languish, became especially famous. At his death it was found that he had made provision in his will for the endowment of a professorship at Amherst. The college also has fallen heir to his library.

He began his literary career by writing children's stories, that were published in the *Independent* and in the *Christian Union*. Before he gave himself up wholly to the theatre, he also essayed verse and short stories. But only three years after his graduation from college, he wrote *Beau Brummell,* and from that date, until his death twenty years later, he was engaged uninterruptedly in turning out the plays that secured him fame and fortune.

He lived in New York and had country houses at various times at Katonah, New York, and at Greenwich, Connecticut. According to the editors of the memorial edition of his plays: "In one respect it may be said that from the time Clyde Fitch began to be regarded as America's most popular playwright, each year found him externally doing the same things —fulfilling contracts, selecting casts, arranging rehearsals, and attending 'openings.' Faster and faster grew the whirl of routine until, during the last year of his life, he was attempting sufficient to undermine the health of the strongest man. Every year found him abroad, noting with the quick eye of the trained expert what was best in the Continental theatres, and meeting Charles Frohman or some other American manager in order to read a manuscript or to talk over an embryo

[1] For a complete list of his plays, see Montrose J. Moses, *The American Dramatist,* Boston, 1911, pp. 171-172.

3

comedy. It was the life of a successful literary man of the theatre, and was filled with interesting associations, correspondence, and travel." [1] It was during Fitch's periodical visits to Venice that much of his writing was done. He was seen there once scribbling for dear life as his gondola swept him along. But he hardly needed the special stimulus of time or place; his ideas for plays were so pressing and so abundant that they forced themselves to the surface for expression. While he waited at the roadside for his automobile, for example, or while he sat with friends at the opera, the impulse to set down his thronging thoughts would not be restrained.

On September 4, 1909, Clyde Fitch died at Châlons-sur-Marne. Though he had twenty years of feverish activity as a dramatist behind him, he was still a young man. He had shown great promise; more than that, performance had not been lacking. His unexpected and untimely death is but another of countless illustrations of the unequal race between Art and Time.

Among the " fifty other plays " referred to at the beginning of this sketch, five stand out as Fitch's most signal achievements in American drama.[2] They are *Beau Brummell,* written at the suggestion of the distinguished creator of the rôle, Richard Mansfield, who in turn had had the character called to his attention by William Winter,[3] *The Climbers, The Girl with the Green Eyes, The Truth,* which was met with greater acclaim in Europe than in the playwright's own country, and *The City,* posthumously produced. Fitch's knowledge of New York types as evidenced in the last four plays and in others like *Captain Jinks of the Horse Marines* and *The Girls* has been compared to O. Henry's. But the range of the writer of short stories was narrower. Fitch was fond, too, of the period play. *Nathan Hale, Barbara Frietchie,* and *Beau Brummell,* in spite of certain frank distortions of fact, exhibit their author's intelligent use of historical material.

We owe the lifelike and artistic delineation of the great

[1] *Plays by Clyde Fitch,* edited by Montrose J. Moses and Virginia Gerson, Boston, 1915, pp. vi-vii.

[2] See William Lyon Phelps, *Essays on Modern Dramatists,* New York, 1920, p. 160.

[3] See William Winter, *Life and Art of Richard Mansfield,* New York, 1910, Vol. 1, pp. 128-136; and William Winter, *Shadows of the Stage,* Third Series, New York, 1906, pp. 212-220.

dandy to the joint researches of Fitch and Mansfield. They had ample data for their study. The real George Bryan Brummell was born June 7, 1778, and baptized at Westminster. Even while at Eton, to which he was sent in 1790, he was known as " Buck Brummell." During his four years at that college he became increasingly popular. His reputation as a social genius and as a wit was made even in these early days. At this period he attracted the attention of the Prince of Wales, later Regent for George III and later still himself King George IV, and was an attendant at the Prince's wedding. He was given a cornetcy in the Prince's, his own regiment, the Tenth Hussars. From Eton in 1784, Brummell went to Oxford, but, disinclined for study, left Oriel College the same year.

He was presently promoted to a captaincy in his regiment, retiring at length from the service in 1798. About that time coming into his fortune, he set up a bachelor establishment in Mayfair. With the Regent as his friend, he became a social power. His taste and authority in matters connected with fashion were acknowledged to be faultless, and though in no sense a fop, he became a dictator of the mode. Leigh Hunt wrote of him: " I remember that Lord Byron once described him to me, as having nothing remarkable in his style of dress, except a ' certain exquisite propriety.' " [1] Even the Prince bowed to his mandates and is said, on one occasion, to have begun " to blubber when told that Brummell did not like the cut of his coat." Brummell counted Byron and Sheridan among his friends in the gay world. The author of *The Rivals* and *The School for Scandal,* second in stage popularity only to Shakespeare, used to send his verses to Brummell. The Beau owed his position no less to his assurance and ready wit than to his supremacy in all that pertained to dress. The two following anecdotes perpetuate certain of his affectations: " He pretended to look upon the City as a terra incognita; and when some great merchant requested the honour of his company at dinner, he replied, ' With pleasure, if you will promise faithfully not to tell.' . . . An acquaintance having, in a morning call, bored him dreadfully about some tour he had made in the north of England, enquired with great pertinacity which

[1] William Jesse, *The Life of George Brummell,* London, 1893, p. 47.

of the lakes he preferred; when Brummell, quite tired of the
man's tedious raptures, turned his head imploringly towards
his valet, who was arranging something in the room, and said,
'Robinson.' 'Sir.' 'Which of the lakes do I admire?'
'Windemere, sir,' replied that distinguished individual. 'Ah
yes,—Windemere,' replied Brummell, 'so it is,—Windemere.'" [1]

He finally quarreled with the Prince. The break is usually
attributed to the Beau's sharp tongue. The famous "Who's
your fat friend?" and "Wales, will you ring the bell?" are
traditional, if not authentic. Brummell did not, as in the
play, lose his place in society. It was only when his gambling
losses overwhelmed him that he was constrained to leave England. He fled to Calais on May 16, 1816, where for a time
in his little home under the ramparts, he gave himself to the
reckless elegance of his old life [2] until a new accumulation of
debts proved once more his undoing. When, a year after
George IV's accession, the new king passed through Calais, he
did not even see his old friend, nor were there any offers of
assistance.

For two years, from 1830 until 1832, Beau Brummell was
British consul at Caen. Here, in 1835, he was consigned to
prison for his debts. The days of his glory were over. His
mind began to fail. He did actually hold "phantom recep-
tions of the beauties and magnates of old days." He became
careless and finally disgusting in his personal habits. His last
days were spent in the asylum of the Bon Sauveur, Caen. On
March 30, 1840, he died and was buried in the Protestant
cemetery of the town.

It will thus be seen that Clyde Fitch follows with considerable fidelity the outlines of the real Beau's character, even
such traditional anecdotes as have been quoted having their
counterpart in the play. Though a play does not have to be
documented, yet a period play must create an atmosphere, and
in *Beau Brummell* the England of the Regency appears to live
again.

Brummell had figured in literature before Clyde Fitch's

[1] William Jesse, *The Life of George Brummell*, London, 1893, pp.
79-80.
[2] *Cf.* The Diary of a Dandy, in John Ashton, *Social England under
the Regency*, London, 1899, Chapter XXXIII.

play. He is supposed to be the prototype of Bulwer's *Pelham,* and the character of Trebeck in Lister's *Granby,* published in 1826, is a portrait of the Beau in his own lifetime, to the accuracy of which he himself bore witness. There was also a two-act play on the subject by Blanchard Jerrold which Mansfield examined and discarded before broaching his idea to Clyde Fitch.[1] Edgar Fawcett in 1887 had also treated the subject in blank verse.[2]

When *Beau Brummell* was produced on Monday, May 19, 1890, at the Madison Square Theatre in New York, it met only with the qualified approval of the dramatic critics. The verdict, printed in the *New York Dramatic Mirror,* pronounced that *"Beau Brummell* is very far from perfection in its dramatic construction. If produced under less favorable circumstances—that is, with an ordinary company—it is questionable whether the piece would have attained any marked attention from the critical fraternity. The principal drawback in the first sample of Mr. Fitch's work as a playwright, is the lack of dramatic action. Of all things, a modern audience abhors a ' talky ' play. It is extremely fortunate, therefore, that the abundance of talk in *Beau Brummell* is not of a tiresome character. On the contrary, the conversation throughout scintillates with witty retorts, partly compiled from authentic sources and partly supplied by the dramatist himself." This opinion is more or less representative of the stand taken by the critics generally in 1890. It was almost always implied that it was Richard Mansfield's acting that lent distinction to the play.

During Fitch's lifetime, the criticism appearing in the newspapers and in the magazines must have made poor reading indeed for the playwright. A later commentator on Fitch has attributed the lack of enthusiasm on the part of the play reviewers to the fact that they left the theatre with a sense of depression due to the circumstance that this dramatist's attack and exposition were, as a rule, superior to his last acts.

[1] Jerrold's *Beau Brummell* was first produced at the Royal Lyceum Theatre in London on April 11, 1859. There are no English scenes in the play at all. It has almost nothing in common with Clyde Fitch's piece of the same name.

[2] *Two Scenes in the Life of Beau Brummell,* in *Songs of Doubt and Dream,* New York, 1891, p. 190.

Neither the novel situations that he invented nor the brilliant
dialogue that he supplied served to counteract the chilling effect of those last acts. More recent appraisers of Fitch's work
have considered him in relation to a larger movement. They
have, generally, conceded his cleverness as a technician, his
unexcelled knowledge of the conditions of the theatre, and his
appreciation of the tastes of the average audience of his all-too-
short day. He is, even more significantly, coming gradually
to be associated with the good fight that has been going on
ever since the days of Bronson Howard for an independent
and artistic native drama.

NOTE

The idea of this play was Richard Mansfield's, and the author gratefully acknowledges his debt to the actor for innumerable suggestions.

This play was first produced at the Madison Square Theatre by Richard Mansfield, on May 19, 1890. The 250th representation took place at the Garden Theatre, on January 30, 1891. The cast on this occasion was:

Beau Brummell............................Mr. Richard Mansfield
The Prince of Wales..........................Mr. D. H. Harkins
Richard Brinsley Sheridan.....................Mr. A. G. Andrews
Lord Manly..................................Mr. H. G. Lonsdale
Reginald Courtenay..........................Mr. Vincent Sternroyd
Mortimer....................................Mr. W. J. Ferguson
Mr. Abrahams..............................Mr. Harry Gwynette
Simpson...Mr. Smiles
Bailiffs............................... { Mr. Gwynette and
                                        { Mr. Ivan Peronette
Prince's Footman...............................Mr. F. F. Graham
Mr. Oliver Vincent.........................Mr. W. H. Crompton
Mariana Vincent...........................Miss Beatrice Cameron
Kathleen.......................................Miss Ethel Sprague
The Duchess of Leamington....................Mrs. Julia Brutone
Lady Farthingale.............................Miss Helen Glidden
French Lodging-house Keeper..................Miss Hazel Selden
Nurse.......................................Miss Genevra Campbell
Mrs. St. Aubyn..............................Miss Adela Measor

THE PERSONS IN THE PLAY

THE PRINCE OF WALES, *heir apparent to the throne of England.*

BEAU BRUMMELL, *prince of dandies.*

RICHARD BRINSLEY SHERIDAN, *playwright.*

REGINALD COURTENAY, *nephew to the Beau.*

MORTIMER, *valet and confidential servant to the Beau.*

MR. OLIVER VINCENT, *a self-made merchant, father of Mariana.*

LORD MANLY, *a fop.*

MR. ABRAHAMS, *a money-lender.*

BAILIFFS.

PRINCE'S FOOTMAN.

SIMPSON, *footman to Beau.*

THE DUCHESS OF LEAMINGTON, *middle-aged, but very anxious to appear young.*

MARIANA VINCENT, *young and beautiful, beloved by Beau and Reginald.*

MRS. ST. AUBYN, *passée but still beautiful—very anxious to captivate the Prince, but unwilling to resign the Beau.*

KATHLEEN, *Irish maid of Mariana.*

LADY FARTHINGALE, *pretty—insipid.*

A FRENCH LODGING-HOUSE KEEPER.

A NURSE.

BEAU BRUMMELL

THE FIRST ACT. FIRST SCENE. *The morning toilet. Mr. Brummell dispatches a proposal of marriage, assists his nephew, and sends for a new tailor.*
SECOND SCENE. *The Beau receives a number of friends, and makes an unfortunate blunder.*

THE SECOND ACT. *A small and early party at Carlton House. Mr. Brummell proposes to an heiress, and reprimands a Prince.*

THE THIRD ACT. *The Mall, and how it came about that Mr. Brummell had a previous engagement with His Majesty.*

THE FOURTH ACT. FIRST SCENE. *Mr. Brummell's lodgings in Calais.*

(Six months later.)

SECOND SCENE. *The attic at Caen. A very poor dinner with an excellent dessert.*

BEAU BRUMMELL

THE FIRST ACT

SCENE ONE

The scene represents the BEAU'S *dressing-room. A cheerful room, furnished more like a lady's boudoir than a man's dressing-room. A handsome dressing-table, covered with a bewildering array of silver-topped bottles, stands at the left. A large cheval-glass stands in front of a bay window opening out on a balcony. The curtains are open. The door at the back leads into the* BEAU'S *bedroom. A table stands at one side, with books and papers in precise order. A door at the left-hand side leads into an ante-room where visitors are detained until the great man wishes to see them.*

MORTIMER, *the* BEAU'S *valet and really confidential servant, is discovered sitting on sofa, head back, face covered with handkerchief; he has evidently been asleep. It is about noon.*

[MORTIMER *removes handkerchief, yawns and speaks.*]
MORTIMER. Up till four this morning! It was pretty lively at the club last night, but I have lost all my beauty sleep to pay for it. I don't know how much longer we will be able to continue this style of living. Our nerves will give out if our credit doesn't. Mr. Brummell only turned over twice and then took to his chocolate. That means he will only be half an hour at his bath—time for a nap. [*Replaces handkerchief. Enter* SIMPSON *through door from ante-room.* SIMPSON *is the regulation footman, with powdered hair and livery.*]
SIMPSON [*at left*]. Mr. Mortimer, sir, Mr. Abrahams has just called. He particularly wishes to see you, sir. [*Going toward* MORTIMER.]

MORTIMER [*starting and removing handkerchief*]. Hang Abrahams, what's he after? Dear me! It can't be that he thinks of collecting those I. O. U.'s of mine. [*Rising.*]

SIMPSON [*who has a great respect for* MORTIMER. *Very deferentially*]. Been losing again, sir?

MORTIMER [*loftily*]. Yes, Simpson, pretty high stakes last night, and one must play, you know.

SIMPSON. Mr. Mortimer, sir, you couldn't propose me in your club, could you, sir?

MORTIMER [*haughtily and then more kindly, as he sees* SIMPSON'S *downcast face*]. No, Simpson, not in your present position, you know; but if you should ever raise yourself, depend upon me to use all my influence for you.

SIMPSON [*gratefully*]. Oh, thank you, sir, I'm sure, [*going*] but what about Mr. Abrahams, sir?

MORTIMER [*seating himself*]. Oh, damn Abrahams! [*Enter* ABRAHAMS *from ante-room, hat and cane in hand.* ABRAHAMS *is the typical Jew money-lender of the period, exaggerated in dress and manner.*]

ABRAHAMS [*advancing just as* SIMPSON *crosses back of table and exits, giving him a look of haughty disdain*]. No, you don't, Mr. Mortimer; no, you don't, not yet. Where's your master?

MORTIMER. Excuse me, where's my gentleman, you mean, Mr. Abrahams. [*Rising.*] I am a gentleman's gentleman; I have no master.

ABRAHAMS [*at left center*]. Oh, you haven't a master, haven't you? Well, now, suppose I was to come down on you with some of your little I. O. U.'s, I wonder then if you'd have a master. Where's Mr. Brummell?

MORTIMER. Mr. Brummell has not yet appeared.

ABRAHAMS [*sitting down as if to wait*]. Inform him that Mr. Abrahams wishes to see him.

MORTIMER [*shocked*]. I repeat, sir, he is not up.

ABRAHAMS. Well, then, my good fellow, it's time he were up. Tell him I said so.

MORTIMER. It is as much as my position is worth, sir, to go to him at this hour. You must call again, Mr. Abrahams.

ABRAHAMS [*rising*]. Call again! Call again! This is the seventh time I've called again.

MORTIMER [*trying now to placate him*]. Yes—eh—if you please, Mr. Abrahams.

ABRAHAMS. No, sir; I must see him now. I'm in need of money myself, and I must get it from Mr. Brummell. My creditors are pressing me, and they force me to do the same. [*Loudly.*] I regret the necessity, but I am determined upon seeing him.

MORTIMER [*who is so shocked he can hardly speak*]. Not so loud, Mr. Abrahams, not so loud. If Mr. Brummell were to hear you, he'd be distressed. Besides, he never tolerates anyone who raises his voice unnecessarily. If he should hear you, you might never be paid.

ABRAHAMS [*aghast at the thought*]. What!

MORTIMER [*hands raised in horror*]. Sh! Sh!

ABRAHAMS. What! [*Whispering in MORTIMER's ear.*]

MORTIMER [*looking at ABRAHAMS out of the corner of his eye*]. Upon my honor, Mr. Brummell was saying only yesterday he thought he would pay Mr. Abrahams.

ABRAHAMS [*a little more calmly*]. Then why hasn't he done so?

MORTIMER. Mr. Brummell only said it yesterday, and Mr. Brummell never does anything in a hurry.

ABRAHAMS. Is four years a hurry? Well, this is the last time that I will be put off. Do you follow me—the last time! And now, when am I to have your little sums?

MORTIMER [*taking out handkerchief and wiping eyes*]. Mine! Oh, I have a wealthy aunt, who is now dying in Clapham, Mr. Abrahams, and I am her sole heir. I fear I must beg you to wait until after her funeral.

ABRAHAMS [*at left center. Really puzzled*]. It is very strange, a very large number of my clients have wealthy aunts who are dying, but they don't die. They all appear to be affected with a most lingering sickness. However, Mr. Brummell has no such relative, and I believe, on consideration, that I will wait for him this morning. [*Sits in chair by table.*]

MORTIMER [*who is now determined to get rid of him, crossing to ABRAHAMS*]. No, really, Mr. Abrahams, you must go. Mr. Brummell would not see you until his toilet is completed; and, indeed, if he would, he could transact no business in *déshabille*.

ABRAHAMS. In what? [*Jumps up.*] Oh, very well, very

well; but advise him this is the last time I will be dismissed without seeing him. The next time I call, I will see him whether he is in desh—desh—or nothing. I will have my money. I will have my money. [*All the while he is saying this,* MORTIMER *is pushing him gently off through the ante-room.* MORTIMER *ushers* ABRAHAMS *off at the left, then crosses to the right center, and turns away with a sigh of relief as* SIMPSON *enters very hurriedly.*]

SIMPSON. Mr. Mortimer, sir, there are a number of people waiting with their accounts to see Mr. Brummell. What shall I say, sir?

MORTIMER [*resignedly*]. Get a list of their names, Simpson, and tell them I'll call around and see them to-day.

SIMPSON. Very well, sir. [*Exit* SIMPSON *through ante-room. A murmur of voices is heard there.*]

MORTIMER. Affairs are very shaky. It was only three days since Abrahams called. According to this he will return again to-morrow. [*Sits in chair in front of dressing-case, makes himself comfortable, and is about to fall asleep when* KATHLEEN *appears at door and peeps in.*]

KATHLEEN [*in door at left. She is* MARIANA'S *Irish maid, very pretty and piquant*]. Pst! Pst! [MORTIMER *starts and listens, then composes himself for another nap.*]

KATHLEEN. Pst! Pst!

MORTIMER [*still seated*]. I did drink pretty heavily last night, but I hardly thought it affected me.

KATHLEEN. Hello!

MORTIMER [*rising*]. Who is it? What is it?

KATHLEEN [*still in door. With pretty impatience*]. Is it all right,—can I come in?

MORTIMER [*laughingly*]. Look here, Kathleen, are you going to indulge in that sort of thing when we are married?

KATHLEEN. Can I come in? [*Comes in a few steps.*]

MORTIMER [*crossing to center*]. Yes, it's all right now. Mr. Brummell is finishing the first part of his toilet; he won't be out for some time yet. Well, what do you want, you little minx? [*Chucks her under chin.*]

KATHLEEN [*tossing her head*]. Minx, indeed! [*Crossing to right.*] I dropped in to find out what's your intentions. Mr. Sheridan's gentleman has become very pressing in his, and won't be held off much longer. Now, is it marriage with you, Mr. Mortimer, or is it a breaking off, Mr. Mortimer? Am I to be worn in your coat like a flower and thrown aside when I'm withered, or am I to be pressed in the album of your affections, Mr. Mortimer? I own there is an air about Mr. Brummell, and I should not be averse to a connection with the family. [*Quite seriously.*]

MORTIMER [*just as seriously*]. And I mean you shall have it, Kathleen, for you would become our position. But the fact is, I can't afford to marry while Mr. Brummell's money matters are so bad. I tell you his social position is like a halo,—it is glory all round him, but there's a hollow in the middle.

KATHLEEN [*with a sudden thought*]. Mr. Mortimer! We must marry Mr. Brummell! First, we must procure a list of the heiresses.

MORTIMER [*slyly*]. I understand there is a heap of money in your family.

KATHLEEN [*dubiously*]. But there's one obstacle—Miss Mariana's affections are already engaged.

MORTIMER. Indeed, to whom?

KATHLEEN. That's what I can't find out. The divvle never signs any of his letters. I can promise you one thing, he isn't very high, and Miss Mariana's father has forbid him the house, and swears she shan't have him. Mr. Vincent, oh, ho! he's all for position and fashion.

MORTIMER [*puts arm around her waist and they walk up and down*]. Then Mr. Vincent would be glad to marry her to Mr. Brummell. We'll enlist him on our side. Now there are two difficulties with Mr. Brummell—first, he is, just at present, very friendly with Mrs. St. Aubyn. Still, I think I can get him out of that predicament, and then you see Mr. Brummell is so demmed particular,—the young lady must be correct to a hair in every respect—

KATHLEEN [*affectedly*]. Lord, Mr. Morty, you needn't worry yourself about that; ar'n't I in her service? And what's the matter with me? She's a very much *a la mud* and [*crosses to mirror at right*] correct in every particular. Mr. Mortimer, do you think you are as becoming to me as Mr. Sheridan's gentleman? [*Beckoning to him; he comes up and looks over her shoulder in the glass.*]

MORTIMER [*putting his arm around her and leading her*

away from mirror]. Look here, Kathleen, no tricks; and what are you doing out at this time of day?

KATHLEEN [*walking to and fro with* MORTIMER]. Why, Miss Mariana sent me over an hour back with this letter [*holding up letter*] for her young gentleman. They correspond through me; faith, I'm turned into a regular post-bag. But I'm afraid I've missed him this time.

MORTIMER [*laughing*]. You will have to miss him quite regularly when we begin to break it off between your young mistress and her lover, and supplant him with my gentleman.

BEAU [*voice in distance from bedroom*]. Mortimer! Mortimer!

MORTIMER. Yes, sir! [*Alarmed.*] That's Mr. Brummell!

KATHLEEN [*starts off left*]. Lord! I'm off. [*Pointing to dressing-table.*] Oh, Morty! Is that where he sits and does it? [MORTIMER *nods.*] Couldn't I see him?

MORTIMER [*with horror*]. What! Before he's finished? Gracious Heavens! No!

KATHLEEN [*crossing to door of ante-room*]. Well, I am going. I'm loath to leave ye; good-by—be faithful. [*Throws kiss. Exit* KATHLEEN. *Enter* BEAU *from door into bedroom. He enters slowly as though it were too much trouble to come in. He is dressed in a yellow brocaded dressing-gown, tied with a heavy yellow cord. It is long, so that only his patent leather pumps with silver buckles show, with just a glimpse of brown and yellow striped socks. He crosses at once to the dressing-table without paying any attention to* MORTIMER, *who bows deferentially and says:*]

MORTIMER. Good morning, sir.

BEAU. Oh, go to the devil.

MORTIMER [*to himself*]. Mr. Brummell is in a bad temper this morning.

BEAU [*seating himself at dressing-table*]. Mortimer, is the sun shining?

MORTIMER [*crossing to window—right*]. Oh, finely, sir. [SIMPSON *enters, bringing soda-water bottle and glass on a tray.*]

BEAU [*simply looks at it and motions it away; exit* SIMPSON]. Any gossip, Mortimer? [*Has taken up hand-glass, and then gently smooths his eyebrows.*]

MORTIMER. None of any account, sir. The Dowager
Lady Slopington ran off yesterday with young Philip Petti-
bone.

BEAU [*now manicuring his nails*]. If it happened yesterday, it must be forgotten to-day.

MORTIMER. And Captain Badminton shot himself in the
Park last night, sir, after losing ten thousand pounds at hazard.

BEAU [*now takes tweezers and pulls out one or two hairs
from his face*]. Very stupid of him; he should have shot himself first—is he dead, Mortimer?

MORTIMER. No, sir.

BEAU. He always was a bad shot. You'll find some of his
I. O. U.'s among my papers; return them to him canceled,
with my compliments. He can use them for plasters. And
who has called?

MORTIMER [*crosses to small table and looks over cards*].
Oh, nobody, sir. To be sure there has been the usual crowd of
people. The Honorable Mrs. Donner came for your sub-
scription to the town charities, and I gave her all you could
spare, sir. Mr. Cecil Serious, the poet, called for permission
to inscribe your name under the dedication of his new volume
of verses. Lord Cowden came to know if your influence might
still be used in the support of his party in the coming elections.

BEAU [*still occupied with his toilet*]. Yes, he can use my
influence. Well, you satisfied them all, I presume.

MORTIMER [*at left*]. I took that liberty, sir. Then there
was a quantity of trades-people with their bills and accounts.
I said you had been out all night with the Prince and really
were not able to see them.

BEAU. Pray, Mortimer, be a little careful of my reputation in your lies. You know common people are apt to look
upon dissipation very differently from persons of fashion. You
may say what you like about the Prince, but handle me a little
delicately.

MORTIMER [*bows, then speaks after short pause*]. Sprague,
the tailor, called again, sir, with his account.

BEAU [*much astonished*]. Again! What insolence! Upon
what previous occasion had he the presumption to call?

MORTIMER. A year ago last month, sir.

BEAU [*with real astonishment*]. What damned impudence!
Mortimer, you may let it be known at your club that he comes

to me no longer. Send for that new tailor—what's his name—
to wait upon me this afternoon. Bring this morning's letters.
[MORTIMER *brings down table with a number of little notes
to* BEAU, *who is still seated at dressing-table.*]

MORTIMER [*holding up a bundle of bills*]. These are bills,
sir. All of them fresh this morning, and some of them more
urgent than usual.

BEAU [*not taking the trouble to look at them*]. Hide them
away somewhere, where I can't see them, and I shall feel as if
they had been paid.

MORTIMER [*pushing forward a bundle of notes*]. Your
private correspondence, this little collection, sir.

BEAU [*still seated, takes up notes, one at a time, and smells
them*]. Patchouli!—phew!—Frangipane!—I believe that smells
like peppermint. I don't know what that is, but it's very unpleasant. Violet!—musk! Take them all away—you may
read them yourself.

MORTIMER [*holding up a yellow lock of hair which he has
taken from an envelope*]. This letter has this little enclosure,
sir.

BEAU [*in interested tone*]. Money?

MORTIMER. Not exactly, sir, although a similar color.

BEAU [*disappointedly—languidly*]. Whose is it?

MORTIMER. Lady Constance Conway's, and she says—

BEAU [*interrupts him*]. Never mind what she says. I believe I did honor her with the request. Write and thank her,
and quote some poetry. Say hers is the most precious lock I
possess. Rather tender little woman, Lady Constance. [*Sentimentally.*]

MORTIMER [*pointedly*]. Is she rich, sir?

BEAU [*sighing*]. No, she's not.

MORTIMER [*opening another note*]. Oh! A note from
Mrs. St. Aubyn. She wants to know where you've been these
two days. She says you are her lover's knot; she's coming to
see you at three this afternoon; bids you be ready to receive
her. She has, besides, down below in a postscript, a myriad
of sentiments which she says belong to you, and she is herself,
unalterably yours, Horatia.

BEAU. The one woman in London with whom it's possible
to have a Platonic friendship. One must have something nowadays, and these other liaisons are so excessively vulgar.

MORTIMER [*very loud as he opens letter*]. Mr. Brummell, sir.

BEAU [*shocked*]. Mortimer, how often have I told you never to startle me?

MORTIMER [*bows an apology*]. Mr. Brummell, sir, here's the memorandum of an I. O. U. for one thousand pounds, given by you to Lord Gainsby at White's three nights ago, for sums lost at hazard.

BEAU [*a little disturbed*]. The deuce, Mortimer. It must be paid to-day; that's a debt of honor. How can we obtain the money?

MORTIMER. I can try Abrahams again, sir, but he was very difficult the last time.

BEAU [*rings bell. Enter* SIMPSON *from ante-room.—Without looking at him*]. Simpson!

SIMPSON. Yes, sir.

BEAU. Go to Mr. Abrahams. Of course, you know where he lives.

SIMPSON. Yes, sir. [MORTIMER *brings table back to place up at right.*]

BEAU. Say Mr. Brummell requests his immediate attendance.

SIMPSON. Very well, sir! [*Exit* SIMPSON.]

MORTIMER [*coming down*]. Mr. Brummell, sir, this can't go on much longer.

BEAU. No, I hope not.

MORTIMER. Everybody's pressing on you, and the only thing that keeps them off at all is your friendship with the Prince, and if anything should happen to that—

BEAU [*quite unaffectedly*]. Nothing could happen to that, Mortimer, and if anything did, I should cut the Prince and make the old King the fashion. [*Rises.*]

MORTIMER. I have been wondering, Mr. Brummell, if I might be so bold, if you had ever thought, sir, of the advisability of a rich marriage.

BEAU. Yes, it has occurred to me occasionally; in fact, it has passed through my mind quite recently that it might be desirable. Only to decide on the person really seems too difficult a task for me to undertake. You would not have me marry a mere money-bag, would you, Mortimer?

MORTIMER [*at left of table*]. But the great Mr. Brummell has only to choose.

BEAU [*staring at him in utter surprise that such a remark should be necessary*]. Yes, of course! But one desires some sentiment. I wouldn't care to make a loan for life and give myself as security.

MORTIMER. Mr. Brummell, sir, have you ever observed Miss Mariana Vincent?

BEAU [*thoughtfully*]. Yes, I have noticed her in the Mall, and I must confess it was to admire her; her person is perfect. Is her matrimonial figure as good?

MORTIMER. I believe it is sixty thousand pounds, sir.

BEAU. Oh, dear!

MORTIMER [*hastily*]. But Mr. Vincent would be ashamed to offer so little to the wife of Mr. Brummell.

BEAU [*musingly*]. Yes, it's a very paltry sum, and Mrs. St. Aubyn—

MORTIMER [*insinuatingly*]. If you could present her to the Prince, Mr. Brummell, don't you think a Platonic friendship might spring up there?

BEAU [*as though thinking aloud*]. She is ambitious, but she is clever and would never forgive a slight. She is a good hater, and if she thought she were being put upon one side, she would make a sly enemy. Well—we shall see. Mortimer, write a letter to Mr. Vincent—make my proposal for his daughter's hand. Be mindful of your language and careful to accomplish it in the most elegant manner, and request an immediate reply.

MORTIMER. Yes, sir.

SIMPSON [*enters at left from ante-room*]. Mr. Reginald Courtenay, sir.

BEAU. Yes, you may bid him come in here. [REGINALD *comes rushing in from ante-room. He is a handsome, bright-faced lad of twenty, dressed simply, in great contrast to* BEAU'S *gorgeous attire.*]

REGINALD [*speaks very loud*]. Ah! Mortimer. [*Crossing to* BEAU, *after placing hat and cane on table, with hand extended.*] Good morning Uncle Beau!

BEAU. Reginald! You are evidently laboring under the impression that I am a great distance off. [MORTIMER *goes into bedroom.*]

REGINALD [*in a much lower tone*]. I beg your pardon, Uncle Beau. [*Bows.*] Good morning. [*Hand extended.*]

BEAU. No, I don't think I will shake hands; men shake hands much too often, especially in warm weather. A glance of the eye, Reginald—a glance of the eye! Did it ever occur to you, Reginald, how thoughtful our Creator was, in giving us bodies, to give them to us naked, so that we could dress and ornament them as we choose?

REGINALD. It had not occurred to me before, Uncle.

BEAU. No, I suppose not.

REGINALD. I trust you are well this morning?

BEAU. No, I've contracted a cold—I suppose everybody will have a cold now. I left my carriage on the way to the Pavilion last night, and the wretch of a landlord put me into the same room with a damp stranger.

REGINALD [goes up, sits on settee at right, with a change of tone and manner]. Uncle, I want your advice and help.

BEAU [goes to REGINALD, and puts his hand on his shoulder and speaks with real affection]. All the advice I have is yours. Reginald, my boy, I trust you haven't gotten yourself into difficulties. You are the one creature in the world whom I love, and I think it would break my heart to see you in any trouble from which I could not free you. Your mother, my boy, was a mother to me for years, and when I lost my sister I lost the best friend I ever had. She saw the heart that beat beneath the waistcoat. Moreover, she helped me always—in every way; if it had not been for her, perhaps even now, I might be in some smoky office in the city—that undiscovered country from whose bourn no social traveler ever returns. [Crosses back to dressing-table.] What is it, Reginald? If you are in debt, I will give you a letter to Mr. Abrahams. If you are in the blue-devils, I will give you one to Mrs. St. Aubyn.

REGINALD [rises and comes down to BEAU]. I am in neither, Uncle Beau; I am in love.

BEAU. Dear me, that's worse than either. How do you know you are?

REGINALD. Why—well—I feel it here! [Indicating heart.] I live only when she is present, and merely exist when away from her.

BEAU [staring at him through his glass]. Reginald, don't talk like a family newspaper. Is your fair one possible?

REGINALD [*indignantly*]. If you mean is she a gentle-woman, she is, and besides, young and beautiful—and—

BEAU [*at right*]. Of course, she would be. But does she return your passion?

REGINALD. She loves me, Uncle.

BEAU. Of course, she would—but—

REGINALD. Her father is opposed to me. He has forbidden our seeing each other; our meetings have to be clandestine, and our mutual correspondence is carried, on through her maid. He wishes a title for his daughter. He is rich and seeks only position in the world of society, while she, ah! she cares nothing for it—only—for—me.

BEAU [*looking at him through glass*]. Reginald, do you know I think you are more conceited than I am.

REGINALD [*at center*]. Oh, no! [*Bowing.*] Oh! Uncle Beau, you, who are so high in favor at the Court, who have Dukes at your elbow and the Regent on your arm, might help me in a worldly way, that I might win over the father. I know that I am dear to you, as you are to me—and that is why I have come to you!

BEAU. And you shall not have come in vain. [*With enthusiasm.*] By my manners! You shall have the girl if I have to plead for you myself. But that will not be necessary. No, I will give you social distinction and prominence much more easily. Come for me in a little while, and I'll walk along the Mall with you to White's. Yes, and be seen with you at the Club window a few moments. Now, my dear boy, can anybody possibly do anything more for you? [*With absolute conviction.*]

REGINALD [*pleased*]. No, Uncle. [*Turning to go.*] Yes, Uncle—you can do one thing more for me. I've left my purse; will you lend me a couple of crowns to take a chair with? I've missed an appointment with the maid, and I wish to return to the Park in a hurry.

BEAU. Reginald, you know I never use silver, it's so excessively dirty and heavy. Ask Mortimer for a couple of guineas as you go out. [REGINALD *starts to go.*] By the way, Reginald, it is just possible that I may enter into the golden bands myself. I am thinking somewhat of a marriage with a certain young lady whose charms, strange to say, very much resemble those you would have described had I permitted you to inflict me.

REGINALD [*laughing*]. You marry! Uncle! You! Your wit makes me laugh in spite of my dolors! Imagine the great Beau Brummell married! Why, Uncle, your children would be little Rosettes.

BEAU [*wincing*]. Reginald, never be guilty of a pun; it is excessively vulgar. I am serious. I think I may marry.

REGINALD [*going to* BEAU *and offering hand quickly*]. Then, Uncle, I am glad for you.

BEAU [*starts, looks at hand with eye-glass*]. Dear me, what's that? Oh, dear, no, Reginald—a glance of the eye. [REGINALD *drops hand.*] A glance of the eye! My boy, you look so like your mother—God bless you! [REGINALD *goes to table at left for hat and stick.*]

BEAU. You will return?

REGINALD [*boisterously, crossing to door at left*]. Yes, shortly.

BEAU [*again shocked at his loud tone*]. Reginald! [REGINALD *stops, returns a step or two, looks at* BEAU *as if to say,* "*What is it?*" BEAU *bows very politely.* REGINALD *remembers he had forgotten himself for a minute, bows, places hat on his head, as he turns, and exits less boisterously.*]

SIMPSON [*enters from ante-room as* REGINALD *exits*]. Mr. Abrahams, sir.

BEAU. Yes, you can let him in here.

SIMPSON [*exits and returns, ushering in* ABRAHAMS]. Mr. Abrahams, sir.

ABRAHAMS [*enters with assurance*]. I understand, Mr. Brummell, that you wished to see me. I had much difficulty in leaving my place of business, but you see I am here.

BEAU [*glancing at him through his glass*]. Ah—Abrahams —ah, yes! So you are, so you are.

ABRAHAMS [*insinuatingly*]. I thought it was likely, sir, that you wished to make a few payments.

BEAU [*dryly*]. I think that's wrong, Abrahams; do you know, I fear you will have to guess again.

ABRAHAMS [*with indignation*]. Well, now, really, Mr. Brummell, I hope you don't want to raise another loan.

BEAU [*pleased that he has surmised it*]. I believe that's right, Abrahams; second thoughts seem to be always the best.

ABRAHAMS [*very loudly*]. Really, Mr. Brummell, sir, I'm sorry, sir, but the fact is I can't possibly— [*Enter* SIMPSON *from ante-room.*]

SIMPSON [*interrupting* ABRAHAMS]. A footman from His Royal Highness, the Prince Regent, sir.

BEAU [*quite unconcernedly*]. Yes, you can let him come in here. [ABRAHAMS *looks at* BEAU, *and backs up a trifle. Enter footman. Stands below door.*]

BEAU [*without looking at him*]. Mortimer, which one is it?

MORTIMER [*who had come in from bedroom*]. Bendon, sir.

BEAU [*at right. Graciously*]. Very well, Bendon.

FOOTMAN [*with great respect*]. Mr. Brummell, sir, His Royal Highness wishes to know if you will be at home this afternoon at four o'clock. If so, he will call upon you to make arrangements for the dance at Carlton House.

BEAU. At what o'clock did you say, Bendon?

BENDON [*with low bow*]. At four o'clock, sir.

BEAU. Say to His Royal Highness to make it half-past four o'clock. [*Exit footman at left, followed by* SIMPSON. ABRAHAMS *is overcome with wonder at this, and looks at* MORTIMER, *who draws himself up proudly.*]

BEAU [*as if recollecting his presence*]. You were saying, Mr. Abrahams, that you could not possibly—

ABRAHAMS [*bowing, changing attitude and tone*]. H'm, ach—hem—that I should be very glad—though I am just now rather pressed myself. How much did you say, sir?

BEAU. How much did I say, Mortimer? [*Enter* REGINALD, *same door.*]

REGINALD [*boisterously rushing to* BEAU, *left center*]. Am I in good time, Uncle?

BEAU [*startled*]. Reginald, how often have I told you to enter a room properly. You came in like—like a—Mortimer, what did Mr. Reginald come like?

MORTIMER [*reproachfully*]. Like a thunderbolt, sir.

BEAU. Ah, yes—like a thunderbolt; very unpleasant things, thunderbolts. Mortimer, have I ever seen a thunderbolt?

MORTIMER. Once, sir.

BEAU. Yes; I once saw a thunderbolt; very unpleasant

things, thunderbolts. You must not come in like a thunderbolt, Reginald.

REGINALD [*looking at* ABRAHAMS]. I beg your pardon, Uncle Beau. Are you busy?

BEAU [*as if startled*]. I beg your pardon—

REGINALD. Are you busy?

BEAU. Busy! Ugh! Never employ that term with me. No gentleman is ever busy. Insects and city people are busy. This—ah—person has come to ask my assistance in some little financial matters, and I think I've rather promised to oblige him. Mortimer, go with this—ah—ah—person. You go with my valet. [ABRAHAMS *bows and bows.*] Yes, quite so, quite so. [*Exit* MORTIMER *and* ABRAHAMS *into ante-room at left,* ABRAHAMS *backing, bowing all the time.*]

REGINALD [*gloomily sitting on sofa*]. I was too late; I missed her.

BEAU. Don't be gloomy, Reginald, or I shall not be able to walk with you. Nothing is more conspicuous than melancholy. [MORTIMER *returns—coughs.*]

BEAU. Mortimer, are you coughing?

MORTIMER [*apologetically*]. Yes, sir.

BEAU [*at right*]. Well, I wish you wouldn't. You wish to speak with me?

MORTIMER. Yes, sir. [BEAU *crosses, bowing in apology as he passes* REGINALD.] Mr. Brummell, sir, everything is arranged satisfactorily, sir.

BEAU. Did you send for the new tailor, what's his name, to come this afternoon?

MORTIMER. Yes, sir.

BEAU. And have you written the letter to Mr. Vincent?

MORTIMER. Yes, sir, all ready to seal.

BEAU. Then seal it and dispatch it at once. And now, Reginald, come with me and you shall see me having my coat put on. [REGINALD *rises. Exit* BEAU *and* REGINALD *into bedroom. Enter* KATHLEEN *from ante-room.*]

KATHLEEN. La! I must come in for a minute. I missed my young gentleman in the Park, and I ventured back to ask how we are to discover who he is. That's what we must do somehow, but how? [REGINALD *enters from bedroom.*]

REGINALD [*coming down*]. Mr. Brummell's snuff-box, Mortimer. [REGINALD *and* KATHLEEN *recognize each other.*]

REGINALD. Her maid!

KATHLEEN [*to* MORTIMER]. Oh, Lord! The very young gentleman himself.

MORTIMER. What!

REGINALD [*at left. Suspiciously*]. What are you doing here?

KATHLEEN [*at center*]. Why, I missed you in the Park, sir—you were too early. [*To* MORTIMER.] Will you say something? But I saw you in advance of me. [*To* MORTIMER.] Give utterance to something! And I followed you here to give you this letter. [*Gives note to* REGINALD. *To* MORTIMER.] I had to give it to him that time.

BEAU [*outside, calling*]. Reginald! [MORTIMER *and* REGINALD *rush* KATHLEEN *off through bay window.* MORTIMER *stands at window after drawing curtain.* REGINALD *crosses to table at left center, and stands back of same. Enter* BEAU *from bedroom.*]

BEAU [*at center door*]. Mortimer, what was that extraordinary commotion?

MORTIMER [*at right, at window, innocently*]. What commotion, sir?

BEAU [*standing in doorway*]. Mortimer, don't be an echo; how often have I told you that servants are born to answer questions, not to ask them? I believe you said the sun was shining? [*Crosses to window.*]

REGINALD [*very loud, stopping him*]. Uncle Beau, your snuff-box. [*Offering box.*]

BEAU [*at center. Starts*]. Ah! I knew I lacked something; I perceived I had on my coat, my fob, my waistcoat, my unmentionables. Dear me, yes, it was my snuff-box— thank you, thank you. [*He does not take snuff-box. He is now fully dressed—long brown trousers, fitting very closely around the leg and buttoned around the ankle, a yellow brocaded waistcoat, brown coat, ruffled shirt with neckerchief, fob with many seals. He crosses to dressing-table and arranges flowers—three yellow roses—in his coat.* MORTIMER *has crossed to table and stands holding hat, gloves and stick.* REGINALD *has the snuff-box.* BEAU *turns from dressing-table, comes to the center.* REGINALD *offers him the snuff-box open.* BEAU *takes a pinch with courteous nod of head.* REGINALD *takes pinch, closes box, hands it to* BEAU, *who holds it in hand.*]

MORTIMER *then hands him gloves.* BEAU *arranges them in hand very precisely.* MORTIMER *then hands stick.* BEAU *puts this in just right position.* MORTIMER *then hands hat.* BEAU *takes it, is about to put it on, then looks at it, stands aghast, and hands it back with no word, but just an expression of complete astonishment.* MORTIMER, *very puzzled, takes it and then sees that he has handed it with the wrong side to put on. Bows very low with an expression of great chagrin. Turns it and hands it to* BEAU. BEAU *takes it, walks to mirror, raises it two or three times until he has it at just the right angle, then puts it on. Turns to* REGINALD.]

BEAU. And now, Reginald, I'll make your fortune for you. I'll walk down the Mall with you to White's. [*Walks to door, followed by* REGINALD, *as*

[THE CURTAIN FALLS.]

THE FIRST ACT

Scene Two

The Beau's *reception-room.* A small room, furnished in
chintz. Chippendale sofa at the right. Large entrance at
back with red striped chintz curtains. Palms in window.
A table on the left holds a standing memorandum tablet.
Small arm-chair back of sofa. Two or three other chairs
scattered around the room. A door at the left. Beau
Brummell *at the rise of curtain is standing by table,
looking at the memorandum tablet through his eye-glass.
He is dressed as in Scene One.* Simpson *draws the curtains at the back, and announces:*

Simpson. Mrs. St. Aubyn, sir! [Simpson *then leaves the
curtains drawn and goes out.* Beau *turns and bows.*]
Beau. Punctual as the day, and twice as welcome. [Mrs.
St. Aubyn *has sailed into the room with an air that plainly
says,* "You and I are to settle some important things to-day."
*She is a very handsome woman of about thirty, beautifully
dressed, and showing in every look and motion the woman
accustomed to homage and command. She carries a fan,
which she uses to emphasize all her remarks.*]
Mrs. St. Aubyn. You received my letter?
Beau [*with another bow*]. And your ambrosial lock of
hair. [Mrs. St. Aubyn *is at first offended, and then laughs
and sits on sofa.*]
Mrs. St. Aubyn. Not mine, my dear Beau; you know I'm
not such a fool. [Beau *is not at all taken aback by the mistake he has made.*]
Beau. Ah, no, I believe I am mistaken; but, my dear
Horatia, one gets things of this sort so mixed; and I plead in
extenuation that the wish was father to the thought. [Beau
sits in chair near table.]
Mrs. St. Aubyn. Have you missed me really these last
two days? Where have you been? It's been so dull without

you, I vow, I could almost have married again. [*Leans forward and speaks very confidentially.*] Now, I want you to do me a favor, will you?

BEAU. Whisper it and it is done.

MRS. ST. AUBYN. Well, then, I will whisper. I want you to get me a card to the dance at Carlton House.

BEAU. The very privilege that I have looked forward to. I desire to present you myself to the Prince, and witness your triumph. An unselfish pleasure, you would say, but I love you too well, my dear Horatia, not to sacrifice myself to your greatest opportunity. [*During this speech, MRS. ST. AUBYN has listened with a slight cynical smile, and now with an air of finality says:*]

MRS. ST. AUBYN. I would not give up your devotion altogether—even for the Prince's. [*With great empressement.*]

BEAU. Take both. Mine you will always have.

MRS. ST. AUBYN. Yet I think my devotion for you overbalances yours.

BEAU. My dear madam, you are too good. Do you know, I fear you will die young?

MRS. ST. AUBYN [*with an air of giving up this contest of wits*]. Oh, the deuce take your fine phrases! If I thought I'd a rival, I'd let the Prince flit somewhere else. You're clever and the Prince isn't. He'll be very dull. Then he'll be harder to keep within bounds. Oh, [*quickly as she sees an almost imperceptible shrug of BEAU'S shoulder*] it isn't that I'm afraid for my reputation—that was damned long ago. But I've certain notions of self-respect which aren't in the fashion and which men don't seem to understand.

BEAU [*very quietly*]. Marry him!

MRS. ST. AUBYN [*with real astonishment*]. What!

BEAU [*taking out snuff-box and taking snuff*]. Marry him.

MRS. ST. AUBYN. It is impossible!

BEAU. With you all things are possible. [MRS. ST. AUBYN *laughs nervously and steals a surreptitious look at herself in a little mirror in her fan.*]

MRS. ST. AUBYN. My dear Beau, I wish you'd make plain sense instead of pretty sentences. What advantages have I to recommend me?

BEAU. I will ask Mortimer to make out a list, but I may name one only—which is all-sufficient. For the past six weeks

—I have admired you. [MRS. ST. AUBYN *rises with a laugh.*]

MRS. ST. AUBYN. Oh, the conceit of the man! But tell me what style of woman is the Prince caught by? [BEAU *rising also.*]

BEAU. To be perfectly frank with you, the Prince admires the fashion, and I—have made you the fashion. I am expecting him here this afternoon. [MRS. ST. AUBYN *gives a shriek of dismay.*]

MRS. ST. AUBYN. Who? The Prince! Gracious, why didn't you tell me? [*Runs to cheval-glass.*] How am I looking? There, there, you needn't answer; I know it is one of my bad days. [BEAU *is really very much upset by this rushing around and rapid talking. Speaks as though quite overcome.*]

BEAU. My dear Horatia, I beg of you not to rattle on so; you've no idea how you fatigue me. [SIMPSON *enters at back and announces:*]

SIMPSON. The Duchess of Leamington, Mr. Sheridan, sir! [SIMPSON *goes out.* MRS. ST. AUBYN *says to herself, as she comes down to chair at right of sofa:*]

MRS. ST. AUBYN. Damme, that woman. [*The* DUCHESS *and* MR. SHERIDAN *enter at back. The* DUCHESS *is a very much painted and bewigged old young woman, dressed in a very light flowered gown, with a very large hat.* SHERIDAN *is still handsome, but no longer young, dressed in black silk knee-breeches, black coat and stockings; he wears the powdered wig instead of short hair like* BEAU'S. *The* DUCHESS *makes low curtsy to* BEAU, *who bows.*]

BEAU. Ah, Duchess, what happy accident! Has your carriage broken down at my door, or do you come out of your own sweet charity? We were just speaking of you. I said you were the best-dressed woman in London, but Mrs. St. Aubyn did not seem to agree with me. [*To* SHERIDAN.] How do you do, Sherry? [*Nods to* SHERIDAN *and, crossing to him, offers him snuff-box.* SHERIDAN *takes snuff.*]

DUCHESS [*as though noticing* MRS. ST. AUBYN *for the first time, says superciliously:*] How d'ye do?

MRS. ST. AUBYN [*haughtily*]. Mr. Brummell pleases to be witty at my expense, Duchess. [*Then to herself.*] I must be on my guard. I don't understand Beau. [*The* DUCHESS *seats herself on sofa.* MRS. ST. AUBYN *is sitting in chair just below sofa.* BEAU *is sitting at chair near table, and* SHERIDAN *is still standing.*]

DUCHESS. Mr. Sheridan and I thought we'd come to tell you the news. We knew you were never up till noon, and thought you might want to hear what's going on. [SHERIDAN *now brings down chair from the back, and sits about center.*]

SHERIDAN. And when we were nearly here we remembered that really there was nothing to tell. There seems to be a lamentable dearth of scandal and gossip nowadays. I don't know what we are coming to. The ladies have absolutely nothing to talk about.

BEAU. Sherry, I hear the "School for Scandal" is to be revived. It returns to us every year like Spring and the influenza.

SHERIDAN [*regretfully*]. Yes, but it won't be played as it used to be.

BEAU [*thankfully*]. No, I hope not.

DUCHESS. Dear me, only think of Miss Motional playing *Lady Teazle* now, at her age! Why is it that *passé* people are always so anxious to act? [*With a little affected giggle.*] I wonder you don't go on the stage, Mrs. St. Aubyn?

MRS. ST. AUBYN [*with great sweetness*]. I never experienced a scandal of sufficient *éclat* to warrant such a step. But you, Duchess, what a success you would have!

DUCHESS. Spiteful creature!

BEAU. How very severe— [SIMPSON *enters at back, and announces:*]

SIMPSON. His Royal Highness, the Prince Regent, sir. [SIMPSON *exits. The* PRINCE *enters; does not remove his hat. All rise.* DUCHESS *and* MRS. ST. AUBYN *curtsy.* SHERIDAN *bows very low and* BEAU *bows rather condescendingly.*]

PRINCE. Ah, Beau, good morning.

BEAU. This is very good of you, sir. The Duchess, I am sure, is a welcome vision. Sherry you know, and you have heard—surely you have heard of the fascinating Mrs. St. Aubyn.

PRINCE. But never have seen half enough.

BEAU. Where will you put yourself, sir?

PRINCE. [*very emphatically says as he crosses to sofa:*] Damme, here. [*He sits on sofa and makes a motion with his*

hand, inviting MRS. ST. AUBYN *to sit beside him. To do this,*
MRS. ST. AUBYN *has to cross in front of the* DUCHESS, *which
she does with a look of triumph, while the* DUCHESS, *in moving to* MRS. ST. AUBYN'S *vacated seat, turns up her nose as
much as to say, " That won't last long." And* BEAU, *having
witnessed all this little byplay, has a little smile as he sees all
is just as he wants it.*]

MRS. ST. AUBYN. I believe, sir, Mr. Sheridan is thinking
of a new play.

PRINCE. Don't you put me in, Sherry, or, if you do, mind
you make me thin. A fat man played me in the pantomime
t'other night, and damme, I had him locked up.

SHERIDAN [*with great deference*]. 'Twas a libel, sir, a
gross libel.

PRINCE. I heard, Beau, from my tailor, this morning, that
you had gotten up something new in trousers. Why the
deuce haven't you told me?

DUCHESS [*with affected girlishness*]. Oh, dear me, what
are the new trousers?

SHERIDAN [*maliciously*]. Why, Duchess, I don't see how
they can possibly interest you.

MRS. ST. AUBYN. Mr. Sheridan, Mr. Sheridan, both your
plays and your conversation ought to be expurgated.

DUCHESS. Come, come, stop all this banter, and Mr. Brummell will tell us.

BEAU [*as though bored by all this chatter*]. You must
excuse me, Duchess; I have contracted a cold.

PRINCE. I'll tell you, Duchess; they're long trousers which
are slit so [*pointing with his cane to his own leg*] at the bottom, and then buttoned tight. Very odd, you see, and striking.

DUCHESS. It might be too striking; don't you think it
depends on the—eh—eh—circumstances? [*She draws her
skirt up very slightly, and strikes her leg with her fan.*]

PRINCE. Damme, Duchess, you're right; and that's just
what I want to know of Beau here, whether he thinks my legs
could stand 'em.

BEAU. Really, my dear fellow, I'm no judge of calves.
[*All laugh.*]

SHERIDAN. You must appeal to the ladies, sir.

MRS. ST. AUBYN [*feigning to hide her face with her fan*].
No, no; I object!

BEAU. Mrs. St. Aubyn means they are little trifles not worth mentioning.

PRINCE. Now, I object. Besides, I've something else to talk about. What think you, Beau, of Tuesday week for the dance at Carlton House? [BEAU *rises very slowly, takes tablet, looks it over.*]

BEAU. Tuesday, Tuesday—yes, I think I might make Tuesday do. [PRINCE *rises, and everybody rises.*]

PRINCE [*to* MRS. ST. AUBYN]. You will not forget, then, siren, the opening quadrille with me. May I take you to your chair? [MRS. ST. AUBYN *makes him a low curtsy.*]

MRS. ST. AUBYN. You make me wish my chair was at my own door, instead of at Mr. Brummell's.

BEAU. That's very good, very good. [MRS. ST. AUBYN *curtsies with a look of triumph to the* DUCHESS. *The* PRINCE *holds out his hand. She places her hand lightly on his, curtsies low to* BEAU, *and retires up to the center door, while the* PRINCE *is making his adieus, which he does by simply nodding to the* DUCHESS *and* SHERIDAN, *most graciously nodding to* BEAU; *and then he takes* MRS. ST. AUBYN'S *hand again and they go off chattering.*]

DUCHESS [*who has witnessed this with ill-concealed envy*]. Now, Mr. Brummell, promise me you'll bow to me at the play to-night. You bowed to Lady Farthingale last week Thursday, and she has given herself airs ever since.

BEAU. After the play, Duchess, after the play. If I looked at you once during the play, I could never bend my attention again to the players.

DUCHESS [*with a girlish giggle*]. And that, Mr. Brummell, would damn the play.

BEAU. Yes, I shouldn't wonder if it did. It wouldn't be the first play I've damned. [DUCHESS *curtsies,* SHERIDAN *bows, and they go off at center door.* BEAU *takes up memorandum tablet and goes toward door, left, reading as he goes.*] Let me see—Thursday, lunch with Lord and Lady Pleasant, then on to Mrs. Hearsays—*pour passer le temps.* Dinner with the Dowager Countess of Alimony, dance at Gordon House, then to the Rag, then to the Raleigh, then to Vauxhall. [BEAU *goes out.* SIMPSON *enters at center door, showing in* MR. VINCENT. VINCENT *is a stout, red-faced man, bluff manner, dressed rather loudly, with brown bob-wig, and he drops his h's.*]

SIMPSON. Whom shall I say, sir?

VINCENT. Never mind introducing me. I'll introduce myself—tell him a gentleman wishes to see him in answer to his message; he'll understand.

SIMPSON. Yes, sir. [SIMPSON *goes out at left door with a look of disdain at* VINCENT.]

VINCENT [*who is in a state of great excitement*]. Well, am I really in the great Mr. Brummell's house? I thought I'd show my appreciation of the honor I feel in Mr. Brummell's suit for my daughter's 'and by answering his message in person. But, really, now I'm 'ere, I'm not sure I've done the right thing. It's perfectly absurd, ridiculous, but I'm slightly nervous. I, the most successful cloth merchant of the day—unreasonable! I must appear at my ease or I shall fail to make an impression. Let me see, what shall I say when he comes in? After greeting him cordially, but with dignity, which is due to my position, I'll tell him in the proper language, with a few figures of speech to show I'm a man of some learning—he's coming. [*Shows great nervousness. Begins to bow very low, moving first on one foot, then on the other, rubbing his hands together.*]

BEAU [*enters from left door; tablet in hand; as he comes on he says:*] Sunday—Sunday!—

VINCENT. He's coming, he's coming.

BEAU. Sunday after service, lunch with Lady Sybilla—Sybilla! She is "*un tant soit peu passé,*" but there was a time, there was a time, when poor Sybilla and I— [VINCENT'S *bowings and movements now attract* BEAU'S *attention, and he looks at him through eye-glass.*]

BEAU [*to himself*]. Ah, yes, the new tailor. [*Aloud.*] I will speak with you presently. I am somewhat occupied just now. [*Resumes soliloquy.*] Dinner with Figgles—silly beast, Figgles, but delicious truffles. [VINCENT *has still continued to bow.*]

BEAU [*looks at him again*]. Would you be so kind as not to wobble about in that way? [VINCENT *stops a moment.*]

BEAU. Thank you. [*Resumes soliloquy.*] Then on to Lady Ancient's—very tedious, but I must go or the poor

woman's rooms will be quite vacant. [VINCENT *has again
resumed his bowing and clasping and unclasping his hands.*]

BEAU [*looks at him*]. Did you hear what I observed?
Would you be kind enough not to wobble about in that way,
and please do not wash your hands incessantly with imaginary
soap, or *chassez* about in that manner? You have no idea how
you distress me. [VINCENT *never stops, growing more and
more nervous.*] How very extraordinary; he does not seem
to be able to stop. Perhaps he is suffering with St. Vitus's
dance. I shall never be able to employ a person so afflicted.
Well, I won't dismiss him at once. I'll turn my back on him
so I can't see him. [BEAU *turns his back to* VINCENT.] Let
me see, where was I—ah—yes, Lady Ancient's very tedious, but
I must go or the poor woman's rooms will be quite empty;
then on to the club.

VINCENT [*very deprecatingly*]. But, sir—

BEAU. I'll speak with you presently. I am somewhat occupied just now, and, although my back is turned, I can feel you
are wobbling about. [*To himself.*] I think I might venture
to play again with my present prospects, Monday—Monday—

VINCENT [*who is now getting restive, and realizes he is
being treated badly*]. But!—

BEAU. Please do not say "but" again.

VINCENT. My lord!—

BEAU. Nothing so commonplace.

VINCENT. Sir—

BEAU. Very well, I suppose I had better speak with him
—the sooner it is over the better. You've come to see me
about my suit, I suppose.

VINCENT. Yes, the honor it confers upon my daughter and
myself—

BEAU. It's affected his head. Does your daughter sew,
also?

VINCENT [*surprised*]. Oh, beautifully, Mr. Brummell,
but—

BEAU. I must ask you to omit your "buts." Now, if you
will stand perfectly still for a few moments, I will endeavor
to ask you one or two questions; but you must try to stand
still, and if you try very hard, you may succeed. But do try
—there's a good man—try, try, try again. [*Aside.*] I'm so
sorry for him. He must suffer so. Well, I won't look at him.

[*Turns away and sits down at table. During all this time* VINCENT *has been bowing, trying to stand still, but not succeeding, owing to his great embarrassment.*] Now, have you any new cloths?

VINCENT. My dear sir, I was not aware that you were at all interested in cloths. [*Looks around for a chair, and goes up to back of room to get one.*]

BEAU. He's violent—he's going to attack me.

VINCENT [*bringing down the chair near to* BEAU]. Yes, there are some very fine new cloths. Now, if you'll allow me—

BEAU. Certainly not, sir; certainly not. [*Aside.*] Poor man, I suppose he never waited upon anyone before.

VINCENT [*can now stand it no longer, and rises*]. This is too much. 'Tis outrageous. I'll not stand it, sir. I am a gentleman, sir.

BEAU. Then why don't you behave like one?

VINCENT. I've come here—

BEAU. Of course, you've come here, that's very evident. You've come in answer to my message, haven't you?

VINCENT. Yes, sir, I've come in answer to your message asking for my daughter's 'and—

BEAU. Your daughter's what?

VINCENT. My daughter's 'and—

BEAU. Your daughter's hand? [*It begins to dawn upon him.*] I beg your pardon.

VINCENT. I came to accept your offer of marriage, but I've altered my intention.

BEAU. Dear me, you are—

VINCENT. Mr. Holiver Vincent, sir.

BEAU [*aside*]. And I thought he was the tailor! [*Aloud.*] A thousand apologies; won't you be seated? I was very much preoccupied. I ask you a thousand pardons—but [VINCENT *has begun to bow and wobble again*] what can you expect if you will wobble about in that manner, my dear *Sir* Oliver! [VINCENT, *indignant, again is soothed by title.*]

VINCENT. Not *Sir* Holiver yet. *Mr.* Holiver—Mr. Holiver Vincent, at your service.

BEAU. I only regret that you did not say so before. [SIMPSON *enters.*]

SIMPSON. Sir, the Duke of York sends word, will you be

so gracious as to take mutton with him to-night? [BEAU *looks at* VINCENT, *who looks pleadingly at him, as much as to say, " Dine with me."*]

BEAU.   Send my polite regrets to His Royal Highness and say, I dine to-night with Mr. Oliver Vincent.   [SIMPSON *exits at center door.   BEAU offers his snuff-box to* VINCENT, *who takes a pinch and snuffs it with a loud, disagreeable noise, which shocks BEAU unspeakably.*]

[THE CURTAIN FALLS.]

THE SECOND ACT

*The ballroom at Carlton House, a large, stately room hung
in yellow damask—yellow damask furniture. On the
right, a door leading into reception room. On the left
are three curtained recesses. At the back a large doorway extends the whole width of room; it is curtained with
yellow brocade curtains, which are looped back, showing
a long hall hung with mirrors; it leads to supper room.
On the stage, at rise of curtain, is the PRINCE, standing near
the center, talking to MRS. ST. AUBYN. The PRINCE is
dressed in black, with the blue ribbon of the Garter;
MRS. ST. AUBYN in elaborate evening dress. SHERIDAN,
the DUCHESS OF LEAMINGTON, LADY FARTHINGALE,
LORD MANLY and other guests are standing at back.*

PRINCE [*a little impatiently, as though he had been welcoming guests until tired*]. Anyone else, damme; I'm ready
to dance. [*Servant enters from the door on the right.*]

SERVANT. Mr. Brummell, Mr. Oliver Vincent, Miss Vincent. [*Servant steps to one side of door as* MR. BRUMMELL
comes in with MARIANA, *her hand resting lightly on his.
The* DUCHESS *then steps forward and takes* MARIANA'S
hand. MR. BRUMMELL *steps back to the side of* VINCENT,
who has followed them on. The DUCHESS *leads* MARIANA
to the PRINCE. *While this is going on,* MRS. ST. AUBYN,
who has stared in amazement, says:]

MRS. ST. AUBYN. What's this presentation for: does it
mean money for the Duchess? She does not need it.

DUCHESS [*as she presents* MARIANA]. Your Royal Highness—Miss Vincent. [*Both curtsy to the* PRINCE.]

PRINCE. This places me deeper than ever in Mr. Brummell's debt. [*The* DUCHESS *and* MARIANA *back away and
retire to the back of room, where they are joined by* SHER-
IDAN. BEAU *now advances to the* PRINCE, *closely followed
by* VINCENT, *who is greatly excited.*]

39

BEAU. Sir, I have the honor to present my friend, Mr. Oliver Vincent.

MRS. ST. AUBYN [*aside*]. It's Mr. Brummell who is at the bottom of this. I think I begin to see.

PRINCE. Mr. Vincent? Is this *the* Mr. Vincent, of the City? For, egad, sir, I am pleased—

VINCENT [*greatly embarrassed*]. Your Highness, sir, the honor is all mine, ah, all mine, Your Highness, thank you for your cordiality, Your Highness. [*Offers the* PRINCE *his hand.* BEAU *quietly throws it up, and motions* VINCENT *away to the back, covering his retreat, as it were, by his own self-possession and the look of humorous appeal which he gives to the* PRINCE.]

MRS. ST. AUBYN. Your Royal Highness, what does Beau mean? Really, sir, I think you take too much from him. They are from the City, these Vincents; you can see its dust on their feet.

PRINCE [*chuckling at his own wit*]. Yes, damme, madam; but it's gold dust.

MRS. ST. AUBYN [*with a slight smile, such as an offended goddess might give*]. Pray, sir, let us have the dance now. [*The* PRINCE *offers her his hand and they take their places at the head of the set.* SHERIDAN *leads the* DUCHESS *to one side.* LORD MANLY *leads* LADY FARTHINGALE *to the other.*]

BEAU [*to* MARIANA]. May I have the delight of leading you out in the dance?

MARIANA. I fear, Mr. Brummell, you will find me but a poor dancer.

BEAU. I know you dance well, or I should not have asked you. I have watched you. One must always judge for oneself. [*He leads* MARIANA *to the head, opposite the* PRINCE. *They dance an old-fashioned quadrille, the end of which is a deep curtsy from the ladies and a bow from the men. The* PRINCE *then goes up to center door, and out through the hall with* MRS. ST. AUBYN.]

PRINCE. Egad! Poor Beau! Your charms have made me false to my friend.

MRS. ST. AUBYN. Ah! But I fear Your Royal Highness is fickle, and may be false to me, too.

PRINCE. Zounds! I could only be that by being false to

myself. [*They are now out of sight. The* DUCHESS *has joined* BEAU *and* MARIANA, LADY FARTHINGALE *and* LORD MANLY. *The latter couple now curtsy and bow and exit through center door, and go down the hall.*]

DUCHESS. I really think it gives one more *éclat* to dance with Mr. Brummell than to dance with the Prince.

BEAU [*quite sincerely*]. I really think it does. [*The* DUCHESS *and* MR. SHERIDAN *then bow, and also go out at center door, meeting* VINCENT, *who bows to them in a most exaggerated way and then comes down toward the* BEAU *and* MARIANA. BEAU *bows in courtly fashion and also goes out through center door, so* VINCENT *and* MARIANA *are left alone.* MARIANA *is a charming type of a young English girl, dressed in white, her hair in soft ringlets, with a wreath of tiny rose-buds.*]

VINCENT. This is the proudest moment of my life! He had heard of me; he recognized me at once, Mariana.

MARIANA [*quizzically*]. Of course, papa, he had read your name on his buttons.

VINCENT. You are mistaken, my dear; I am not a tailor, I am a cloth merchant. Did you notice how cordial His Royal Highness was? [*Regretfully.*] I was too stiff with him, much too stiff, but Mr. Brummell would have it so.

MARIANA [*still trying to make a jest of it*]. Quite right, papa; you needed your dignity and His Royal Highness did not.

VINCENT. Think, Mariana, what a difference to-day from yesterday. Yesterday, I was Vincent, of the City—to-night, I am Vincent, of the Court. It is a proud position, my dear; think of it, Holiver Vincent, the Prince's friend! No more "The Hoak, the Hash, and the Bonny Hivy Tree." No more "A Weary Lot Is Thine, Fair Maid." [*Imitates the playing of a piano.*] No more going to sleep after dinner. No, my dear, we'll read our names every morning, several times over, in the Court Journal. It'll be a staggerer for your Aunt Jane at 'Oundsditch.

MARIANA [*sadly*]. I think, for my part, we are very well as we are, and very happy. And I like the old songs, and I like my old father just as he is.

VINCENT. Pooh! My child, I am ambitious, and, if you marry the Beau, in a year from now, I may wear a coronet—

a coronet. [*Makes a gesture as though placing a coronet on his head.*]

MARIANA. Uneasy lies the head that wears a crown, papa, and how much are you going to give for the coronet? Anybody can buy one nowadays. Give your money for it, by all means—but not your daughter's happiness. [*Crossing and going up toward center as though to end the discussion.*]

VINCENT [*follows her and speaks pleadingly*]. Mariana, I have been a kind father to you. My heart is set upon the accomplishment of this thing. You have ever been a dutiful child.

MARIANA [*turning quickly*]. And you shall ever find me so. But I hold, papa, that a woman's heart alone should guide a woman's choice.

VINCENT [*turns away vexed*]. Yes, I know—but—

MARIANA. Still, my affection for you shall largely influence my decision. Go, my ambitious father. [*Goes to him and puts her hand on his shoulder.*] I will see what I can do to win the coronet for your head.

VINCENT [*delightedly kisses her forehead*]. That's a good child. [*He goes up and out through center door.*]

MARIANA. If I can only tear the arrow from my heart. [*Walks slowly up and down.*] No dream of greatness, no wish even of my father's, should for one instant weaken my devotion to Reginald if I could believe him true to me. But he has ceased to write; I hear of him only in social dissipation. He is gay and merry, and Mariana is forgotten. Since I cannot be happy, there is only my dear old father to be pleased. And yet—and yet— [*Starts and turns as BEAU, the DUCHESS and MR. VINCENT enter from the center door.*]

DUCHESS [*as she comes gaily down*]. *Ma mie,* you are very fortunate, I vow—you will be the talk of the town tomorrow—to have pirouetted with our Beau here. 'Tis no small favor, I assure you—and one his Beauship has never yet bestowed upon his doting Duchess—you naughty, naughty Beau! [*Shakes her fan at BEAU.*] And I must say, *ma mie,* you comported yourself right well, right limber and nimbly for a débutante. Though I am no bad executante on the tips of my toes myself, i' faith. [*Gives a little pas seul.*]

BEAU [*putting up glasses and looking at her critically*]. Ah, Duchess, all you need is a ballet skirt and a tambourine. But, egad, we forgot the Prince—the Merchant Prince—we have just left the title! Permit me, my dear Duchess, to present to you the money. Mr. Oliver Vincent—Her Grace, the Duchess of Leamington.

DUCHESS [*as she curtsies to* VINCENT, *who bows very low*]. Deuce take me, Mr. Brummell, have you ever known me to refuse a presentation to money?

BEAU. No, my dear Duchess, and I have known you to become very familiar with it at the card-table without even a formal introduction.

DUCHESS. Beau, I vow you're a brute. [*She crosses to* VINCENT *and they go up a little.*]

BEAU [*crossing to* MARIANA]. You hear that, Mariana. I am a brute, 'tis true, and I am looking forward to a conjunction of Beauty and the Beast. [*Turning to the* DUCHESS.] Duchess, shall Sir Money conduct you to the cardroom?

DUCHESS [*smiling at* VINCENT]. With pleasure, if he'll stay there with me.

BEAU. No fear of that, for your Grace is sure to put him in your pocket.

DUCHESS. Incorrigible! Come, Mr. Vincent, your arm, your arm; 'fore Gad, we are routed. [*Takes* VINCENT'S *arm; they turn to go.*]

BEAU [*stopping them*]. One moment, my dear Vincent. [BEAU *bows to* DUCHESS, *who joins* MARIANA, *and they stand talking, while* BEAU *speaks to* VINCENT.] My valet has neglected placing my purse in my pocket, and I am going to allow you the privilege of lending me five hundred guineas before you run away with the Duchess.

VINCENT [*heartily*]. Certainly, my dear Mr. Brummell, certainly, sir, take ten— [*Puts his hand in his pocket.*]

BEAU [*with a look of horror*]. Not here, my good sir, not here—in the card-room.

VINCENT [*going up to the* DUCHESS]. My arm, madam, my purse and myself are entirely at your service.

DUCHESS [*taking his arm*]. I only need one of them; but come, come, I see you are quite a courtier. *Au revoir,* Beau. [*To* MARIANA, *as she waves a kiss.*] *Ma chère!* [*Curtsies to the* BEAU, *waves her hand airily to* MARIANA, *and goes off with* VINCENT.]

BEAU. Your most humble and devoted slave, Duchess.

MARIANA. You do not follow the cards, Mr. Brummell?

BEAU. They are too fickle; I am always unlucky.

MARIANA. Unlucky at cards, lucky in love— [*Stops abruptly, vexed that she has mentioned the word " love."*]

BEAU. That is why I am here.

MARIANA [*a little coquettishly*]. Well, what sort of a hand shall I deal you?

BEAU [*with great meaning*]. Yours!

MARIANA [*with equal meaning*]. Are diamonds trumps?

BEAU [*reproachfully*]. No. Hearts!

MARIANA [*lightly*]. I haven't one in the pack.

BEAU. Nay, but you deal your cards badly.

MARIANA. That is because I have chosen Nature, not Art, to be my mistress.

BEAU. By my manners! I've a mind to bring Dame Nature into fashion again.

MARIANA. Then there's not a woman here could show her face.

BEAU. But you. And if you would deign to be seen always on my arm—

MARIANA. Mercy! Mr. Brummell, I fear you would wear me as you do your coat, and throw me aside when I'm wrinkled.

BEAU [*with a shudder*]. Don't mention wrinkles; they give me the jaundice.

MARIANA [*seriously*]. I cannot but remember that only one short week ago every bench in the Mall, every lady's tea-table, every *entr'acte* of the play was the occasion for reportings of Mr. Brummell's fancy for the Honorable Mrs. St. Aubyn.

BEAU. You cannot imagine I have not favored some women more than others. Mrs. St. Aubyn was clever and amused me. We passed our time in laughter, not in loving. [MRS. ST. AUBYN, *who has entered at back, hears this last remark.*]

MRS. ST. AUBYN. I fear I am *malapropos,* but I will be deaf and blind. [*She comes down the center, while* VINCENT, SHERIDAN, LADY FARTHINGALE *and the* DUCHESS *enter also at center door.*]

MARIANA. It would be a pity, madam, to destroy two faculties which serve you to such good purpose. [*Crosses and passes* Mrs. St. Aubyn *with a slight bend of her head, and joins* Vincent.]

Beau. Oh, that's very good. [*To* Mrs. St. Aubyn, *as he crosses to her.*] Don't you think that's very good? [*They stand together, apparently talking,* Mrs. St. Aubyn *very angrily.*]

Vincent [*to* Mariana]. A most bewitching woman that, but I'm sorry she would insist upon hunting Mr. Brummell, for I knew you wouldn't want to be interrupted. I did all I could with politeness. I took her to every other room before this. [Mariana *and* Vincent *go out at center door, as* Lord Manly *comes rushing on, almost running into them.*]

Lord Manly [*he is a fop of the period, and quite a little the worse for drink*]. My dear Beau! My dear Beau! [*A little louder.* Beau *pays no attention to him.*] My dear Beau!! [*Still louder.* Beau *finally looks at him.*] Lord Crawlings is cheating at the card-table. It is a fact! He has cards up his sleeve. What shall I do?

Beau. Cheating at the card-table?

Lord Manly. Yes; he has cards up his sleeve.

Beau [*thoughtfully*]. Cards up his sleeve!

Lord Manly. Yes. What shall I do?

Beau. Well, if he has cards up his sleeve, bet on him.

Lord Manly [*with a blank stare*]. Oh—thank you. [*He joins* Lady Farthingale *and offers her a chair, which she refusing, they stand conversing with other guests.*]

Lady Farthingale. If Mr. Brummell marries Miss Vincent, he'll have no more difficulty in paying for his clothes, though I hear he's sadly in debt now.

Sheridan. Poor Beau! He will never be able to forget the old gentleman's cloth; it will be like riding to wealth on a clothes-horse.

Duchess [*who has been looking down the hall*]. Lord, Mr. Sheridan! They are starting for supper. You can do as you please, but I want an oyster. [Sheridan *and* Duchess *go off at center door, followed by* Lady Farthingale, Lord Manly *and other guests.*]

Mrs. St. Aubyn [*to* Beau, *who was starting to go*]. I insist upon a few words with you.

Beau. Your wishes are my commands. [*He is now stand-*

ing in the door, center, so he can look down the hall. Mrs.
St. Aubyn *is walking angrily back and forth.*]

Mrs. St. Aubyn. I found myself quite *de trop* when I
entered the room a few minutes ago.

Beau. You speak of impossibilities.

Mrs. St. Aubyn. Pray, spare me; I overheard your last
speech.

Beau. You mean you listened to what I said.

Mrs. St. Aubyn. Well, if I did—I begin to see through
you now.

Beau. Happy me!

Mrs. St. Aubyn. Did you think me blind when you presented these Vincents to the Prince?

Beau [*bowing to some imaginary guests down the hall*].
How do you do? Who could think those eyes blind?

Mrs. St. Aubyn. You presented me to the Prince, not
for my own sake, but for yours. 'Twas a pleasant way to be
rid of me.

Beau. No way with such a destination could possibly be
pleasant.

Mrs. St. Aubyn. You have puffed the Prince with the
conceit that he is driving you out of my affections against your
will. Suppose he were to know the truth?

Beau. Royal personages are so rarely told the truth that
if he did hear it he would not recognize it. How do you do!
[*Again bowing to some imaginary person.*]

Mrs. St. Aubyn. What would become of his friendship
for you, do you think, and what would you do without it?

Beau. He would have my sincere sympathy.

Mrs. St. Aubyn. Suppose I were to inform him?

Beau [*again bowing*]. How do you do, my dear Lady
Betty; how do you do? Yes, presently—with great pleasure
—h'm. [*Turning and apparently paying attention to* Mrs.
St. Aubyn *for the first time.*] My dear Horatia would not
be so foolish as to ruin herself. Would the Prince, do you
think, still care for you if he thought I no longer admired
you? He affects you now for the same reason he wears my
coats, because I have made you as I made them—the Fashion.

Mrs. St. Aubyn [*triumphantly*]. But there's something
that binds one faster to a man than the button of a coat.
There is, my dear Beau, such a thing as marriage.

BEAU. Oh, yes, to be sure! There, my dear madam, I bow to your vast experience [MRS. ST. AUBYN *makes an impatient movement*], but, when it comes to a question of the Prince's wedding coat, I fear you will find the buttons are sewed on with a very light thread.

MRS. ST. AUBYN. There you are wrong. You seem to forget, my dear Beau, that the Prince already dotes on me. We are both playing a little game—you and I—but I am persuaded I shall win, for I stake on a heart. [*Sweeps past* BEAU *with a superb gesture, toward the left.*]

BEAU [*very quietly*]. Your fortune will turn, for you stake on a knave.

MRS. ST. AUBYN. What will take my knave when the king is out of the pack?

BEAU. Why, then, I think a queen might turn up. [*Before* MRS. ST. AUBYN *can crush him with the reply that is on her lips,* VINCENT *enters.*]

VINCENT. Ah, 'ere you are, my dear Mr. Brummell; you are losing your supper, and Mrs. St. Aubyn, too, is depriving the feast of its most brilliant hornament.

BEAU. Yes, truly, it is too selfish of Mrs. St. Aubyn. Mr. Vincent, Mrs. St. Aubyn must permit you to conduct her to the supper-room.

MRS. ST. AUBYN [*sarcastically*]. Surely, Mr. Vincent did not do *me* the honor of leaving the table to search me out.

VINCENT. 'Fore Gad, madam, though I did see a vacant seat next His Royal Highness, in truth I came to look for my daughter.

BEAU. Mrs. St. Aubyn will hardly permit the chair which awaits her next to the Prince to remain vacant. [*Takes* MRS. ST. AUBYN's *hand and hands her with great* empressement *to* VINCENT.] Meanwhile, Mr. Vincent, I will go through the rooms for your daughter. [MRS. ST. AUBYN *stops, gives* BEAU *a look, is about to make a scene, then thinks better of it, and lets* VINCENT *lead her from the room.*]

BEAU. You amused me once, but you do so no longer. No, you're clever; yes, you are clever, and you dress to perfection, but Mariana has all your charms and more—a heart! Horatia St. Aubyn, your day in the world is waning; Mariana's reign begins. I will go and inform her so. She cannot be insensible to my regard, to my love, for, strange to say, I begin to think I do love her. Yes, I believe I do. [*Quite seriously.*] And I think I love her madly—yes, I do, I love her madly. [*Stands for a moment in deep thought; then walks slowly off through center door down the hall.* MARIANA *enters from door down right from reception room. She has a note in her hand.*]

MARIANA. Kathleen has conveyed to me my own letter to Reginald unopened. She says he has left his lodgings, and his landlady does not know when he will return. I am afraid men are not what they are represented to be. [*Sits down in chair near the door at right.* LORD MANLY *comes on through hall and center door. He is slightly intoxicated.*]

LORD MANLY. Ah! Miss Vincent! What happiness.

MARIANA [*annoyed*]. Here's another!

LORD MANLY. Won't you drink something? I mean eat something?

MARIANA [*not looking at him*]. Thank you, I care for nothing! There can be no mistake; Kathleen vowed she delivered the letters.

LORD MANLY. You won't eat, and you won't drink— most 'straordinary! What *will* you do?

MARIANA. I will dispense with your society, sir. [*As she rises, she looks at him.*] I do believe he is intoxicated.

LORD MANLY. She's coy! She's coy! No, fair creature, I have follolled—follolled—I have follolled—most 'straordinary I can't say follolled—I have follolled you from room to room to find you.

MARIANA. And, having found me, you may leave me, sir!

LORD MANLY. Leave you! Never! Never will I stir from this sacred spot. [*In his endeavor to stand quite still, he staggers and almost falls over.*] I mean the sacred spot where you are. Miss Vincent, I adore you! Fact. All you do, I see through rosy-colored glasses.

MARIANA. Wine-colored glasses you mean, sir. Let me pass!

LORD MANLY. No, fair tantalizer. [*Nods his head with great satisfaction.*] Good word—tantalizer. I will speak; my heart is full.

MARIANA. There can be no doubt about the fullness.

LORD MANLY. Here on my knees [*looks at knees*]—egad, look at my knees. I have four knees instead of two knees—

but, no matter—here on all my knees [*kneels, almost falling*]
I will pour out—

MARIANA. More liquor, sir! You do not need it.

LORD MANLY. You cannot ignore me, my love, my passion, my *adorashion*—I mean adoration—Miss Vincent—I—
[BEAU *has come on through center door. Unperceived, he
comes down, takes* LORD MANLY *by the ear, making him rise
and stagger back.*]

BEAU. My dear Miss Vincent, how unfortunately unconventional.

LORD MANLY. Mr. Brummell, sir, you are no gentleman.

BEAU. My good fellow, you are no judge.

LORD MANLY. My honor, sir, my honor!

BEAU. Fiddlesticks! Come, trot away, trot away. You
may apologize to Miss Vincent to-morrow.

LORD MANLY. You apologize to me now, sir.

BEAU. I never had occasion to do such a thing in my life.
[*Walks up and looks off down the hall.*] Now trot away; I
think I see the Prince approaching.

LORD MANLY. Proach aprincing!—I mean Prince approaching. Miss Vincent, it is with deep regret I say adieu!
[*He stumbles to door at right and goes off.*]

BEAU [*coming down and offering* MARIANA *a chair. She
sits*]. I heartily congratulate you, my dear Miss Vincent, on
having escaped a scene. Nothing but the regard I bear you
could have persuaded me to so nearly incur a possible fracas.
Lord Manly was born with a silver spoon in his mouth, and
he has thought it necessary to keep that spoon full ever since.
But now that we have found one another, may I not be permitted to continue the conversation where it was broken off?
I desire to speak with you seriously. I wish to make a confession. I want to tell you what perhaps you know—when
I first sought your hand, I did not bring my heart. I admired
you, 'tis true, but I did not love you—not then—not madly!
I was—I am so deeply in debt, so hemmed in by my creditors,
so hard pressed on every side, it was necessary for me to do
something to find the wherewithal to satisfy their just demands,
or sink under my misfortunes and give up forever the life of
the world which had become my very breath and being. The
one means at my disposal to free myself from my difficulties
was a marriage. I knew your fortune and I sought you out.

The admiration I entertained for you the first few days deepened into esteem, and finally expanded into love—mad love! That is why I have rehearsed this to you. At first it was your fortune which allured me—but now it is yourself!

MARIANA. Mr. Brummell!

BEAU. Yet, were you penniless, I would not wed you.

MARIANA [*rising in astonishment*]. Mr. Brummell!

BEAU. Because I would not drag you down to share this miserable, uncertain lot of mine. No! I would seek you once to tell you of my love, and then step aside out of your path, and never cross it again. I would not willingly, purposely encompass your unhappiness.

MARIANA [*slowly*]. I begin to believe in you.

BEAU. I remember no other word that you have spoken. May I have the delight of pressing my very unworthy lips to your very dear hand? [MARIANA *is about to give* BEAU *her hand; then suddenly withdraws it.*]

MARIANA. I think, Mr. Brummell, I would rather you did not.

BEAU [*thoughtfully*]. I believe you are right. Yes, I am quite sure you are! Thank you. You have saved me from doing something very commonplace.

MARIANA. You are not angry, sir?

BEAU. I believe it is exactly fifteen years since I last lost my temper—but, Mariana, I still await your answer. It is a new sensation for Brummell to be kept waiting.

MARIANA. Will you leave me, sir, to consider my decision? I pray you, Mr. Brummell, give me a few moments here—alone. [*She motions toward recess farthest down stage, and crosses toward it.*]

BEAU. I would refuse you nothing. I will await your pleasure in this other recess, and seek you here in five slow minutes. [*He motions toward the recess, the farthest up stage, and with a low bow to* MARIANA *goes in and draws the curtain.*]

MARIANA [*holding the curtain which closes the recess where she is standing*]. I cannot bring myself to say yes to him, although a certain sympathy pleads in his behalf, and joins with pride to prompt me against Reginald, who has neglected me. Why has he not replied to my letters? 'Tis very soon to be forgotten! Oh, Reginald, to be absent when most I needed you! You are no better than the men of the world. Father is right. Mr. Brummell shall have his answer. [*The* PRINCE *and* MRS. ST. AUBYN *enter at center door, so much engrossed in each other that they do not see* MARIANA.] Oh, how provoking! [MARIANA *hides in recess and draws the curtain.*]

BEAU [*who has also looked out at that moment*]. How very annoying! I shall have to play Patience on a window-seat, and wait.

MRS. ST. AUBYN. Yes. I must own to you, my sentiments toward Mr. Brummell are greatly altered. Until I met you—can you believe it?—I positively thought him a man of some parts.

BEAU [*from the window*]. Really, really!

PRINCE. Goddess! Of course, he has been much with me, and naturally smacks somewhat of my wit.

BEAU. Ah, that's very good! Very good!

MRS. ST. AUBYN. But only as a false echo does, for he has none of your delicate pleasantry.

BEAU. No, thank goodness, I haven't.

MRS. ST. AUBYN. He mimics you in dress, in everything, but, then, you know, he never had your figure. [*The* PRINCE *and* MRS. ST. AUBYN *go toward middle recess and seat themselves.*]

BEAU. Heaven forbid!

MRS. ST. AUBYN. He really has no taste.

PRINCE. He showed that when he chose Miss Vincent for his marked attention.

MRS. ST. AUBYN. And do you think so, too? Why, I know Miss Vincent is an insignificant little thing, whose name has never been associated with any gentleman of quality, but, though without mind or manners, she has money, sir. She dresses like a guy, but her clothes, like the clouds, have silver lining.

MARIANA [*with a hasty look out of the curtain*]. I wish I could escape by the window.

BEAU. I've half a mind to crawl out of the window, but I might be observed. There's no resource but to try to go asleep.

PRINCE. You are a flatterer and a coquette.

MRS. ST. AUBYN. No; only a woman—and under a spell.

PRINCE. Damme, that sounds very fine. I should like—

MRS. ST. AUBYN.   Well?

PRINCE.   I should like to be one of those little words that kiss your lips and die.

BEAU.   One of my pet speeches—number five.

MRS. ST. AUBYN.   Beware, sir, let me warn you—remember, I have been married once already.

PRINCE.   'Fore Gad, madam, I wish that you would marry twice.

MRS. ST. AUBYN.   Never! Now! To be sure, I once thought there was something like love engendered in me by Mr. Brummell, but now I know it was not real love; it was only a shadow.

PRINCE.   Why do you think that?   [*At this moment* VINCENT *enters from the center door. All the curtains of the different windows are drawn so he can see no one.*]

VINCENT.   I cannot keep away any longer; she's been sensible and accepted him, or they'd have been gone long before this. [MRS. ST. AUBYN *moves the curtain a little, with a slight exclamation.*]   There they are in the recess behind the curtain. Oh, he's clever—Mr. Brummell—very clever.

MRS. ST. AUBYN.   I tremble to acknowledge, even to myself, the dictates of my own heart.   Ah, sir, I conceive you know only too well who reigns there now.

VINCENT [*who apparently cannot hear*].   I should just like to hear a word to see how the great Mr. Brummell makes love.   I wonder would it be wrong now to listen a bit?   Why should it be—am I not her father?   It's my duty, and I will. [*Comes further down and listens.*]

PRINCE.   Siren!   You make me drunk with joy!

MRS. ST. AUBYN.   No; let me recover myself.   You have bewitched me, sir.   I must resist your fascinations, and not forget the difference in our rank.   Fashion would condemn me.

PRINCE.   Damn Fashion!

VINCENT.   Oh!   Mr. Brummell a-damning Fashion.   How he loves her!   How he loves her!

MRS. ST. AUBYN.   Ah! sir, we women are so frail, so easily beguiled!

PRINCE [*falling on his knees*].   By Heaven, I will not lose you!

VINCENT [*joyfully*].   He's on his knees!   He's on his knees!

PRINCE. Superb! sumptuous! beautiful woman! [*Kisses her hand.*]

VINCENT. He's kissing her! He's kissing her!

PRINCE. I swear I will marry you!

VINCENT [*who can restrain himself no longer, rushes forward and draws curtain aside*]. And so you shall! Bless you, my—[*Sees the* PRINCE *and* MRS. ST. AUBYN. *Falls back.*] Oh, Lord! The Prince! [*All guests enter at center door.*]

PRINCE [*rising, indignantly*]. What do you mean, sir? Confound your damned impudence! Will someone show this gentleman—

BEAU [*who has come slowly down*]. Oh, take his blessing; it won't hurt you.

PRINCE. Damn his blessing!

BEAU. Be composed, my dear Wales, or you'll make a fool of yourself.

PRINCE [*too exasperated to take from* BEAU *what he usually thinks all right*]. Oh, I am tired of your deuced impertinence, too, Beau. Step aside, step aside!

BEAU [*slowly handing his snuff-box to the* PRINCE]. My dear Wales, first you lose your equilibrium, and now you lose your temper. Take a little snuff.

PRINCE. Damn your snuff! [*Knocks snuff-box out of* BEAU'S *hand.*]

BEAU [*puts up his glass and looks quietly at him*]. Very bad manners, very bad. I shall have to order my carriage. Wales, will you ring the bell? [*Everybody is aghast at* BEAU'S *daring. The* PRINCE *stands petrified.* BEAU *holds out his hand to* MARIANA, *who has been standing in the recess, half fainting. She comes forward, bows low to the* PRINCE, *and backs to the door, followed by her father, who is pitifully dejected. As* BEAU, *with a last look at the* PRINCE *through his glass, turns and walks toward the door,*

[THE CURTAIN FALLS.]

THE THIRD ACT

*The Mall, St. James Park, the great promenade where, every
day, all London walks. There are benches on each side
of the stage under the trees. At the back, ladies and
gentlemen can be seen walking.*

MORTIMER *comes on from right-hand side, and walks up and
down impatiently. After a little,* KATHLEEN *appears in
a great hurry.*

KATHLEEN. Oh! You're there, are you?

MORTIMER [*indignantly*]. Am I here? You're half an
hour late.

KATHLEEN [*airily*]. Well, what do you expect? Aren't I
a woman? Say, what's the matter with your face? You have
an awful gloomy expression of countenance.

MORTIMER [*laughing*]. You little minx. Well, how goes
it?

KATHLEEN [*crossing to bench and sitting down*]. Why,
bad. I can't for the life of me keep one lie from spoiling the
other. Say, is all this true about Mr. Brummell and the
Prince?

MORTIMER. Yes. We've quarrelled.

KATHLEEN. And did the Prince cut ye's?

MORTIMER. No; we cut the Prince, and on account of you
Vincents, too. The Prince is deuced put out with Mr. Brummell, [*crosses to bench and sits*] so Bendon told me. It's all
abroad, and I left a swarm of creditors at the house, and,
worse still, there are two bailiffs after him. [KATHLEEN *gives
an exclamation of horror.*] We must hurry on this marriage,
Kathleen, or you and I'll be ruined. We must take pains to
keep Mr. Brummell and his nephew apart, for he's that partial
to him there's no telling what he mightn't do if he was to
discover Miss Mariana and Mr. Reginald were lovers.

KATHLEEN. And we must see to it that Miss Mariana
and Mr. Reginald don't meet, else he'd explain how he'd never

received any of her letters. I kept them all carefully, for I thought it might comfort him to read 'em after she was married to Mr. Brummell. But I must be off. [*Rises.*] Good morning, me Lud. [*Makes very deep curtsy.*]

MORTIMER [*bowing very low*]. Till this evening, me Lady.

KATHLEEN. Till this evening. [*Turns to go out, and meets* REGINALD *face to face.*]

REGINALD. Ah! Kathleen, where have you been this last week?

KATHLEEN [*is very much perturbed;* MORTIMER *has retreated to the back of the Mall, and has disappeared*]. Here, sir, here.

REGINALD. Will your mistress be in the Park this morning?

KATHLEEN. No, sir; she left town to-day, sir.

REGINALD [*a little wistfully*]. Was she—in good spirits, Kathleen?

KATHLEEN. Oh, beautiful, sir! She skipt with joy.

REGINALD [*gives* KATHLEEN *money, and then slowly walks away*]. I cannot understand it. I am sure there is some mistake.

KATHLEEN [*looking at the coin disdainfully*]. That's mighty small pay for a mighty big lie. Bad cess to him! [*She walks off at the right with a toss of her head. As she disappears,* REGINALD *comes down as though to call her back, but she has gone, and he turns to see* MORTIMER.]

REGINALD. Ah, Mortimer, is Mr. Brummell well?

MORTIMER [*very respectfully, hat in hand*]. No, sir. Not at all, sir. He can see no one, sir.

REGINALD. But he will see me?

MORTIMER. Excuse me, sir, but he especially mentioned your name, sir; he could not even see you.

REGINALD. Will he not be in the Mall this morning?

MORTIMER. No, oh no, sir.

REGINALD. Well, tell him I will visit him to-morrow. [REGINALD *goes off down path to the right.*]

MORTIMER. That was a tight squeeze. I expect him here any moment. I must see him and warn him of the bailiffs, if he only arrives before they do. [MORTIMER *goes off hurriedly by a path to the left.* BEAU *enters from the lower left-hand side, and walks slowly to the center, followed by* MOR-

TIMER. MORTIMER *seems quite out of breath.* BEAU *is dressed in dark green silk knee-breeches, green coat, black silk stockings, buckled shoes, frilled shirt and neckcloth; wears two fobs, carries cane with eye-glass in the top; has gray high hat of the period, yellow waistcoat, yellow gloves, large red boutonnière.*]

MORTIMER. Mr. Brummell, sir! [BEAU *starts, turns, lifts cane slowly, looks at* MORTIMER *through glass on top, then turns away and continues his walk.*]

MORTIMER [*very deferentially, but firmly*]. Mr. Brummell, sir!

BEAU [*without turning*]. I think there is some mistake.

MORTIMER. Excuse me, sir, but I *must* speak to you.

BEAU. You forget, Mortimer, servants in the street are like children at the table,—they may be seen, but must not be heard.

MORTIMER. I have not forgotten, sir, but this is serious.

BEAU. Serious! then it is sure to be unpleasant—wait till I take some snuff. [*Takes snuff very quietly, and with much ceremony replaces box; then nods to* MORTIMER *and listens.*]

MORTIMER. Sir, your quarrel with the Prince is already common talk.

BEAU [*brushing a little snuff off his ruffles*]. Ah, poor Wales!

MORTIMER. There was a crowd of creditors at your door when I left, sir.

BEAU. That is neither new nor serious.

MORTIMER. But they were angry and would not go away.

BEAU. Why did you not send them off?

MORTIMER. Sir, we've been sending them off for the past two years, and now—they won't *be* sent. Besides, sir, there are two bailiffs who swore they'd have you if they had to take you in the Mall.

BEAU. Impossible!

MORTIMER. I fear not, sir; one is from Mr. Abrahams.

BEAU. Here? In the Mall? I would rather perish! There is no help for it. [*To himself.*] I must make a shield of my marriage. I blush to do it, for it would seem to leave a blot upon my love for Mariana, but a blot upon that love is better than a blot upon the name of Brummell, the name she is to wear. [*Aloud to* MORTIMER.] Mortimer!

MORTIMER. Yes, sir.

BEAU. You must hasten back and meet them, these dogs of bailiffs; you must prevent them by telling them of my marriage to the daughter of Mr. Oliver Vincent. That prospect should satisfy them. Promise them all they demand—and added interest. [BEAU *starts to go off at the right-hand side;* MORTIMER *also moves off to the left.*] Promise them everything. [MORTIMER *stops and bows respectfully, then starts again.* BEAU *moves on a few paces, then stops again.*] Promise them anything! [MORTIMER *again stops and bows.* BEAU *moves on again, and* MORTIMER *also starts again to go.* BEAU *stops suddenly.*]

BEAU. And, Mortimer! [MORTIMER *stops, and comes back a few steps.*] You must not go unrewarded [MORTIMER *looks pleased and expectant*]; promise yourself something! [BEAU *walks slowly off at the right-hand side and* MORTIMER, *with low bow, replaces his hat, and goes quickly off at the left side.*]

MORTIMER [*as he exits*]. Yes, sir! [VINCENT *and* MARIANA *enter from the upper left-hand entrance.* MARIANA *is dressed simply but prettily in a light flowered silk gown and poke bonnet, with a parasol.*]

VINCENT. We'll be sure to meet him here somewhere. You must do it all, Mariana. He was just as haughty with me last night after we left Carlton House as he always was. You wouldn't have thought he had just sacrificed himself for me.

MARIANA. Sacrificed himself for *you,* papa?

VINCENT. Isn't it sacrificing himself for him to give up his position in the world? And isn't that what he has done to resent your father's insult?

MARIANA [*trying to lighten the seriousness of the situation*]. I fancied he did it partly on my account, papa.

VINCENT. Of course, you little rogue, it was for us both, but it's you alone who can repay him. He hasn't a penny, and this rupture with the Prince has brought down all his creditors upon him. With the money your dowry will bring him [MARIANA *turns her head away, biting her lip*], he can pay off his creditors and defy the Prince. Without it he can do neither, and is utterly ruined.

MARIANA. I realize, father, that it is through us this sudden calamity has come upon Mr. Brummell. It was you, papa, who were to blame. Why did you bring down the curtain before the comedy was over?

VINCENT [*a little irritably*]. Come, come, Mariana, you have too teasing a temper.

MARIANA [*seriously enough now*]. Ah, my dear father, I only want to help you by making light of the matter. Come [*taking his arm and crossing slowly toward the right*], let us find Mr. Brummell. I am not blind to the fact that it was by protecting you and me he exposed himself to insult. Well, he shall not suffer for it. Father, I promise you that I will accept his hand!

VINCENT. And I feel sure that it will mean happiness for you in the end. Wait here [*seats MARIANA on bench at right*] a moment, and I will return with Mr. Brummell. [*VINCENT exits at the upper right-hand path.*]

MARIANA. Yes, yes. I must hesitate no longer. I must think now only of my father, and not remember Reginald, who has neglected me. Gratitude and sympathy shall take the place of love in my heart. [*MRS. ST. AUBYN enters from right-hand entrance, dressed very exquisitely in white,—large white hat; she carries a fan.*]

MRS. ST. AUBYN. Ah, Miss Vincent! Is Mr. Brummell with you? [*Makes a very slight curtsy.*]

MARIANA [*rising and curtsying*]. No; my father.

MRS. ST. AUBYN. And you have him to thank for the scene last evening. It is he Mr. Brummell has to thank for the Prince's displeasure.

MARIANA [*anxiously*]. Madam, and is the Prince still angry?

MRS. ST. AUBYN [*with great relish*]. He is furious, and swears he will never forgive him. There is, I think, only one person who could influence him in Mr. Brummell's behalf, and that person—is—myself! [*Crosses triumphantly in front of MARIANA, with a sweep of her fan on the last word.*]

MARIANA [*eagerly going a little toward her*]. Then, surely, you who have been such a good friend of Mr. Brummell will use your influence in his behalf. Indeed, if I am not wrong, it was through Mr. Brummell that you met the Prince. Your smoothing this quarrel, then, will be but a fair return to him.

MRS. ST. AUBYN. You forget I am a woman of fashion. We take all we can get, but we never give anything. No, only on one condition shall I persuade the Prince to hold Mr. Brummell again in favor.

MARIANA [*with quiet scorn*]. Ah, I see, a condition. Then you women of the world condescend to sell, if you will not give.

MRS. ST. AUBYN [*angrily*]. You would do better not to ruffle me. My condition is this: If you will promise to relinquish Mr. Brummell, I will make the Prince promise not to cut him, as he has sworn to do publicly to-day. [*Looks triumphantly at* MARIANA, *then turns away as though to give her time to consider.*]

MARIANA. I would I could accept this proposition, but I cannot, I cannot! 'Twould be the greatest injustice to Mr. Brummell. I must not forget that he did not hesitate to sacrifice himself for me and my father. I spoke to her of making him a return. Let me not shrink then from making as just a one myself. [*Then speaking to* MRS. ST. AUBYN, *who has turned toward* MARIANA.] What right have you to ask anyone to give him up?

MRS. ST. AUBYN. He sought my favors before you enticed him from me.

MARIANA [*very quietly*]. I do not believe that.

MRS. ST. AUBYN [*angrily*]. You are uncommonly insolent. [*Then changing her tone to one of condescension.*] Well, even if it were not so, I should still have the right to ask you. You seem to forget the difference in our position. [*She sweeps past* MARIANA *with a grand air toward the right. At this moment* BEAU *enters from the right-hand side; he has overheard the last speech. He crosses to the center, bowing to* MRS. ST. AUBYN *as he passes her, and with a very low bow to* MARIANA *says:*]

BEAU. It is you, Mrs. St. Aubyn, who forget. It is greatly to the credit of Miss Vincent if she can overlook a difference your present conduct makes so very marked.

MRS. ST. AUBYN [*with a very low curtsy*]. I will repeat to you what I have just said to Miss Vincent.

BEAU [*airily*]. Pray do not fatigue yourself, madam.

MRS. ST. AUBYN. You will learn that I know how to remain a friend when once I become one. I offered Miss

Vincent the chance of regaining for you the Prince's friendship.

BEAU. And your price?

MRS. ST. AUBYN [*in a low tone*]. Yourself.

BEAU [*to* MARIANA]. And you, you refused? [MARIANA *bows her head.*] It would have been most unflattering, madam, had Miss Vincent disposed of me so cheaply.

MRS. ST. AUBYN [*who is now enraged almost beyond the bounds of endurance*]. Are you mad? Do you know to whom you are speaking? You are somewhat rash, sir. Discard me, and the Prince shall know *all*.

BEAU. He knows so very little at present, the knowledge of anything would be largely to his advantage. And yet—I cannot imagine you will tell him—*all*.

MRS. ST. AUBYN. Your raillery is ill planned. A woman scorned—

BEAU. Pray spare us, Mrs. St. Aubyn; you were never intended for tragedy—it does not become you—and it produces [*pause*]—wrinkles.

MRS. ST. AUBYN [*has now recovered her composure*]. Mr. Brummell, I bid you adieu—you have taught me how to smile even when—tush—I am a woman of fashion! [*Crosses to left, passing* MARIANA.] Miss Vincent, I wish you joy. [*With an exaggerated deep curtsy.* MARIANA *curtsies. Looks off up the left path, and calls:*] Manly—Lord Manly. [MANLY *comes on, raises hat, bows.*] Lord Manly—your arm—your arm. [*They go off arm in arm.*]

MARIANA [*sinking down on bench*]. Your regard and protection leave me too much in your debt.

BEAU. Pray let that debt weigh no more heavily on you than do my debts on me. One smile of yours had overpaid me.

MARIANA. If your creditors were as easily satisfied as you are, sir, I should be prodigal of my smiles.

BEAU [*crossing to* MARIANA'S *side*]. Ah, Mariana, if your smiles were the coinage, egad, I think I should turn miser.

MARIANA. You are not practical, sir. I must make you so.

BEAU. I am your slave, and the chains I wear are no burden. May I indeed hope that you will accept my humble service? That you will be my wife? [*Stands hat in hand.*]

MARIANA. Yes, Mr. Brummell, I honor and respect you. [*Gives her hand to* BEAU.] I will be your wife.

BEAU [*kissing her hand*]. And may I hope you will learn to love me a little?

MARIANA. I do indeed hope so. [*Aside.*] Or make myself forget.

BEAU [*putting on his hat with a buoyant gesture*]. Come, Mariana [MARIANA *rises*], honor my arm—and we will tell the whole world of our—of *my* happiness. [*They go off at left-hand path.* VINCENT *enters from the right.*]

VINCENT. I can't find him anywhere. I'm afraid he's hiding, poor fellow, from those bailiffs, and doesn't dare show his face lest he be taken. Where's Mariana? Has she changed her mind and gone? No, she gave her promise she'd accept him, and I can trust to her word. I'll search for her now, and perhaps, by so doing, I may find him. [VINCENT *goes out by upper path, left-hand side.* TWO BAILIFFS *enter from upper right-hand path. They are villainous-looking creatures; one limps—the other has a patch over one eye, and both have very red noses; they are dressed in ragged clothes.*]

FIRST BAILIFF. Our gentleman's so fine we mustn't bother our eyes with winking, or he'll slip through our fingers.

SECOND BAILIFF. Not if I know it. This is the most fashionable affair of my life. Look here—who's this? [*He points to the left-hand path. They both quickly withdraw behind a tree.* BEAU *enters from the left.*]

BEAU. I'll leave her to inform her father. I must find Mortimer; he should have returned by now. What if he should not have met those bailiffs—if they should still be at large. Zounds! [*He sits on bench at right.*]

FIRST BAILIFF [*in a low tone*]. That's him!

SECOND BAILIFF. Lud—ain't he scrumptious! We ought to have a pair of silver sugar-tongs to take him with. [*They come down, one behind the other.*]

FIRST BAILIFF. Mr. Brummell, sir!

BEAU [*looking up*]. The devil!

FIRST BAILIFF. No, sir, the bailiff.

BEAU. What is the difference? [*The* BAILIFFS *look at one another in amazement.*]

FIRST BAILIFF. We've been looking for you, sir.

BEAU. I am so sorry you have put yourself to that trouble, and you must not speak to me here. Do you realize what you are doing? Suppose some one were to observe you. My valet will attend to you.

FIRST BAILIFF. Oh, we'll take care of your valet later; it's you that we've got a couple of papers for this morning. I represent your landlord, sir! [BEAU *lifts his cane with great deliberation, and looks at him through the glass.*]

BEAU. Are you the best he can do?

FIRST BAILIFF. You have lived in his house three years, and he considers it's time as how you paid a bit of rent.

BEAU [*as though to himself*]. The ungrateful wretch! The very fact of my having resided in his house should be more than sufficient remuneration.

SECOND BAILIFF [*comes up in front of* BEAU, *while* FIRST BAILIFF *retires a little, shaking his head as though completely puzzled*]. And I am here for Mr. Abrahams and several other gentlemen.

BEAU. You remind me of the person in the theatre whom they call the super, who represents the enemy on the march or the company in the ballroom. We will dispense with your company, sir.

FIRST BAILIFF [*coming up again*]. That won't do, Mr. Brummell. You must pay, or come along with us. [*Makes vague gesture of thumb over shoulder.*]

SECOND BAILIFF [*making same gesture as he withdraws again*]. Yes, pay, or come along with us.

BEAU. You men must be mad; the Prince will be here presently, and I will speak to him. [*Rises.*]

FIRST BAILIFF [*obsequiously*]. Oh, if His Royal Highness will help you, sir, of course we won't press matters.

BEAU. See that you do not. And now [*looking at them through his glass*], trot away, trot away, and walk in Fleet Street; the Mall is really no place for you. [*He turns, lifts his boutonnière so he can inhale the perfume of the flowers, and then walks away with great deliberation. They stand staring after him for an instant, stupefied.*]

FIRST BAILIFF. We'll keep our eye on our gentleman, just the same. These little rumors about the Prince and him might be true after all, and if they are, why, we won't walk in Fleet Street alone. [*He pulls a black bottle out of his pocket, takes a drink, and then hands it to the* SECOND BAILIFF, *who also takes a drink; then they go off in the same direction* BEAU *went. The* DUCHESS, LADY FARTHINGALE, LORD MANLY *and* SHERIDAN *come on from the left-hand path.* LORD MANLY *and* LADY FARTHINGALE *cross to the right-hand bench.* LADY FARTHINGALE *sits,* MANLY *stands by her side. Three ladies and gentlemen come on at the back and stand there, apparently chatting or listening to the* DUCHESS.]

DUCHESS. Where can Beau have disappeared to? It's near time for the Prince to be out, and I wouldn't miss observing the meeting for worlds. Pray, Sherry, give us your opinion—will he cut him or not? [*The* DUCHESS *has been flying around, looking for* BEAU *in every direction.*]

SHERIDAN. Really, Duchess, I cannot say what the Prince will do. He's too great a fool for me to put myself in his place.

MANLY. Damme, of course he'll cut him, and, moreover, Beau deserves it.

SHERIDAN [*decidedly*]. Then, for my part, I say, let's move on.

DUCHESS [*equally decided*]. We'll do no such thing. We must see for ourselves, so that we can trust our own ears and know how to treat Mr. Brummell accordingly. Besides, if we observe it, we can inform others of the affair correctly, and there will be some merit in that. [SHERIDAN *moves away to the right, with a shrug of his shoulders.*]

LADY FARTHINGALE. Mr. Brummell will never be able to stand it if he's injured. I should not wonder now if he fainted!

DUCHESS. Dear me, do you think so? [*Face falls as though disappointed.*] I don't know, I'm afraid not.

SHERIDAN [*impatiently*]. He's more likely to resent any insult, I'm convinced.

DUCHESS [*most excited, rushes to* LADY FARTHINGALE]. What! A duel! Oh, Lud, Lady Farthingale, only think— a duel! Deuce take it, where can Beau be? I'm afraid the Prince will arrive first.

SHERIDAN [*sarcastically*]. My dear Duchess, prithee be calm; you are too great an enthusiast.

DUCHESS [*looking off at the right*]. Here comes Mr. Brummell, I vow. Do you notice anything different in his manner of walking?

SHERIDAN [*monocle in eye, looks off in direction* BEAU *is supposed to be*]. He seems to have the same number of legs as formerly. [*He crosses over to the left.*]

DUCHESS. Oh, you may rail at me, Sherry, but it's no laughing matter for Mr. Brummell, I can tell you.

LADY FARTHINGALE [*rising so she can see better*]. He's coming—he's coming!

DUCHESS. Lud, we must not expose ourselves! We must at least feign utter ignorance of the affair. [BEAU *enters.*] Ah, Beau! [*The ladies curtsy, the men raise their hats.*]

BEAU. Still loitering, Duchess? I was so afraid you would have returned home. [*He joins* SHERIDAN *on the other side.*]

DUCHESS [*aside to* LADY FARTHINGALE]. You hear? A hint for us to go, but he'll not hoodwink his Duchess. [*To* BEAU.] We were just going, but we'll rest a moment for another chat with you.

BEAU. Too good of you, Duchess. Are you not afraid to risk your—what's that called, Sherry? [*Touching his cheek.*]

SHERIDAN [*much embarrassed*]. Complexion.

BEAU. Yes, your complexion in the sun. [*Chats with* SHERIDAN. DUCHESS, *very angry, does not know what to say until* LADY FARTHINGALE'S *speech gives her a chance to show her spitefulness.*]

LADY FARTHINGALE. Here comes His Royal Highness!

DUCHESS [*looking off at the right*]. The Prince! Is he truly? I didn't expect him this morning. Beau, the Prince is coming.

BEAU [*indifferently*]. Is he really? Where's the music? In the play the Prince always comes on with music. Let's be going, Sherry, there's no music. [*Takes* SHERIDAN'S *arm, and they move off to the left.*]

DUCHESS [*meaningly*]. What, Beau, you wouldn't leave before His Royal Highness comes?

BEAU [*seeing there is no escape, meets his fate gallantly*]. By my manners, no! Sherry, let us meet him. [*They turn and start to the right, as the* PRINCE *enters with* MRS. ST. AUBYN *on his arm. The* DUCHESS *has retreated back to where* LADY FARTHINGALE *is standing.*]

DUCHESS. The deuce, did you hear that, Lady Farthingale? [BEAU *and* SHERIDAN *reach the center and stop. The* PRINCE *and* MRS. ST. AUBYN *pass directly by* BEAU, *although he*

stands, hat in hand, and the PRINCE *addresses* SHERIDAN.
BEAU *replaces hat and listens with an amused expression.*]

PRINCE. Sup with me to-night, Sherry, after the play.
Mrs. St. Aubyn and the Duchess will be there with us, and,
egad, we'll make a night of it. [SHERIDAN *can only bow
acquiescence, and the* PRINCE *and* MRS. ST. AUBYN *move on
a little way.* BEAU, *lifting his glass, looks after them and
says to* SHERIDAN:]

BEAU. Sherry, who's your fat friend? [SHERIDAN *is
divided between delight and amazement at his daring, and
consternation at thought of the consequences, and whispers in*
BEAU'S *ear.*]

PRINCE [*who has stopped short*]. Well—damn his impudence!

BEAU [*affects not to hear or understand* SHERIDAN]. I beg
your pardon, who did you say? I had no idea he looked like
that. Is it really? You don't say so? Dear, dear, what a
pity! What a pity! [*Takes* SHERIDAN'S *arm and they go
off at the right,* BEAU *with his usual imperturbable air, and*
SHERIDAN *visibly shaking and dejected. The* PRINCE *and*
MRS. ST. AUBYN *are at the left, the* PRINCE *speechless with
rage, and* MRS. ST. AUBYN *trying to say something consoling.*]

DUCHESS. Well, I've had all my pains for nothing.

LADY FARTHINGALE. But, Duchess, did you see?

DUCHESS. See what? There was nothing to see! [*With
a chuckle.*] Lud, Beau got the best of it.

MRS. ST. AUBYN. Duchess, you look ill. Doesn't the air
agree with you, or is it the daylight?

DUCHESS [*loftily*]. I hope, my dear Mrs. St. Aubyn,
you'll never look worse. [*With a deep curtsy.*]

MRS. ST. AUBYN [*with affected horror*]. Heaven forbid!
[*The* PRINCE *and* MRS. ST. AUBYN *exit at left. All the people at back exit.*]

DUCHESS. Come, let's be going. [LORD MANLY *offers
one arm to the* DUCHESS, LADY FARTHINGALE *takes his other
arm. They move off toward the left.*] Where can Beau
have disappeared to? Of course, it's of no interest to us, only
I must say it was uncommonly ill-natured of him not to make
more of a scene for our sakes, you know. [*They all go out.*
BEAU *and* SHERIDAN *enter from the right, followed by the*
TWO BAILIFFS. SHERIDAN *speaks as they come on.*]

SHERIDAN. Your marriage, my dear Beau, will redeem your misfortune, and it is the only thing that will. [*They have reached the center by this time, and* BEAU *sees the* BAILIFFS. *He stops, puts up his glass, looks at them, and says:*]

BEAU [*shaking his finger at* SHERIDAN]. Sherry, Sherry, who are these fellows following you? [SHERIDAN *turns and sees the* BAILIFFS, *and becomes much agitated.*]

BAILIFF. Mr. Brummell, sir! [BEAU *sees it's no use to try to deceive* SHERIDAN.]

BEAU. Zounds! Proceed. Sherry, I will join you in a moment. Well, my good men! [SHERIDAN *hurries off, shaking his head sadly.*]

BEAU. You donkeys, would you ruin me?

BAILIFF. Come, come, we've had enough of your airs, now. You'd better come along with us quietly. [*Places finger on* BEAU'S *shoulder.*]

BEAU [*moves away*]. For Heaven's sake, don't put those hands on me! Why don't you wear gloves? [BAILIFF, *who had retreated a step, comes closer.*] And don't come so close. You are too hasty and ill-advised—you have no manners. [BAILIFFS *retreat in real confusion and astonishment.*] There's one resource, I must tell them. [*He takes out snuff-box, and takes snuff with great deliberation, and does not speak until he has returned box, brushed his lace ruffles,—then he turns to them.*] Had you met my valet he would have delivered to you my message. It was to the effect that the banns of marriage between the daughter of Mr. Oliver Vincent and myself are to be published in St. James's on Sunday. As the son-in-law of the merchant prince, I can not only satisfy your master's demands, but handsomely remember you yourselves. Now, trot away, trot away, anywhere out of my sight. [*Turns away.*]

BAILIFF. We've heard one of your fine stories before, and we don't go till you prove what you say.

BEAU. How very annoying! [*Looks off at left and sees* MARIANA. *His face lights up.*] Here comes Mariana. Here is the young lady herself. Withdraw and you shall have your proof. [BAILIFFS *look at each other.*]

FIRST BAILIFF [*a little doubtfully*]. Well!

SECOND BAILIFF [*still more doubtfully*]. Well!!

FIRST BAILIFF. Well, we'll see what it is, eh? [*They exit at the back left.* BEAU *walks down to the right, brushes his shoulder where the* BAILIFF'S *hand had rested, turns and crosses toward left as though to meet* MARIANA, *and suddenly stops.*]

BEAU. What! [*Looks again as though he thought himself mistaken.*] Reginald and Mariana! Mariana and Reginald! [*Shakes his head as though to dispel the thoughts that would come. Then walks slowly toward the path at back, leading off to the left.* MARIANA *enters hastily, followed by* REGINALD, *both much agitated.*]

REGINALD. I have been wretched beyond the telling—my letters left unanswered, not one word from you in fourteen days!

MARIANA. My letters and appeals unanswered is what you mean, sir. I wrote you even up to yesterday, and Kathleen vowed that she delivered all the notes till then.

REGINALD. To whom did she deliver them? 'Twas not to me.

MARIANA [*with a cry of joy*]. What, you did not receive them? Then Kathleen has played me false. Oh, Reginald, what I have suffered in wrongly thinking you untrue to me.

REGINALD. Such doubt of me was cruel, Mariana, but [*lightly*] come, ask my pardon and see how quickly I'll forgive you. [*Comes to her and tries to take her hands, but* MARIANA *draws away.*]

MARIANA. No—no! I cannot, I cannot.

REGINALD [*misunderstanding*]. Then see, I'll forgive without the asking.

MARIANA [*still refusing to let him take her hand*]. Reginald, what will you think? How can I tell you? It is too late now.

REGINALD. Too late! What do you mean?

MARIANA. I have promised myself to another. [BEAU *is seen at back, head bowed, his attitude one of utter sadness.*]

REGINALD [*forcibly*]. You must break that promise. To whom has it been given?

MARIANA. To Mr. Brummell.

REGINALD. Mr. Brummell! [*In shocked surprise.*] Great Heavens! Mariana, he is my best friend—my benefactor.

MARIANA. No—no!

REGINALD. My mother's only brother. It is he who, since her death, has cared for me most tenderly, and, all my life, has shielded me from every harm.

MARIANA. He is overwhelmed now by his difficulties. His creditors are like bloodhounds on his track. He has sacrificed himself for me in defense of my father. Through me alone can he be rid of his distresses.

REGINALD. And he loves you. I know that, too, and you, do you love him?

MARIANA [*reproachfully*]. You should not ask me that.

REGINALD [*taking her hands*]. You are right! But I cannot give you up, nor can I see my uncle ruined; he is the one man in the universe from whom I would not steal your love. 'Tis you who must decide.

MARIANA. And I have done so. I am his. [BEAU *comes down to the center.* REGINALD *and* MARIANA *draw back on each side.*]

BEAU. No—no, I give you up; I release you from your promise. [*The* BAILIFFS *enter and stand at back, listening.*]

MARIANA [*starting forward*]. Sir!

BEAU. Take her, Reginald! [*He holds out his hand to* MARIANA, *who is about to give him hers, when she stops, and withdraws her hand.*]

MARIANA. No, I am yours. I will not be released. Our love would not be happiness if it entailed your ruin. Reginald has told me that he owes to you his life. My father and myself have greater cause for gratitude to you than I can say. I hold you to your vows.

BEAU. Impossible; I now release you.

REGINALD [*sees the* BAILIFFS]. Great Heavens, the bailiffs! You shall not sacrifice yourself for us. I join with Mariana against myself, and say that she is yours.

BEAU [*looks at him with great affection*]. No—no! [*Brushes an imaginary speck from his sleeve.*] I love you both too well to come between your young hearts' happiness.

MARIANA [*in a last effort to change him*]. And yet you loved me! [BEAU *takes a step toward her with a look of love and reproach.*]

BEAU. Mariana! No, [*lifting his hat and turning away*] I must leave you.

Reginald. You shall not; we will speak to Mr. Vincent and he will help you.

Beau [*reprovingly*]. I have no claim whatever on Mr. Vincent. [Bailiffs *standing at back give a nod to each other.*] Take her, Reginald; wear her very near your heart for my sake. [*Hands* Mariana *to* Reginald.] And now I would accompany you further, but I cannot—not now. [*With a slight, almost imperceptible turn toward the* Bailiffs.] I happen to have a very pressing engagement—with—with—His Majesty! [Beau *turns, after a very ceremonious bow to* Mariana *to the right, and moves off. The* Bailiffs *have come down, and follow him closely; one of them taps him on the shoulder.* Beau *stops for an instant, then takes out snuff-box, and takes snuff, and walks slowly off with the greatest dignity.* Mariana *hides her face on* Reginald's *shoulder as*

[THE CURTAIN FALLS.]

THE FOURTH ACT

Scene One

A lodging house at Calais—a room at the top of the house. The shabbiest furniture, bare floor, window at the back with rude settle in it; the tops of neighboring houses can be seen from the window. A large fireplace with small fire is at the right, with a door below, leading into another room. A table stands in the middle of room with a chair each side. Another door at the left leads into the hall. Beau *is discovered sitting in front of fireplace with his back to the audience. He is dressed in a yellow brocaded dressing-gown, apparently the same one worn in Act I, but with its glory gone,—faded and worn, torn in places. He wears old black slippers, with white stockings and brown trousers, " slit so at the bottom and then buttoned tight." His hair is a little gray, his face thin and worn. At the rise of curtain* Mortimer *enters from hallway. He, too, shows the wear and tear of poverty. All his jauntiness has gone; he is shabbily dressed. After waiting a minute to see if* Beau *will notice him, he speaks:*

Mortimer. Not a letter, sir. No answer to those we sent over a month ago. Only one to me from Kathleen, to say if I don't return immediately she will take to Mr. Sheridan's gentleman for good, and enclosing me the passage-money over. [Beau *turns a little and looks at him, as though to see if he is going.*] I—I—gave it to the bootmaker, whom I met at the foot of the stairs with a bailiff as I came in. [Beau *sinks back in his chair again, satisfied that* Mortimer *will not leave him.*]

Beau. If you would not use it for yourself, Mortimer, you might at least have bought a *paté* for dinner instead; we should have had something to eat, and we could have made the bailiff stop and dine with us. Could you make no further loans? [*His voice is harsh and strained.*]

70

MORTIMER. No more, sir. I tried everywhere. No one will trust us any more.

BEAU. Mortimer, what will become of us? Think what the finest gentleman of his time is undergoing. It's enough to drive one mad.

MORTIMER. Have you nothing more to sell, sir? [BEAU *rises and comes to the table. He has a snuff-box in his hand— a small black one, in great contrast to the jeweled box he carried in the earlier scenes.*]

BEAU. My last snuff-box. You would not have me dispose of that, Mortimer—a paltry trifle that would bring nothing. No, there is nothing, Mortimer. Everything belongs to that wretched female creature who dignifies this hovel with the name of lodgings. [*Loud knocking is heard at the door, which is thrown violently open, and the* LANDLADY *stalks in. She is a very determined-looking woman, short and stout, with a red face and a pronounced moustache. She is dressed in a rather short blue skirt, heavy shoes, blue denim apron, black blouse with white neckerchief, a white cap with broad frill. Stands with arms akimbo, looking at* BEAU *disdainfully.*]

BEAU. Talking of angels! Good morning, my dear madam. So courteous of you to come. It is not my reception day, but you are always welcome. Mortimer, offer this good lady a chair.

LANDLADY [*speaks with French accent*]. Chair, humph! Your Mortimer had better offer me some money, some rent money, or I'll have you both shown to the door, do you hear? [*Rapping on table;* BEAU *starts as though in distress at each loud rap.*] That's what I come to say. [MORTIMER *now offers her a chair.*] No, I thank you, I'll stand! It's my own chair, and I will not wear it out by sitting in it.

BEAU. Then sit in it yourself, Mortimer; I cannot permit you to stand; you are tired. I'm so sorry, my dear madam, that I have nothing to offer you; the supplies for which Mortimer went out a short time ago have not yet arrived.

LANDLADY [*sneeringly*]. Supplies! Not yet arrived! Well, when they do they will not pass my door, I'll tell you that. [*Hammers on table again.*]

BEAU [*wincing*]. Do, my dear madam, do help yourself. And speaking of helping yourself reminds me, would you mind returning some of my shirts? I am sure you cannot wear them yourself. Mortimer!

MORTIMER. Yes, sir.

BEAU. How many were there in the wash last week?

MORTIMER. Twelve, sir.

BEAU. Yes—now if you wouldn't mind returning—Mortimer!

MORTIMER. Yes, sir.

BEAU. How many shall I require for the remainder of the week?

MORTIMER. Five, sir.

BEAU. Yes, if you would not mind returning five, I think I might manage for the remainder of the week.

LANDLADY [*who has been restraining her wrath with difficulty*]. I'll do nothing of the sort, sir, and I'm sick of your fine manners. I want more of the money, and less of the politeness. [*With an exaggerated bow, mocking* BEAU.]

BEAU [*taking snuff*]. You mean, my dear madam, you want more of the politeness and less of the money.

LANDLADY [*furiously*]. What! You dare insult me? Pay me to-day, or out into the street you go! Your polite talk may do good there. It may do for the stones, but it will not do for the flesh, not for this flesh. Pauper! Pauper! Bah! [*She shouts the last three words, and as she gets to the door on " Bah," bangs door and goes out. At the word " Pauper,"* BEAU *stands as though turned to stone.*]

BEAU [*very slowly*]. Mortimer.

MORTIMER. Yes, sir.

BEAU. What did she call me?

MORTIMER [*half sobbingly*]. Pauper, sir.

BEAU [*sinking into chair by right of table*]. Pauper!

MORTIMER. I am afraid, sir, she's in earnest.

BEAU [*quite simply*]. She had that appearance. Mortimer, we must find the money somehow, or I must leave Calais to-night.

MORTIMER [*hesitatingly*]. That packet of letters, sir, for which you have had so many offers from publishers.

BEAU. What packet, Mortimer?

MORTIMER. Your private letters of gossip and scandal from people of the Court. I know you have been averse, sir—

[*His voice dies away, as* BEAU, *drawing himself up, gives him a withering glance.*]

BEAU. Mortimer, you surprise me. I thought you knew me better. No. I would rather suffer anything than live by sacrificing the reputation of those who once befriended me. [*Opens drawer in table, and takes out packet of letters tied with a faded ribbon. Fondles them for an instant,—then goes to fireplace, kneels and throws them into the flames.*] There they go, Mortimer. There they go—and almost any one of them might break a heart or blast a reputation. And see how swiftly they vanish,—as swiftly as would the reputations which they are destroyed to save.

MORTIMER. I was wondering, sir, if it would do to appeal to His Majesty. He might overlook what happened when he was Prince. He passes through Calais to-day, sir.

BEAU [*rising and coming to table*]. I have thought of it, Mortimer, but I fear it would be in vain—well, we might try. Go to him, Mortimer, go to him, and take him [*pauses to think what* MORTIMER *can take, and feels snuff-box in pocket; takes it out and handles it lovingly*]—take him this snuff-box. [*Gives* MORTIMER *the box. Hardly has it left his hands, however, when he reaches out for it again.*] That is, you might take him the box, but, perhaps, you'd better not take him the snuff. [*MORTIMER gives* BEAU *the box.* BEAU *picks up a paper lying on the table, saying:*] Bills, bills. [*Makes the paper into a cornucopia, and empties the snuff from the box into it; then taps box on the table, loosening any remaining particles of snuff with his finger; then looks at table and scrapes any remaining there into the cornucopia; finally hands box to* MORTIMER.] Give it to him with your own hands,—say Mr. Brummell presents his compliments. And if that fails, like everything else—why, then—

MORTIMER. And what then, sir?

BEAU. Then, [*taking snuff elegantly from cornucopia*] then, Mortimer, I can starve. And I promise you I shall do it in the most elegant manner. And you—you, Mortimer, must return to that Japanese girl; what's her name?

MORTIMER [*tearfully*]. Kathleen, sir.

BEAU. Yes. Kathleen. [*Knock at door.* MORTIMER *opens it and starts back astounded.*]

MORTIMER. Mr. Vincent, sir. [VINCENT *enters, puffing from the climb upstairs.*]

BEAU [*is astonished and annoyed; puts the cornucopia of snuff hastily into his pocket, and draws his dressing-gown around him*]. Mr. Vincent! My dear sir! Why, how did you find your way here? You should have been shown into the reception-room, or my drawing-room, or my library; you find me in my morning-gown, in my morning-room. I make a thousand apologies.

VINCENT. Don't, don't; I was passing through Calais and I just happened in. Phew, you're pretty high up here!

BEAU. Yes; the air is so very much purer. Will you be seated, Mr.— It is still *Mr.* Vincent, is it not? [*To himself:*] He must not know my want, my poverty; I could not suffer this man's pity or compassion.

VINCENT [*sits at left of table*]. Before I forget it, let me ask you to do me the honor of dining with me to-day.

BEAU [*with an involuntary drawing-in of the breath*]. Dine! At what hour?

VINCENT. I always dine at five o'clock.

BEAU. Thank you; but I fear you will have to excuse me. I could not possibly dine at such an hour. [*Turns from table, and goes up toward window.*]

VINCENT [*aside*]. Not changed much in spirit, but in everything else— [*Aloud.*] Well, Mr. Brummell, you must lead a dull life of it here in Calais.

BEAU [*still at window, and jauntily*]. You forget, Mr. Vincent, that by living in Calais I do what all the young bucks do—I pass all my time between London and Paris.

VINCENT. Witty as ever, Mr. Brummell. The sea air does not dampen your spirits.

BEAU. No; and I use none other. That is the reason I have nothing to offer you. Had I known of your coming I should have been better prepared to receive you. [*Comes down and sits at right of table.*]

VINCENT [*looking around the room*]. You must be hard pressed for money, if you don't mind my saying so.

BEAU [*very hastily and airily, and rising*]. Oh, no! You have quite a mistaken notion of my affairs, because you miss certain useless articles given away as pledges—[*swallows a word*] ahem—of gratitude for favors shown me. I always pay a debt, Mr. Vincent, when it's a social one.

VINCENT. But those other debts which rumor says are overwhelming you again. Now, if you'd let me pay them—

BEAU [*sits at right of table. In a very cold tone*]. Thank you, thank you. No doubt you intend to be kind, but you are impertinent. [VINCENT *turns away rebuffed and disappointed.* BEAU *to himself:*] No, I will not be so humiliated by *her* father. I would rather tell a little lie instead. [*To* VINCENT.] I assure you, since the renewal of my friendship with the Prince, now His Majesty!— [*Makes a slight bow at "His Majesty."*]

VINCENT [*coming down, delighted*]. Friendship with His Majesty!

BEAU. What! Has not rumor told you that, too? She's a sorry jade, and sees only the gloomy side of things. Then, I suppose you have not heard that the King has pensioned me! [*Takes handkerchief from pocket; it is full of holes.*]

VINCENT. But—

BEAU. I see you still have that very unfortunate habit of "butting." Why, how, how, without a pension, could I keep up this establishment? [*Holding up the tattered handkerchief in his trembling hand, he says, aside:*] If he can tell me that he will help me more than he knows.

VINCENT. All the more reason, then, why you should return to London and marry my daughter.

BEAU. Are you still obstinate on that point? Do you still refuse her to Reginald? [*Knock is heard at door.*]

VINCENT. There is Mariana. I told her to join me here.

BEAU [*rises in consternation, draws his dressing-gown around him, looks down at it*]. Mariana—Miss Vincent, coming here. Mr. Vincent, one moment, one moment, Mr. Vincent, one moment. [*Goes hastily to door at right, bows to* VINCENT, *and exits.* MARIANA *enters from hall door at left.*]

MARIANA. Is he here? Have you succeeded?

VINCENT. My child, we have heard false reports in town. He has a pension from His Majesty. He is friends with the King. Dear me! I hope I haven't offended him.

MARIANA. A pension, papa! [*And then as she looks*

around the dingy room.] Are you quite sure he's not deceiving you?

VINCENT. Quite sure; he could not deceive me.

MARIANA. Then, father, there is no further need for me to make the sacrifice you demanded, and which Mr. Brummell's need did justify.

VINCENT. By no means. I am all the more determined on it.

MARIANA. I also am determined now, and say I will not marry him.

VINCENT. Tut, tut! Hush, he's coming—he's somewhat changed. [BEAU *enters. He has put on his coat—a shabby, full-skirted brown coat. Has dingy black neckerchief on. Bows very low to* MARIANA.]

BEAU. Good morning, my dear Miss Vincent. I trust the stairs have not fatigued you. You should feel at home, so high up among the angels.

MARIANA [*shows she is much affected by* BEAU'S *changed appearance*]. I am most pleased, sir, that we find you happy with the world and with yourself. We had feared otherwise.

BEAU. I lead a charmed life; even now, you see, it brings you to me.

MARIANA. And has it brought your nephew, too, sir?

BEAU. That may be your privilege.

MARIANA. I trust it may be, or else that you will bring him back to me. [*As she says this, she turns away and goes up toward the window with* VINCENT, *who shows he is not pleased at this speech. At this moment,* REGINALD *enters quickly, throwing hat on table as he goes by, and rushing up to* BEAU, *holds out his hand eagerly.*]

REGINALD. Uncle!

BEAU [*with great affection*]. Reginald! [*Then recollecting himself.*] No, Reginald, a glance of the eye. Reginald, my boy, you here, too!

REGINALD. I heard yesterday of your distresses—

BEAU [*hastily interrupting him*]. Do you not see Miss Vincent and her father? [REGINALD *turns, sees* MARIANA, *and crosses to window to her, where they stand eagerly talking.* VINCENT *goes toward hall door, evidently very anxious to get* MARIANA *away.*] I might have accepted it from him, but he has come too late. This Vincent shall not know the truth.

But Reginald shall have Mariana, and Vincent shall give her to him.

VINCENT. I think, my dear, you had better go and wait downstairs for me.

BEAU. No, no, let Miss Vincent remain; my nephew will entertain her [REGINALD *and* MARIANA *at this begin talking more confidentially*], and I wish to consult you privately in my room for a few moments.

VINCENT. Now, my dear Mr. Brummell, I must insist on Mariana's retiring.

BEAU. And I must insist that Miss Vincent remain. I see your manners have not improved. I will not detain you a moment. I wish to ask your advice. I hear an earldom is soon likely to become vacant. Now, who's eligible?

VINCENT. An earldom!

BEAU. You know more about matters in town than I, and I wish to be prepared in case my influence should be needed. Now, what name would you suggest?

VINCENT [*gasping*]. You honor me, Mr. Brummell!

BEAU. Very likely, but I wish you wouldn't gasp so. Indeed, I do honor you in asking you for your daughter's hand— [REGINALD *and* MARIANA *start and look around.*]

VINCENT [*bows very low*]. Mr. Brummell!

BEAU. For my nephew! [REGINALD *and* MARIANA *turn again toward window, relieved.*]

VINCENT. My dear Mr. Brummell, you know I am opposed to that, and I hope to persuade you—

BEAU [*significantly*]. Who is eligible for the earldom— exactly—and I think—mind, I say I think—we both have the same person in mind. But, first, I must persuade you who is eligible for your daughter. [*He bows to* VINCENT *and motions him to door at right.*]

VINCENT [*speaking as he goes*]. Gad! Zounds! An earldom! If this should be my opportunity at last. Mariana *shall* marry the boy if he wants it. [*Exits.*]

BEAU [*turns to speak to* MARIANA *and* REGINALD, *and finds them so absorbed in each other they do not even see him. He attracts their attention by knocking a chair on the floor. They start guiltily apart*]. My dears, I am about to draw up the marriage settlement, and, perhaps, I'll make my will at the same time and leave you everything. [*They both bow.*]

I will now allow you to settle the preliminaries by yourselves. [*They immediately retire again to the window, and are once more absorbed in each other.* BEAU *stands watching them for a few minutes, then turns away, puts hand over his eyes and totters off.*]

MARIANA [*coming down left of table*]. But I don't understand, do you?

REGINALD [*coming down to her side*]. I don't desire to. I take the fact as it is. [*Kisses her.*]

MARIANA. I think you take much else besides, sir. Aren't you a trifle precipitate?

REGINALD. No, this is the first preliminary. [*Puts arm around her waist.*] I think I shall linger over the preliminaries.

MARIANA. But has my father relented?

REGINALD. Surely! Or why did you come here?

MARIANA. We heard Mr. Brummell was in great distress, and we came to help him, but we found the rumors were false; his friendship with the King has been renewed.

REGINALD. Thank Heaven! Then his troubles are at an end.

MARIANA. My father still clung to the idea of our marriage.

REGINALD. And you?

MARIANA. That question is superfluous, sir. Have I not allowed the first preliminaries to be settled? [BEAU *and* VINCENT *enter—*VINCENT *a little ahead of* BEAU. *Also* MORTIMER *comes on dejectedly from hall door.*]

BEAU. Reginald, give me your hand. [REGINALD *crosses to him.*]

VINCENT [*who has crossed over to left of table*]. Mariana, come to your father. Are you still bent on marrying him?

MARIANA. You mean, papa, that he is still bent on marrying me, and that I—I am not unwilling.

VINCENT. She is yours, sir.

REGINALD [*coming back to* MARIANA]. Mine!

MORTIMER [*goes up to* BEAU *at right of table, and hands him snuff-box*]. It was returned without a word, sir.

BEAU [*in a loud tone*]. Beg Her Grace to excuse me this afternoon.

MORTIMER. Yes, sir.

REGINALD. You will dine with us, Uncle Beau, on board the vessel?

BEAU. Thank you, but I fear you will have to excuse me, and now pardon me if I ask you to retire. I happen to have a very pressing engagement.

MARIANA. When will you be in London, sir? You will be there for our wedding?

BEAU. I hope so—and you must accept some little present, some little trifle, some little token of my affection and regard—some—some—remembrance. Now what shall it be? Eh? What shall we say? [*They all look around the room, which is, of course, bare of all ornament.*] What do you really think you would like best—hum? [*Absently fingers the snuff-box which* MORTIMER *brought him.*] Ah, yes, this snuff-box —it has just been sent to me by—His Majesty. [*Hands* MARIANA *snuff-box, which she takes with deep curtsy and goes back to* REGINALD, *showing it to him.*]

VINCENT [*at door as he goes out*]. I shall probably hear from you, Mr. Brummell?

BEAU [*absently*]. Ah, yes, perhaps—good-by. Reginald, [REGINALD *comes to him;* BEAU *places his hand on* REGINALD'S *shoulder*] God bless you— [REGINALD *picks up hat from table and crosses to door.* MARIANA *comes down, gives hand to* BEAU, *curtsies;* BEAU *raises hand to his lips.* MARIANA *draws it away, backs toward door, makes another curtsy, turns to* REGINALD, *and they go off gaily, apparently talking to each other.* BEAU *puts hand over eyes, staggers back, and leans against table for support.*]

[THE CURTAIN FALLS.]

THE FOURTH ACT

Scene Two

*An attic room. Sloping roof. Walls discolored with the
damp. Paper peeling off. Window at the back. A bare
deal-table over near the left, with one chair at its side.
Another chair stands down near the front, at the right-
hand side. Another chair stands at the back, near window. There is a door at the right and one also at the left.*
BEAU *enters at the right-hand door. You can hear him for
some time before he enters, stumbling up the stairs as
though feeble. He stands for a moment at the door,
bowing very low. He is very shabbily dressed—his hat
battered—his boots gray.*

BEAU. I thought I saw the Prince there, [*pointing to
chair*] there! The boys mocked me in the streets—they threw
stones at me. No wonder; there has been no varnish on my
boots for days. They refused to give me a cup of coffee or
a macaroon. They would rather see me starve—and starve
so in rags. [*Sits in chair.*]

MORTIMER [*enters from door at left*]. Shall I announce
dinner, sir?

BEAU [*starting*]. No, Mortimer, I have only just come in,
and you forget this is Thursday, when I always entertain.
[*Sinks into a reverie.*]

MORTIMER. Poor Mr. Brummell! He's getting worse
and worse. Lack of food is turning his head instead of his
stomach. But I don't dare oppose him when he's this way.

BEAU. Mortimer!

MORTIMER. Yes, sir.

BEAU. I could get nothing for us to eat, Mortimer, nothing—and they refused to wash my cravats!

MORTIMER. Oh, Mr. Brummell, sir, what shall we do?
We will starve, sir.

BEAU [*severely*]. Mortimer, you forget yourself! Who
has called during my absence?

MORTIMER [*goes up to the window-ledge, and brings down an old broken plate with a few dirty cards*]. These cards won't last much longer. I have been bringing him the same ones on Thursday for the last year. [BEAU *has fallen asleep.*] Mr. Brummell, sir! Mr. Brummell, sir! [*He puts plate directly in front of* BEAU.]

BEAU [*starts and looks at plate*]. The—the—card tray.

MORTIMER. We've—lent it, sir! [*He pushes cards forward with his thumb and finger, as* BEAU *takes them one by one and lays them back on plate.*]

BEAU. Duchess of Leamington—thank goodness, I was out. Lord Manly—do we owe him anything?

MORTIMER. No, sir.

BEAU. Why not? Mrs. St. Aubyn—and I missed her—no matter! They will all dine here this evening.

MORTIMER [*taking plate back to ledge*]. Dine—that's the way we eat—the names of things—but it is very weakening—very weakening.

BEAU. Mortimer!

MORTIMER. Yes, sir.

BEAU. Light the candelabra. [*Begins to sing very low in a quavering voice:*] "She Wore a Wreath of Roses."

MORTIMER. Yes, sir. [*He goes to window-ledge, and brings down to table two pewter candlesticks with a little piece of a candle in each one. He lights both and then with a quick look at* BEAU *blows out one.*] He'll never know, and if it burns, there will be none to light the next time.

BEAU. Mortimer!

MORTIMER. Yes, sir.

BEAU. Is my hat on?

MORTIMER [*choking back a sob*]. Yes, sir.

BEAU [*lifts hat with elegant gesture; his hand drops and hat falls to the floor; he rises*]. Mortimer, I hear carriage wheels—carriage wheels! Observe me, Mortimer, am I quite correct? Are there creases in my cravat? I would not wish to make creases the fashion.

MORTIMER. Mr. Brummell, sir, you are quite correct.

BEAU. To your post. Bid the musicians play. [*Bows as though welcoming guest.*] Ah, Duchess, you are always welcome! And in pink! You come like the rosy morning sunshine into the darkness of my poor lodgings. Lord Manly!

And sober—truth is stranger than fiction. The Duchess's
smiles should have intoxicated you. Mrs. St. Aubyn—Your
Majesty! [*Bows very low.*] Pray, sir, honor my poor arm.
Permit me to conduct Your Majesty to a chair, whilst I receive my less distinguished guests. [*Walks to chair with
imaginary guest on his arm.*] My dear Lady Farthingale, how
do you do? As beautiful and as charming as ever. [*Backs
up a little and knocks a chair over.*] I beg ten thousand
pardons! My dear Lady Cecilie, how you have grown and
how beautiful. [*With vacant stare.*] Shall we dine? Dine!
Shall we dine? Permit me to escort Your Majesty to the
table where we dine! [*Goes to chair and escorts the imaginary
king to the table.*] Yours is the honor and mine, Lady Cecilie,
my charming *vis-à-vis.* Mariana—Mariana—always nearest
my heart—always. Mortimer—Mortimer!

MORTIMER [*who has been leaning against the wall with
head on arm*]. Yes, sir.

BEAU. His Majesty waits! [*Bows to right and left.*]
Enchanted! Enchanted! [*Waits until, apparently, they are
all seated, and then sits.*] I trust you will find these oysters
agreeable; they arrived but this morning from Ostend. Bird's-
nest soup. It is very hot. I am very particular to have
the soup hot on these cold evenings. This is very good
melon.

MORTIMER [*who has been pretending to pass things*].
Melon, sir.

BEAU. Duchess, I trust you are fond of ortolans stuffed
with truffles. Brown—and glazed. My chef—my chef—
[*Voice dies away.*]

MORTIMER. His chef! If only we had something to cook,
I should not mind the chef. [*Sinks in chair.*]

BEAU. Mariana, let me fill your glass, and drink with me.
My dear. My own always. My only dear one! [*His head
sinks on chest, and he falls asleep.*]

KATHLEEN [*after a pause, putting her head in at the door
and saying very softly:*] And may I come in?

MORTIMER [*rising in bewilderment*]. Kathleen! And has
it gone to my head, too?

KATHLEEN [*half crying*]. No, but to my heart!—or to
yours—for they've gotten that mixed I don't know which is
which. [*They embrace.*]

MORTIMER [*in alarm, fearing* BEAU *may wake*]. Hush!

KATHLEEN. Miss Mariana that was, Mrs. Reginald Courtenay that is, is out in the hall, and him with her. [MARIANA *and* REGINALD *come in at door.*]

MARIANA. Is he here? [*Gives a low, horrified exclamation at* BEAU'S *changed appearance.*]

MORTIMER. Yes, madam, but I fear the sudden surprise of seeing you will kill him.

REGINALD. But the King is in town with his suite. We came with him, and they followed us here immediately.

MORTIMER. The King!

MARIANA. Yes, Mortimer; your master's and your troubles are over. [MARIANA *and* REGINALD *cross to other side of table, away from door.*]

KATHLEEN [*aside to* MORTIMER, *as she goes up to window*]. I am not so sure but yours are just beginning.

KING [*appearing at door*]. Zounds—is this—

MORTIMER [*bowing very low*]. Your Majesty, I beg your pardon, but—sh—sh—

MRS. ST. AUBYN [*at door*]. Dear me, you don't—

KING [*turning to her*]. Sh—sh—

DUCHESS. But how—

KING [*goes through same pantomime, turning, putting finger on lip and saying:*] Sh!

LADY FARTHINGALE. Where is Mr. Brummell?

KING [*as before*]. Sh! Sh!

LORD MANLY. Well—

KING [*as before*]. Sh! Sh!

MORTIMER. If Your Majesty will pardon me, I think I could suggest something. Mr. Brummell has just been imagining you were all dining with him. I think if you were to take your places at the table, when he saw you the truth would gradually come to him. [*They all sit—*KING *at left,* MRS. ST. AUBYN *next, then the* DUCHESS. MARIANA *and* REGINALD *are at the right.*]

MORTIMER. Mr. Brummell! [*Louder, as* BEAU *does not move.*] Mr. Brummell, sir!

BEAU. Duchess, let me send you this saddle of venison; it's delicious. [*Wakes, looks around, and sees* MARIANA.] Mariana! Mariana! Reginald! [*They come to his side.*] Pardon me for not rising; I think I must have forgotten my manners. You won't leave me, Mariana? You won't leave me, will you, will you?

MARIANA. No, Mr. Brummell.

BEAU [*sees* MRS. ST. AUBYN.] Mrs. St. Aubyn, you—you forgive?

MRS. ST. AUBYN [*very gently*]. And forget, Mr. Brummell.

BEAU [*sees the* KING]. Your Majesty! Mortimer!

MORTIMER. Yes, sir.

BEAU. Is this real—is it—is it?

KING. Yes, Beau, you've hidden from all of us long enough —but now we've found you we don't mean to lose you. We sup with you to-night; to-morrow you dine in London with us.

BEAU. Dine! [*Drawing in his breath, appreciatively.*] Dine— [*Then remembering.*] At what hour?

MORTIMER [*bowing and whispering to the* KING]. At eight, Your Majesty, at eight!

KING [*with a nod of understanding*]. At eight o'clock.

BEAU. Mortimer, have I any other engagement?

MORTIMER [*with fear and trembling*]. No—oh, no, sir!

BEAU. I shall have much pleasure. Mortimer!

MORTIMER. Yes, sir.

BEAU. Mortimer!

MORTIMER. Yes, sir.

BEAU. Should anybody call, say I have a very pressing engagement with—with—His Majesty. [*His head falls, and he sinks into chair, supported by* MARIANA *and* REGINALD. *All rise.*]

[THE CURTAIN FALLS.]

THE COPPERHEAD.*

A Drama by

AUGUSTUS THOMAS

From a Story by Frederic Landis in Two Epochs of
Two Acts Each

The Copperhead, by Augustus Thomas, is a freely rendered dramatic version of Frederic Landis's tale, *The Glory of His Country.* Mr. Thomas's first experiment with the story was a one-act play put on at the Lambs' Club in New York. There it was acclaimed by the professional audience privileged to see it. The success of the play in its short form gave Mr. Thomas the idea of using the same material, with certain additions, for a four-act play in the nature of a chronicle history. "The difficulty, from a dramatic point of view," as Mr. Thomas has told the present editor, "lay in putting into action the incidents described, in that they covered two periods with an interval of some forty years. This lack of unity, however, became an attraction in the play as it enforced the dramatic presentation of these two periods, so widely different in habit of thought, point of view, speech, and custom. The first two acts deal with the early period of the Civil War, Lincoln's call for volunteers, and the exciting events that followed the beginning of the conflict. The second period is very near our own time and deals entirely with the consequences of those events upon the circumstances of the third generation. In Mr. Landis's story, the old man Shanks dies as he imparts his lifelong secret to his friends and enemies. In the play, for reasons which will be evident, the author has him live and makes the satisfactory conclusion of the drama depend upon this." At a time when the fortunes of America in the Great War still hung in the balance, the appeal of this play, the theme of which is silent and self-sacrificing patriotism, was instant and effective.

Mr. Lionel Barrymore created the part of Milton Shanks when the play opened in Hartford, Connecticut. It came to New York, to the Shubert Theatre, on February 18, 1918, and played until the arrival of the warm weather. It then made a tour of the country, which was only interrupted by Mr. Barrymore's engagement to come to New York to play with his brother John in *The Jest.* In the opinion of Mr. Thomas, there is no other American actor so well able to suggest both the youth of the early period and the character of the old man in his eighties as Mr. Lionel Barrymore.

The Copperhead reflects several circumstances of the playwright's own life. In Mr. Thomas's autobiography, which he calls *The Print of My Remembrance,* he recounts his very earliest recollections: "Another happening of that Homeric day is a fair where my mother holds me high in the crowd that I may see a child impersonating the old woman who lived in a shoe, and had so many children she didn't know what to do. That little girl with the cap and spectacles is Nellie Grant, selling her dolls to buy clothes for soldiers." In *The Copperhead,* Sue Perley and Mrs. Bates describe the booths that are to be set up at the church fair:

"Sue. If we can get dolls enough by to-morrow we are going to have the old woman that lived in a shoe.
Grandma. Have what?
Mrs. Bates. The S'Louis papers say at their fair Nellie Grant, the Gineral's little dotter, was the old woman—a shoe as big as Elsie's bed for her house and dozens of dolls all over it."

In Act I, Ma says, "I stud here by this well with my arms round yer neck, Milt, when Joey was only three—holdin' yer *back* that time from Mexico." Mr. Thomas's own father had gone to the Mexican War and had participated in the Doniphan Expedition.

In Mr. Thomas's study in New York at the present time, hangs the copy of the Lincoln life mask which plays so important a part in the last act of *The Copperhead.* Mr. Thomas received this mask from the son of the sculptor who made it. In this same last act, Shanks is made to say: "Colonel Hardy and me was boys together. Our Congressman give me an appointment to go to West Point, but Tom Hardy ought 'o had it. Besides, 'twasn't convenient for me to go to West Point jest then, so I resigned it fur him." It is a fact that Mr. Thomas as a boy was tutored by the local Methodist minister and won an appointment to West Point which he had to decline for domestic reasons.

Mr. Thomas's interest in Lincoln dates back, of course, to the days of the Civil War. In *The Print of My Remembrance,*[1] he writes:

[1] Augustus Thomas's *The Print of My Remembrance* is now run-

"Before the war my father was associated with Mr. W. N. Wells, among others, in the formation of the Republican Party in the St. Louis district. They were in occasional correspondence with Mr. Lincoln at Springfield, not yet the great emancipator, but just a clever debater who was attracting attention in the West. One of those original letters, addressed to Mr. Wells, not to my father, is between two panes of glass in a frame and a folder in my library. It does not add much to the volume of Lincoln's product, but as it has been in print only in connection with my play, *The Copperhead,* this extract may have for many a genuine interest:

'All dallying with Douglas by Republicans, who are such at heart, is at the very least, time and labor lost; and all such, who so dally with him, will yet bite their lips in vexation for their own folly. His policy which rigorously excludes all idea of there being any *wrong* in slavery, does lead inevitably to the denationalization of the Constitution; and all who deprecate that consummation and yet are seduced into his support, do but cut their own throats. True, Douglas *has* opposed the administration on one measure, and yet *may* on some other; but while he upholds the Dred Scott decision, declares that he cares not whether slavery be voted down or voted up; that it is simply a question of dollars and cents, and that the Almighty has drawn a line on one side of which labor *must* be performed by slaves, to support him or Buchanan is simply to reach the same goal by only slightly different roads.

Very respectfully,

A. LINCOLN.'"

The character of Grandma in *The Copperhead* suggests to a reader of the autobiography Mr. Thomas's own grandmother. Mr. Thomas sketches her thus: "Grandmother's opinion was the most decisive in our family. I had no way of knowing it wasn't so in the nation. Her impatience with McClellan and Grant and even Lincoln seemed to have an effect. At any rate, things happened when she got mad enough. She permanently affected my early admirations."

There must, indeed, be many reflections of Mr. Thomas's early years in this historical play. His earliest year was 1857; his birthday, January 8; the place of his birth, a little house in the outskirts of St. Louis, Missouri. He was the son of Elihu Baldwin Thomas and Imogene Garrettson Thomas. The little boy, Augustus, went to the public schools for six years, between the ages of six and twelve. He writes of this

ning in *The Saturday Evening Post.* It is to be published in book form in the fall of 1922. It is one of the most interesting and important texts for the study of American drama.

period himself: " I had an almost uninterrupted attendance at regular sessions of the St. Louis grammar schools. . . . When I finished I had a card publicly given me for my recitation of *Marco Bozzaris*. The scene is indelible. . . . I can see my teacher now, the bunch of lilacs on her desk and just behind her the Tropic of Capricorn. It had been there all winter, but never so plain as on that fragrant morning in the spring of 1868, with the girls in white and ribbons, and through the open windows trees and grass and cowbells, and beyond the sky line of a great round world turning upon its own axis once in every twenty-four hours, except in February, which has twenty-nine. The safety of our republic rests upon our public schools."

Part of the lad's education was carried on in legislative bodies. After leaving school, he was first a page in the Missouri Legislature, and, after that, page in the Reconstruction Congress of 1870, the Forty-First. During his winter in Washington, he did his first dramatic writing, condensing from memory the *Rip Van Winkle* that he had seen Joseph Jefferson act. His play was performed in a stable converted to the uses of a little playhouse. On this amateur stage the boy also acted in his own versions of *The Lady of the Lake*.

On his return to St. Louis, Augustus Thomas went to high school, and with another boy began the publication of a magazine called *Scratches and Sketches*, which for various reasons lasted for just five weeks. He also joined a dramatic club, for which he wrote his first full-length play called *Alone*. At about this same period he wrote another play for amateurs called *A Big Rise*. Speaking of these and other outlets for his energy in the days of his youth, Mr. Thomas writes in *The Print of My Remembrance*: " My youngish readers . . . may infer . . . that the big value is the self-expression obtained; that the debating society, the dramatic club, the singing school, the art class, the pursuits that invite brain to the finger tips, and to become articulate, are the interests that make life eloquent. They may even come to have opinions and to believe that the amount of self-expression encouraged and protected in any country is the measure of liberty in that country."

In remembering his boyhood, Mr. Thomas records how permanently reading and learning poetry by heart influenced his development. His father said to him, "What you fill your head with in that fashion now will stay with you for a long while. It is a good plan to select the best." Mr. Thomas recalls with gratitude the well-chosen selections of the old McGuffey School Readers that, as the oldsters will testify, contained a wide range of selections from the best in literature.

As he grew to manhood, Mr. Thomas's interest in amateur theatricals became more and more active. They proved the point of departure. Presently he was earning his living, first as the assistant treasurer in a theatre in St. Louis, then with a company on the road. To that theatre in St. Louis where he was employed came some of the greatest actors of the day, who helped on his education in things connected with the stage.

Mr. Thomas's experiences outside of the theatre have included six years in the freight department of a railroad, two years at the study of law, and work as a writer and illustrator for the St. Louis *Post Dispatch,* the St. Louis *Republic,* the Kansas City *Times,* the Kansas City *Mirror,* the North-western *Miller,* and the New York *World.*

Editha's Burglar, dramatized in 1887, from a copy of *St. Nicholas* in which Mrs. Burnett's story had appeared, was the first of Mr. Thomas's plays to be produced professionally and to be shown in New York. Mr. Thomas's first permanent work in New York was at the Madison Square Theatre with A. M. Palmer, the well-known manager, who engaged him to take the place of Mr. Dion Boucicault as play-doctor. Boucicault, an Irishman, had for many years written or adapted plays for the American stage.

For many years Mr. Thomas has been a prominent figure in Democratic politics. He it was who in 1908 seconded the nomination of William Jennings Bryan under circumstances which have been thus described:

"Guessing the probable source of the great American play is a game which each may play to his taste—genius comes when it comes and blows where it listeth. In the small hours of that night at Denver in 1908, when the Democrats nominated Bryan for the third time, somewhere in that delirium of band music, howling, and oratory which dragged on until the dawn came up out of the prairies, Mr. Augustus Thomas arose as a delegate from New York to address the convention. I well remember . . . the cheery sound, after the strange æolian noises that had preceded them of those terse authoritative words. The author of *Arizona* fulfilled at that moment, better perhaps than any of our other play-writers could have done, the American notion that the artist should also be a good citizen. And the 'great' American play, one suspects, is likely to come from some such type of man—not from the Ivory Tower nor 'Broadway,' but closer to the firing line." [1]

At the present time Mr. Thomas is perhaps the most sought-after toastmaster in America. His talents are not confined to forensic oratory.

An interesting appraisal of his work as a playwright is this statement of William Winter's, written some time ago:

"The genius that is manifest in the plays [the best plays of Augustus Thomas] is that which intuitively comprehends human nature, its strength and its weakness, its temptations and its trials; which sees the whole vast current of humanity, the diversified characters, pathetic or antipathetic; the blessings and the cruelties of condition; which discriminates between good and evil, being aware that those elements are strangely commingled in every human creature; and which can seize and reproduce the points and moments when circumstances long fluent in a hidden drift and feelings long intensifying themselves in concealment break suddenly into view and become motives and vehicles of action—that being the one absolutely and imperatively essential constituent of drama." [2]

The following is a complete list of Mr. Thomas's plays:

Alone	*New Blood* (1894)
The Big Rise	*A Proper Impropriety* (1893)
Combustion	*The Music Box* (1894)
The Burglar (1889)	*The Hoosier Doctor*
Editha's Burglar (1887)	*The Man Upstairs*
A Night's Frolic (1890)	*The Meddler*
Reckless Temple (1890)	*Matinée Idol*
A Woman of the World (1890)	*Chimmie Fadden*
A New Year's Call (1891)	*Soldiers of Fortune* (1900)
Surrender (1893)	*On the Quiet*
Alabama (1891)	*The Jucklins*
For Money (1892)	*Arizona* (1898)
A Man of the World (1889)	*Oliver Goldsmith*
After Thoughts (1890)	*Colorado*
Colonel Carter of Cartersville	*That Overcoat*
(1892)	*The Earl of Pawtucket* (1903)
The Capitol (1894)	*The Other Girl* (1902)
In Mizzoura (1893)	*Mrs. Leffingwell's Boots* (1903)

[1] Arthur Ruhl, *Second Nights*, New York, 1914, p. 321.
[2] William Winter, *The Wallet of Time*, New York, 1913, Vol. II, p. 529.

No playwright since Bronson Howard has analyzed his own practices as a dramatist so carefully as has Augustus Thomas. Six of his plays have been printed with prefaces explaining in every case how the particular play came to be written and what circumstances developed the course of character and action. These prefaces show how a play like *In Mizzoura* was written to provide Nat Goodwin with an opportunity to star; how the action of *Oliver Goldsmith* is a tissue of eighteenth century relations and circumstances, the fabrication of which was suggested by Stuart Robson's resemblance to Noll; how *The Earl of Pawtucket* grew out of an attempt to fit the amusing mannerisms of Lawrance D'Orsay into a comedy; how *The Other Girl* was intended in the first place especially to exercise the talents of John Drew and Lionel Barrymore; how *Mrs. Leffingwell's Boots,* a very light comedy of manners, owed its origin to a dinner party balked by a blizzard and to a table fountain that once sprayed itself inopportunely in the direction of Francis Wilson, a guest at Mr. Thomas's board; and, finally, how *The Witching Hour* was "built to carry a theory." These six prefaces are illuminating documents for the student of American drama.

Mr. Thomas considers the creative processes connected with plays like *The Copperhead* or *Oliver Goldsmith* less interesting, if we interpret him rightly, than the creative processes involved in writing other kinds of plays. In discussing his work on *Oliver Goldsmith,* Mr. Thomas expresses himself thus: " It is largely a ' scissors and paste-pot ' undertaking, and is the least difficult and least commendable of a playwright's performances, excepting, perhaps, the dramatizing of a novel, which it strongly resembles. The finished product, dependent as it is upon research, can never have the value of a play written by equal experience and based on observation, but dramatic literature would nevertheless be the loser if we eliminated such plays as *Richelieu, David Garrick, Edmund Kean, Amy Robsart, Beau Brummell, Nathan Hale, Tom Moore, Disraeli* and the like, all made after much the same fashion."

An interviewer once put the following questions and received the following answers from Mr. Thomas:

"What would you say are the elements that go to make up a distinctively American play?"

"An American play might be thoroughly American and at the same time universal. I believe that a pl..y could be written with such a sure seizure of primal and eternal relationship as to make it go in Japan as well as in America. The things that so distinguish American plays as a class from the plays of other countries are the absence of the morbid consideration of the sex question and the absence of recognition and admission of stratified social ranks. . . ."

"What should you say is the one quality that makes a play popular in this country?"

"There is no particular quality that has the field to itself. Any play will succeed in America which hopefully entertains; and, if I were to be called upon to name the most valuable quality in a play, I should say its expression of an ideal sufficiently above the level of its audience to attract them and not so far above that level as to be considered apocryphal or discouraging." [1]

In the autumn of 1915, following Charles Frohman's loss on the *Lusitania,* Mr. Thomas was made Art Director of this manager's reorganized companies. He carried the burden of this work for two years. Mr. Thomas was at one time president of the Society of American Dramatists. He is a member of the American Academy of Arts and Letters.

[1] Van Wyck Brooks, *Augustus Thomas, The World's Work,* New York, 1909, Vol. 18, page 11885.

THE COPPERHEAD

CAST OF CHARACTERS

(In the order of their appearance)

FIRST EPOCH

JOEY SHANKS	Raymond Hackett
GRANDMA PERLEY	Eugenie Woodward
MA SHANKS	Doris Rankin
CAPTAIN HARDY	Albert Phillips
MILT SHANKS	Lionel Barrymore
MRS. BATES	Evelyn Archer
SUE PERLEY	Gladys Burgette
LEM TOLLARD	Ethelbert Hales
NEWT GILLESPIE	William C. Norton
ANDREWS	Harry Hadfield
SAM CARTER	Chester Morris

ADDITIONAL CHARACTERS IN SECOND EPOCH

MADELINE KING	Doris Rankin
PHILIP MANNING	Thomas Corrigan
MRS. MANNING	Grace Reals
DR. RANDALL	Hayden Stevenson

SYNOPSIS

FIRST EPOCH—1861-63.
    Act I. *The dooryard of Milton Shanks.*
    Act II. *The Same. Two years later.*

SECOND EPOCH—*Forty years later.*
    Act III. *The dooryard of Milton Shanks.*
    Act IV. *The living room.*

    Scene laid in southern Illinois.

CHARACTERS IN PART ONE

JOEY SHANKS .... Aged 16
GRANDMA PERLEY .... " 76
MA (MRS. SHANKS) .... " 34
CAPTAIN HARDY .... " 36
MILT SHANKS .... " 36
MRS. BATES .... " 30
SUE PERLEY .... " 14
LEM TOLLARD .... " 38
NEWT GILLESPIE .... " 30
ANDREWS, *a minister* .... " 60
SAM CARTER .... " 24

PART I

ACT I

SCENE

The dooryard on the Illinois farm of MILTON SHANKS.
At the stage, right, is a porch raised six inches from ground
attached to the lean-to kitchen of SHANKS' house, the roof
of which disappears to the right. Under the porch down
stage is a window with a door in second entrance. Behind
the porch a rail or other rough fence straggles across
stage. The back drop shows a half hilly country with the
wet stubbly earth of early spring. Painted on the center
of this drop is a sycamore tree sufficiently distinctive to
help identify the same drop under July color and vegeta-
tion in Act Two.
On the stage at the corner of the house up right is a small
lilac bush which shows three years advance in Act Two,
and is a good lilac tree of forty odd years of age in the
last two acts. To the left of stage in second plane is
rough log curb to well fitted with bucket on a long sweep
with a fulcrum at the side of well and tail of sweep
running off to the left. Above this well is a young apple
tree, bare, to be in foliage and fruit in Act Two, and to
be a stalwart, old, gnarly apple tree in the last two acts.
The wings at the left are bushes. The whole dooryard
is filled with a litter of neglected farm material, such as
grindstones, plow, bits of harness, a broken wheel, the
running gear of a wagon, and the like.

DISCOVERED

JOEY, a boy of sixteen. He is dressed like the son of a poor
farmer of 1861. Joey is molding minnie balls over a char-

98

coal fire, using one mold as a second one cools, and drop-
ping the finished product into a bucket. He is impatient
and fretful.

After a mold or two, GRANDMA PERLEY *enters from the road.*
GRANDMA *is seventy-six—a farmer's woman of the time.*
She smokes a crock pipe with a reed stem.

GRANDMA. Is that you, Joey?

JOEY. Yes'm.

GRANDMA. Where's your ma?

JOEY. Sewing—inside.

GRANDMA. You seem cross about sumpin'.

JOEY. I want to be drillin' and they *detailed* me doin' this.

GRANDMA. Drillin'!

JOEY. Yes.

GRANDMA. " Detailed " ye. Have you volunteered?

JOEY. You bet I've volunteered.

GRANDMA [*in approval*]. Well, then, you go drill—I'll
do that for you.

JOEY. Maybe you wouldn't know how, Mrs. Perley.

GRANDMA. Yes, I would.

JOEY [*explaining*]. This is hot lead. A drop of it'll burn
right thro' yer shoe before you kin kick it off.

GRANDMA. I know.

JOEY. You pour it in these holes with this iron spoon.

GRANDMA. Lord, boy, don't teach yer gran'mother how to
suck aigs! I molded bullets fer Andrew Jackson. Where's
yer knife to trim 'em?

JOEY. This is it.

GRANDMA. All right. Run along and drill.

JOEY [*with sample*]. But these ain't exactly bullets.
They're minnie balls. That ring around 'em is to fasten the
paper cottridge onto. Here's one with the cottridge on it.

GRANDMA. I know all about it. And the ring holds mutton taller that turns into verdy grease—an' you can't volunteer unless ye got front teeth ter tear the cottridge paper to
let the powder out when you ram the cottridge home.

JOEY. That's right, grandma.

GRANDMA. In 1812 every man had a powder-horn. This
idear of the powder fastened right on the bullet is twice as
quick.

JOEY. And the sharp nose on the bullet makes 'em go further.

GRANDMA. Let a Yankee alone for inventions. Go on and drill, my boy.

JOEY. Thank you, grandma. [*Enter* MA. *She is a beautiful, dark-haired drudge, aged thirty-four. She carries a coat.*]

MA. Where you goin', Joey?

JOEY. Ter drill.

MA. I want you.

JOEY [*going*]. They ain't time, ma, now—honest they ain't. [*Exit. He runs off behind the house.*]

GRANDMA. Let him alone, Mrs. Shanks. I told him I'd spell him at these molds. It's wimmen's work, anyhow, at war times.

MA. You're spoilin' him.

GRANDMA. A boy 'at wants ter volunteer has a right ter be spoiled—some.

MA [*hesitating*]. I wanted to match these button-holes— but I 'spose I kin measure 'em from the bottom.

GRANDMA [*rising*]. Why, I'll try it on fur yer.

MA. Will that do it?

GRANDMA. Why not? Kain't tell from my shoulders whether I'm wearin' breeches or not, kin you? An' anyhow, I'm smokin' a pipe man fashion. [*They try on the coat.*]

MA. I hate ter see a coat pucker when it's buttoned.

GRANDMA. No need to have it pucker.

MA [*kneeling*]. I'll jest put a pin at each place. [*Does so.*] Joey hed no right to unload that work onto you.

GRANDMA. I molded bullets before they ever invented a shot-tower. I was only twenty-five years old at Fort Dearborn and we wimmen all molded 'em—big and little. Jim Madison had let the English set the red-skins onto us and thet meant more to the wimmen—I tell ye—than it did to any man.

MA [*finishing*]. Thank you, grandma.

GRANDMA [*resuming work with the bullet-mold*]. Any war will always mean more to the *wimmen*. It's easy enough to *fight,* and easy enough to die. Stayin' behind with yer stummick empty—an' yer hands tied—an' yer hearts a-breakin', is the perfect torment.

MA. We kin hope and pray this won't be a real war.

GRANDMA [*shakes head*]. No fool's paradise, Martha. Men that own niggers ain't a gonta git skeered 'cause Mr. Lincoln jumps at 'em and hollers "Boo." He's got a bigger job than Jim Madison hed, and thet lasted two years. These hellions are right on the ground—in the very midst of us—some of 'em's livin' right here in our own state, an' to git 'em out'll be like—bugs in a rope bedstid.

MA [*going toward house*]. Two years! Joey'll be eighteen before then.

GRANDMA. Yes—if he lives.

MA [*turning, alarmed*]. If he lives! Why, Grandma Perley!

GRANDMA. An' I'll be sevinty-six—if *I* live.

MA [*on porch*]. Come in and hev some tea, won't you?

GRANDMA. No, thank you. I've got my pipe and this hot lead brings back old times a bit. [*Enter* HARDY, *in captain's uniform. A soldier follows, without uniform.*]

HARDY. Good-afternoon. Is Milt at home?

MA. Good-afternoon, Captain. He's inside. [*Calls.*] Milt—here's Captain Hardy.

HARDY. Good-afternoon, Mrs. Perley.

GRANDMA. How de do, Captain.

HARDY [*goes to the well curb*]. Doing your share, I see.

GRANDMA. Tryin' to, Captain—an' I'll keep the wimmen o' this neighborhood at sumpin' as long as the trouble lasts. [*Enter* SHANKS, *with baby, which* MA *takes.* SHANKS *is a farmer of thirty-six.*]

SHANKS. Afternoon, Captain Tom.

HARDY. You've got a wagon and two horses, Milt?

SHANKS. I hev—yes.

HARDY. My company's got orders to move. The ammunition and supplies will need four wagons to carry them.

SHANKS. Well, I kain't stop yer takin' mine, if you mean that.

HARDY. I don't want to *take* it. We'll *hire* it—and we'll pay *you* for your time, too.

SHANKS [*shakes head*]. I couldn't go myself.

MA. Why not, Milt?

SHANKS. I don't hold fur this coercin' of the Southern people—I don't.

HARDY. You hold for the North defending itself when the South begins shooting, don't you?

SHANKS. I don't really know as I do. They haven't come into our territory any—*yit!*

HARDY. They're threatening the arsenal at St. Louis.

SHANKS. Well, Missouri's a slave State, ain't it?

HARDY [*impatient*]. I can't do your thinking for you now. I want your team.

SHANKS [*hands up*]. Well, you've got the power.

HARDY. Can't you persuade him, Mrs. Shanks?

MA. I'm afraid, Captain, that his head's turned with these secession sympathizers. He's wearin' one of their copper buttons.

GRANDMA. The Tories tried that " sympathizin' " business in 1812. We burnt one o' their newspaper offices and run some o' *them* theirselves over the line ter Canada.

HARDY [*writing*]. I'll take your team, Milt—but I'll give you a Government warrant that'll get you the money for it.

SHANKS. Make it in ma's name, Captain. In my eyes, it'd be blood money.

MA. Will you eat the provisions I buy with the blood money?

SHANKS. Not if you keep 'em separated from what I bring in, I won't.

HARDY. There, Mrs. Shanks. 'Tisn't their value, per-haps, but that's the Government rate.

MA. Thank you.

HARDY [*to* SHANKS]. Show us your team.

MA. Oh, Captain, these buttons—does it matter if I sew clear through the facin's? I kain't pick up one piece, tailor-fashion.

HARDY. Not a bit. Tie them on, if you want to. Come, Milt? [*Exit with* SHANKS *and soldier.*]

GRANDMA. Hardy's more tender with Milt than Nathan Heald would a been.

MA. Who?

GRANDMA. Captain Nathan Heald commanded at Dear-born. A militia man talked meal-mouthed like Milt done jest now, and Nathan Heald took his sword hilt butt end and knocked out all his teeth. [*Enter* MRS. BATES *from road back of house, carrying a blue coat she works on.*]

MRS. BATES. Ain't that Captain Hardy?

MA. Yes. What's the matter?

MRS. BATES. I forget which side of a man's coat the button-holes go on.

MA. Why, the left side.

MRS. BATES. Air you sure?

GRANDMA. Ain't you never made no clothes fur yer own men folks?

MRS. BATES. Not soldier clothes, I ain't.

GRANDMA. Well, the left side fur button-holes—right side fur buttons. Men are all one-handed. Wimmen's clothes button with the left hand so they can have their right arm to carry a baby.

MRS. BATES. Jim *said* I was wrong. I've sewed this button-hole slip the tailor gave us, on the wrong side.

GRANDMA. Rip it off.

MRS. BATES. I've cut thro' the cloth that's over it.

GRANDMA. Never mind. They'll find some left-handed man. [*Enter* SUE, *a girl of fourteen.*]

SUE. Oh, Mrs. Shanks!

MA. What is it, Sue?

SUE. The men are going away.

GRANDMA. Why ain't you at the church pickin' lint?

SUE. My bundle's all done. They're going right away.

MRS. BATES. They'll have to wait for this coat, I reckon.

GRANDMA [*rising*]. You sure? [*To* SUE.]

SUE. Yes, grandma.

GRANDMA. Then they better have what's done of these. [*Begins to trim the bullets and collect them.*]

SUE. Oh, grandma! Bullets! [*Reënter* SHANKS.]

GRANDMA. Yes, bullets.

SUE. That don't seem like woman's work.

GRANDMA. In a real war, everything's woman's work, from bringin' 'em into the world right up to closin' their eyes.

MA [*shocked*]. Oh, Mrs. Perley! [MRS. BATES *also shrinks and exclaims.*]

GRANDMA. Oh, you wimmen with yer " faint an' fall in it " high falutin's are what's makin' the fool peace talk amongst the men. [*Goes to gate with bucket.*] " Close their eyes "— yes. A man plows and threshes and grinds hisself to death in sixty years and ye call it the Lord's will. I *don't*. It's what he dies *fur* that tells the tale. I lost a husband at Fort Dearborn, and a father at Detroit, and a brother on Lake Erie—different ages then, but equal now, 'cause they died fur Freedom—fur Liberty. [*Exit*.]

SUE. Gramma ought a been a man. [*Exit*.]

MA. Take this child; I gotta finish these buttons. [SHANKS *takes baby to house*.]

MRS. BATES. What's Milt so downcast about?

MA. The army has took our team. [*Points off left*.]

MRS. BATES. Oh—there comes Lem Tollard.

MA [*going*]. Yes. Another rebel sympathizer. Will you come inside?

MRS. BATES. No; I'll go home and fix this coat if I kin. [*Exit* MA *left in house*. LEM TOLLARD *enters left at back. He is a tough Illinois farmer of 1861, with scowl and underjaw, easily dressed and about thirty-eight years old*. MRS. BATES, *going, looks at him. He touches his hat*. MRS. BATES *exits*. LEM *looks cautiously over fence and comes into yard; reconnoiters house and whistles signal toward porch. Evidently gets attention inside and beckons*. SHANKS *comes from house, sees* LEM, *looks back into house, meets* LEM *left center*.]

SHANKS. What'd you find out?

LEM. These fellers air gonta march in a day or two, from the looks o' things!

SHANKS. Where to?

LEM. Missouri, I'd say. That visitin' member of our Lodge that's here from Indiana understands telegraphin'—kin read it by ear.

SHANKS. By ear?

LEM. You bet! He kin jest lean against a depot an' tell nearly every word the machine's a sayin'. He picked up "Camp Jackson"—and "St. Louis"—and "Government troops from Quincy" goin' to the Arsenal there in St. Louis. Company from here is goin' to Quincy. Now, what's our move?

SHANKS. Why do we have to do anything?

LEM. Why, Camp Jackson's our people.

SHANKS. Air they?

LEM. Yes, at St. Louis.

SHANKS. Why, then, we oughta git word to 'em, I suppose—but, jeemunently—how?

LEM. I've been to St. Louis in my time, with hides and taller.

SHANKS. Then you're the man to go, I'd say.

LEM. I'm ready to go, but it entitles me to railroad tickets and my keep while I'm away.

SHANKS. Naturally.

LEM. An' no use callin' a meetin' if you gimme *your* word fur it that the circle makes it up to me when I git back.

SHANKS. I give you my word fur it, Lem.

LEM. All right. [*Starts off; stops; returns.*] An' see here, Milt, your boy Joe—

SHANKS. What about him?

LEM. He's still drillin' with Newt Gillespie's outfit—like I said he was.

SHANKS. Why not, if it amuses him? No guns, and Joe's only sixteen and a little over.

LEM. Every man or boy we keep out of it, the better.

SHANKS. Besides, Joe's drillin' and cheerin' keeps suspicion off o' me. Lord, his mother's sewin' uniforms for Hardy's Company! What do we care?

LEM [*not convinced*]. You may be right. [*Pause.*] An' if any suspicion falls on me fur this St. Louis trip, you're my witness that I went there on business o' some kind fur you.

SHANKS. You did. There's a mule auction there, I've heard.

LEM. There is—Tenth and Biddle Street.

SHANKS. Well, how's this? These troops has took my team, and you went there to buy another team fur me?

LEM. Why didn't I get 'em?

SHANKS. The army's buyin' 'em. That's a good reason. Price went up. Everything is goin' up, ain't it?

LEM [*pause*]. I'll write you a letter about 'em—through the post-office—sayin' that, and you *keep* it.

SHANKS. 'Nuf said. [*Enter* MA.]

MA [*on porch*]. Well, Lem, what is it?

LEM. Good-mornin'.

MA. The President's called fur seventy-five thousand volunteers. Did you see it?

LEM. I'm thirty-eight years old.

MA. So's Captain Hardy.

LEM [*fishing*]. And my insteps ain't strong.

MA. *Your* insteps air all right, ain't they, Milt?

SHANKS. They air, thank Gawd, but not fur any *un*holy cause like an army against our own countrymen.

MA [*to* LEM]. I see *you're* wearin' one o' them copperheads in yer button-hole, too.

LEM [*regarding button*]. The Goddess of Liberty—yes.

MA. Liberty, is it? I notice that every brute that's ever turned a dog loose after a poor black slave runnin' past here from the Ohio River, is wearin' one of 'em.

SHANKS. Oh, politics ain't fur women, ma!

MA. They always have been in this house until Fort Sumter was fired on—an' I never looked for you to eat yer own words, Milt Shanks.

SHANKS. I ain't eatin' my words. I'm fur peace, that's all—peace. I've got two children ter support.

MA. Ye hed one when the Mexican War broke out, an' yer was devil bent to go to *that*.

SHANKS. Mexicans is different—but not our own countrymen. [*Turns.*] Don't mind her, Lem.

MA. An' as fur protectin' yer children, that's what I'm askin' yer ter do. It's the *shame* of it that's drivin' Joey into the volunteers—the shame of it.

LEM [*contradicting*]. No, no. Just boys' ways, Mrs. Shanks.

SHANKS. They don't want men as old as us.

MA. Then why don't you say jes' that, and stop yer peace hypocrisy and throw away that copperhead off o' yer button-hole?

LEM. That shows we're united, too, Mrs. Shanks. The lovers of liberty air united.

MA. We understand round here that you owned a nigger yerself 'fore you left Kentucky.

LEM. In Kentucky everybody owned 'em 'at could afford it.

MA. *That's* a lie, Lem Tollard.

SHANKS. Ma, how kin *you* know?

MA. I've heard Abraham Lincoln say it was. [*To* LEM.]

An' I call you mighty poor company, even fur Milt Shanks.
[*Enter* GILLESPIE *and* ANDREWS, *a preacher. Both carry
some new uniforms.*]

GILLESPIE. Sorry to rush you, Mrs. Shanks—

MA. What is it, Mr. Gillespie? Good afternoon, Brother
Andrews.

ANDREWS. Sister Shanks.

GILLESPIE. Got to have everything that's finished.

ANDREWS. The Company has orders to march.

MA. Thank God that temptation's goin' away from Joey
at last. They're done, Newt. Only bastin' threads to take
out. [*Exit.*]

GILLESPIE. Don't stop fur that. Any feller they fit kin
pick out the threads.

SHANKS. Where air you goin'?

GILLESPIE. What the hell's that to you? Excuse me,
Brother Andrews. [*To* SHANKS.] Git a gun an' fall in,
like you oughta, and you'll find out.

LEM. Don't answer him, Milt. [*Exit.*]

ANDREWS. The military men are not permitted to give
information of that character, Mr. Shanks.

GILLESPIE. *He* knows that well enough—and we wouldn't
give it to the enemy if we did. [*Reënter* MA *with two suits
of blue.*]

MA [*handing clothes*]. Nothin' to brag on, Newt, fur
looks—but they won't blow apart.

GILLESPIE. *You* oughta have a right ter wear 'em yerself,
'stead o' sech as him.

MA. That spot'll wash out. It's only a little curdled
milk—stummick teeth. I had to take her up a while when I
was sewin' last night.

GILLESPIE. Fur stummick teeth and curdlin', my woman
gives 'em lime water. [*Enter* HARDY.]

HARDY. Make haste, Gillespie.

GILLESPIE [*salutes*]. Jest foldin' 'em, Captain. Come on,
Brother Andrews.

ANDREWS [*to* HARDY]. I'd go with you, Captain, if I
were young enough.

HARDY. I'm sure you would, sir. [*To* GILLESPIE.]
Where's the rest of your squad?

GILLESPIE. All over town.

ANDREWS. Twenty ladies been sewin'. [GILLESPIE *salutes. Exit with clothes, on run.* ANDREWS *follows.*]

HARDY. Thank you, Mrs. Shanks.

MA. God bless *you,* Tom Hardy!

HARDY [*pauses and pleads*]. Come on, Milt.

SHANKS. 'Tain't possible, Tom. [HARDY *looks at* MA.]

MA. I've told him I'd git on—Joey's as good at sixteen as a man twenty-one. [*The baby cries off right. Exit* MA.]

HARDY. You wanted to go with me in '47.

SHANKS. That was different, Tom.

·HARDY. And you wanted to go to *West Point* when I did.

SHANKS. Yes—

HARDY. I wish you had gone. [*Pause.*] Did you hear Colonel Grant muster in our Company last week?

SHANKS [*shakes head*]. I wasn't there.

HARDY. He said a dead rebel would be *envied* compared to the man on the Northern side who stayed home and gave comfort to the enemy. [*Pause.*] They tell me, Milt, you've been making that mistake yourself—comfort to the enemy.

SHANKS. I don't know as I have.

HARDY. That button shows it.

SHANKS. It stands fur peace and the liberty our fathers won.

HARDY. How did our fathers win their liberty?

SHANKS. Why—fightin'.

HARDY. Exactly! And the fight isn't over. Come on! Remember who's calling—our own candidate—our own neighbor—our own friend—Lincoln.

SHANKS. Lincoln wasn't fur war when we elected him. He's lettin' 'em make him jest an instrument in the devil's hands. [*Enter* MA *with baby.*]

HARDY [*hand to* SHANKS' *throat*]. Stop! [*Pause.*] I'd shoot another man that said that. [MA *exclaims. Pause.*] I'm sorry, Mrs. Shanks—sorry.

MA [*pause*]. *I'm* sorry, Captain. [*Enter* JOEY.]

JOEY. Mother—mother—

MA. Well, Joey?

JOEY. You gave Newt Gillespie my uniform.

MA. 'Twasn't yours, dear.

JOEY. Why, you made it to fit me—didn't you?

MA. I tried it on you, boy, to get it straight; that's all.

JOEY. Captain Hardy, 'tain't fair! I'm as good in the drill as any man in your company.

HARDY. You're only sixteen, Joe.

JOEY. Goin' on seventeen. I'm in the same class at school with Sam Perley and Jim Evers and Henry Bates. They're goin'. *I* cut wood and swing a scythe and lift a bag of oats with any of 'em.

HARDY. Well, there'll still be wood to cut, Joey, and farm work to do back here.

JOEY. And the uniform *fits* me—my own mother made it.

MA. For the army, Joey—not for you.

JOEY. Why, mother, you put yer hands on my face and said: "Don't ever disgrace it, boy."

MA. Yes—like I'd say fur the flag. [HARDY *starts.*]

JOEY. Don't go, Captain. If *she* says yes? Say yes, mother—say yes!

MA. Why, Joey, me and Elsie needs *some*body. I ain't despaired yit of yer father goin'.

JOEY. Why— [*Pause.*] Has he changed his mind? [*Pause.*] Dad?

SHANKS [*pause*]. I can't go—I can't—knowin' everything as I do.

HARDY [*to* MA]. Good-by. [*Goes quickly.* JOEY *throws himself on the well curb in tears. After a pause* MA *walks to him and puts her hand on his shoulder.* JOEY *turns at her touch and buries his face in her lap as he kneels. With the baby in her arms, the three make an effective group.*]

MA [*pause*]. Joey—Joey— [*The boy looks up.*] I used ter carry *you* this way, dearie.

JOEY [*rising*]. Well, I kud carry you, now. [*Reënter* GRANDMA, *without her pipe.*]

MA. That's what I'm askin' you ter do, son.

JOEY. But not tied ter yer apron-strings, ma. All the fellers that air goin' air doin' it fur their folks at home—defendin' *them.*

GRANDMA. Gimme that child. Yer plumb tuckered out. [*Takes baby.*]

MA. Kain't you say nothin', Milt Shanks?

SHANKS. I'm fur peace. I've said that time and agin. Joey's heered me. [*Exit* GRANDMA *with baby to house.*]

JOEY. *I* ain't fur peace when they're shootin' at the flag!

SHANKS. But I understand a boy's feelin's, too. When I was sixteen, I'd o' felt jest the way Joey does.

MA. Yer urgin' him to go?

SHANKS. No, by God, I ain't urgin' him! He don't seem ter need it. I only say it's natural, and as long as I live— [*Pause.*] I'll remember that my boy— [*Pause and control.*] I'll remember he was natural and manful.

JOEY. Kain't yer see *I* got ter do it?

MA. Yer only sixteen, Joey.

JOEY. I'm strong as twenty an' a blamed sight quicker.

MA. Yer might git wounded.

JOEY. I been wounded by a pitchfork—and Perley's dog bit me. I " *heal up* " quicker'n a feller o' twenty!

MA. Some boys will git *killed,* Joey. I kain't let you go at sixteen.

JOEY. If I hang round till I'm older, you'll only git fonder of me, an' if a feller is gona be killed, what's the difference sixteen or twenty?

MA [*to* SHANKS]. Yer see how he's a-strainin' ter git away, Milt. I ain't *sendin'* either of yer— [*To* JOEY.] But you won't go, Joey, if yer father goes, will you? [*Watches* SHANKS *anxiously.*]

JOEY. We couldn't *both* leave you and Elsie, of course.

MA. There, Milt. [SHANKS *shakes head.*]

JOEY [*in a burst*]. God A'mighty, ma, let me have one parent I kin look up to! Quick! Please, 'cause some other feller'll git my uniform in a minute.

MA. It's big enough fer yer father. You git it—and we'll see about who goes with the Company.

JOEY. Aha! Bully! [*Exit; runs off back of house.* MA *watches him out of sight, her hand to her lips. Then turns.*]

MA. I know Captain Hardy will send him back, an' then —*then* you'll jest hev ter take his place, Milt.

SHANKS. God bless you, ma. Yer like the wonderful women that put the stars in the flag, an' I ain't worthy ter undo the latchets o' yer shoes—but I kain't go inter this army.

MA. "The stars in the flag!" [*Pause.*] I stud here by this well with my arms round yer neck, Milt, when Joey was only three—holdin' yer *back* that time from Mexico, and yer talked about "the stars in the flag" then. I thought you wuz the handsomest thing in the whole State of Illinois and I prayed God to make our boy hev some of your spirit instead of mine when he growed up to be a man.

SHANKS. Sorry I talked about 'em agin—but it's kind o' the same subject, after all.

MA. We ain't hed riches, and I've hed some sickness, but I've kind o' lived on my respect and trust in you, Milt. Don't tell me that everything I loved you fur is dead in you.

SHANKS. I've loved yer, too, Martha!

MA. I think you hev.

SHANKS. An' I still do.

MA. Well, I'm tryin', Milt.

SHANKS. I still do. Fur time and eternity [*pause*] an' without wantin' ter harp on the same subject—jest as sure as the stars *air* in the flag, you'll look inter my face some time, an' admit I was right.

MA. Never—never! [*Exit to house.* SHANKS *lifts his hands to Heaven in protest, pulls himself together and cleans up the charcoal furnace outfit. Enter* LEM *quickly.*]

LEM. Milt!

SHANKS. Hello!

LEM [*excited*]. They're gonta march *to-day*—not to-morrow.

SHANKS. Air they?

LEM. Yes. I got to git out on to-night's train fur St. Louis.

SHANKS. I 'spose yer hev—really.

LEM. No chance to see anybody. How much money you got on you?

SHANKS [*counting*]. I'll see. Six bits.

LEM. Great Scott! Well, give it to me. If you can scrape up any more, bring it to me at the depot. [*Starts; stops.*] An' remember yer obligation—"a brother Knight's wife, or parents, or any dependent on him." [*Holds up right hand as taking oath.*]

SHANKS [*with same sign*]. "Or any dependent on him."

LEM. Look in at my place now and agin.

SHANKS. Yes—I will.

LEM. Here's Gillespie, runnin'. I told you! [*Enter GILLESPIE on a run.*]

GILLESPIE. Any ammunition here?

SHANKS. Ammunition? [*Exit* LEM *significantly.*]

GILLESPIE. Minnie balls. Your Joey was moldin' 'em. [*Enter* ANDREWS, *evidently following* GILLESPIE.]

SHANKS. Oh, Mrs. Perley took *them.* [*Calls.*] Mrs. Perley—Mrs. Perley!

GILLESPIE. Where to?

SHANKS. She'll tell you. [*Enter* GRANDMA.]

GRANDMA. What is it?

GILLESPIE. Minnie balls—Joe Shanks was makin'.

GRANDMA. Why, you tarnation idiot—I gave 'em to you yerself!

GILLESPIE. When?

GRANDMA. In that horse bucket.

GILLESPIE [*going*]. Hell's bells! I packed 'em with the harness. [*Exit.*]

GRANDMA [*calling after*]. Two bullet molds layin' on top of 'em. [*Going.*] Ye'd think the rebels was ambushin' 'em. [*Exit after* GILLESPIE.]

SHANKS. They're gettin' ready.

ANDREWS. Yes.

SHANKS. Brother Andrews—see here. [*Comes down excitedly and with caution.*] You brought me a letter in March.

ANDREWS. Yes, Milt.

SHANKS [*looks off after* LEM]. Callin' me—*East!* [ANDREWS *nods.*] I don't know if you guessed what was wanted of me, and my wife ain't—nur Joey, nur anybody. Yer mustn't hint it if *you* do—not even to *me*. [*Pause.* ANDREWS *nods.*] But I was told down there that, in a pinch, I could turn ter you, and you'd take orders from me. [ANDREWS *nods.*] Lem Tollard's gittin' the evenin' train fur St. Louis—ter give warnin' ter rebel troops there in Camp Jackson, that Union reinforcements is comin'. You kin beat him by buggy or horseback to Mattoon and the regular Express from there on.

ANDREWS. I understand.

SHANKS. At the St. Louis Arsenal, the Union troops air under Captain Lyon—L-y-o-n. Git ter him personal. He'll know what ter do—whether ter move faster hisself or jes' ter head off Lem.

ANDREWS. So I say *you* told me?

SHANKS [*nods*]. A farmer by the name of Shanks. [*Impressively. A bugle blows assembly.*]

ANDREWS. I'll follow instructions minutely. [*Reënter* SUE.]

SUE. Mr. Shanks—Mr. Shanks!

SHANKS [*turning*]. Yes, Sue.

SUE. Joey wants his other shirt and a pair of sox.

SHANKS. What's the matter?

SUE. The Company's going. He's going with 'em. [ANDREWS *exits.*]

SHANKS. His shirt and sox. Ma—ma! [*Anxiously toward house. Reënter* GRANDMA. *A drum heard in distance.* SHANKS *stops and listens.*]

SUE. That's them.

GRANDMA [*heroically*]. We're comin', Father Abraham, a hundred thousand strong.

SHANKS. God A'mighty! [*Exit.* SUE *runs to fence. Enter* MRS. BATES.]

MRS. BATES. Where's Mrs. Shanks?

SUE. Inside. I've told 'em, Mrs. Bates.

MRS. BATES. My Henry's in the Company, and they're goin' without supper. [*Enter* MA.]

MA. They're just drillin', ain't they?

SUE. No'm, they're really going, Mrs. Shanks. Joey sent me. [*Enter* SHANKS *with small bundle.*]

MRS. BATES. Here they come. [*Fife and drum effect, increasing with scene until it finishes in song.*]

MA. Where's Joey? He can't be with 'em!

SUE. I can see him, Mrs. Shanks. I see Joey. He's with 'em. [SHANKS *goes into road and looks.* MA *comes down right, excitedly.*]

MA. God! Dear God! [*Raises her hands.*]

GRANDMA [*with her*]. Yer his mother. Don't fergit that. Let him see you givin' courage to him as he goes by. [SHANKS *comes down from road and gives* SUE *the bundle for* JOEY; *then exit left rather haunted. Chorus of approaching Company breaks into "John Brown's Body."*] You nursed him an' you brought him into the world. Come, keep up his heart! [*Takes* MA *up.* GRANDMA *goes into road and meets Company. The women and* SUE *indicate approach of Company. The Company, in rather irregular uniforms, swings by, singing;* GRANDMA *waves her apron, leading them in an in-spired and symbolic manner.* SHANKS *sneaks on above well and hides in bushes. Presently* JOEY *passes; he slips from line a moment and kisses* MA, *then runs and catches up his place.* MA *leans against the fence and the women fan her. The scene may be enlivened by old men and children trailers.*]

[CURTAIN ON SONG.]

ACT II

SCENE

Same set as Act One, but over two years later. A lilac bush at upper corner of house is two years larger but without bloom. The month is July. The back drop shows same topography as Act One but the field is of ripening corn. On the post of the porch a cardboard shield of the U. S. Arms is tacked in lieu of a flag.

TIME

Twilight, fading into moonlight; Friday, July 3, 1863.

DISCOVERED

MA *ironing by the charcoal furnace. Her ironing board is laid on the backs of two kitchen chairs. There is a basket of damp linen and a pile of ironed nearly dry. The baby* ELSIE, *now some three years old, is on an improvised bed of chairs, on porch, with a piece of " quadrille " mosquito net over her.* GRANDMA *sits by knitting sox.*

MA. About time fur her medicine, ain't it?
GRANDMA. I'll see.
MA. You set still; I'll see. [*Steps to door.*] Yes—after time.
GRANDMA. I'll give it to her. [*Takes up from floor a tumbler covered with a plate, holding a spoon.*]
MA [*bending over bed*]. How is mammy's precious now? Don't wake up, darling—Grandma Perley's just gonta give it a nice spoonful of the cool water—
GRANDMA. Open mouggy— [*Gives medicine.*] The angel!

MA. Now, lay down, dear, and mammy'll make the beautiful house again. Keep out the nasty flies and skeeters. [*Fixes net.*]

GRANDMA. Seems easier.

MA [*resuming work*]. Yes.

GRANDMA. Beats me; six little sugar pills melted in a tumbler o' water— [*Shakes head.*]

MA. There's *sumpin'* about 'em.

GRANDMA. Don't allow 'em in the army.

MA. Might be better if they did. I hear they're dyin' like flies in the hospitals.

GRANDMA. Kain't believe all we hear, Martha. They said Stonewall Jackson was killed early in May.

MA. Well, wasn't he?

GRANDMA. I doubt it. Six weeks has gone by and Joe Hooker has hed to fall back; looks to me like that yarn about Jackson was jest to throw our folks off their guard—and " shot by his own men."

MA. May be—

GRANDMA. Sounds fishy. An' where's all the help we was gonta git from the four million niggers?—'mancipation's been out six months.

MA. Maybe the niggers didn't git it—most of 'em. Kain't read, an' the Rebs wouldn't *tell* 'em, *would* they?

GRANDMA. P'raps not— [*pause*] and Grant! Why ain't he stirrin' hisself? Sometimes I think them yarns about his drinkin's more truth than poetry. Lord—if I'd only been a man!

MA. Well, it's a siege, Joey says in his letters—if a man's ever been a drinkin' man, seems ter me that'd drive him to it agin—jest settin' an' settin' outside the city—waitin' an' waitin' —day in—day out—even hotter'n this place, too.

GRANDMA. Lord pity 'em!

MA. 'Cause that's the real South—Vicksburg is.

GRANDMA. Oughta be some breeze from the river, I'd think.

MA. Joey don't speak of it.

GRANDMA. How long's it been fur Joey?

MA. Two years and two months since he marched past that gate.

GRANDMA. I mean at Vicksburg?

MA. Oh! 'Bout six weeks now—since the siege begun. [*Pause; going.*] I kin tell exactly by his letters. [*Exit.*]

GRANDMA. Six weeks is near enough. [*Calls.*] Lord! I ain't timin' bread in the oven by it. [MA *returns with bunch of letters from the house.*]

MA. I think this is the one. [*Opens letter. Reads in bitter silence a moment.*]

GRANDMA [*pause*]. What's the matter now?

MA [*pause; shakes head*]. 'Bout his father.

GRANDMA. Well, don't let's git on that subject agin.

MA [*studying letter and biting lip*]. When the news of it got into the army—some o' the men from here had papers with the trial in 'em— [*Looks up in agony.*] Joey's father! My baby's father—

GRANDMA. Evil company kin bring any man down, but I'll stake my hope o' salvation that Milt Shanks didn't do the murder.

MA. Not his fault if he didn't. He'd fired two shots— his revolver showed that at the trial.

GRANDMA. I don't know. They didn't hang him—at any rate.

MA. What comfort kin Joey git from that? The *verdict* was hangin', and they'd a hung him only the governor committed all o' their sentences ter life in the penitentiary—life— life—in the penitentiary. He knowed about it comin' from day to day—but it was a thunderbolt to Joey. He says— [*Reads.*] "If I could jes' put my arms around you, mammy."

GRANDMA [*going to her*]. Now, quit that, Martha. You started to find out when Vicksburg commenced. Lord, we've all got troubles.

MA [*bracing up*]. I know— [*With other letter.*] It's a lead pencil, and I can't make out the writin' now—it's gittin' so dark, besides.

GRANDMA. An' yer tuckered out with yer ironin'.

MA. Only my back—it'll ease up when I lay down. [*Enter* MRS. BATES *and* SUE *to back of fence.*]

MRS. BATES [*calling*]. Good evening. [MA *runs to bed and sings lullaby—" Old Dog Tray."*]

GRANDMA [*signals silence*]. The child's asleep.

MRS. BATES. Sorry.

GRANDMA. All right, I guess. [*Enter* MRS. BATES *to yard. Enter* SUE; *she carries a tin lantern, unlighted.*]

MRS. BATES. I brought some rennet fur her. [MA *nods thanks.*]

GRANDMA. That's good.

SUE. We're goin' down to the church.

GRANDMA. Why?

MRS. BATES. Fixin' the booths fur to-morrow.

MA [*joining them*]. I'm so sorry I can't go along and help.

MRS. BATES. Lord knows you got yer hands full.

GRANDMA. Ain't hed her supper.

MRS. BATES. What!

MA. It's too hot fur supper.

GRANDMA [*to* MA]. Where's yer tea kettle?

MA. I've got cold tea.

SUE. Let me git it, Mrs. Shanks.

MA. It's in the well—I'll get some glasses. [*Starts.*]

GRANDMA. You'll set still. I'll git the glasses. [*Puts her in chair. Exit.* SUE *goes to well. A little cry from the bed.*]

MA [*resigned*]. I guess she's waking. [*Gets* ELSIE.]

SUE. Did we wake her, do you 'spose?

MA. She's slept a good while, anyway. [*Reënter* GRANDMA *with glasses, glass sugar bowl, brown sugar and spoons.*]

MA. Come, dearie, Auntie Bates brought Elsie, oh, such good supper. Mother'll hold her little girl on her lap while she eats it. [MA *sits at ironing board and feeds* ELSIE. MRS. BATES *stands.* SUE *brings tea from well.*]

GRANDMA [*slyly indicating* ELSIE]. It's a good plan to change the subject now—we git on better when you don't notice us— How many booths you got? [*Pours tea.*]

MRS. BATES. Oh, a dozen, I should think.

SUE. If we can get dolls enough by to-morrow we're going to have the old woman that lived in a shoe.

GRANDMA. Have what?

MRS. BATES The S'Louis papers say at their fair Nellie Grant, the Gineral's little dotter was the old woman—a shoe as big as Elsie's bed for her house and dozens of dolls all over it.

GRANDMA. How old's Grant's dotter?

MRS. BATES. Only three or four.

GRANDMA. Well, don't that beat the Dutch. I'll bet it took like hot cakes.

MA [*coaxingly*]. Not here, dearie—that's way off where the sun goes to bed and hot cakes ain't near so nice as Auntie Bates' custard.

GRANDMA. Little pitchers have big ears. [*Enter* ANDREWS *from left at back.*]

MA. There's Brother Andrews.

GRANDMA. A minute later'n he'd a caught me smokin'.

MRS. BATES. Good evening.

ANDREWS. Good evening—may I come in?

MA. Of course—yer always welcome, Mr. Andrews. [ANDREWS *enters yard. He shows elation.*]

ANDREWS. There's some wonderful news on the telegraph wires.

GRANDMA. What is it? [MA *and* MRS. BATES *chorus* "Tell us"—*and* "Good news?"]

ANDREWS. Vicksburg's surrendered.

SUE.
MA.   } [*together*] { Hooray!
MRS. BATES.   Thank God!
                           Oh, Mr. Andrews! [*The twilight goes into moonlight.*]

GRANDMA. God bless ole Grant.

ANDREWS [*fervently*]. Amen—amen, Sister Perley.

MA [*pause*]. And—Joey, too—

ANDREWS. Yes, Joey, too, and all our brave boys in blue. The news comes pretty direct altho' it hasn't been officially confirmed.

GRANDMA. Then hold on, don't count your chickens too soon.

ANDREWS. Oh, I believe it's true—true.

MRS. BATES. Why, Brother Andrews?

ANDREWS. I've expected it right along. The prisoners that have been passing through here give awful reports of their starvation in Vicksburg—eating dogs—anything—and just to think of the glorious way it comes—to-morrow will be the Fourth of July and, praise be to God, we've our bell for the meeting house.

GRANDMA. The bell's come?

ANDREWS. Come? Why, it's up in the belfry, Sister

Perley. Some folks want us to ring it every day for twelve o'clock, but we'll begin with the Sunday service and the Wednesday prayer meetings, except, of course, if this surrender's true we'll ring in the glorious Fourth.

MA. And maybe Joey kin git a furlough now.

ANDREWS. Of course he'll git a furlough.

MA [to ELSIE]. Buvver Joey comin' home to Elsie and Muzzer.

GRANDMA. The news makes us all fergit our manners—will you hev some cold tea, Brother Andrews?

ANDREWS [hesitates]. Why—

SUE. Right out of the well—awfully good.

ANDREWS. Thank you—yes.

MA. You're sure they'll let him come?

ANDREWS. Positive. After that splendid bravery in recovering the flag.

GRANDMA. What was that, Brother Andrews?

ANDREWS. In one of the Rebels' attempts to break through a Union color bearer was struck—Joey not only supported the man but kept the flag flying, too— Didn't you know of it?

MA. Well, not so fine as that—one o' Joey's letters said—" Jim Evers was hit with a bay'net while he was carryin' our flag and I was so close to him that I caught him when he fell over—" That jes' seemed natural kindness.

ANDREWS. Caught him! Why, Joe fought like a wildcat.

SUE. Joey!

MRS. BATES. Well! Well!

GRANDMA. I'm ready to believe it, 'cause at Fort Dearborn the dare devils was always the boys.

MA. Who told you about it, Brother Andrews?

ANDREWS. Why—well—it's a little embarrassing—but Joey's father told me.

MA. His father?

GRANDMA [discounting it]. Oh! [MRS. BATES and SUE relax also.]

MA [pause]. I thought maybe you'd got it straighter'n that. I guess Joey's letter's about right.

ANDREWS. And then again when General Grant was holding a council of war with Admiral Porter on a gunboat in the river—the Rebels knew it somehow and made a sally. Joey swam out to the boat and carried the news to Grant—Grant hustled back in his skiff and rallied our men, who were retreating. Grant sent for Joey the next day and made a world of fuss over him— Yes, indeed.

MA. Did you git all that from his father, too?

ANDREWS. Well—yes.

GRANDMA. 'M. [*The women again go cold.*]

SUE [*pause*]. Well, Joey's *spunky,* jest the same.

MRS. BATES [*pause*]. Sue and I were just goin' down to the church—are there many there?

ANDREWS. Oh, yes.

SUE [*suddenly*]. Oh—we've settled about the rebel states, Mrs. Shanks.

GRANDMA. How!

SUE. Well, you see, I'm on the platform as the Goddess of Liberty—and I say like this: [*Recites*]

"Within the field of blue a cloud I see,
The lightnings threaten over Liberty,
My daughters, come! Ye thirteen brave I bore—
And come, ye younger, making thirty-four." [*Breaks.*]

'Cause there's thirty-four states altogether—then these dear little girls—thirteen walkin' two and two—six couples an' then single that cute baby of Mrs. Ransom's, hardly bigger'n Elsie—she's Rhode Island. Then the other states accordin' to their dates of admission, all with blue sashes, except the rebel states, *wherever* they are, have red sashes—and don't you think this is too beautiful?—heavy bands of smoke-colored tulle blindfoldin' their eyes, meanin' error. These darlin's! None of 'em over ten! Why, I jest *cried* at rehearsal.

GRANDMA. Well—I'm comin' to see you if I'm able to walk. You git me a ticket— What are they, Mrs. Bates?

MRS. BATES. Two bits. [GRANDMA *gets shin plaster pocketbook and produces twenty-five cents.*] Thank you. [*Stows the paper in similar book.*] Come, Sue, we're awfully late now.

MA. Elsie thanks you for her supper, Auntie Bates.

MRS. BATES. She shall have more to-morrow— Good-by. [*Exits with* SUE.]

GRANDMA. Good-night—

MA. Why do yo' 'spose Milt wanted ter make up that ridiculous stuff about Joey?

ANDREWS. It's true—every word of it. Grant wanted to know what he could do for Joey—well, one way and another the dear boy told him everything—and on Joey's account Milt has been pardoned, Mrs. Shanks.

MA [*pause*]. Pardoned!

ANDREWS. Pardoned—

MA [*prompting*]. You mean from hangin'—to penitentiary for life.

ANDREWS [*shakes head*]. That was done at the time of their conviction—for the whole band—but Milt has been set free.

MA. How do you know—who told you?

ANDREWS. Milt told me.

MA. In the prison?

ANDREWS. Here—Milt's back in town.

MA. He's foolin' you. He's broke out, ain't he?

ANDREWS. Pardoned—by the Governor—I've seen his papers. [MA *gives* ELSIE *to* GRANDMA.]

MA. In town? [ANDREWS *nods.* MA *gets up—walks nervously—stops. Pause.*] It's time Elsie was in bed—will you undress her, Mrs. Perley—I've got to talk to Brother Andrews alone.

GRANDMA. Come with grandma, darlin', an' she'll tell you about the fairies. [*Takes* ELSIE *to porch.*]

MA. I'll bring her medicine when it's time. [*Exit* GRANDMA *with* ELSIE. *Pause.*] Where is he—now?

ANDREWS. Waiting for me.

MA. Why?

ANDREWS. For some message from—his wife.

MA. *Am* I his wife in the eyes o' Gawd?

ANDREWS. Aren't you? For better—for worse—

MA. It's the law in Illinois when a man's convicted of *murder* it sets his wife free.

ANDREWS. Do you ask to be free?

MA. I don't ask anything any more fur myself, Brother Andrews. [*A candle is lighted inside the house.*]

ANDREWS. Well, it won't help Milt to cast him off, will it?

MA. I'm thinkin' about the children and—I ask *you*—

ANDREWS. If you ask me—you'll send word to your husband to come home.

MA [*pause*]. Home— [*Pause.*] What if Joey's here on his furlough? What then?

ANDREWS. I wish you might have seen Milt's face when he told me of Joey's bravery.

MA. I'm thinkin' what Joey's face must a been when he wrote me the letters after his father's trial reached the army— [*Shakes head.*] I know why Joey was willin' to swim out to a gunboat—or foller Jim Evers and his flag in the front ranks —his letter says—"Don't you never shed a tear fur me, mammy —if it—comes to—me." My Gawd! Think of a boy of nineteen writin' that-a-way!

ANDREWS. He'll feel different, now, when he comes to know that his heroism gives his father another chance at life— let me tell Milt to come home.

MA [*pause*]. I'll see him.

ANDREWS. Good.

MA. But I'll have to git used to the notion of it some— before I'll say jest what I will do—one way or the other— [*Pause.*] I'm gonna kneel down by my baby's bed an' ask Gawd. [*Distant gun. MA sits on the ironing chair, with her head bent to her knees, and buries her face in her hands. A country band strikes up in the distance, "Rally Round the Flag."*]

ANDREWS [*pause*]. The news is confirmed, I guess. [*Goes to MA.*] Come, Martha—God's doing it all his way—we can't be downhearted about anything. [*MA rises and, slowly nodding, exits. ANDREWS watches her off, then wipes his forehead and puts on his hat. He slowly turns to go. The village band still plays. He stops at sight of somebody. It is SHANKS. SHANKS enters, left, behind fence. SHANKS shows more than three years' added age—his hair is perceptibly gray —and he is more worn in body.*]

SHANKS. Well?

ANDREWS. She'll see you. [*SHANKS crosses toward house. Pause.*]

SHANKS. She's kneelin' by the bed.

ANDREWS. One minute. [*Looks down the road cautiously. Returns.*] I've a letter for you.

SHANKS. From her?

ANDREWS. From Washington—I didn't even *mention* it to you in the village because—it didn't seem safe. [*Hands letter.*]

SHANKS. You might jes' stand at the gate. [ANDREWS *stands watch.* SHANKS *opens letter and reads by the light from the door. He puts letter in pocket.* ANDREWS *returns.*] I'm ordered to Pennsylvania. [*Pause.*] What's been going on there?—we didn't git much news in Joliet.

ANDREWS. Hooker has succeeded Rosecrans in command—but Lee's driven him back— [*Pause.*] Harper's Ferry's been taken by Lee—things generally pretty gloomy.

SHANKS. My letter hints there's some underground leak—through this crowd I'm with. [*Hand goes to lapel.*] They took our buttons away from us in jail.

ANDREWS [*ominously*]. 'Twouldn't be safe to wear one now.

SHANKS. I reckon not—I didn't feel very safe even without mine—down there to-night.

ANDREWS. The county *is* very bitter.

SHANKS. Whata they say about me bein' pardoned and Lem Tollard kept in for life?

ANDREWS. Very few of them know it yet.

SHANKS. It's gonna make it hard in Pennsylvania, I cahilate.

ANDREWS. Joey's good work should explain it.

SHANKS. Maybe. [*Pause.*] Tollard ain't a murderer in heart—fact none of 'em—jes' wrong-headed—an' war's war— [*Pause.*] If anything happens to me—Brother Andrews—I mean—permanent—

ANDREWS. I understand, Milt.

SHANKS. Why, then—I'd like her to really know— [AN-DREWS *nods.*] She's fine. [*Pause.*] Mighty fine—like the wonderful women that— [*Pause—chews—wipes nose.*] An' the back wash of it when she knows why—and everything'll be twice as hard 'cause she's awful tender-hearted—so make her understand that I sensed all of it and was proud she done her part this way—

ANDREWS. I shall.

SHANKS. Show her that ef she hadn't suffered and suffered plenty—my work wouldn't a looked gen-u-ine.

ANDREWS. She'll know.

SHANKS. And Joey— [ANDREWS *nods.*] Tell her 'twas really me that got word to Grant at Columbus, Kentucky, that Van Dorn was behind him, an' saved thousands o' Union lives —like as not Joey's amongst the lot. [MA *comes from house— peering into the lesser light.*]

ANDREWS. Well, good-night.

MA. You, Brother Andrews?

ANDREWS. Yes, Martha.

SHANKS. An' me. [*General pause.*]

ANDREWS. I'm just going— Good-night, Milt. [*Affectionately pats his shoulder and goes. At intervals from now on a small cannon fires salutes.*]

MA [*pause*]. Yer pardoned?

SHANKS. Yes—by the Governor.

MA [*points after* ANDREWS]. He says 'count o' Joey.

SHANKS. Yes.

MA. Well— Don't that mortify you completely?

SHANKS. 'Twould if I didn't believe Joey'd understand my side of it—some day.

MA. Your side was Peace—wasn't it?

SHANKS. As fur as I could make it—yes.

MA. Yer empty revolver showed two of the shots was by you.

SHANKS. I pinted over their heads—besides, I know I didn't hit anybody.

MA. You didn't tell that at yer trial, did ye?

SHANKS. What use? And then I couldn't strive to throw all the blame onto Lem and the others.

MA. Yer doin' it now, ain't you?

SHANKS. I reckon I am—come to think of it—but— [*Pause.*]

MA [*pause*]. But what— Ef you've got anything to say fur yerself—fur Gawd's sake, Milt—

SHANKS. I'm doin' it now 'cause I care more fur what you think about my bein' a murderer, Martha—than what the law court thought—

MA. I'd like ter believe ye, Milt.

SHANKS. If ye could—it'd be mighty fine.

MA. Ye've been untruthful so often.

SHANKS. Ter you, Martha?

MA. Yes, to me—about nearly every trip you made after

you turned copperhead somethin' didn't gee. Where was you and Lem Tollard an' yer crowd takin' them stolen horses?

SHANKS. Kentucky.

MA. For rebel guerrillas, if the truth's known, wasn't it?

SHANKS [*nods*]. Confederate cavalry—yes.

MA. And when the Sheriff's posse headed you off—you killed two of 'em.

SHANKS [*shakes head*]. Our crowd—not me.

MA. Am I to try an' make the neighbors believe that?

SHANKS. My God—no—no— [*Pause.*] I ain't talkin' fur the neighbors—besides, they won't be neighbors o' mine.

MA. They won't—

SHANKS. I cahilate ter go East in a day or so—an' git work when the harvestin' begins—the war's made farm hands scarce—folks say.

MA. East? [SHANKS *nods.*] Fur good?

SHANKS. Well—while the war's on, anyway.

MA. And after the war?

SHANKS. I hope ter be near you—[*pause*] and the children—ef I kin.

MA [*pause*]. Have you hed yer supper?

SHANKS. Yes, thank you— I'd like a drink, though— [*Moves to well.*]

MA. Here's tea—and it's been cold.

SHANKS. Thank you. [*Returns, takes tea.*] How's Elsie?

MA. Ailin' some—the heat and the flies—but she made a good supper—and is sleepin'.

SHANKS. Would it wake her if I—looked at her?

MA. No—talkin' would—an' ye better wait till Grandma Perley comes out.

SHANKS. What d'ye hear from Joey?

MA. Here's his letters— [*Sorts them.*] 'Twould do you no good to read these— [*Lays them aside.*]

SHANKS. Where's the last one?

MA [*handing letter*]. I'll get Grandma Perley out the other way. [*Exit.* SHANKS *watches her off—drinks tea from bucket—opens a letter and reads. The village bell tolls very distantly.* SHANKS *adjusts himself to its novelty and resumes reading. The sound of a cantering horse approaches—* MILT *moves from light to shadow.* SAM CARTER, *a soldier, rides on and stops back of fence, pauses, dismounts and ties. Soldier enters yard to light—calls into house.*]

SAM [*calls*]. Hello!

SHANKS [*speaks*]. Good evening.

SAM [*inquiring*]. Shanks?

SHANKS [*into light again*]. Hello, Sam. [*A distant gun.*]

SAM [*pause—nodding off*]. That's fur Vicksburg's surrender.

SHANKS. Yes.

SAM. What are you doin'—round here?

SHANKS. Well—I have been away, but—

SAM [*pause*]. In trouble—we heard, in the army.

SHANKS. Yes—considerable—but, somehow—'count Joey doin' so well—I—I—was—released—

SAM. He did do well— [*Awkwardly.*] Come up by the gate. [*They go up.*] Whoa, boy—Whoa! [*Goes to horse.*]

SHANKS. Where air you from now?

SAM. Vicksburg—but I left there two days ago with some prisoners and wounded—steamer *Forest Queen* to Cairo—When did you hear from Joe?

SHANKS [*down with letter to light*]. Last week.

SAM. How was Joe?

SHANKS [*reading*]. All right—an' mighty hopeful about Grant's winnin'.

SAM. Joe—Joe's dead.

SHANKS. Dead! [*Looks slowly at letter and back.*]

SAM. Yes—awful sorry.

SHANKS. Who told you so?

SAM. I saw him.

SHANKS. Saw him—killed?

SAM. No—but afterwards—in his coffin.

SHANKS. You mean—they buried him?

SAM. We fetched his body home on our boat to Cairo—and box car over here.

SHANKS. Kain't be no mistake? Joseph Taylor Shanks?

SAM [*nods*]. Son o' Milton Shanks.

SHANKS [*nods helplessly*]. That's right. [*Reënter MA.*]

MA. Yer kin come in now, but walk on yer toes.

SHANKS. Sam Carter's here—

MA. Oh— How are you, Sam?

SAM. Good evening.

SHANKS. —with bad news, Martha.

MA [*quickly*]. Bad news! From Joey?

SHANKS. Yes.

MA. Give me the letter. [*Takes letter quickly from* MILT.]

SHANKS. That's the one you gave me—Joey—couldn't write *his*self— My God, Martha, it's terrible— [*Cannon— bell. The village band plays " When Johnnie comes Marching Home."*]

MA. Terrible? Hurt bad?

SAM. He's dead, Mrs. Shanks.

MA. Oh, Gawd— Oh, Gawd!— [*Crosses, in agony, to corner of well—falls, kneeling on it—she sobs a bit, then, realizing that* JOEY *had that place before he went away, she caresses the curb and weeps.*]

SAM [*after pause*]. Yer oughta say somethin' to her—

SHANKS. Joey wouldn't want ye ter do that, ma. [*Bends over her.*]

MA [*shrinking from him*]. Fer Gawd's sake, Milt Shanks —don't tetch me—yer unclean—yer unclean— [*She rises. She presses* JOE'S *letter against her face and so, sobbing, crosses to ironing board, gets other letters, and exits.*]

SHANKS [*pause*]. You said—in a box car.

SAM. Unloaded—in the depot now.

SHANKS. I'll go there. [*Starts.*]

SAM [*interposes*]. I wouldn't, Milt.

SHANKS. Why not?

SAM. Newt Gillespie's with it—he's wounded, himself, slightly.

SHANKS. Well—'twon't hurt fur me to be there, too—by his coffin—

SAM. 'Twon't be pleasant, 'cause that's one reason Newt come along— 'Fore he died Joe said, " Don't let my father see me—even in my coffin—'' Boy was kinda feverish but Newt takes it serious—and Newt wouldn't 'low you even if you went there— [*He mounts.*] My advice is to take it comfortable as you kin— [SAM *rides off.* SHANKS *watches him off—looks at sky—comes into light—looks painfully into house—stands irresolute—goes into road with intention of go-*

ing to Joey—*feels the pull of the stricken wife—stops—returns into light and is looking into house. In distance, " Johnny Comes Marching Home."*]

[CURTAIN.]

CHARACTERS IN PART TWO

Milton Shanks .... Aged 78
Madeline King, *his granddaughter* ..... " 22
Philip Manning .... " 28
Mrs. Manning .... " 48
Col. Hardy .... " 76
Dr. Randall .... " 34
Newt Gillespie .... " 78
Lem Tollard .... " 78

PART II

ACT III

SCENE

Set same as preceding acts but showing lapse of forty years and some improvement by money. The lilac bush is now tall as the house and is in bloom—spring flowers in beds. The ground cloth has become a lawn. The well-sweep is replaced by super-structure and pulley wheel. Small trees are big. Vines cover the porch. The cornfield suggests Villa acreage instead. There is a picket fence where the rails were. Lawn furniture.

DISCOVERED

Empty stage. Piano heard. Enter SHANKS—aged seventy-six —white-haired and bowed. He is in his shirt sleeves. He crosses up to gate—goes outside, and examines R.F.D. box. Opens letter—to himself, reads. Consults watch. The song stops.

SHANKS [*calls*]. Some letters fur you, dearie.

MADELINE [*off*]. From Boston?

SHANKS. One is. [*Enter MADELINE. This part is for the same actress who does MA in Acts One and Two—but with complete change of character from drudge woman to bright girl and from dark hair to blonde.*]

MADELINE. Big envelope?

SHANKS [*hands mail*]. Yes.

MADELINE [*showing contents of letter*]. A copy of my certificate, grandpa.

SHANKS [*brightly*]. From the Normal?

MADELINE. Yes. That ought to satisfy the board, hadn't it?

SHANKS [*smiles*]. Some.

131

MADELINE. What's the best way to present it?

SHANKS. One way's ter send it or take it to their meetin' to-night—other way is take it round this afternoon to the separate members.

MADELINE. I could do both.

SHANKS. 'Course ye could.

MADELINE [*in delight*]. Oh! If I get it, grandpa—

SHANKS. You ain't jes' sayin' that 'cause it tickles me— air ye?

MADELINE. No, indeed—why, look around us—no grain elevators—no noisy railroad yards—no cobble stones—and sixty dollars a month, here, is as good as eighty in the city—and maybe I'd get some singing, too.

SHANKS. Wouldn't count on that for money— Lemme see yer certificate— [*Takes it*—MADELINE *opens other letters—is earnest over one. Pause.*] I've got to go to the village—I kin show this to some of 'em.

MADELINE. The village? Why?

SHANKS. There's a man I want ter see comin' in on the train—or you could go along, too.

MADELINE [*shakes head*]. My doctor's coming.

SHANKS. Yer doctor?

MADELINE. The specialist—that treated my throat last winter.

SHANKS [*frightened*]. Why, darlin'—ye ain't ailin' agin?

MADELINE [*affectionately. Laughs and pets him*]. No, grandpa—a friendly visit— He's down this way on another call, he says.

SHANKS. Doctors unsettle me. An' I don't want any o' their blamed experiments on th' only treasure God A'mighty's spared me—no.

MADELINE. I don't need one—I never will down here. It's only the soft coal in the city!

SHANKS [*with certificate*]. I'll go in Philip Manning's office with this and ask him to tell his mother about it.

MADELINE. We can wait until the meeting for Mrs. Manning—she's for me, of course.

SHANKS. But maybe this'll give her a chance to pull some wires this afternoon.

MADELINE. That's so.

SHANKS. And give Philip a chance. He ain't on the board, but he's a power jest the same.

MADELINE. You bet.

SHANKS. You know, Maddy, I sicked Philip into politics.

MADELINE. Yes, I know.

SHANKS. D' I ever tell you that?

MADELINE. Often, grandpa, yes.

SHANKS. Years ago, in a town meetin'—he stud up and said sumpin'—I fergit what it was—an' I sent fur him— Jest a slip of a boy no older than yer Uncle Joey was. I said— "Young man, you take an' ole feller's advice you'll go inter politicks—you got everything fur it—voice and hair—blue eyes" —an' now, by Jim-min-nee, he's in the legislature—I know it— [*Enter* PHILIP *and* MRS. MANNING, *left, behind fence.*]

PHILIP. Good afternoon.

MADELINE [*very pleased*]. Oh— How-de-do.

SHANKS. Why, Philip—jest talkin' about you—afternoon, Mrs. Manning.

MRS. MANNING. Good afternoon, Miss Shanks.

MADELINE. My certificate has come from Boston.

MRS. MANNING. Good.

MADELINE. Come in.

PHILIP. We're on our way to Colonel Hardy's.

MADELINE. Just a minute—your coat, grandpa.

PHILIP. Nonsense—never mind your coat, Mr. Shanks.

SHANKS [*on porch*]. Got to go to the village, anyway. [*Exit.* MRS. MANNING *and* PHILIP *come through gate.*]

MRS. MANNING [*with certificate*]. This completes our hand. I'll make a motion that applicants for the position of teacher must show a normal school certificate— That will dispose of Mrs. Simpson.

PHILIP. Yes, mother, if the motion passes—but we want to be sure. Hardy's our man to see. [*Reënter* SHANKS *with coat on.*]

MRS. MANNING. Why Colonel Hardy so importantly? He isn't on the board.

PHILIP. But as president of the village he appoints the board—and the majority will want to please him. Politics every time.

SHANKS. Hardy—Hardy's a stiff-necked feller—allers was.

MRS. MANNING. Don't you like Colonel Hardy, Mr. Shanks?

SHANKS. I do—but Hardy ain't very friendly.

PHILIP. Then all the more reason for us to see him.

MRS. MANNING. Do you think he'd favor Mrs. Simpson for the place?

SHANKS. Well, you see—she's a widder and her father's a Grand Army man—Hardy's a Grand Army man, too.

PHILIP. That's so.

MRS. MANNING. Her old father's one of my objections to Mrs. Simpson. I'm a great believer in heredity myself.

SHANKS. We got a little heredity ourselves. Madeline's Uncle Joey was in Hardy's company. Ef he'd a lived he'd a been a Gran' Army hisself.

PHILIP. That's a good point for Hardy.

SHANKS. Oh, he ain't forgot it. Hardy ain't the forgettin' kind. [Consults watch.] I hope you'll excuse me; I got ter meet a man at the train.

MRS. MANNING. Certainly.

SHANKS [going]. Madeline kin make ye feel more at home than I kin, anyway. [Exit.]

MADELINE. Please sit down. [They sit.]

PHILIP. Now let's hold a council of war. We're going to get you that teacher job if I have to set fire to the school house. What strings can we pull?

MRS. MANNING. There are only five votes—three men and Mrs. Voorhees and myself— One comfort, my dear, the women are for you.

PHILIP. Tompkins is a regular crony of Gillespie's—sure for Mrs. Simpson.

MRS. MANNING. So's Wheeler. Our only hope is the third man, Baumer.

PHILIP. What's his line of goods?

MRS. MANNING. He gives Swedish massage and tunes pianos.

PHILIP. Tunes pianos— Probably recommends some make on commission, doesn't he?

MRS. MANNING. I think he does.

PHILIP [rising]. Good. I'll consult him about a piano this afternoon.

MRS. MANNING [shakes head]. He knows I have one.

PHILIP. Not for you—some friend of mine getting married. And then—[*indicates* MADELINE] and let's see—I wonder if he knows you sing? [MADELINE *shrugs.*]

MRS. MANNING. He must. The whole village is talking of your singing last Sunday—the first morning service I've missed in months.

PHILIP. Well, there's another drag—brother artist—and I'll tell him if we can get you to live here there'll be regular concerts—you'll want a new piano—the best he can find, and for every concert it'll have to be freshly tuned and massaged and everything— Oh, I'll get Baumer.

MRS. MANNING. They're raving about your voice.

MADELINE. How lovely!

PHILIP. And they've never really heard it. I was at church Sunday morning. Come in and sing one of those lovely ballads for mother, now, and we'll go on about our campaigning.

MRS. MANNING [*rising*]. Please.

MADELINE [*as they start toward house*]. It's pleasanter out of doors, and you'll hear just as well. [*Exit.*]

PHILIP [*on porch*]. Personally, I enjoy seeing it done.

MRS. MANNING. Don't embarrass her, Philip.

PHILIP [*returns*]. Girls aren't embarrassed nowadays, mother, because men like to look at them. [*With lover's fervor.*] Isn't she adorable? [*Song begins.*]

MRS. MANNING. Sh— [*After a few bars of song*—COLONEL HARDY *enters, left, back of fence. He is the* CAPTAIN HARDY *of the first part of play, and now about seventy-five years old.*]

PHILIP [*seeing* HARDY]. There's Colonel Hardy! [*Calls.*] Colonel! [HARDY, *who has crossed, stops up right.* MRS. MANNING *rises.*]

PHILIP [*in tone intended not to interrupt singer*]. Mother and I were just going to see you, Colonel.

HARDY [*lifting hat*]. Mrs. Manning— [MRS. MANNING *gives hand.*]

PHILIP [*nodding to house*]. That's Miss King singing. Have you met her?

HARDY. No.

PHILIP [*opening gate*]. Come in.

HARDY. No, thank you.

PHILIP. Business—Colonel—for the village—

MRS. MANNING [*persuading*]. Yes.

HARDY [*indicates yard*]. It's forty years, Mrs. Manning, since I set foot on that ground.

PHILIP [*playfully*]. But Miss King's only about twenty— aren't visiting the third generation with the sins of others— are you, Colonel? You know that's a divine prerogative—

HARDY. I refuse to speak to Mr. Milton Shank— [*Song stops.* MRS. MANNING *turns back to porch.*]

PHILIP. He's gone to the village.

HARDY. No? [*Reënter* MADELINE.]

MADELINE [*laughing*]. It's a very sentimental selection, but—[*slows down as she sees the stranger*] Philip is rather partial to it.

MRS. MANNING. Miss King—I want Colonel Hardy, our village president, to meet you.

MADELINE [*coming on*]. You're very good.

MRS. MANNING. Miss Madeline King, Colonel Hardy.

HARDY [*lifting hat*]. Miss King!

MADELINE. Won't you come in, Colonel? You're one of my story book heroes—

HARDY [*reserved but pleased by her*]. Indeed?

MADELINE. Colonel Hardy's a name as large as George Washington in our household—an uncle of mine was in your regiment— Do come in a moment— [HARDY *enters. Chairs are readjusted.*]

MRS. MANNING. Colonel Hardy heard some of your song— [*To* HARDY.] This is Miss King's certificate from the Normal School—Boston—

HARDY. I won't sit down, thank you—I'm on my way home. [*With certificate.*] Oh, yes— Well, you've evidently been very industrious, Miss King.

MADELINE. Very fortunate, Colonel . . . so far. My ambition now is to be allowed to stay here.

HARDY [*attempting humor*]. Well—I've some influence with the police.

MADELINE. They haven't bothered me—yet—

PHILIP. They may!

HARDY. Yes— They're both young.

MADELINE [*shakes head*]. It's the shop-keepers— I've got work in Chicago—but I can't coax grandpa away from this place—and I'd rather come to him—I do know how to teach school.

HARDY [*musing, and studying her*]. 'M. [*Pause.*] Your grandfather likes it here?

MADELINE. Adores it— I had an awful time getting that picket fence—the old rails had been there when Captain Tom Hardy leaned on them—Sam somebody tied his horse there, when Vicksburg surrendered.

HARDY [*pause*]. The other candidate before the school board has lived here always.

MRS. MANNING. Exactly—she'll perpetuate every local blemish.

HARDY. Her father has lived here—

MADELINE. Well, my grandfather—and grandmother—until Vicksburg "came along," as grandpa says—

HARDY. I knew your grandmother, and it's a pleasure to meet you— The school board matter is mere—gossip with me: I'm not a member. [*Extends hand.*]

MRS. MANNING. Philip and I will walk with you a ways and elaborate the gossip.

HARDY. Delighted.

PHILIP. I'll follow, mother, and relieve you in a few minutes. I'm a terrible muff at gossip.

HARDY. He's boasting.

PHILIP. And the sidewalks in your man's town, Colonel, aren't organized for three. . . .

HARDY [*at gate*]. My dear Philip—that's what recommends them— Come, Mrs. Manning. [*Exeunt* MRS. MANNING *and* COLONEL.]

PHILIP [*easily*]. No school like the old school.

MADELINE. I think your mother's wonderful.

PHILIP. Father was all right, too—[*pause and smile*] and the further back you go the better we get—

MADELINE [*smiling*]. I wasn't thinking in that direction.

PHILIP. Fine! Let's talk about me. [*Sits.*]

MADELINE. You should hear grandpa. He thinks he put you into the legislature.

PHILIP. I think so, too.

MADELINE. And in his mind and heart he's got you all nominated next fall for Congress.

PHILIP [*seriously*]. Really! [MADELINE *nods and smiles.*]

Funny, but Hardy's been putting that congressional bee into my bonnet, too.

MADELINE. Why not?

PHILIP. Oh, I'm in favor of it—but I might get a glorious licking and be assigned to go on in very private and depressing obscurity here.

MADELINE [*reproving*]. One doesn't win by feeling that way, Mr. Candidate.

PHILIP. I got in the legislature feeling that way.

MADELINE [*pause*]. You said " depressing obscurity! "

PHILIP. Well?

MADELINE. Do you mean the life in this place?

PHILIP. Principally.

MADELINE. I don't call it depressing. I think it's beautiful. I love every minute that I can stay here.

PHILIP. You're not a man—with ambition.

MADELINE. Lincoln was. He lived only a few miles over that way.

PHILIP. But Lincoln wanted to go to Washington.

MADELINE. I don't believe he did—very much. Grandpa says he didn't. And just a few miles further over that way is Whitcomb Riley. " 'Long the banks of Deer Crick's good enough for him."

PHILIP. I'm not a poet.

MADELINE. Grandpa says you are.

PHILIP. Does he?

MADELINE. Yes.

PHILIP. Did he mean it for a knock or a boost—?

MADELINE. Boost, I hope.

PHILIP. Good— [*Pause. Earnestly.*] I've got a notion to tell you something, Madeline King.

MADELINE. Poetry?

PHILIP [*nods*]. The first day I saw you—after you came back from Boston—this same time two years ago—I was to make the Decoration Day speech at the soldiers' monument next day and I was scared blue—I didn't have a single idea—but I drifted by here on the other side of the road— You were standing near the gate—[MADELINE *nods*]—that big lilac bush behind you— There'd been a shower and " the sun had come out with a flagon of amber and drenched the whole world in ambrosial wine."

MADELINE [*in real appreciation*]. Oh, that's wonderful.

PHILIP. It seemed a vision. A symbol of the beauty that must be eternal—and—I—had—my—speech— [*Smiles—relaxes.*]

MADELINE. We heard you make it. That's when grandpa decided you were a poet. You said something about the sadness of the flowers fading, but the unbearable thing would be if the Spirit of Spring itself should pass from the world— Then about those young people there growing old, but there would always be on earth the spirit of youth—and from that to the soldiers dying but forever the spirit of Liberty—living— and so on—didn't you?

PHILIP. Yes—but all the time I was thinking of you and that lilac and the golden sunlight over you and, dog-gone it, Madeline, it's haunted me in committee rooms and courts and railroad trains. Do you know, I jumped up to Chicago from Springfield last session and went to church just to look at you singing.

MADELINE. When?

PHILIP. In February.

MADELINE. Why didn't you speak to me? ·

PHILIP. When it was over the aisle was crowded and before I could get to you—you went out the stage entrance.

MADELINE [*solemnly, shaking head*]. That isn't what we call the side door of a church.

PHILIP. I want you to get this teacher job if you want it— but whether you do or don't—I've just got to have you with me, Madeline—

MADELINE [*pause*]. Of course— [*Pause.*] Any woman would be complimented, Mr. Manning—

PHILIP. Would she, Miss King?

MADELINE. Yes, Philip— [PHILIP *nods solemnly.*] Complimented by your—your—attention—

PHILIP. I'm asking you to marry me, you know.

MADELINE [*pause*]. I couldn't— [*pause*] quite leave grandpa—now.

PHILIP. Don't leave him—if the place is good enough for Lincoln and Whitcomb Riley, I'll stand for it. Say yes.

MADELINE [*regarding him*]. You're a funny—creature.

PHILIP. Well, I'll throw that in along with the poetry— but principally I want you to think about my law position and my general health. You're just playing the mischief with both of 'em. . . . [*Pause. He puts out his hand.* MADELINE *studies him; then quietly lays her hand in his.*] It's a bet, is it?

MADELINE [*hushed*]. Yes—it's a bet! [*He kisses her hand. Then with a better idea, goes to fence and looks right and left—returns. Rising.*] No.

PHILIP. Not a God's soul in sight but one stranger, and he's a block away. [*Embraces and kisses her.*]

MADELINE. Don't any more—don't [*breaks away*] —but I'm awfully happy.

PHILIP [*pause*]. I can think of about a million things in my life I wish I hadn't done.

MADELINE. Stage doors?

PHILIP. No—mostly stupid things, like thinking there wasn't a God. [*Laughs tenderly. Enter, from right back,* DOCTOR RANDALL. RANDALL *looks over the fence as though to identify the place—sees* MADELINE.]

RANDALL. Why! Miss King! [MADELINE *goes to gate.*]

MADELINE. Doctor Randall—this is wonderful. [*Shakes hands.*]

RANDALL. Yes. [*She brings him through the gate.*]

MADELINE. Mr. Manning—let me introduce Doctor Randall, of Chicago.

PHILIP. Pleased to meet you, sir.

RANDALL. Mr. Manning. [*Shaking hands.*] Haven't we met before?

MADELINE. Mr. Manning is our member of the legislature.

RANDALL. Judiciary Committee?

PHILIP. Yes.

RANDALL. That's it—I'm on the Pardon Board.

PHILIP. Of course. Stupid not to remember you.

MADELINE. Sit down.

PHILIP. I promised to follow mother, you know. [*To* RANDALL.] Honoring our metropolis by any lengthy visit, Doctor?

RANDALL. Leaving to-night.

PHILIP. Oh—may see you later at that. [*Smiles to* MADE-LINE.] Good-by. [*Exit right.*]

MADELINE. Awfully good of you to think of me.

RANDALL. I had a professional call at Moline this forenoon —seemed a crime to be so near and not see you—and this amusing coincidence of your address.

MADELINE. What?

RANDALL. The name—" care of Mr. Milton Shanks "—

MADELINE. My grandfather.

RANDALL. I thought likely—we're old acquaintances.

MADELINE. Grandpa and you?

RANDALL. Yes. Had half a dozen conferences at Springfield—since I've been on the Pardon Board.

MADELINE. What about?

RANDALL. Some old fellow he's interested in. But isn't it strange that in all our talks about him you never mentioned his name?

MADELINE. I don't know. He's gone to the station now to meet someone.

RANDALL. That's me, I fancy. I wrote him by the same mail.

MADELINE. Yes?

RANDALL. I got off at the crossing. Brakeman said I'd save time. [*Indicates bag.*] Nothing to carry.

MADELINE. Then your visit isn't mine, after all?

RANDALL. Entirely yours—grandfather is just an excuse.

MADELINE. Did you need an excuse?

RANDALL. A man's self-respect needs one, when a girl's turned him down annually for years.

MADELINE [*smiles*]. I've known you only two years, Doctor.

RANDALL [*pause*]. Really? [*She nods.*] Those refusals seemed a year apart.

MADELINE. That's better.

RANDALL. How's the voice?

MADELINE. Fine, thank you.

RANDALL. You know, I don't want to talk physiology to you, but even a great voice is sometimes improved by marriage.

MADELINE. That's the most expensive treatment you've ever recommended.

RANDALL. I offer it free.

MADELINE [*shaking head*]. 'Twouldn't be fair.

RANDALL. To you?

MADELINE. To either of us.

RANDALL. I wouldn't ask you to give up your work.

MADELINE. I can't do things by halves.

RANDALL. Not even—better halves?

MADELINE. Not even better halves. I love the Church work and the City now, but when I marry I'll want something more like—this [*stretches out her arms*]—the sky to the ground all about me.

RANDALL [*in coaxing cadence*]. Suburbs—

MADELINE [*shuddering*]. Ugh!

RANDALL [*pause*]. The lake front would give us an horizon view half way round.

MADELINE [*pause. Shakes head*]. I'm—sorry. [*Pause. Maternally.*] Dear Doctor [*puts hand on his arm*]—I haven't told anyone about it—not even grandpa—but I'm engaged to be married now—

RANDALL [*pause*]. Afraid to tell grandpa?

MADELINE. No. [*Pause.*] I haven't seen him since it happened. [RANDALL *looks at her—looks off—looks at her—pause—nods off inquiringly after* PHILIP—MADELINE *slowly nods " yes."*]

RANDALL. Ten minutes too late.

MADELINE. No, dear Doctor; I've been in love with him over a year. [*A pause.* RANDALL *gets a railroad yellow time-table from his pocket and begins to consult it.* MADELINE *covers the time-table.*] Please wait and see grandpa. I do want your opinion about him.

RANDALL. 'Tisn't my specialty—but—I get a bit of it.

MADELINE. It seems to be only the Civil War—and that's all right, too, except the siege of Vicksburg.

RANDALL. Was he at Vicksburg?

MADELINE [*shakes head*]. His boy—my uncle on my mother's side—was killed there.

RANDALL. Union army?

MADELINE. Yes; and some of the explanation may be there. Grandpa wasn't in the Confederate army but a sympathizer. Folks—well, not so much now—but they used to blame him for it—kinda cruelly.

RANDALL. I see. [*Pause. Reënter* SHANKS.]

MADELINE [*going to him*]. Grandpa, I'm glad you're back. This is my good friend, Doctor Randall, of Chicago.

SHANKS. When you had your sore throat?

MADELINE. Yes.

SHANKS. Madeline never told me the name, or I'd known it. How'd I miss you?

RANDALL. I got off at the crossing.

SHANKS. Sit down, Doctor. How do you think Madeline's looking?

RANDALL. Looking? Why, heart-breakingly happy, sir.

SHANKS. Heart-breaking?

MADELINE. He's laughing at me, grandpa, because I've been foolish enough to tell him a secret—but I'll not let him laugh at you, too. I'm engaged, grandpa.

SHANKS [*unhappy at the idea that the man is* RANDALL]. Why—

MADELINE. To Philip Manning.

SHANKS. To Philip—well, I'm happy, too. That [*to* RANDALL] —that'll keep her here [*to* MADELINE] unless you go to Washington. [*To* RANDALL.] The young man's in the legislature. 'Fact, you've heard him talk at your commission.

RANDALL [*nodding*]. We met here to-day.

SHANKS. Engaged. So you don't care anything about the teacher's position, then?

MADELINE. Oh, but I do—all the more. I've got to be perfectly independent—so that Philip shan't feel too sure about it. [*All laugh.*]

SHANKS. I reckon you've seen her more'n her grandfather has—livin' in Chicago.

MADELINE. Not quite, grandpa.

RANDALL. It must be fairly lonely by yourself. What do you do here, Mr. Shanks, when she's away?

SHANKS. Well—I read. [*Pause.*] An' I think considerable—an' I cook some—besides, a good deal of it's habit.

RANDALL. Yes; these machines of ours are very adjustable things.

SHANKS. Machines?

RANDALL. Our bodies.

SHANKS. Yes, but I cahilate it's more a man's ideas—how he thinks. Automobiles go along that road now, but I've seen cavalry ridin' by in the sixties—an' cannons—four horses to 'em. General Logan—"Fightin' John," they called him, rested hisself in that chair yer sittin' in—Madeline's grand-mother give him a drink o' water. [*Conscious of the well.*] Automobiles go by here now, but sometimes I kin see Logan and the cavalry plainer. How do you account for that?

RANDALL. Deeper impressions.

SHANKS. Madeline's mother played roun' under them lilac bushes—Madeline played under 'em. Somehow I see the mother cl'arest—an' along in May, when the smell of 'em comes in the winder—'bout sundown—why, I can't say it makes me downhearted 'xactly—but if I was a woman, by thunder, I'd jes' cry, I reckon. [*Smiles.*]

MADELINE [*going to him*]. Dear grandpa—I won't leave you alone so much any more.

SHANKS. Nonsense—why, she's spent years in Boston pre-parin' herself. [*To* MADELINE.] Don't you fret about me.

RANDALL. You say Logan sat in this chair?

SHANKS. Yes; Fightin' John.

RANDALL. Was your son with Logan?

SHANKS. With Grant.

RANDALL. Killed at Vicksburg.

SHANKS. You heared of Joey? [RANDALL *looks at* MAD-ELINE.]

MADELINE. Yes, grandpa.

SHANKS. Oh— [*Muses.*] Yes, Vicksburg. [*In low under-tone.*]

RANDALL. A hard siege, I believe.

SHANKS [*annoyed*]. Grant didn't push it.

RANDALL. Didn't, eh?

SHANKS. No.

RANDALL. Tell me about it.

SHANKS. It's all as fresh as yesterday. You see, the coun-try'd been waitin' for Grant ter do sumpin'. [*As the glint of madness comes in* SHANKS' *eyes* MADELINE *puts her hands together in distress.* RANDALL *gestures silence.*]

RANDALL. Waiting for Grant—

SHANKS. Yes. So I went down there myself. I sez to him, "What's the delay, General?" I recollec' he was settin' on a camp stool smokin', and—

MADELINE [*goes to him*]. Grandpa.

SHANKS [*feeling her touch*]. Yes, dear.

MADELINE. You were here when they brought Uncle Joey's body home, weren't you? Here with gramma.

SHANKS. Yes, here.

MADELINE. Then you couldn't have been at Vicksburg, could you? [*Brushes his hair back.*] That's just the dream again, grandpa—the dream.

SHANKS [*pause. To* RANDALL]. Ever have a dream that way? Takes hold o' you perfect—till sumpin' brings you out of it.

RANDALL. I know about them, a little. Yes.

SHANKS. It's all right, dearie. Excuse me; I'll be all right in a minute. [*Goes up left fence.*]

MADELINE. I had to interrupt him. It hurts me so when that delusion comes over him.

RANDALL. Ever violent with it?

MADELINE. Never—excited a little in telling it—I used to believe him when I was a child.

RANDALL. The son's death was a blow, of course, but—

MADELINE. And his wife at the same time.

RANDALL. Wife died? [MADELINE *nods.*] Oh!

MADELINE. And neighbors hostile because of his politics.

RANDALL. I see.

MADELINE. Joey—his son—enlisted on the Union side and wouldn't even speak to grandpa.

RANDALL. Well, that was pressure enough, God knows.

MADELINE. Take a walk with me. [SHANKS *returns.*]

RANDALL. Yes—if you wish it.

MADELINE. I'll get a hat. [*Exit to house.*]

SHANKS. And yer letter, Doctor—kind o' excited me some —brought back old times.

RANDALL. Made you happy, I hope.

SHANKS. I can't tell you how much. The pore feller's been in there thirty-eight long years—and night and day I've thought about him—been workin' on his case thirty years— fifteen different legislatures.

RANDALL. Still—his first sentence was death.

SHANKS. War times, Doctor—and war-time hate. If he'd just had on a different suit of clothes when we got inter that fight—he'd a been a prisoner o' war and set free in two years— jist as Philip Manning said ter yer board.

RANDALL. Does Tollard find any of his old friends living?

SHANKS. He ain't been here, to my knowledge.

RANDALL. Hasn't?

SHANKS [*shakes head*]. Your letter was the first hint I had he was free.

RANDALL. It must have startled you.

SHANKS. Don't tell her.

RANDALL. I won't.

SHANKS. She knows the folks here have been aginst me purty hard—but I've kept all that prison talk and—sentence o' death business out of her life—and I'm gonna see him first an' tell him not ter talk, 'cause if he ain't got any place else to go, I plan ter take him in here—yes, sir.

RANDALL [*gives hand*]. You're a Christian gentleman, Mr. Shanks.

SHANKS [*shakes hand*]. Some back-slidin'—I used horrible language durin' the war. [*Enter* GILLESPIE *in Grand Army uniform, back left.*]

GILLESPIE. Shanks.

SHANKS [*turns—pauses*]. Well, Newt?

GILLESPIE. Busy?

SHANKS. I've got a friend visitin' here. [*Enter* MADELINE.]

MADELINE. I'm going to walk up and meet Mrs. Manning, grandpa. [*Sees* GILLESPIE.]

GILLESPIE [*pause*]. That's her—ain't it?

SHANKS. Madeline—this is Mr. Newt Gillespie—

MADELINE. How do you do, sir?

GILLESPIE [*pause*]. Elsie's daughter?

SHANKS. Yes.

GILLESPIE. I knowed yer grandmother, young woman.

MADELINE. I never saw her.

GILLESPIE. Well, anybody 'at ever did would a knowed she was your grandmother. Don't lemme keep you—because us men has some business.

MADELINE. We'll go, then—come, Doctor. [DOCTOR *opens gate, exits with* MADELINE.]

GILLESPIE. I don't call on you very of'en, Milt.

SHANKS. No.

GILLESPIE. But I ain't like Hardy—I ain't tongue-tied.

SHANKS. You said business, Newt—

GILLESPIE. The school board votes to-night—for a new

teacher—my dotter has earned the place by years o' primer school work—and she's substituted satisfactory in this job— the old settlers here ain't gonna be patient with any move to cubflank her.

SHANKS. I think it's gone too far ter do anything but leave it ter the board.

GILLESPIE. 'Tain't gone too far fur your girl ter withdraw.

SHANKS. I kain't ask her to do that.

GILLESPIE. Oh, yes, ye kin.

SHANKS. Well— [*Pause.*] I won't.

GILLESPIE. You will, Milt.

SHANKS. Well, just remember, Newt—I didn't gee and haw about it. I tell you once for all—flat-footed—no.

GILLESPIE [*pause*]. Grover Cleveland's been president twict—an' I ain't aimin' ter dig up the bloody shirt agin, but when little children air under a teacher's influence murder ain't a nice subject to have in their minds. This'll be my argument ter the school board to-night if you compel me.

SHANKS [*pause*]. I respect that coat ye got on, Newt, and that cord round yer hat— Them are naytional—but it's a mystery ter me sometimes how the war ever was won with souls as little as yours is behind the guns.

GILLESPIE. I'll tell ye, Milt—an' yer welcome to repeat it. It's 'cause the souls on the other side was the size o' yourn— [*Pause.*] Now yer kin go ter yer church Sunday— and sing " Fur sech a worm as I "—but Elsie's daughter withdraws.

SHANKS [*pause*]. 'Twasn't murder, and you know it. They wair shootin' on both sides—fast as any pitched battle.

GILLESPIE. That's all been adjudicated by the courts an' one of yer gang is still servin' a life sentence fur it at Jolliet.

SHANKS. No—he's pardoned now.

GILLESPIE. Lem Tollard?

SHANKS. Yes.

GILLESPIE. Who contrived that?

SHANKS. The unanimous pardon board—that gentleman walkin' with Madeline is a member of it.

GILLESPIE. Pardoned? [SHANKS *nods.*] Well—that don't hurt my argument— [*Chews excitedly.*] On the contrary— [*Pause.*] An' it'll jes' set tongues a waggin'—I don't hev to be personal at all—it'll be only foresighted fur the board to shun it in the school house— Ye've jist histed yerself with yer own pattard—I told you you'd withdraw. [*Enter* Lem, *right. He is seventy-eight—but a fierce and burning seventy-eight—sullen and patient.*]

Lem [*inquiring*]. Gillespie!

Gillespie [*pause*]. That's my name.

Lem. *You* know me, don't you? [*To* Shanks.]

Shanks. Yes—'cause I been expectin' you—but we're both changed a heap—come in. [*Extends hand.*]

Lem [*refuses hand but enters*]. Expectin' me?

Shanks. Yes.

Lem. Why?

Shanks. Well—you lived here—

Lem. Not for thirty-eight years I ain't—by God!

Shanks. I've kept count of 'em and I went before every legislature we've had—an' ter every governor up to this time.

Lem. I knew some bastard must a been at work ter keep me there. [*Pause.*] Ye didn't stay inside there long yourself, did you?

Shanks. Sorry yer bitter about it, Lem—but I ain't found much to choose between—outside or in—except the last year or so—

Lem. You expected me—'cause I lived here.

Shanks. Yes.

Lem. Listen ter this, Gillespie—'cause it's gonna be important—and short— [*Pause.*] I've come 'cause *you* live here—'cause I've figured out who fixed it so the cavalry was in them especial bushes waitin' for us—I've figured why I was invited ter the arsenal in St. Louis and shet up till Camp Jackson was captured—I've figured why several plans of ours come out the little end o' the horn—figured it— Listenin', Gillespie?

Gillespie. I am.

Lem. Now listen and watch, too—when I hand you what's comin' to you, Milt—it's gonna be in the guts. [*Enter* Philip *and* Madeline.] Why? Because there it ain't immediate and you have time, God damn you, to suffer and be sorry. [*Draws gun.* Philip *has been ready from word " guts" and grabs* Lem *from back.*]

Madeline. Grandpa— [*Runs to* Shanks.]

Philip. Give that to me! [*Quickly gets gun and throws*

Lem *from him to ground. Enter* Randall *and* Mrs. Manning.]

Mrs. Manning.   Philip—Philip—what's the matter?

Randall.   Tollard—what's this mean—your pardon's conditional on good behavior.—Now go. [Tollard *goes out gate; waits for* Gillespie.]

Gillespie.   I've heard his case—[*to* Shanks] and he ought a killed you—by God! You're more a murderer than he is— you was sentenced to be hung and they ought a hung you forty years ago— [*To* Mrs. Manning.] School board! This is the kind o' scandals you're tryin' to introduce with your Boston idears—

Madeline.   To be hanged—why, grandpa—Philip—

Gillespie.   Damned ole jailbird—firebrand and horse thief and copperhead! Once a copperhead—always a copperhead— [*Exit.*]

Shanks.   Maddy—Maddy, dear—it had to come some time—you got ter gimme a minute ter collect my idears. I ain't afraid o' death, Philip—but I couldn't leave her this way!

[CURTAIN.]

ACT IV

Scene

Cheap Illinois rural interior—but neat. The room is rectangular except that upper left corner is obliqued for a chimneypiece and cheap wood mantel of a low ivory in color. The back wall has an exterior door, right, and window, left. A second window is up, right, in side wall.

A door to kitchen is down, left. The wallpaper is neutral. There are hartshorn blinds and cheap muslin curtains looped back. A much worn rug or ingrain carpet—preferably rug—covers entire floor.

Combined bookcase and desk, right. Desk is open and full of the accumulated scraps of years. Chair at desk. Leaf table, center, closed and covered with faded red cloth. Piano between door and window. Two mid-Victorian hair chairs at table. Rocker above fireplace. Black walnut buffet, left. Cheaply furnished. The mantelpiece carries a Rogers' group—and some China peasants. The fireplace has a wallpaper screen in it, a rusty iron fender is in place, and blowers. In upper right corner is a furnished " whatnot." The pictures on wall are framed prints of sentimental stuff. An oval frame of walnut molding over fireplace holds photo of boy of sixteen in Federal uniform. Center table has a lamp. Volk's life mask of Lincoln hangs on mantel panel over fire opening —Lincoln's hand is in bookcase desk. Through back door is seen ceiling of porch, which may be a small piece hung to about height of door. The back drop beyond gives an oblique of left side of first set adjusted to angle of that set—house.

Discovered

Madeline *putting away the supper dishes on dresser. She takes off apron and brings writing material from desk to table. Lights lamp.*

[MADELINE *turns at sound of step on porch.* PHILIP *appears.*]

PHILIP [*pause*]. Good evening.

MADELINE [*with restraint*]. Good evening.

PHILIP. May I come in?

MADELINE. Yes.

PHILIP [*enters*]. Well—that's something. [*Pause.*] Shake hands? [*Extends hand.*]

MADELINE. Yes.

PHILIP. Feeling better?

MADELINE. Seeing better, I think.

PHILIP. Couldn't be looking better—unless perhaps you'd consent to smile.

MADELINE [*bitterly*]. Not in this place. When I've got him away from these people who can carry hatred for a lifetime—got him safe with me in the city—perhaps.

PHILIP. Only two old geezers in their dotage—ignorant and primitive. One of them just turned loose from jail. Why care about them?

MADELINE [*shakes head*]. Colonel Hardy, the biggest man in the town, hasn't spoken to him in nearly forty years. And to think I was ignorant of the martyrdom he was suffering!

PHILIP. But it's over now, isn't it?

MADELINE. Is it? Who's been here to see him since it happened? The afternoon's gone by and only the string of morbid gossips gaping past the house.

PHILIP. I've been here.

MADELINE. Your mother hasn't.

PHILIP. Well, mother's peculiar—mother believes—

MADELINE [*pause*]. In heredity—

PHILIP. Mother believes there are times when people want to be alone—besides, to tell the truth, that shindy of ours rather shook mother's nerves. She never saw anybody pull a gun before—and—

MADELINE. Nor heard any one called a murderer.

PHILIP. I fancy not. But mother's all right. She said: "My heart just aches for poor little Madeline." [MADELINE *sits and covers eyes.*] I told her 'twasn't best to pull much of that—and you see I'm right. Don't cry, dear, unless it comforts you. [*Pause.*] Must be a deuce of a strain. [*Arm about her.*]

MADELINE [*moves away*]. Please don't do that.

PHILIP. We're engaged, aren't we? [MADELINE *shakes her head. Pause.*] Well, I am—and I've got witness. That Doctor friend of yours congratulated me—said you'd told him.

MADELINE. Did your mother congratulate you?

PHILIP. Not yet—but she will.

MADELINE. Did you tell her?

PHILIP [*pauses—shakes head*]. She heard the Doctor. [MADELINE *looks at him. Pause.*] I was planning to cushion it—even if that scrap hadn't have happened.

MADELINE. Naturally—

PHILIP. I mean for any girl. When a fellow's an only child and his mother's a widow, she— [*Shakes head.*] Well, for a thing like this you got to kind o' blindfold 'em and back 'em into it. Mother thinks now that I don't love her— [*shakes head*] and I kind o' hoped I'd bring up my average with you.

MADELINE [*pause*]. You may tell her she has nothing to fear.

PHILIP. Ha! You don't know my mother. When I tell her that you're making her conduct an excuse for throwing me over, she'll be in here asking you what you mean by it. I want you to marry me because you love me and—appreciate me, and not just to get rid of mother.

MADELINE [*smiles*]. Oh, Philip!

PHILIP [*pleased with smile*]. *That's* the girl I'm going to marry.

MADELINE [*tasting her tears*]. That's the girl that's— breaking her heart—because you're not.

PHILIP [*pause*]. Why, Madeline, I'd insist on your keeping your contract with me—if you'd been in jail. You can't cancel it because this story turns up about your grandfather.

MADELINE. I saw the horror on your mother's face when grandpa couldn't deny the stories—copperhead and horse thief and murder and penitentiary—

PHILIP. But, Madeline, some of our best families can't stand a show-down on grandfathers. Why—

MADELINE. No, no—I love him and I'll take him away and protect him—but I won't burden your career with that— a public man just starting—his success—a—

PHILIP. Where is your grandfather now?

MADELINE. In town somewhere.

PHILIP. I've got a car out here. Come with me. We'll pick him up and a ride will do you both good. [MADELINE *shakes her head. A step is heard. They turn. Enter* RANDALL.]

RANDALL. Good evening.

PHILIP. How are you?

RANDALL. I don't mean to intrude, but I've an appointment here with Mr. Shanks. [*Consults watch.*]

PHILIP. I'm glad not to leave Madeline alone, Doctor. [*Pause.*] That engagement on which you congratulated me is disturbing her just at present. I wish you'd tell her that in politics a man's father cuts very little ice and when it comes to grandfathers, that most of the voters never had any. [*To* MADELINE.] He'll tell you I'm right about it. [*Exit.*]

MADELINE. Where did you leave grandpa?

RANDALL. On his way to Colonel Hardy's—if that's the name.

MADELINE. Why there?

RANDALL [*shakes head*]. Something about an election to-night.

MADELINE. At the school board?

RANDALL. I think so.

MADELINE. Poor grandpa. He mustn't be humiliated by that. Oh, dear!

RANDALL. What is it?

MADELINE. I'd applied for the appointment as school teacher, but I don't want it now—and I wish grandpa wouldn't say any more about it.

RANDALL [*pause*]. Our friend [*nods off*] says your engagement is disturbing you some way. What does he mean?

MADELINE. I've broken it.

RANDALL. On account of—this—trouble to-day?

MADELINE. Yes.

RANDALL [*pause*]. 'M! [*Pause.*] Why, as I remember it, Mr. Manning behaved rather sympathetically.

MADELINE. His mother didn't.

RANDALL. Well [*pause*]—it's hard for me to be an enthusiastic advocate, but maybe it's just as unfair to blame him for mother as it would be to blame you for grandfather.

MADELINE. She's never liked grandpa. I was only twelve when she took me away from him.

RANDALL. She took you?

MADELINE. Well, sent me.

RANDALL. Why?

MADELINE. School—and music lessons in Boston. Their family comes from there.

RANDALL. What was her reason?

MADELINE. She heard me singing in here as I was washing dishes one day. I must have been bawling, because she stopped her carriage and turned back and then came in.

RANDALL. Did she have her son with her?

MADELINE. No.

RANDALL. Carriage? [MADELINE *nods*.] By taking you away from your grandfather, you mean that she financed your school period?

MADELINE. Yes—and that's one of the things I'm going to repay. That must have hurt grandpa, too—because he's awfully fine and delicate about such things—but what's a girl of twelve know? Can't you go to Colonel Hardy's and find grandpa?

RANDALL. Yes, but let's be sure that's what we want to do. Don't you think that unpleasantly suggests a lack of responsibility and—

MADELINE. Yes—of course—you mustn't go—

RANDALL [*pause*]. This—this indebtedness you imply to Mrs. Manning—was that—did that influence you in entering into this engagement with her son?

MADELINE. Rather the other way—but that's over now. She's been against the other woman who is applying for the teacher's place—against her because her father, Mr. Gillespie, is—rather ordinary—but grandpa's education isn't any better— and I couldn't [*shakes head*]—with this—this new talk about him— No, it's over—over—all of that— [*Throws it from her.*]

RANDALL. I'm not going to be so gauche as to urge my interest again—at a moment like this—but I want you to be conscious of me as a kind of rainy day proposition—one of those consolation backgrounds—like an accident policy when one feels the automobile skidding.

MADELINE. Dear Doctor, your proposals are all so—so—

RANDALL. Indefinite?

MADELINE. Practical—to improve my voice, or live on the lake front, or guard against skidding—but I do like you.

RANDALL. And my dear mother is *buried*—in Ann Arbor. [*Enter* GILLESPIE.]

GILLESPIE. Where's Mr. Milton Shanks?

MADELINE. He's not at home, and I wouldn't let you see him if he were.

GILLESPIE. He left word at my house that if I wasn't a coward, to come here soon as I got home.

MADELINE. Doctor—

RANDALL. Well, we'll tell him you called.

GILLESPIE. I won't trouble you, stranger. I'll wait for him.

MADELINE. Not in here, Mr. Gillespie.

GILLESPIE. Sidewalk suits me—unless it's just another copperhead trick ter keep me away from the school board. I'll stay right out here till that meets—and then I'll be back agin when it adjourns—at the gate. [*Exit.*]

MADELINE. Doctor—

RANDALL. Nothing to fear, Madeline. An old fellow like that! Why, his wind goes at the first real exertion. Besides— [*Voices outside.* PHILIP *and* GILLESPIE.]

MADELINE. Grandpa— [*Runs to door*—RANDALL *with her.*]

RANDALL. Mr. Manning again.

GILLESPIE [*outside*]. Half a dozen fellers heered him. By God, I never tuk a dare from a copperhead in the army times.

RANDALL. Your grandfather isn't there. Come away.

MADELINE. I can't stand any more fuss. [PHILIP *and* MRS. MANNING *appear.*]

PHILIP. Here's mother, Madeline. I'll be right back myself. [*Exit.* MRS. MANNING *enters.*]

MRS. MANNING. Madeline!

MADELINE. Mrs. Manning—

MRS. MANNING. Dear Madeline, you don't doubt my affection for you?

MADELINE. 'Tisn't a question of that, Mrs. Manning. I know your pride, too. I'm not going to shame it.

MRS. MANNING. Philip wants us to go on as though nothing had happened—and wants us not to let this business stampede our meeting to-night. The whole matter can be put over a week. Philip's a lawyer and—

MADELINE. What can a week change, if it's all true?

MRS. MANNING. Perhaps it isn't.

MADELINE. Perhaps it is. Grandpa hasn't denied it.

MRS. MANNING. He hasn't?

MADELINE. No. [*Voices outside.*]

SHANKS [*voice emerging*]. Yes, I said so. Come in, Philip.

RANDALL. That's Mr. Shanks. [SHANKS *and* PHILIP *appear.*]

SHANKS. Inside, Gillespie— [PHILIP *enters and goes to* MADELINE, *who avoids him—down left.*] Inside— [*Enters.* GILLESPIE *enters.* SHANKS *looks about at others—hesitates.*]

GILLESPIE. If I wasn't a coward, I'd come. Well, I'm here.

SHANKS. I've asked Colonel Hardy to come here.

PHILIP. Mr. Shanks!

SHANKS. Yes, Philip.

PHILIP [*impulsively*]. There's my hand, sir.

SHANKS [*taking hand*]. Yes.

PHILIP [*pause*]. You can tell whether I like you or not, can't you?

SHANKS [*in pain of grasp*]. Yes, Philip—I kin—but don't keep it up any longer'n you haf to. [*Straightens his cramped fingers.*]

MRS. MANNING. I've just got to be straightforward with you, Mr. Shanks.

SHANKS. Best way—allers—if ye kin—straightforward!

MRS. MANNING. Were you ever—convicted on a criminal charge?

SHANKS [*pause. Nods*]. Once.

MRS. MANNING. That man said the penitentiary.

GILLESPIE. An' I said so, too.

MRS. MANNING. I hate to add a moment to your unhappiness, Mr. Shanks. [*Pause, during which* SHANKS *suffers quietly.*] I'm perfectly willing to concede that there was some mistake about it—that you were probably innocent of the charge, but—

SHANKS [*shakes head*]. No, I took 'em—me and some other fellers workin' for the South. Them was war times, recollec', an' they wanted the horses fur John Moseby in Kentucky. 'F I'd been in the army, it'd been all right, but I was—I wasn't in the army. [*Pause.*] So— [*Throws up his hands.*]

MRS. MANNING. You must believe I haven't meant to hurt you, Mr. Shanks!

SHANKS. Course. Yer jist thinkin' about yer boy.

MRS. MANNING. That's all.

PHILIP. Never mind about me.

SHANKS. That's all 'at matters now. I don't care about myself. Two other fellers was convicted 'long with me. One of 'em's gone now; you saw the other one to-day—so I don't have to say anything fur them. But I would— Folks called 'em "copperheads," but they thought they was workin' fur their country, same as folks on the other side. Grant understood. He gave every feller his side-arms and his hoss at Appomattox. Grant said: "You'll need the hosses, boys, to plant yer crops." That's what Abe Lincoln would o' said, too. Er— [*Pause.*] Sorry, Philip [*pause*]—awful sorry.

PHILIP [*hands on* SHANKS' *shoulders*]. Over fifty years ago, Mr. Shanks. It's a damned shame to dig it up now. There's a moral statute of limitations and I hope that in fifty years I'll have as clean a heart. [*Strikes* SHANKS *on breast.*]

SHANKS [*pause and tender regard*]. Taller'n me. He—he used to put his hands on my shoulders. I wish Hardy'd come—but there's somethin' we kin do while we're waitin'. [*He goes to desk—gets old revolver in paper, unwraps it. There is a tag which his grasp hides.*]

MRS. MANNING. Is that loaded?

SHANKS. Four barrels—yes.

GILLESPIE. I didn't bring any gun.

SHANKS. You kin have this one, Newt. [*To* MADELINE.] Dearie, git the corkscrew for me. [MADELINE *goes for old folding corkscrew in buffet.*] Philip.

PHILIP. Mr. Shanks.

SHANKS. At my trial, this was marked Exhibit B. Two barrels fired. The rest are just as we left 'em. Take that corkscrew, Philip, and pull out the wads and the powder, 'cause they never was any bullets in 'em. I didn't say that at the trial, 'cause I—didn't want to lay the blame all on the others—but I ain't a murderer, Madeline.

MADELINE. Of course you aren't, dear.

GILLESPIE. You've had thirty-eight years ter git out the bullets yerself.

SHANKS. That's so—and I only want to convince Madeline about that. I've never told her a story.

PHILIP. I believe you, too.

GILLESPIE. Well, I don't—and it's time fur your school board meetin', Mrs. Manning. [*Enter* HARDY.]

SHANKS. Come in, Colonel Hardy, come in, sir. Sit down, Mrs. Manning. A short horse is soon curried, and my business won't keep the men standin' long. [HARDY *comes down, bowing to company*.] Sit down, Maddy, dear—you kin stan' by her, Philip. [*Pause as group arranges itself*.] Doctor Randall. [*Pause*.] Philip. [*Pause. Defers to* MRS. MANNING *slightly*.] Colonel Hardy and me was boys together. Our Congressman give me an appointment to West Point, but Tom Hardy ought a o' had it. Besides, 'twasn't convenient for me to go to West Point jest then, so I resigned it fur him. 'Fore that, we went together to a school where Abe Lincoln come and talked to us. We both knowed him from that time on until he was elected President—ain't that so, Colonel Hardy?

HARDY [*severely*]. Yes.

SHANKS [*gets mask from mantel, blows dust from it*]. Lincoln! We was together at his house, 'fore he started for Washington. A sculpture man was there to take a plaster Paris model of his face. Most folks think this is a after death thing, but Colonel Hardy and me saw it took—jes' throwed the soft plaster on his face and let it git hard. Lincoln sittin' in a armchair, like you are. [*To* MRS. MANNING.] In this box [*gets it from desk*]—where I have my letters and keepsakes—is a model of Lincoln's hand—the hand that wrote the emancipation of slavery. [*Pause*.] The sculpture man sent me these hisself, so they're genuine. That stick's a piece of broom handle Lincoln sawed off while—Volk [*reads name on cast*]—that was the sculpture feller's name—while Volk was mixin' plaster in a washbowl. [*Shows hand by his own*.] Bigger man'n me, every way. [*Pause*.] All of the statues of Lincoln nowadays is copied from this [*pause*]—so, you see, we knowed him. [*Pause*.] Then the war broke out. Hardy tuk a vow to support his country, I took one to destroy it. Hardy's company marched off—my Joey, only sixteen, along with 'em. His mother leant agin the fence an' the women fanned her—an', my God—he looked like a soldier! [*Regards picture—suggests march. To* PHILIP.] You was probably thinner at sixteen yerself.

PHILIP. Yes—I was.

SHANKS. I was peekin' from some bushes—cud o' almost teched him as they marched by [*pause*]—blue eyes— [*To* MRS. MANNING. *Pause.*] His mother never said a word—cried quite a spell. Well, us Knights o' the Golden Circle—

GILLESPIE. Copperheads—

SHANKS [*pause*]. Golden Circle—we sent help to the South—all we could—and we pizened cattle, and I went to Richmond—Virginy—twict. Time went on an' Vicksburg come and one night a feller galloped into town hyar and hitched. "When'd you hear from Joe?" sez he. "Last week," I sez. "How was he?" sez he, a-foolin' round tightenin' up his girth. "All right," sez I, and he sez: "Joe's dead." [*Pause. To* MADELINE.] I kin see yer gramma yet, a-cryin' by the well, pettin' the corner of it where Joey'd been. Bym' by, I leant over to tech her, but she drawed away, a-tremblin' and a-sayin': "For Gawd's sake, Milt Shanks, yer unclean!" [*Pause. To* MRS. MANNING.] His mother [*pause*]—two or three days she was pinin'—with her face agin the letters he'd wrote home, and then— [*Pause.*] At the church—instead of the trouble I expected from the neighbors, they was all strange-like an' kind, 'cept when I went to look in the black coffin under the flag, where Joey was. Newt Gillespie took me by the arm and— [*Pause.*] You tell 'em, Newt, what you said to me.

GILLESPIE. I hev told 'em—more'n once.

SHANKS. Tell her. She never heered it.

GILLESPIE. I'd give my word 'fore he died.

SHANKS [*to* MADELINE]. His word to Joey.

GILLESPIE. Yes. He said: "If you take me back, don't let him see me. If he on'y fought on the other side, I'd o' been proud, even if he'd been the one that shot me—but no copperhead." An' I did. Right in the church, I jes' tuk him by the arm and said: "It was his particular last request—" quiet-like, as I'm talkin' now, and led him out o' the church. An', by God, I'd do it agin!

MADELINE. Oh, grandpa!

SHANKS. That left only little Elsie, yer ma—an' she was so little I couldn't leave her alone, and I was carryin' her on my arm. Newt Gillespie was the only man 'at spoke to me—and in the whole United States—yes, in the whole world—only one man wrote to me. [*Pause.*] I kep' his letter—natural— [*Gets letter from box.*] I'm gonna ask Colonel Hardy ter read it. [*Takes letter from old flag and hands it, open, to* HARDY.] Careful, Colonel. It's a keepsake with me. An' then that's all I've got to say. If 'twasn't fur Madeline and Philip—and I know they're lovin' each other and separatin'—

HARDY. My God! Who's crazy—you or I— Milt Shanks! Milt Shanks!

RANDALL. What is it, Colonel?

SHANKS. Read it, Colonel Hardy.

HARDY [*reads*]. "Executive Mansion, Washington, April 11th, 1865. Mr. Milton Shanks, Millville. Dear Milt: Lee's surrender ends it all. I cannot think of you without a sense of guilt, but it had to be. I alone knew what you did—and, even more, what you endured. I cannot reward you—man cannot reward anything worth while—there is only One who can. I send you a flag handkerchief. [SHANKS *unconsciously touches the flag.*] It is not new, but you will prize it the more for that. I hope to shake your hand some time. Your friend, A. Lincoln."

SHANKS. Colonel, do you recollec' the time you druv me to the train in March o' sixty-one?

HARDY. Very well. You went to look at cattle.

SHANKS. That's what I told you. I wuz called to Washington by Lincoln, an' two days later, at night, in his library—White House—he walked over to'erd a winder, and, without turnin' round, he says: "Milt—" [*Pause.*] Funny I remember a clock tickin' on the mantelpiece— [*Pause.*] I sez: "Mr. President—" [*Pause.*] "Milt, how much do you love yer country?" [*Pause.*] "I cahilate I'd die for it," I sez. [*Shakes head.*] "Thousands o' boys is a-cryin' to do that." Then he turned round. "Would you give up sumpin' more'n life?" [*Pause.*] "Try me," I sez. The President run his hands through his hair an' went on: "It means to be odious in the eyes of men *and* women—ter eat yer heart out—

alone—fur you can't tell yer wife—ner chile—ner friend."
[*Pause.*] "Go on," I sez. [*Pause.*] "The Southern sympathizers are organizing in our State—really worse than the
soldiers. I want you ter jine them Knights o' the Golden
Circle—ter be one of them—their leader, if you kin. I need
you, Milt. Yer country needs you." [*Pause.*] Hadn't been
two minutes since he was laffin', but he lifted his hands, and it
seemed we wuz the only folks in the world [*pause*]—and that
clock [*pause*]—funny I remember that. [*Pause.*] "I'll do
it," I sez. [*Pause.*] He tuk a little flag out o' his pocket—
like as not this very one—put it on the table like I'm puttin'
it. [*Pause.*] "As Chief Magistrate of the nation, I'll muster
you inter the nation's service," he said. He laid my hand
where the blue is and all the stars, and put his hand over mine.
[*Business suggested with cast.*] Only open, of course [*uses
his own hand*]—and said nothin' [*pause. Nods.*]—jes' looked
in my eyes—an' looked— [*Pause.*] Well, I jined 'em.
[*Pause.*] It was terrible, when I couldn't tell the boy [*looks
at* PHILIP]—when he marched off. [*To* MRS. MANNING.]
Sixteen, you know—blue eyes— [*Pause.* MADELINE *takes
his hand and kisses it. The action startles him a little.*] It
ruined the Governor that pardoned me out o' Joliet, where I
was convicted to—but I've allers figured he had his orders
from Washington—same as me—an' couldn't talk about it.
An' even when Vicksburg come, and Joey was dead, why, the
war wasn't over.

HARDY.   But, damn it, in all these years we've despised you,
why haven't you told?

SHANKS.   Told who? Couldn't tell Joey or his mother,
and, with them gone—tellin' anybody seemed so—so useless.
Only now, when it's separatin' her an' Philip an' spoilin' her
election—in the school board—

HARDY.   Her election! Why, damn it, that story'd elect a
wooden Indian! [GILLESPIE *grabs* SHANKS' *coat.*]

RANDALL.   What are you doing?

GILLESPIE.   Take that off. This coat don't belong on me.

SHANKS.   Newt—not yer Grand Army coat?

GILLESPIE.   Git in it! Here's the hat. [*Goes to door,
carrying* SHANKS' *coat.*] Bring him to that meetin'. I'm a
damn fool, but, by God, I ain't no skunk! [*Exit.*]

MADELINE.   Oh, grandpa!

SHANKS [*loving the coat*]. The blue—

RANDALL. The hat, Mr. Shanks!

SHANKS. An' a cord round it. If they was only a lookin' glass.

MRS. MANNING. Come, Colonel. [HARDY *crosses to* SHANKS—*returns the letter. The two men join hands in speechless emotion a moment.*]

SHANKS [*forgiving*]. Tom! [HARDY *pats* SHANKS' *shoulder and moves on. With flag.*] All right, now, to carry this, ain't it?

PHILIP. I should say it was!

SHANKS. God! It's wonderful—[*pauses and inhales*] to hev friends agin! [*Goes.* PHILIP *takes* MADELINE *in his arms*—MRS. MANNING *watching them from right.*]

[CURTAIN.]

DULCY *

A COMEDY IN THREE ACTS

By

GEORGE S. KAUFMAN

and

MARC CONNELLY

(With a Bow to Franklin P. Adams) [1]

* Copyright, 1921, by George S. Kaufman and Marc Connelly.
Dulcy is reprinted in this volume by the kind permission of G. P. Putnam's Sons, the original publishers. All dramatic rights are controlled by George C. Tyler, New Amsterdam Theatre Building, New York. It may not be acted, either by professional or amateur companies, without permission and the payment of royalty.

[1] The editor thanks F. P. A. for permission genially granted to "take anything you like" from The Tower.

There is hardly any kind of source, novels, poetry, chronicle histories, biographies, or old plays that Shakespeare did not draw upon for his plots, his characters, his local color, and even his great passages of poetry; but since modern journalism dates only from the eighteenth century, and feature journalism developed in the nineteenth century, and "colyumists" have flourished and multiplied only in the twentieth, it is safe to assert that George S. Kaufman and Marc Connelly were strictly original in using the "Dulcinea" of Franklin P. Adams for dramatic purposes.

Within easy recollection, Mr. Adams has conducted columns in three New York newspapers, *The New York Mail, The New York Tribune,* and *The World.* There have been other notable column conductors, beginning with Eugene Field, who was the first one, and coming down to Bert Leston Taylor, for whose posthumous collection of poems F. P. A. has written such a gay and touching foreword. Then there is Don Marquis, who presides over The Sun Dial in *The Sun.* There are other favorites, too, in various parts of the United States.[1]

To the present generation of readers, it seems fairly evident that future historians of "columning" in America will rank high among the brilliant achievements of Don Marquis the delineation of that inimitable lady of intellectual pretensions, Hermione, and her "Little Group of Serious Thinkers." Hermione was born and grew to full artistic maturity in The Sun Dial; and the same historians will place on a neighboring pinnacle Dulcinea, who in June, 1914, sprang fully panoplied in platitudes to a place of power and position in The Conning Tower, the column conducted by F. P. A. in *The New York Tribune.*

So many beastly things happened in the summer of 1914 that it is pleasant to stop and contemplate the emergence of laughter-provoking Dulcinea. On June 4, 1914, there appeared the following item in The Conning Tower:

[1] Other well known "colyumists" are Edwin Meade Robinson, Christopher Morley, Judd Mortimer Lewis, S. Jay Kaufman, S. E. Kiser, Kenneth C. Beaton, and Frank Stanton.

"PROBABLY FANNING ONLY MAKES HER WARMER

How are Don Juan's dates for this week? I'd like to take him to Dulcinea's Del Taboso's for tea smafternoon and let her spring 'You know, hot tea is really more cooling than iced tea in warm weather' on him."

Dulcy was followed up the next day in a series of items like this:

"IT ISN'T THE PLACE, THOUGH, IT'S THE PEOPLE

Sir: Tell Don Juan I can produce one upon a day's notice guaranteed to say: 'I want to go somewheres where it's quiet, *this* summer.' "

and

"OH, IT'S A FINE TOWN TO VISIT BUT NO PLACE TO LIVE IN

Sir: Dulcinea tells me she knows Don Juan, and that he told her New York, for a man, is really as comfortable a place as any to spend the summer."

Three days later, F. P. A. printed more interpretations under the heading:

"DULCINEA AND THE BROMIDAN TOUCH

M. L. E. Each Spring she says: 'I like to do Coney Island just once every summer, and that's enough.'

Sartor. Perhaps she 'lives in Europe, but only exists in America.'

Helen. I know her. She 'doesn't care for money for its own sake—only for what it will buy.'

R. C. M. 'You don't need to care much what kind of people are there, Dulcinea, if you have your own crowd.'

We feel certain that Dulcinea doesn't care much about what kind of room she gets at that summer resort. 'One is never in one's room except to sleep, you know.' "

Presently F. P. A. was having Dulcinea send to The Conning Tower letters describing her stay at Bromidlewild. She would write, for example:

"At Bromidlewild they have had some new stationery designed. The shield shows a bromide tablet, dormant on a field of parsnips.

Motto: Dulcy far niente."

or

"Last night was one of those nights in the country that makes you feel so sad, you don't know why. So I went up to my room and read some poetry. Don't you just *love* Poe? His poems are so musical, especially 'The Bells,' and 'The Raven' is a wonderful thing. He must have been awfully distressed to have written that. It might seem funny to you, but I've always thought he had his own life in mind when he wrote and that it is symbolic of his passion for drink and the remorse that followed. Then again there's Browning, —so entirely different, but so true to life."

F. P. A. even allowed Dulcinea to attempt her own Horatian paraphrase, here reprinted:

"IN A MANNER OF WRITING

Horace: Book I, Ode 38.

'Persicos odi, puer, apparatus—'

By Our Own Dulcinea

Honestly, Fred, I simply detest the new Persian styles. And I can't bear those linden-tree hats. And don't, please, Fred, go looking for expensive American Beauty roses. I like plain myrtle heaps better. It's the intention; not the cost of a gift, I always say.

I'd rather have a glass of cold water, too, than all the fancy drinks in the world.

Good-by! Be good."

On July 4, 1914, the following prophetic notice appeared in The Conning Tower:

"THE SAILING AWAY OF G. S. K.

SIR: I told Dulcinea I'd be in England and she said to give her regards to the king. . . . Imagine me with five weeks of Towers to read when I come back! [*Exit laughingly.*] G. S. K."

On July 7, another contributor wrote as follows:

"SIR: Dulcinea and I went down to see G. S. K. off on the Kroonland. She thought the slow boats were lots more fun, the fast trips don't seem like really crossing the pond at all. She wanted to know if I didn't wish *I* was going too, but thought she'd rather see America first. . . . The officers' uniforms were awfully handsome, and she thought a sailor's life must be awfully healthy, always out in the salt air. But they say they're terribly superstitious."

So we arrive finally at the meeting of Dulcinea and G. S. K., as George S. Kaufman is known, when he writes as contributor to F. P. A.'s The Conning Tower.

In August, 1920, George C. Tyler, the manager, needed a comedy for Lynn Fontanne, Ellen Terry's charming pupil. Mr. Tyler invited George S. Kaufman and Marc Connelly to write a play for this English actress. Only ten characters were to be introduced. The authors exceeded this limit by one. To quote Mr. Kaufman, "We had a great break of luck with it—the various parts fell into place all in one Sunday afternoon. It was written in less than five weeks in the belief that it would go into rehearsal immediately. That was August of 1920. The theatre shortage held us up until February of the following year, when the play opened in Chicago."

Both authors are journalists. Marc Connelly comes from Pittsburgh, where he did newspaper work for six or seven years, during the last one of which he conducted a humorous column in *The Gazette Times*. He has lived in New York ever since. Mr. Connelly is a reporter on *The Morning Telegraph,* has done a number of Sunday stories for *The New York Times* and other papers, and has been a frequent contributor to *Life*.

George S. Kaufman was also born in Pittsburgh, in 1889, a year before Mr. Connelly. They both studied in public schools in Pennsylvania. At one time Mr. Kaufman thought of becoming a lawyer, but he found the law "too dry." Mr. Kaufman is now in the dramatic department of *The New York Times*. He has in the past been connected with *The New York Tribune, The New York Mail,* and *The Washington Times,* conducting columns on the last two. On these various newspapers, he has also been reporter, rewrite man, and copy writer. "Incidentally," Mr. Kaufman confesses, "as Dulcy herself might say, the newspaper training is elegant for stage writing—it teaches you not to repeat."

As a matter of poetic justice, one more fact should be chronicled in connection with *Dulcy*. On February 20, 1922, another comedy in three acts by George S. Kaufman and Marc Connelly, called *To the Ladies,* was produced at the Liberty Theatre in New York. In this play, according to the appreciative reviewers in the Calendar of The New York Drama League, " the authors of *Dulcy* have given us another bright, clean, hilarious comedy. They have turned the tables, and in the place of the bungling, bromidic wife tangling up the affairs of a self-reliant husband, we see a quick-witted little wife smoothing out the ineptitudes of a conceited blockhead of a husband."

DULCY

CHARACTERS

Produced by George C. Tyler and H. H. Frazee, at the Cort Theatre, Chicago, February 20, 1921, with the following cast:

DULCINEA .... Lynn Fontanne
GORDON SMITH, *her husband* .... John Westley
WILLIAM PARKER, *her brother* ...... Gregory Kelly
C. ROGER FORBES .... Walter Clark
MRS. FORBES .... Constance Pelissier
ANGELA FORBES .... Norma Lee
SCHUYLER VAN DYCK .... Gilbert Douglas
TOM STERRETT, *advertising engineer* . Elliott Nugent
VINCENT LEACH, *scenarist* .... Howard Lindsay
BLAIR PATTERSON .... George Alison
HENRY .... Harry Lillford

Produced at the Frazee Theatre, New York, August 13, 1921, with the same cast:

ACT I

The scene is the living-room in the suburban home of DUL-CINEA and her husband—in Westchester County, within commuting distance of New York. It is a room that is splashing rather than merely striking. The furniture, for no particular reason, is old Italian, but most of it is hidden beneath beautiful and variously colored batiks and drapes. Over the divan, for example, is a golden brocade, and on it three blue pillows. Across the grand piano is a red drape, and on it a blue book. The window curtains are also of blue; there are two or three striking lamps in the background, and the tinted walls are covered here and there by a couple of good-looking tapestries. There are no pictures, for DULCINEA is nothing if not modern. On a platform at the rear, where the stairs begin to ascend, stands a great blue urn, filled with hydran-

170

*geas. On a cabinet at one side is an iridescent bowl
containing tea roses; at each side of the cabinet stands
a floor candlestick of Italian design. In a word, the
room is* DULCY. *If there were a telephone* DULCY *would
have it covered with a cute little doll—but this is a play
without a telephone.*

*In addition to the stairs there are three means of exit—at the
rear are French windows which open onto the lawn and*
DULCY'S *cherished garden; at the right is a door that
leads to the interior of the house, and at the left another
that leads to the hallway and the outer door.*

*The time is five o'clock on a Friday afternoon in late summer.
The French windows are closed, subduing somewhat the
light in the room. The rising curtain reveals* WILLIAM
PARKER, DULCY'S *brother, stretched out in an easy chair,
reading a magazine. After a moment* HENRY, *the butler, enters. He goes up to the windows, opens them, and
comes back to* BILL.

HENRY. Mr. Smith has just come in, sir.

BILL [*after a pause, not looking up from his magazine*].
Yeh?

HENRY. Yes, sir.

BILL. My sister with him?

HENRY. Oh, no, sir! Mrs. Smith is at her Friday afternoon club, over at Mrs. Kennedy's. [HENRY *picks up a
magazine from the floor and puts it on the table.*]

BILL [*getting to his feet*]. What time's dinner?

HENRY [*hesitates*]. Seven-fifty, sir.

BILL. Seven-*fifty?* My God!

HENRY. Yes, sir.

BILL. Oh—James!

HENRY. Henry, sir.

BILL. Henry?

HENRY. Yes, sir.

BILL. Henry. [*He pauses.*] Who else is coming to this
—week-end? I mean, besides Mr. Forbes, and—ah—his wife
and daughter?

HENRY. I'm not certain, sir. I've rooms ready for a
number, sir.

BILL. M'm. Well— [*Enter* GORDON SMITH, DUL-

CINEA's *husband. He is an alert young business man, with worry just beginning to set on his shoulders.*]

GORDON [*as he enters*]. Good evening, Bill. You're early.

HENRY [*turning away from* BILL]. Yes, sir.

BILL. Hello, Gordon. [BILL *lights a cigarette.* HENRY *goes out;* GORDON's *eyes follow him.*]

GORDON [*looks around, yawns, stretches*]. Been here long?

BILL. Oh, not so very. It was sort of dull in town, so I thought I'd come out early.

GORDON. Of course—glad you did. [*He takes another moment to stretch, then drops onto the sofa.*] Tired to-night.

BILL [*observing a folded newspaper in* GORDON's *pocket*]. What's that—the *Sun?*

GORDON. No—*Post.* [*He hands him the paper*—BILL *drops into a chair with it. There is a considerable pause while* BILL *reads and* GORDON *indulges in another yawn.*] Dulcy not home yet, huh?

BILL [*reading the paper at the same time*]. No. She's—across the street—some place. Mrs. Kennedy's, I think.

GORDON. Oh, yes. It's a—Friday afternoon thingmajig.

BILL [*still with the paper*]. M'm.

GORDON [*another pause; musters up some energy*]. Well! How's business?

BILL [*puts down the paper and looks at him*]. What?

GORDON. I say, how's business?

BILL [*as though announcing a death*]. Haven't you heard?

GORDON [*a bit cheerily*]. Oh, I don't know—I have an idea it may be picking up presently.

BILL [*tapping the newspaper*]. You've been reading Mr. Schwab. [*He quotes.*] "Steel Man Sees Era of Prosperity."

GORDON. Well—I think he's right at that.

BILL. Yes. [*A pause.*] Rockefeller expects to break even this year, too.

GORDON. Just the same, I look for an improvement. [*Earnestly.*] Bill, if it could just be arranged that all the outstanding accounts could be absorbed by the banks, and then turn those into accounts payable—

BILL [*interrupting*]. I know. You mean—things would be better if we weren't all broke.

GORDON. That's one of the things that holds us back—pessimism.

BILL. How's the artificial jewelry business? If any?

GORDON. Well, it's—looking up a bit.

BILL. Anything new on Forbes' merger?

GORDON. It's coming along. It's practically settled, I think, that I'm to go in with him.

BILL. That's great. I hadn't said anything, but I rather felt that you were up against it, when I saw you last week.

GORDON. Thanks, old man. I—was, a bit.

BILL. You'll be all right if this deal goes through?

GORDON. I think so. It will end this fighting among us smaller men.

BILL. How many of you are going into this pool?

GORDON. About half the trade. I'm to get sixteen and two-thirds per cent of the stock of the combine.

BILL. Just for the factory?

GORDON [unwillingly]. Well, the plant *and* the pearl formula.

BILL. Oh, I see.

GORDON [justifying himself]. Of course, that means a cash payment when the papers are signed, and that will just about see me through.

BILL. You think that's enough—sixteen and two-thirds? Those pearls of yours are pretty good, you know, even if they *are* imitations.

GORDON. I know—but I'm up against it. I've got to take what he gives me, or have that crowd to fight. Forbes is a tough customer.

BILL. That's hard luck.

GORDON [doubtfully]. Of course, I *may* be able to do something with him over the week-end.

BILL. Huh?

GORDON. He's coming out here, you know.

BILL. So I understand.

GORDON [looks at his watch]. They're driving up from town.

BILL. Uh-huh. [Thoughtfully.] Bringing his wife and —daughter, too, isn't he?

GORDON. Yes. They're going to stay over Sunday.

BILL. I didn't know you knew them that well.

GORDON. Well, I don't—except Forbes—in a business way. [He pauses.] I wasn't keen for it.

BILL. Well, then—

GORDON [*rises*]. Well, Dulcy thought it would be nice to have them out here, and—well—

BILL [*as* GORDON *pauses*]. Yes, I know. [*There is a pause.*] Does he play Russian bank? [HENRY *enters with the afternoon papers, which he puts on the table.* GORDON *watches him narrowly, and believes that he detects* HENRY *looking furtively at him.* HENRY *departs again.*]

GORDON [*paying no attention to* BILL'S *question*]. Did you notice that?

BILL. What?

GORDON. The way he looked at me.

BILL [*lightly*]. Henry?

GORDON. Didn't Dulcy tell you?

BILL. She's over at Mrs. Kennedy's.

GORDON. Well—he's an escaped convict!

BILL [*with a start*]. He's—what?

GORDON. No—I don't think that's just what I mean. It's a—suspended sentence. Dulcy got him off by—*you* know. Promised to take care of him, and give him work, and—

BILL. What's his line?

GORDON. He's a—butler.

BILL. I mean, what *was* his line?

GORDON. Oh! He—wrote a little check or something.

BILL. And the judge turned him over to Dulcy?

GORDON. After she made about twenty trips to town, and exhausted the judge, and used up a hundred dollars' worth of my lawyer, and—

BILL. She does things right.

GORDON. Oh, well, I suppose it's all right. After all, there *was* some doubt about him. Dulcy went to see his wife and family, and—she felt pretty badly over it— [*Door bell rings.*]

GORDON. Here they are!

BILL. The Forbeses?

GORDON. Yes.

BILL. Better send them over to Mrs. Kennedy's, so that Dulcy can receive them.

GORDON. Darn it!—the man coming *here,* with a business deal on. I don't like it! [*Enter* HENRY.] It looks too much as if I were trying to—

BILL. Oh, I don't know. [HENRY *crosses and goes out at the other side.* BILL *watches him off.*] Are you always sure he's coming back?

GORDON. I don't like mixing business with social affairs.

BILL [*solemnly*]. Why don't you make Dulcy lay off?

GORDON. Why don't I? How *can* I?

BILL [*after considering it*]. I never thought of that. [*Enter* HENRY.]

HENRY. It's a Mr.— [*Enter* TOM STERRETT, *a very-much-alive young man. He is the kind of youth who pulls weights in his bedroom every morning, and who feels that a vigorous good health is the first aid toward business success. His business is advertising. He could tell you hundreds of interesting facts about type psychology, direct sales drives and national conferences; and would, if you gave him half a chance. He believes in Presence and knows he has it.*]

STERRETT [*brushing past* HENRY *with an Open, Sesame! smile*]. I beg your pardon! I'm Mr. Sterrett!

BILL [*first looking at* GORDON *to see if he knows him; sees he does not*]. That's fine.

GORDON. You're looking for—Smiths? [HENRY *departs at this point.*]

STERRETT. Yes, sir. I'm expected to meet Mr. Forbes here. Your man says—

GORDON [*a bit more cordial*]. Oh! Mr Forbes hasn't arrived yet—I'm expecting him very soon. [*Extending his hand.*] I am Mr. Smith.

STERRETT [*inflicting a brisk hand-shake*]. Smith Pearls?

GORDON. Ah—yes.

STERRETT. I follow your campaigns. Your advertising.

GORDON. This is Mr. Parker, my brother-in-law.

STERRETT. How are you, sir! [*Shaking his hand vigor-ously.*] Didn't I meet you at the A. C. A. Convention?—in Detroit last summer? [*Renewing the hand-shake with the explanation.*] Advertising Clubs of America?

BILL [*returning the shake with interest*]. I'm afraid not.

STERRETT [*very quickly*]. Sorry, my mistake.

BILL [*adopting* STERRETT'S *snappy style*]. It's all right! Have a cigarette! [*He whips out his case; clicks his heels with military precision.*]

STERRETT [*accepting one and glancing at it*]. Ah! C &

G! Thanks! [*Pulls forward a chair, sits, and lights his cigarette.*]

GORDON [*knowingly saying the unnecessary*]. Won't you —wait?

STERRETT. Surely! Mr. Forbes left word at his office for me to meet him here. It's about some contracts that have to be—

GORDON [*somewhat more cordially*]. Oh, I see. You're in the Forbes organization?

STERRETT [*with a trace of reproof*]. Oh, no! I handle Mr. Forbes' advertising. S. S. Q. & L. Agency.

BILL [*airily*]. Oh, the S. S. U. & L.!

STERRETT [*correcting him*]. S. S. Q. & L. Simpson, Simpson, Querrida and Lawford.

BILL [*taking a moment to digest it*]. That's fine.

STERRETT [*hitching his chair towards* SMITH]. Have you followed our Forbes copy, Mr. Smith?

GORDON. Well—to a degree—yes.

STERRETT [*a bit disappointed in* GORDON; *turns to* BILL]. You're interested in advertising, Mr. Parker?

BILL. I buy the *Saturday Evening Post*.

STERRETT [*missing it by sixty feet*]. But speaking generally of the other media—

BILL. I'm afraid I don't know much about advertising. In fact, I've never *been* in Detroit.

STERRETT [*answering without thinking*]. Well, that's too bad. [*Realizing he hasn't understood.*] Huh? [*Thinking he understands.*] Oh, yes—great town! Town that's made itself through advertising! [*He consults watch.*] What time do you expect—ah—Mr.—

GORDON. Mr. Forbes and his family will be here presently.

STERRETT. Oh, is Mr. Forbes' family coming?

GORDON. Yes, they're going to spend the week-end.

STERRETT. Mr. and Mrs. Forbes?

GORDON. Yes.

STERRETT. And Miss Forbes?

GORDON. Yes.

BILL. Are you a friend of the—family's?

STERRETT. Oh, yes! [*A pause.*] Yes, indeed!

BILL [*giving* GORDON *a significant look*]. H'm.

STERRETT. What was that?

BILL. I didn't say anything.

STERRETT. Oh, beg pardon, I'm sure.

GORDON. Well—ah— [*He is saying what seems to be expected of him.*] You must stay for dinner, Mr. Sterrett.

STERRETT. Many thanks. If I won't be—

GORDON [*a bit curtly*]. That's splendid.

BILL. Yes—that's fine. We generally need one more for Dulcy's parlor games, don't we?

STERRETT. Now, I want to be sure I'm not intruding.

GORDON. Not at all. We're only too glad to have you. [DULCINEA *enters through the French window. She is dressed in a gown that is just a bit too much for an afternoon gathering; she carries an armful of flowers, and she is in her customary bubbling good humor.*]

DULCY. Hello, everybody!

BILL. Hello, Dulcy.

DULCY. M'm! It's nice and cool in here, isn't it? You know, if there is any breeze going at all, we get it in this room. [*She has a way of speaking an age-old platitude as though it were a wise and original thought—a little thing casually tossed off in the course of conversation.*] Don't we, Gordon, darling? [*She kisses him.*] Did you have a good day at the office? Send for Henry to fix these, will you? [*She indicates the flowers.*] Aren't they pretty?—right out of my own garden. [BILL *comes down to her.*] Hello, Willie. [*Kisses him.*] Whom have you been doing? Eh? [*She laughs loudly at her own joke.*]

GORDON. Dulcy, this is Mr. Sterrett. My wife.

DULCY. Oh, how do you do? [*Shaking hands somewhat appraisingly.*]

STERRETT [*with great assurance*]. How do *you* do!

DULCY [*trying to estimate* STERRETT'S *position in the scheme of things*]. Have you been over the grounds? Gordon, you must show Mr. Sterrett over the grounds.

GORDON. Mr. Sterrett is a friend of the Forbeses.

DULCY [*as this explains* STERRETT *to her*]. Oh, the Forbeses—really! Oh, that *is* nice! [*Then with a bit of panic.*] Have they come? Where are they? Why didn't you tell me! [*She rushes up toward the staircase, then toward the windows.*] Upstairs or in the garden or where—

BILL [*holding up his hand*]. Now—wait.

DULCY [*coming to* BILL]. But what are they going to think? My not being here—how rude—why, if they—

BILL. Now, wait—wait! [*She finally pauses.*] The Forbeses are not here.

DULCY. Well, why didn't you tell me so in the first place? After all, Willie, I'm not a mind reader.

GORDON. Mr. Sterrett has come to see Mr. Forbes on a matter of business.

BILL. And since he is also a friend of *Miss* Forbes—

GORDON. I've invited him to stay for dinner.

DULCY [*none too pleased, particularly about* STERRETT'S *being a friend of* ANGELA'S]. Oh! So, you're a friend of Angela's—that's lovely! Yes, you *must* stay! [HENRY *enters and stands awaiting instructions.*] Just take pot luck with us, Mr. Sterrett. I always say that anyone can drop in— I think that's the nicest kind of a household, don't you? [*This one is No. 213, Series L, but* DULCY *utters it as though no one had ever thought of such a thing before.*]

STERRETT. Why, yes. You know, I have a dear old aunt—

DULCY [*not waiting to hear*]. Oh, Henry, get some vases for these flowers—then I'll arrange them. I think arranging flowers is quite a knack, don't you, Mr. Sterrett? Some people can do it, and others can't, you know . . . it's just like an ear for music. Either you have it, or you haven't it, and there you are!

BILL. Mr. Sterrett is in the advertising business—not the music business.

STERRETT. Oh, but what she says is very true—very true, indeed. But as I was saying—this dear old aunt of mine— I—ah—she— [DULCY *is giving the flowers to* HENRY *and pays no attention.* STERRETT *fails to make an audience either of* SMITH *or* BILL.] I—ah—suppose I wait in the next room for Mr. Forbes?

DULCY. Of course. Henry, show Mr. Sterrett into the library. There are some lovely books there. My books are my best friends, Mr. Sterrett.

STERRETT. Thank you. [*He departs—and glad of the opportunity.*]

DULCY. Henry, fix up the little green room for to-night. Fix it nicely.

HENRY. Yes, ma'am. [*He follows* STERRETT *off.*]

GORDON. He's not going to stay to-night!

DULCY [*has picked up an evening paper, and is already absorbed in it*]. No, darling, but someone else is.

BILL. Still another?

DULCY [*with the paper*]. Oh, what do you think? Mrs. Harper was acquitted! I always say, if a woman is good looking, no jury on earth will convict her.

GORDON. Dulcy, never mind that. Who else is coming?

DULCY [*immersed in paper*]. " A demonstration that lasted fifteen minutes greeted the acquittal of Mrs.—"

GORDON. Dulcy!

DULCY [*slowly, as she scans the article*]. I just want to see what she wore.

GORDON. Dulcy, listen to me!

DULCY. Well, dear?

GORDON. Who else is coming?

DULCY [*putting paper down*]. You'll never guess.

GORDON [*tiredly*]. I'm sure I've no idea, Dulcy.

DULCY [*going to him*]. Schuyler Van Dyck!

BILL. Schuyler Van Dyck!

DULCY. One of *the* Van Dycks, and he's worth millions!

GORDON. Schuyler Van Dyck's coming *here!*

DULCY. Yes—isn't it wonderful! He's a marvelous man, and you ought to hear him play the piano. You'd never think he was a Van Dyck—he's so democratic.

BILL. Where the devil did you meet *him?*

DULCY. Oh, several places, and this afternoon he was at Mrs. Kennedy's and played for us. He had a lot of invitations, and he accepted mine. [DULCY *returns to the table and replaces the newspaper neatly, then gives the sofa cushions a touch.* GORDON *follows her, speaking as he goes.*]

GORDON. But, my dear, having this man here with Forbes —how do we know it's going to—

DULCY. Oh, but it will—Mr. Van Dyck's a business man too, darling. He owns all kinds of things—railroads—railroads—I think—some of them are. He'll help entertain Mr. Forbes with them.

GORDON. But Forbes isn't the kind of man that wants to be entertained. That's just it!

DULCY. Darling, leave Mr. Forbes to me. [*Puts arm around him.*] I've got a *real* surprise for you!

GORDON. Another one?

DULCY. A wonderful one! Just for you!

BILL. One thing that Dulcy never learned is the difference between a surprise and a shock. [HENRY *returns with a bowl and a vase of flowers.*]

DULCY. You shut up, Willie.

GORDON. But what is it? Has it got to do with Forbes?

DULCY. Yes, darling, and it's something that's going to help you a great deal with Mr. Forbes. [BILL *goes solemnly to* GORDON *and shakes his hand.*]

BILL. Sometimes I think our family must have adopted Dulcy. [*He makes a melancholy exit.*]

DULCY. Oh, Henry! There'll be two more for dinner.

HENRY. Yes, ma'am.

DULCY. That makes—nine, doesn't it?

HENRY. Yes, ma'am. [HENRY *goes upstairs.*]

DULCY. I love a big table, don't you, Gordon? There's something so hospitable about it. [*She is looking around for the spots at which to place the flowers.*]

GORDON. Nine? Then there's still another coming—besides Van Dyck?

DULCY [*with the air of someone revealing a great secret*]. Yes!

GORDON. What are you trying to do—solve the housing problem?

DULCY [*picking up vase of flowers*]. Just wait, darling! You'll be so excited! [*Breaking the big news over* SMITH'S *shoulder.*] Vincent—is coming!

GORDON [*at sea*]. Vincent?

DULCY. Yes. Isn't it *wonderful?* [*Puts the vase on the piano.*] That looks pretty, doesn't it?

GORDON [*trying to recall*]. Vincent—Vincent—who the devil is Vincent?

DULCY [*indicating the bowl*]. Or do you think this one ought to go over there and that one here?

GORDON [*annoyed*]. I don't know. Who is this man?

DULCY. Well, you don't need to get angry at me, darling, just because I want to make the place look nice.

GORDON. I'm not angry—but—

DULCY. I'm doing it for you, darling. You know, with Mr. Forbes coming—

GORDON. I know, but—tell me about this man—

DULCY. *Vincent Leach?* Don't you remember? You and I met him at Mrs. Peabody's last week—you know, the big scenario writer.

GORDON [*faintly recalling*]. Oh, yes. Is *he* coming here?

DULCY. Yes! Isn't it wonderful? [*Picks up the bowl from the table and starts toward piano with it.*]

GORDON. But look here now—Dulcy, will you leave those flowers alone, and come here and talk to me?

DULCY. Just a minute, darling. [*She replaces the vase on the piano with the bowl, then takes the vase back and puts it on the table.*] A time and a place for everything. There! [*She seats herself on his lap.*]

GORDON. But, dear, why do you want to mix this man Leach up with Forbes? Van Dyck may be all right, but—

DULCY. Ah! That's the secret!

GORDON. But I don't like—secrets. This isn't a—game.

DULCY. Promise you won't tell! Cross your heart!

GORDON. Yes, yes.

DULCY. Well, then—Vincent and Angela— [*she kisses him*] —like each other.

GORDON. You mean—Forbes' daughter?

DULCY [*nodding*]. Isn't it wonderful? So I invited them both here so they'll have the whole week-end together. And at the same time he can meet her parents. You never can tell what will happen.

GORDON. But, Dulcy, dear, you don't know Angela so well, and—this man Leach—what do you know about *him?*

DULCY. I know all about him. He's a big scenario writer, and just the man for Angie. He's—he's so practical, and she's a dreamer. Opposites should marry—you know that, darling.

GORDON. But, Dulcy, now—

DULCY. And what else do you think? I'm going to get him to help me with some of *my* scenarios while he's here.

GORDON. But why, dear—?

DULCY. To make them better.

GORDON. No, no—I mean—why are you trying to match this fellow Leach with Angela? What do *you* care about it?

DULCY. Don't you see?

GORDON. No.

DULCY. Can't you guess?

GORDON. No.

DULCY. Well, if Angie *likes* Mr. Leach, and marries him—

GORDON. Yes?

DULCY. And *I* fix it—

GORDON. Well?

DULCY. Well—I'm your wife— [GORDON *springs up in alarm, dropping* DULCY *off his lap*.]

GORDON. Now, Dulcy dear—

DULCY. That will make Mr. Forbes so grateful that he'll have to give you more than sixteen and two-thirds of the percentage.

GORDON. Good heavens, Dulcy! Now—

DULCY [*ecstatically*]. I figured it all out myself!

GORDON. But, now wait! [*He paces the floor*].

DULCY. Gordon, darling—don't be upset about it. I know they ought to marry—I just know it. It's a woman's intuition. [*A pause*.] Just as I knew I ought to marry you, dear. [GORDON *stops*.] It was because I loved you, darling, and wanted to help you, and—and—

GORDON [*going to her and embracing her*]. Yes, and you do help me.

DULCY. Well, then—

GORDON [*tenderly*]. And you're not sorry that you married me, instead of Arthur, with all those millions?

DULCY. You're going to have millions, too, dear—at least thousands. And I loved you—not Arthur. [*She buries her head on his shoulder*.]

GORDON. Dulcy, dear. [*He kisses her neck*.]

DULCY. And I'd love you if you didn't have a cent, and—and stand by you, and help you. You do want me to help you, don't you?

GORDON [*reluctantly*]. Why—I—ah—yes—ah—

DULCY. Well, then, let me!

GORDON. But you don't understand, dear. Try to see my position.

DULCY. But I do see it. You need Mr. Forbes' help and I'm going to get it for you.

GORDON. I need it in a business way. And as it's only in

a business way, I feel that I ought to handle it alone—in office hours. Don't you see?

DULCY [*turning away on the verge of tears*]. I feel almost as if I were being—exiled.

GORDON [*embracing her*]. Well, you mustn't—you aren't being exiled. Just realize that in this particular affair you're my silent partner, and a very important one, too. Don't you know, dear, if it weren't for you I couldn't go to town day after day and fight! There!—you're really helping me all the time, by just being *you*. [*He steps back from her.*] Furthermore, don't you remember that you promised me that you'd let me manage my own business matters?

DULCY. When?

GORDON. Three months ago? When we came back from our honeymoon?

DULCY. Why, I never did.

GORDON. The time that you practically discharged my secretary?

DULCY [*remembering*]. Oh!

GORDON. You thought Shepherd was dishonest simply because he wore a heavy black moustache.

DULCY. Oh, Gordon, darling, I know I've done some silly things, but when I married you, dearest, I did promise to stand beside you all my life and love you and help you, and that's what I think I ought to do now. That's why I'm doing it.

GORDON. But, Dulcy—

DULCY. Well, Mr. Forbes *is* taking advantage of you and I'm not going to let him—that's all!

GORDON [*desperately*]. But that isn't the point! In the position that I am I have to go ahead with it. I wouldn't want anything to happen. [*Pleading affectionately.*] Don't you see, dear, if I'm not in that merger, I'll lose—everything!

DULCY. But only sixteen and two-thirds per cent—it's such a funny number, too. I don't see why you couldn't get a nice even number—like twenty-five. [*She pauses.*] Or fifty! But sixteen and two-thirds—they could never divide it. [BILL *returns.*]

BILL. Well, has she fixed it?

DULCY. We've been all through it quietly, Willie, and it's settled.

GORDON. Now, Dulcy, you must listen—

DULCY. Now—now—not another word. Just let—let—sleeping dogs lie and everything is bound to come out all right. It always does. [*She looks toward the window.*] Oh, here's Mr. Van Dyck! [*Rushing to the window.*] Come right in this way, Mr. Van Dyck! That's right—here you are! [SCHUYLER VAN DYCK *enters through the French window. He is aristocratic in bearing and well dressed. He has a bag of golf-clubs over his shoulder and is carrying a suitcase.*] Well, you found the way, didn't you—you're like me—you've got a bump of location! Henry will take your things—where's Henry?—Willie, send for Henry! My, this is lovely! [BILL *pulls the bell cord.*] So glad to see you in our own little nest, Mr. Van Dyck. [VAN DYCK *has put his suitcase and golf-bag down.* DULCINEA *leads him down to* GORDON.] This is my husband, Mr. Van Dyck. Mr. Van Dyck, Gordon, that I've been telling you so much about. [*As an afterthought.*] And my brother, Willie. [HENRY *comes downstairs.*]

VAN DYCK [*as he shakes* SMITH'S *hand*]. Mr. Smith, how do you do, sir?

GORDON. I'm very pleased to know you, Mr. Van Dyck.

DULCY. Henry, take Mr. Van Dyck's things. So glad you brought your golf clubs. We'll see that you use them. [BILL *has circled down to* VAN DYCK *and offers his hand.*]

BILL [*quietly*]. My name is Parker.

VAN DYCK. I'm delighted, Mr. Parker. [BILL *retires again.*] I'm very much afraid that I'm intruding.

GORDON. Why, not at all!

DULCY. Intruding! I should say not! [HENRY *has picked up the bags and is awaiting* VAN DYCK *on the stairs.*]

VAN DYCK. Mrs. Smith was so—so very gracious as to ask me to be your guest. May I—accept with a proviso?

GORDON. Why, certainly.

VAN DYCK. It is barely possible that some business matters will call me back to town. In that event— [*He smiles his rare smile.*] I hope you will pardon me.

DULCY. Of course! We all understand business here—don't we, Gordon, darling? Business before pleasure!

VAN DYCK. You're very good.

DULCY. Henry, show Mr. Van Dyck to his room. Henry

will show you, Mr. Van Dyck. [*It is not in her nature to say a thing* ONCE.]

VAN DYCK. Thank you—if I may. I shall rejoin you presently.

DULCY [*calling to him as he goes upstairs*]. Dinner at eight-twenty!

BILL. Eight-twenty? Have you been reading *Vanity Fair* again?

DULCY. Everybody dines at eight-twenty, Willie. It's continental. [DULCY *turns to her husband.*] Well, how do you like Mr. Van Dyck? Nice, isn't he?

GORDON. He's all right, I guess.

DULCY. Wait till you hear him play the piano. A lovely touch, and so soulful.

BILL. Don't forget to ask him to play. [HENRY *comes down the steps.*]

DULCY [*going to* BILL *and sitting beside him*]. Dear, no—right after dinner. We're going to have a nice musical evening. Music after eating helps digestion. All the new doctors say so. [HENRY *departs again.* BILL *looks after him uncomfortably.*]

BILL. Dulcy!

DULCY. Well, Willie?

BILL. When you took this butler out of Sing Sing—

DULCY [*rising*]. Sing Sing? He wasn't in Sing Sing!

BILL. You didn't go way out to Leavenworth, did you?

DULCY. Now, I know just what you're going to say, but it isn't true. Just because Henry made one false step doesn't mean he's going to make another. If you ask me, I think there's enough sorrow in the world without trying to make things worse. Every cloud has a silver lining, and—so has Henry.

BILL. Yes. The question is, how did he get it?

DULCY. It doesn't matter in the least—he's all right now. He promised me. Besides, he has to report to the probation officer every week, and tell him everything he does.

BILL. Oh, he *has* to tell him everything?

DULCY. Every week.

BILL. You don't think he has any—secrets?

DULCY. You must be more tolerant, Willie. You know, there's so much good in the best of us—and so much bad in the worst of us—well, it ill behooves the best of us— [*She floundors, but is saved by the door bell.*]

GORDON. Here are the Forbeses!

DULCY. Wait, Gordon—let that poor Henry answer! The trouble with the world, Willie, is that it doesn't give the under-dog a chance! Live and let live—is my motto. [HENRY *returns to answer the bell.*]

BILL. I surrender. [*A pause.*] Oh, Dulcy! [HENRY *goes out at the other side.*] Why don't you raise his salary?

DULCY. I have!

GORDON. Now remember, Dulcy, just leave Forbes to me —and—don't forget this is a very important business matter—

DULCY. Now, don't worry, darling. Worrying is the very worst thing you can do—everybody says so. I was reading where Dr. Crane said it in the *Globe* the other day—by worrying you can catch things. [HENRY *opens the door. The voices of the* FORBESES *are heard; they enter. First,* MR. FORBES—*then* MRS. FORBES—*then* ANGELA. *The greetings are ad lib.* DULCY *shakes hands with each, passing them to* GORDON, *who does likewise.*]

DULCY. Well, here is Mr. Forbes now, and Mrs. Forbes! How charming you look! Green's your color! [*She turns to* GORDON *to tell him about it.*] Green's her color, darling! And Angela!! You've come to see me at last! My, such red cheeks! Just like two ripe apples! [FORBES *is already deep in business talk with* SMITH, *but* DULCY *turns to him blithely.*] Mr. Forbes— [FORBES *turns to her.*] Did you have a nice ride out from the city? Awfully pretty, isn't it—Westchester? [FORBES *agrees with a nod—is about to turn back to* SMITH.] Did you come out the short way or the long way?

FORBES [*it is already evident that* DULCY *is going to be just the person for him.*] Ah—what was that?

DULCY. Did you come out the short way or the long way?

FORBES. Ah—let me see. [*A pause.*] Do *you* know, Eleanor?

MRS. FORBES [*his second wife; a very feminine person of about thirty-five; good looking and a bit flighty*]. What, dear?

FORBES. Mrs. Smith was just asking if—

DULCY. Did you come out the short way or the long way?

MRS. FORBES. Which is the way through Hartsdale?

DULCY. Oh, that's the short way—you should have come

the long way. No, I think that *is* the long way, isn't it? Hartsdale?—Yes. No—

GORDON [*diplomatically*]. Well, it doesn't really matter.

DULCY. No, no—both ways are awfully pretty. [*She has said this to* MRS. FORBES, *and* FORBES *and* SMITH *have turned immediately to each other to renew their conversation. They haven't a chance.*] Though I don't suppose *you* got much chance to look at the scenery, did you, Mr. Forbes—driving the car? Don't you think driving is awfully hard work, Mr. Forbes?

FORBES. Why, no, I rather like it.

DULCY. Like it? Really! Oh! Well, it wouldn't do if all our tastes were alike, would it? [*Turns away just as* HENRY *enters.*] Henry, take the things right up—you know the rooms. [DULCY *turns to* MRS. FORBES.] Mrs. Forbes, you and your husband are to have the shell-pink suite. It looks just like a bridal suite. [MRS. FORBES *giggles and* DULCY *laughs with her.*] The bridal suite! Oh, Mr. Forbes— [*She goes to him.*] Mr. Forbes—you and your wife are going to have the bridal suite! [FORBES *tries to understand the joke, but without success.*] And, Angie—Oh, there you are! I forgot you and Willie were old friends. Naughty, naughty! [HENRY *is on the stairs with the bags.*] Well, how is little Angie! My, what a pretty necklace! It's new, isn't it? Pearls, too! [*This registers with* HENRY.]

ANGELA. Father gave it to me for my birthday.

DULCY. Your father. Really—wasn't that sweet of him? [*To* FORBES.] Your own manufacture?

FORBES. Oh, no!

DULCY. Real pearls! Angela, fancy your having a string of real pearls! Isn't that wonderful! [*Remembers* HENRY'S *presence.*] Take the bags right up, Henry.

BILL. Yes, Henry. [HENRY *goes.*]

DULCY. Angie is going to have the cutest little room of all! Just wait till you see it!

ANGELA. Oh, thank you. [VAN DYCK *comes downstairs.*]

DULCY [*turning* ANGELA *away as if for a confidence*]. And wait till you see what else I've got for you! *You'll* be surprised, and—oh, here's Mr. Van Dyck! [*In her element.*] Mrs. Forbes, Mr. Van Dyck!

MRS. FORBES. How do you do?

DULCY. And Miss Forbes—

VAN DYCK [*bowing*]. Miss Forbes! [ANGELA *bows.*]

DULCY. And Mr. Forbes—Mr. Schuyler Van Dyck of New York.

VAN DYCK. C. Roger Forbes?

FORBES. I'm certainly glad to know you, Mr. Van Dyck. I believe I know something of your interests. In fact, I just missed meeting you at the International Metals conference last week.

VAN DYCK. Yes? Well, I hope we can have a little chance to talk down here. I'm very much interested in jewelry.

DULCY [*with a triumphant look at her husband*]. You see, Gordon?

FORBES [*aware that something is going on*]. What's that?

GORDON. Oh, it was just—ah—that is, Mrs. Smith thought— [HENRY *comes downstairs.*]

DULCY. Oh, we're all forgetting Mr.—What's-his-name—in the library—a gentleman to see you, Mr. Forbes, on business. Henry, tell the gentleman in the library to come in. [HENRY *departs again.*]

GORDON. It's your advertising man.

FORBES. Oh, yes—Sterrett. [ANGELA *turns sharply at the mention of the name.*] I took the liberty of leaving word for him to come here—I had to get away early.

GORDON. Why, certainly.

DULCY. And so that you'll have lots of time to talk business, I've invited him to stay for dinner. [*She looks proudly toward her husband as though asking approbation for this remark.* GORDON *is pleased with her for the first time.*]

ANGELA. Oh! Mr. Sterrett is going to stay for dinner?

DULCY. Yes—because he's a friend of *yours,* Angie, dear. [*Quickly.*] *And* because of the business, of course. Well, what do you girls say? Shall we leave the men to talk business? Wouldn't you like to see your rooms? You haven't been over the house at all, you know.

MRS. FORBES. Why, we'd love to.

DULCY. Gordon, darling, you must show Mr. Forbes and the others over the grounds. [*She is shepherding* MRS. F. *and* ANGELA *toward the stairs.*] You get a beautiful view from the lawn, Mr. Forbes. And don't forget to show him the garden, darling—all our vegetables are out of our own garden, Mr. Forbes. Then later *you* must see the garden, Mrs. Forbes—and Angie. You know, there's nothing like country life, is there? Out next to Nature, you know. We're just gypsies—regular gypsies. New York is a wonderful place to visit, but I wouldn't like to live there. [*They go up the stairs.*]

BILL [*breaking the spell*]. All in favor of the garden, say " Aye."

GORDON. Smoke?

FORBES. Thanks. [*He selects a cigar.*]

VAN DYCK. Thank you. [*Takes a cigarette.* FORBES, *after a glance around the room, heads for a stiff chair.*]

GORDON [*indicating an easy chair*]. Oh, sit here, Mr. Forbes!

FORBES. Thanks—I prefer a stiff chair—my back, you know. [STERRETT *returns.*]

STERRETT. Ah! Good afternoon, Chief!

FORBES. Hello, Sterrett. Too bad to make you come way out here, but—

STERRETT. Not at all—not at all! Particularly, as Mr. Smith has insisted on my staying to dinner. Has Angela come?

FORBES [*patting him on back*]. Oh, yes, she's come. You've met Mr. Parker?

STERRETT. Oh, yes.

FORBES. And Mr. Schuyler Van Dyck?

STERRETT. Mr. Schuyler Van Dyck?

VAN DYCK [*shaking his hand*]. Mr. Sterrett.

STERRETT. I've heard of you, Mr. Van Dyck.

VAN DYCK. Yes?

STERRETT [*crisply*]. Yes, sir. They tell me you have advertising interests, on the q. t.

VAN DYCK. Well, it's—it's possible, yes.

STERRETT. I'm an advertising man myself.

VAN DYCK. Really?

BILL [*helping along*]. S. S. Q. & L. Agency.

STERRETT. Yes, I personally handle all of Mr. Forbes' business.

VAN DYCK. That so?

STERRETT. Yes, sir. I've made the nation Forbes-conscious.

BILL. Forbes—what?

STERRETT. Forbes-conscious. I have made Forbes Jewelry Products a part of the country's buying habit.

FORBES. It's wonderful—wonderful what the younger generation is doing in a business way.

GORDON. It certainly is.

FORBES. Why, when I was breaking into business, sir, do you think that a young man like that would have been entrusted with the handling of such important matters?

GORDON. No, sir.

FORBES. No, sir—he would not! Would he, Mr. Parker?

BILL [*with a look at* STERRETT]. No, sir, he would not!

FORBES. But to-day, not only is he entrusted with them, but he is actually given the preference over an older man. I find myself doing it.

STERRETT. Oh, I don't know, Chief. I'm no unusual specimen—that is, so far as my youth is concerned. Mozart was composing at fifteen; William Cullen Bryant wrote *Thanatopsis* when he was nineteen; Homer did part of the *Iliad*—

BILL [*rising*]. Suppose we *all* go out and look at the garden?

GORDON. Yes, that's a good idea.

FORBES. If you don't mind, I'll put my car in your garage.

GORDON. Certainly.

FORBES. That is, if there's room.

GORDON. Oh, plenty. Our car isn't here at present. It's being repaired.

BILL [*to* VAN DYCK]. You must find it rather a relief to get away from business occasionally.

VAN DYCK. Yes, just to relax. It's very wonderful.

FORBES [*turning back to* VAN DYCK]. I imagine you've been kept pretty well tied down lately. [*All except* STERRETT *have strolled up to the window.*]

VAN DYCK. Well, yes—to a degree. Of course, I have things pretty well systematized.

FORBES. Of course.

GORDON. Now, right here at the left is where the garden begins. You can see for yourself— [*They go out through the windows—*SMITH, FORBES, VAN DYCK *and* BILL. STERRETT, *somewhat puzzled at losing his audience, decides to go along.* ANGELA *comes down the stairway.*]

ANGELA [*very impersonally*]. Oh, hello, Tom!

STERRETT. Angela! I'm here, you see!

ANGELA [*selecting a magazine*]. Yes, I see.

STERRETT. Well, aren't you glad to see me?

ANGELA. You came to see father, didn't you?

STERRETT. Why, no—that is—yes—but—

ANGELA. Have you seen him?

STERRETT. Yes, but—that was business and—

ANGELA. I know—it's always business with you men. You're all alike.

STERRETT. You talk as though you'd examined the whole city.

ANGELA. Well, I did know another man who was just like you.

STERRETT. Who is he?

ANGELA [*looking up from the magazine for first time*]. Oh, don't be silly. I shouldn't tell you even if you weren't so rude. I simply say you are all alike. Your idea of romance is to sit in the moonlight and talk about the income tax.

STERRETT [*sitting beside her*]. Now, look here, Angela— you know I'm crazy about you, and I've told you what I'll do for you. I'll devote my entire life to you.

ANGELA. And give up business?

STERRETT [*swallows*]. Well, you wouldn't want me to give it up, would you? Right at the beginning of my career! Why, when your father signs these new contracts—

ANGELA [*throwing the magazine down beside her and rising*]. Contracts! Bother the contracts! It's always contracts!

STERRETT. But they mean our future.

ANGELA. *Our* future? I didn't know that *we* were going to have any!

STERRETT. Well, we are! You just watch me! I've always got what I was after in business, and—

ANGELA. Well, I'm not—business!

STERRETT. I—I didn't mean just that, Angela.

ANGELA. Oh, sometimes I feel that I don't ever want to talk to another business man in my life!

STERRETT. I notice that you don't mind talking to a moving picture man, though!

ANGELA [*wheeling*]. What do you mean by that?

STERRETT. I saw you with that bird Leach at the Biltmore yesterday.

ANGELA. Well, what of it? Mr. Leach is a very charming man.

STERRETT. He's got a swelled head!

ANGELA. He's entitled to one.

STERRETT. Look here—has he been making love to you?

ANGELA. Well, at least he hasn't been talking business.

STERRETT. Now look here, Angela—

ANGELA. Oh, Tom, don't be silly! If I didn't know any more about girls than you do, I'd go some place and learn! That other man talked business, too, and that's why I—what does a girl care about business, and things like that? She wants something else in her life—that's what makes her a girl! She wants romance—and a thrill—and something real—and she wants a man to be like all the heroes she ever read about—if she cares about him at all! It may be foolish and all that, but that's what she wants and she's bound to have it! She wants someone to tell her how wonderful she is—whether she is or not—to sweep her off her feet and—carry her away—and— [*One look at* STERRETT'S *face tells her that all this has been wasted.*] Oh, I'm going out into the garden! [*She flounces through French window.* STERRETT *follows.*]

STERRETT. Now look here, Angela! I didn't mean— [*Enter* FORBES *and* SMITH. FORBES *looks back after* AN- GELA *and* STERRETT.]

FORBES. Smart chap, Sterrett.

GORDON. Yes, he—seems to be.

FORBES. Wide-awake! That's what I like about him.

GORDON [*eager to agree*]. Yes, wide-awake chaps certainly have an advantage.

FORBES [*bluffly*]. Now, that's the kind of a man I'd like for a son-in-law.

GORDON [*mindful of* DULCY'S *plans*]. Son-in-law?

FORBES. Yes. Good business head. No foolishness, like most young people. Substantial—that's what I mean. Lord knows, Smith, I'm just as tolerant as anybody, and a little bit more so, but if there is one thing I can't stand it's this frivol-headed, gad-about way of doing things they've got now-a-days.

GORDON. Oh, absolutely. Yes, indeed.

FORBES. Damn it—they—they play with life—they don't

work. And it's not just the young people that have notions. The worst of it is that—oh, well, what's the use! [*He pauses.*] That reminds me. I must apologize for not answering that letter of yours. My wife comes into my office occasionally and uses my stenographer—the one that writes English. [*He tries to appear half-joking.*] All day yesterday. She likes to write little stories and movie scenarios. Of course she never sells them.

GORDON. Well—ah—probably she's just—seeking self-expression.

FORBES. Yes, I suppose so. She's quite young—Angela's step-mother, you know. [DULCY *and* MRS. FORBES *come downstairs.*]

DULCY. Come right down, Mrs. Forbes. Well, here we are! No more business now! It's time to play! [*To* FORBES.] You know one thing poor Gordon has never learned is how to play! He takes everything so seriously. Now, what I like to do is cut loose once in a while—just be children again. Don't you, Mrs. Forbes?

MRS. FORBES. Yes, indeed—away from everything.

DULCY. Gordon, darling—why don't you take Mrs. Forbes for a stroll out in the garden before dinner—she hasn't seen it yet. [GORDON *realizes this would leave* DULCY *with* FORBES.] Wouldn't you like to see it, Mrs. Forbes?

MRS. FORBES. Indeed, yes.

DULCY. Gordon!

GORDON [*turning to* MRS. FORBES.] Why, of course.

MRS. FORBES. It's awfully good of you. You have a beautiful place here. There are some lovely places in Westchester, aren't there? [MRS. FORBES *and* GORDON *go through the window,* GORDON *looking back nervously at the possibilities he is leaving.*]

DULCY. I've got the most wonderful day planned out for you to-morrow, Mr. Forbes! You're going to play and play and play!

FORBES [*alarmed*]. Me! Thank you very much—but you know I—

DULCY. Oh, but you play golf, don't you?

FORBES. Well—ah—thank you. It's been so long since—

DULCY [*pursuing him*]. You'll love our links—they're wonderful!

FORBES. Yes, but I've been having a lot of trouble with my back lately and—

DULCY. Oh, really! That's too bad! What you need is exercise. It would be the finest thing in the world for you. Now, you play nine holes of golf with Mr. Van Dyck first thing in the morning.

FORBES. But, really, Mrs. Smith—

DULCY [*indulgently*]. You remind me so much of Gordon —that poor darling. All men are children. You know *he* gets hardly any exercise at all—he works so hard, the poor boy. I don't suppose he's told you, Mr. Forbes, but he's really got a lot of things on hand.

FORBES. Why, no—

DULCY. You might just as well know—it isn't only the pearl business. He has lots of other interests, too.

FORBES. What's that?

DULCY. It's really asking too much of him to make him give up all these other things to come into the jewelry combination—that is, unless it were made worth his while. [DULCY *effects her master stroke.*] Of course, if he just got sixteen and two-thirds per cent, he couldn't afford to give up all his time to it—no! [VAN DYCK *and* BILL *come strolling through the window.*] He'd have to look after his other things, too, and you'd be the loser.

FORBES. Why, I didn't know he had any other— [*Door bell rings.*]

DULCY. Oh, there's Mr. Leach now! [*Calling.*] Gordon! Gordon, bring Angela in! [*She sees* VAN DYCK.] Are you having a nice time, Mr. Van Dyck? We want everybody to have a nice time. [GORDON *and* MRS. FORBES *return.* HENRY *enters to answer the door bell.*]

VAN DYCK. Oh, delightful!

DULCY. You're to play eighteen holes of golf with Mr. Forbes the first thing in the morning. [FORBES *is delighted.*]

VAN DYCK. That will be splendid!

GORDON. Now—now, *I* have a suggestion.

DULCY. Well, what is it?

GORDON. Suppose that to-morrow we just let everybody go the way they want to, and— [*Enter* HENRY, *followed by* VINCENT LEACH. DULCY *swings down to greet him.*]

DULCY [*with great enthusiasm*]. Oh, *here* he is!

LEACH. Mrs. Smith, dear lady— [VINCENT LEACH *is young, very languid, a bit effeminate.*]

DULCY. Ladies and gentlemen, this is Mr. Vincent Leach, the great scenario writer! [FORBES *looks up, puzzled and annoyed.* BILL *is merely puzzled.* VAN DYCK *is politely interested.* GORDON *is all but crazy with apprehension.* MRS. FORBES *is quite in her element.* DULCY *passes* LEACH *over towards* MRS. FORBES.] Mrs. Forbes, Angela's step-mother!

LEACH [*enthusiastically*]. Oh, how do you do!

DULCY. And *Mr.* Forbes, her real father! [FORBES *rises slowly—his dislike has been immediate and intense.* LEACH *does all the bowing.*] And Mr. Van Dyck! [*They bow.*] You've met Gordon, haven't you? [LEACH *shakes* GORDON'S *hand.*] And my brother, Willie.

BILL. Parker—William.

DULCY [ANGELA *and* STERRETT *appear in the windows*]. Oh, here she is! Well— [*She leads* ANGELA *down to* LEACH.]

ANGELA. Why, Mr. Leach!

LEACH. *Miss* Forbes!

STERRETT [*with cold emphasis*]. How do you do, Leach?

LEACH. Oh, how are you?

DULCY. Didn't I tell you I'd have a surprise for you?

FORBES [*to* ANGELA, *as she stands with her hand still in* LEACH'S, *to* STERRETT'S *great annoyance*]. Oh, then you've met Mr. Leach before?

ANGELA. Oh, yes!

DULCY. Why, didn't you know about it? Mr. Leach showed us through his studio the other day. He almost kidnapped your Angela, and made a motion picture star out of her.

FORBES [*not quite succeeding in being pleasant about it*]. Oh, is that so?

DULCY. We saw his new picture being taken. Oh, tell us about it, Mr. Leach! [*Whispering loudly to everyone.*] Mr. Leach is a scenario writer—a scenario writer.

LEACH [*correcting her*]. If you will pardon me, not scenario writer—scenarist—really.

BILL [*in mock comprehension*]. Oh, scenarist!

LEACH. It's the more modern term. The scenarist of to-day is quite different from the scenario writer of yesterday.

DULCY [*in her element*]. Mr. Leach says the motion picture business is still in its infancy.

LEACH. The surface has hardly been scratched. The possibilities are enormous, and the demand for new people—new writers— [*He turns to* MRS. FORBES.] Oh! Mrs. Smith tells me that *you* are writing for the films, my dear Mrs. Forbes!

MRS. FORBES. Well, I'm—trying to—

LEACH. Well, you go on writing—don't give up—don't let anyone discourage you. [FORBES *turns away with a mild attack of apoplexy*.] That was my experience. I just kept on and on until—well, you see.

BILL. What?

DULCY [*in a quick aside*]. You shut up, Willie!

LEACH [*to* MRS. FORBES]. Yes, you just keep on writing. [*Then generously taking them all in*.] All of you—and go and see the pictures. See them and see them and see them. [*To* MRS. FORBES *and* VAN DYCK.] Study them! [*To* MR. FORBES.] Learn how they're made! Now in my last picture, *The Sacred Love*—you've all seen that, I take it?

DULCY. Oh, yes—a wonderful picture!

MRS. FORBES. Yes!

ANGELA. I saw it twice. Once with you, Tom.

STERRETT. Was *that* his picture?

LEACH. There were some points in that—did you see it, Mr. Forbes?

FORBES [*wild within*]. No, I—I don't believe I did.

LEACH. Really! You must come to one of our trade showings at the Hotel Astor—

FORBES. What?

LEACH. Just a moment. [*Consults note-book*.] At the Hotel Astor, next Tuesday, at 3:30. Of course, it's—it's only a little thing. We're going to do some big things later. The possibilities—

BILL [*ever helpful*]. Are enormous.

LEACH [*falling for it*]. Oh, *very* big . . . you'd be surprised! Yes, we're going to do some of Shakespeare's things next.

DULCY. Shakespeare's? Well— [*Her arms are around her husband's shoulders and she shakes him to pick up the cue*.]

GORDON [*coming to*]. Really!

LEACH. Yes, I'm at work on his continuity now. I was telling my director yesterday—I said, you know, Shakespeare had a tremendous feeling for plot. Of course, the dialogue is stilted for modern audiences—but then, you don't have to listen to that in the pictures. But he's still the master.

DULCY. He's going to organize his own company next.

BILL. Who—Shakespeare?

DULCY. No, Willie! Mr. Leach.

LEACH. Yes—the Vincent Leach Productions, Inc. The stock will be placed on the open market very soon.

DULCY. Mr. Van Dyck can tell you how to do it! He owns lots of moving picture companies—don't you, Mr. Van Dyck?

LEACH. Is that so?

VAN DYCK [modestly, as always]. Well, I'm interested—in a small way.

LEACH. I'd enjoy talking to you about it later. [To MR. FORBES.] And how about you, Mr. Forbes? Didn't I hear that *you* were interested in pictures?

FORBES [turning away and smothering the line]. I don't care a damn about pictures.

LEACH [not believing his ears]. What's that?

FORBES. I said, I make jewelry.

LEACH. Well, of course, that's very necessary too, in its way. [FORBES' mouth opens—GORDON rises hurriedly.]

GORDON. Dulcy!

DULCY. Ah—let's play a rubber of bridge before dinner! It's so nice and soothing. [Patting LEACH for fear he has been offended.] Let me see— [To MR. FORBES.] Mr. Forbes, you play bridge, don't you?

FORBES. No, I'm afraid not.

DULCY. Oh, yes, you do—you're just modest. Mr. Forbes— [She is picking the card players out with cool intent.] And Mr. Sterrett—and Gordon— And I'll make the fourth. Mr. Leach. [He is absorbed in ANGELA.] Mr. Leach. [He turns.] Why don't you and Angela go out on the lawn and see the view?

GORDON. Dulcy, dear—

DULCY. Where the Japanese garden is going to be?

ANGELA [giving LEACH her hand]. Come on, Vincent.

LEACH [putting her arm through his]. Yes, I'd love to

see you framed against the glowing splendor of a twilit garden. [ANGELA *and* LEACH *go out through the window.*]

BILL. My golly, the man even makes love in subtitles!

FORBES. I'll see if my car is still in the garage. I'll come back—I think. [*He goes out through the window.*]

GORDON [*to* DULCY]. Now, now, you see— [*He goes out quickly after* FORBES.]

BILL [*up in the windows*]. You know, this is probably going to be the first week-end party on record that ended on Friday night. [*He departs, lugubriously.*]

STERRETT. I think I'll go back to my book.

DULCY [*somewhat weakly*]. We'll be starting the game in a minute, Mr. Sterrett. [STERRETT *disappears.*] Well, I'll get the bridge things. [*She turns in the doorway—only* MRS. FORBES *and* VAN DYCK *are left on the stage.*] Two's company and three's a crowd! [*She goes.*]

MRS. FORBES [*rising with a self-conscious laugh*]. I must go and dress for dinner.

VAN DYCK. Oh, please don't go—I've been wanting to have a chat with you. I've been hearing all about you this afternoon.

MRS. FORBES. All about me? From whom?

VAN DYCK. Mrs. Smith.

MRS. FORBES. Oh!

VAN DYCK. So you see, I was prepared to be interested—even before I met you.

MRS. FORBES [*sitting*]. And now the disappointment?

VAN DYCK [*sitting beside her*]. Oh, far from it. I find you even more interesting than I had anticipated. You have depths.

MRS. FORBES. Are you going to—fathom them?

VAN DYCK. If I may.

MRS. FORBES. And how are you going about it? [FORBES *is seen strolling behind the windows at back*].

VAN DYCK. That's *my* secret. But tell me, first—you've been married just a short time?

MRS. FORBES. Not so short—four years. Why? [FORBES *comes down into window; sees and hears.*]

VAN DYCK. Mrs. Smith tells me that you are becoming quite a novelist.

MRS. FORBES. Oh, but I'm not yet. I only—

FORBES. Is that you, Eleanor? [VAN DYCK *rises*.]

MRS. FORBES. Yes, dear.

FORBES. Oh!

VAN DYCK. I shall see you later, I hope.

MRS. FORBES. I hope.

VAN DYCK [*attempting to relieve the tension*]. I suppose you get a good many ideas for your writings from your husband? [*The tension is not relieved*. VAN DYCK *departs through windows*.]

FORBES [*looking from* VAN DYCK *to his wife*]. Well!

MRS. FORBES [*rises*]. Well?

FORBES. What did *that* mean?

MRS. FORBES. Why, nothing!

FORBES. Isn't it enough to have Angela go prancing off with that—brainless—conceited—motion picture jack-ass?

MRS. FORBES. Mr. Leach, do you mean? Why, he's a charming man, and very successful.

FORBES. Bah! And on top of it, I come in here and find you—spooning with Van Dyck.

MRS. FORBES. Why, Charlie—how can you say such a thing!

FORBES. My God, didn't I see it!

MRS. FORBES. But, Charlie, dear—

FORBES. I tell you this whole place is going to drive me crazy! I didn't want to come here anyhow! I had a backache, and I wanted to stay home and rest.

MRS. FORBES. But you couldn't refuse—

FORBES. And instead of that I've got to get up at some ungodly hour in the morning and go out and play golf. If there is one thing I hate more than anything else in this world, it's golf—unless it's bridge or moving pictures!

MRS. FORBES. Now, Charlie, dear—when you're here as a guest—

FORBES. If I could think of a good excuse, I'd go back to town to-night with Sterrett, and take Angela and you with me.

MRS. FORBES [*alarmed*]. But, Charlie, you can't do that when—

FORBES. Don't you suppose I see that woman's plan to throw Angela and that—that film thing together!

MRS. FORBES. But I tell you he's a most charming man.

FORBES. And I tell you, if it weren't for Smith and our business relations I WOULD go back to-night!

MRS. FORBES. But, Charlie—you can't be so rude! [*Enter* GORDON.]

FORBES. Sh! That reminds me—Oh, Smith!

GORDON. Yes, sir.

FORBES. Mr. Smith, Mrs. Smith has been telling me something of your other business activities.

GORDON. Other business activities? Why—

FORBES. And it came as something of a revelation to me.

GORDON. But Mrs. Smith couldn't have meant— [VAN DYCK *returns and joins* MRS. FORBES.]

FORBES. As you may have been aware, my agreement to admit you on a sixteen and two-thirds basis was founded on the expectation that you would give all your time to the new enterprise.

GORDON. Yes, of course, Mr. Forbes.

FORBES. In the circumstances your business and your services would hardly be worth that amount to me.

GORDON. But, my dear Mr. Forbes—you—you don't understand. Mrs. Smith— [*Enter* DULCY, *bubbling over.*]

DULCY. Oh, here are the bridge players! Come right in, Mr. Sterrett. [*Enter* STERRETT *and* HENRY, *carrying the card table.*] Henry, put the table right here. You know, I hope you men don't mind playing with me—I'm not very good. I always say I don't really play bridge, I play *at* it. But I do love it, and after all, that's what counts, isn't it?

FORBES [*worn out*]. Yes.

DULCY. That's right, Henry, put the chairs around. Now, I think Mr. Sterrett will sit there. [*Indicating chair opposite her.*] I shall sit here. Let's see—that makes you my partner, Mr. Sterrett. You don't mind, do you?

STERRETT [*beyond minding anything*]. Not at all. [STERRETT *takes one final look out the windows after* ANGELA.]

DULCY [*to* FORBES]. He *had* to say that. You know I'm an awfully unlucky player—I never have a finesse go right. Well, unlucky at cards—lucky at love— [*Turning to* GORDON.] Lucky at love, Gordie, darling. You're here, of course. [GORDON *is evidently worrying about what* DULCY *could have said to* FORBES. FORBES *keeps turning uneasily for a sight of his wife and* VAN DYCK. DULCY *starts to deal.*] Now look at me—I'm dealing when I ought to be shuffling! [*She gathers up the cards and shuffles awkwardly.*] Come along, Mr. Sterrett! We're going to beat them! Bring that chair. [STERRETT *starts to follow her directions. Three more miserable men have never been seen.*] Is everybody happy? [*The curtain starts slowly down.*] Somebody tell me—which is higher—a heart or a spade? I never can remember. And do you discard from strength or weakness, Mr. Sterrett? Of course it doesn't matter— [*She continues her chatter, as*

[THE CURTAIN FALLS.]

ACT II

*The scene is the same as Act I; the time is immediately after
dinner, on the same day. Although it is evening, the
French windows at the rear still stand open. The stage
is in semi-darkness—only one or two of the lamps are
lighted—but a shaft of moonlight shoots through the
windows. The dining room, at the left, is brilliantly
lighted, and the chatter of many people, with the
clink of glasses and the occasional scrape of a chair, can
be distinctly heard. For an appreciable period after the
rise of the curtain only the sound of this merry gathering
can be heard. Over the others the voice of* VINCENT
LEACH *rings out clearly—"I said to Mr. Breitenstein,
'Don't you worry about those German films.'" Then the
babble drowns his further remarks.*

DULCY, *resplendent in a golden evening dress, presently
enters, peering back as though expecting someone to follow
her. She beckons excitedly to someone in the other room,
and* MRS. FORBES *enters.*

DULCY [*in excited tones*]. Isn't he wonderful?

MRS. FORBES [*also flushed with excitement*]. Who?

DULCY. Vincent Leach! [*Banteringly.*] Ah, you thought
I meant Mr. Van Dyck, didn't you? Ah, ha!

MRS. FORBES [*confused*]. Why—I didn't know—

DULCY. Now, now! It doesn't take a brick wall to fall
on *me*. But seriously, he's mad about her!

MRS. FORBES [*with just a touch of apprehension*]. Do you
really think so?

DULCY. And she hasn't taken her eyes off him since he
arrived! I tell you, they're in love!

MRS. FORBES [*looking off*]. There *is*—something about
him. The only thing is—

DULCY. I wouldn't be surprised if they became engaged—
right here in my house. Wouldn't that be nice, after my
bringing them together?

Mrs. Forbes. But you're sure it's all right—positive that Mr. Leach is—

Dulcy. Of course, I am—he's just the man for Angela. Ssh! Here's Mr. Sterrett! [*The two women draw up against the wall as* Sterrett *enters. His hands are deep in his pockets, and he is sore. He looks back as he enters, then starts across the room. A few steps further he looks back again, as* Angela's *laugh is heard. He stalks out the windows.* Dulcy *titters.*]

Dulcy. He's mad! Let's see what happened! [Angela *comes running on. She is happily excited, being pursued.* Leach *follows her, capturing her at the piano, and holding her with her back toward him, giving* Mrs. Forbes *and* Dulcy *a chance to escape into the dining room unseen.*]

Leach. Now I've got you!

Angela. And what are you going to do with me?

Leach [*turning her around*]. I'm going to tell you—how wonderful you are.

Angela [*liking it*]. Oh, my!

Leach. You are! You're like a beautiful warm dawn— just your magic presence— [Van Dyck *and* Mrs. Forbes *stroll on together.*]

Angela [*stopping* Leach]. Ssh!

Van Dyck. But surely if one has a talent it should be developed.

Angela. Shall we sit down? [Leach *makes a gesture towards the chairs by the piano.*] Oh, not there—here. [*She bounces over to the stairs and sits behind the hydrangeas.* Leach *takes his place beside her.*]

Mrs. Forbes [*convinced by now she is a potential George Sand*]. But I'm afraid I'm just a dabbler and always will be.

Van Dyck [*sitting beside her*]. Ah, but I'm sure you're wrong! You must be wrong. [*Enter* Forbes *and* Gordon. *All of the men, except* Sterrett, *are in evening clothes.*]

Forbes. Well, as a straight business proposition I must say— [*He sees his wife with* Van Dyck, *and stops short.*] Huh! [Van Dyck *gets up from the easy chair.*]

Van Dyck. Sit here, Mr. Forbes.

Forbes. No, thank you. I prefer a stiff chair.

Gordon. Here you are, Mr. Forbes. [*Enter* Bill.]

Bill. Everybody ready for a nice musical evening? [Ster-

RETT, *still sulking, comes in silently through the French windows.* DULCY *enters at the same time, and immediately takes characteristic charge of the situation.*]

DULCY. Well, this is going to be jolly, isn't it? Let's have a little light on the subject. [*She switches on the lights.*] Let me see— Yes, everybody's here. [MRS. FORBES, *anxious to relieve the tension maintained by her husband, leaves* VAN DYCK *and follows* DULCY. DULCY *puts her arm around her.*] I love a big house and lots of company. If only it were a winter night, we could gather around the fireplace and tell ghost stories. [FORBES *has made up his mind to sit and has headed for the stiff chair.* DULCY *seizes him.*] Oh, no, Mr. Forbes—you must take the easy chair—that's for you —yes. [*She pulls him across to it.*]

FORBES [*cursing the conventions of chivalry*]. But I really would rather—that is—

DULCY. Now, not a word—I know you're polite and want to leave it for me, but I insist on your having it. [GORDON *tries to head her off but his efforts are unavailing.* DULCY *forces* MR. FORBES *into the chair.*] I wouldn't dream of anyone else's having it but you. Now sit right in it—that's right —way back! It's awfully comfortable—just the thing after eating. [MRS. FORBES *has seated herself;* VAN DYCK *is entertaining her.*] It'll rest you for to-morrow—for your horseback riding.

FORBES [*in great alarm*]. Horse-back!

DULCY. Yes, didn't you hear us talking about it? In the afternoon. We're making up a party to go to the Sound and you're in it. [*Enter* HENRY *with coffee, on a tea wagon. He pushes it across to* DULCY.] Well, who's for coffee? Coffee—coffee! [BILL *has wandered over to the piano and has seated himself.* DULCY *pours.*] It's a lovely ride to the Sound. You'll go, won't you, Mr. Van Dyck?

VAN DYCK [*with* MRS. FORBES]. What's that? Oh, yes —yes, indeed.

DULCY [*whispering*]. You and Mrs. Forbes can go together. [FORBES *turns around to locate his wife and daughter.*] I'll ride with *Mr.* Forbes. Here you are, Henry. [HENRY *serves.*]

GORDON [*to* FORBES]. Now this was what I wanted to

show you. These are our Number Three's; we are turning
these out at an extremely low price, and the German formula
can't touch them. Just examine these. [FORBES *puts on
glasses and does so.* HENRY *returns for two more coffees;
he offers one to* FORBES, *who refuses.*]

DULCY. We're going to have a lovely day for it to-morrow. Did you see that sunset? Angela, you and Mr. Leach
are to go along, too. And Mr. Sterrett—where is that Mr.
Sterrett?

STERRETT [*behind her*]. I'm here.

DULCY. Oh! There you are! I'd almost forgotten you.

STERRETT [*submerged in gloom*]. That's all right.

DULCY. It's too bad you can't stay over, Mr. Sterrett.
I'm sure you'd enjoy it. [HENRY *serves* ANGELA *and* LEACH,
who both accept. His offers to BILL *and* STERRETT *are refused.*] You know, the paper says rain for to-morrow, but
it's always wrong. I have the worst luck with the weather
whenever I go any place. When I take my umbrella it never
rains, and if I don't take it— [BILL *has started on a solo of
" Chop Sticks" as an anodyne.*] Come away from the piano,
Willie. . . . Mr. Van Dyck is going to play us something—
aren't you, Mr. Van Dyck?

VAN DYCK. Why—ah—a little later. [BILL *starts another one-finger solo.*]

GORDON. If you'll examine those you'll see that they are
the same grain and luster as the Hammond Number Six.

DULCY. Oh, do stop, Willie!

FORBES. Mmm. [*A pause.*] Angela! [*There is no answer.*] Angela!!

ANGELA [*coming to*]. Yes, father.

FORBES. Just let me see those pearls of yours for a minute,
will you?

ANGELA. Yes, father. [ANGELA *and* LEACH *rise.* LEACH
reaches as if to remove the pearls, but ANGELA *hands him her
coffee instead and removes the pearls herself.* HENRY *steps up
to* ANGELA *to relieve her of the pearls. She gives them to
him.* BILL *strikes a bass note three or four times in warning,
rising as he does so.* DULCY *and* GORDON *rise, their eyes on*
HENRY. HENRY *gives the pearls to* FORBES; DULCY *gives a
huge sigh of relief.* ANGELA *and* LEACH *resume their seat on*

the bench again. BILL *sits again at piano. Quiet is restored.*]

DULCY. Are you ready now, Mr. Van Dyck—it's your turn!

VAN DYCK. Oh, really, I—I don't think that I should play. Mr. Forbes and your husband would much prefer to discuss jewelry, I'm sure.

DULCY. Oh, no, they wouldn't! Would you, Mr. Forbes? [*He is studying the necklace.*] Mr. Forbes!

FORBES [*looking up*]. Huh?

DULCY. Wouldn't you like to hear Mr. Van Dyck play the piano?

FORBES. Oh, yes—yes.

DULCY. You see—and I know Mrs. Forbes wants you to play—don't you, dear?

MRS. FORBES. Oh, yes.

DULCY. And *I* do! And Willie— [*Another solo of* BILL's *is obtruding.*] Get away from the piano, Willie—and Mr. Sterrett. Now, Mr. Van Dyck—

VAN DYCK. Well, if you insist. [VAN DYCK *seats himself and starts to play. The selection is the Chopin Prelude, Op. 28, No. 4.*]

DULCY [*seated*]. What was that little thing you played at Mrs. Kennedy's this afternoon? [*She listens.* GORDON *and* FORBES *are discussing jewelry in low tones.*] No—that wasn't it. It's lovely, though. Carries me right away. [GORDON *and* FORBES *become audible.*] Quiet everybody—quiet! [*After a look at her they lower their tones, but not enough to satisfy* DULCY.] Ssh! [*She rattles some noisy bracelets.* FORBES *turns and looks at her.* DULCY *giggles at him.*] Oh, Mr. Forbes! I thought it was my husband. [DULCY's *wandering eyes light upon a box of candy, the wrapping still on it. She makes a weak attempt to turn her eyes away from it and then picks it up and tears off its paper noisily, whispering across to* MRS. FORBES.] Candy that Mr. Leach brought! Yes—wasn't it nice of him? [*She removes cover and ribbon, opens box and offers some to* MRS. FORBES *and* STERRETT *in hoarse whisper.*] Take some! [*They signal refusal. She reaches it towards* FORBES.] Want some candy, Mr. Forbes? [FORBES *looks around, but does not understand.* DULCY *creeps across to him.*] Some candy? Sherry's! Delicious! Molasses! [*She is heavily sibilant.* FORBES, *unable to hear, leans toward her. She reaches the box further toward him. After seeing the candy he refuses.*]

FORBES. No, no, thank you. [*Returns to his chair.* GORDON *coughs and is hushed.* DULCY *takes a piece of candy from the box and tastes it; does not like it, looks about to make sure no one is observing—replaces it.* BILL *rises, comes down and selects two pieces.*]

DULCY. Ssh!

BILL [*whispering*]. What?

DULCY. Ssh! [*The music suddenly stops.* DULCY *drops candy and applauds.*]

BILL. Ssh! [*The music begins again.*]

DULCY [*in a whisper to* MRS. FORBES]. I thought he had finished. [VAN DYCK *strikes the remaining chords.* DULCY *rises.*] Lovely!! [*Long drawn out.*]

MRS. FORBES. It was adorable!

ANGELA. I loved it!

LEACH. It was—beautiful. It made me think of Araby and the moon-soaked desert. [*He loses himself in the desert for a second.*] Did you see *The Virgin of Stamboul?*

BILL [*promptly*]. No.

DULCY. No—I don't believe I did, either.

LEACH. That's too bad. You know, some of *my* new picture is being laid in the desert, and that would be wonderful music for it.

DULCY [*getting an inspiration*]. Oh!

BILL. What's the matter?

DULCY. I have an idea. [BILL *moves toward the door.*] Why not have Mr. Leach tell us the story of his new picture, while Mr. Van Dyck plays the music for it?

GORDON [*springing up*]. But—but, Dulcy—

DULCY. It'll be just like a moving-picture theatre!

LEACH [*with fake modesty*]. Oh, but really—I don't think that I should—of course, it *would* be interesting.

ANGELA. Oh, please tell it, Vincent! [*She gives a look at* STERRETT.]

STERRETT. Yes, do! [*Turns away.*]

MRS. FORBES. I'd love to hear it, and so would my husband. [*She throws her husband a look.*]

DULCY. Well, now you can't refuse.

LEACH [*with no thought of refusing*]. Since you demand it.

DULCY. Oh, good! Now everybody take their places! Mr. Van Dyck, you go back to the piano! [*They all take seats.*] Mr. Leach, you tell him what kind of music you want! [BILL *stands motionless and noiseless.*] Be quiet, Willie. Now, I'll sit here.

BILL. Mr. Leach. [*A pause.*] How many reels is this picture?

LEACH. There are eight! [BILL *sinks into his chair.*] It's an extra-super-feature, not released on the regular program!

BILL. How long does each reel take?

LEACH. Oh, about fifteen minutes.

FORBES [*looks up*]. Two hours?

BILL. To tell it?

LEACH. Oh, no, to show it. I can give you what *we* call an outline in half an hour—well, three-quarters at the most.

BILL. That's much better—three-quarters. That's fine!

DULCY. Now keep quiet, Willie, or he won't tell it. What's the name of the picture, Mr. Leach?

GORDON [*striking match*]. We can have a smoke, anyhow.

FORBES. Thanks.

LEACH [*with a winning smile*]. Of course, I must have absolute silence. [FORBES *looks at him.*]

DULCY. Of course. Tell us the name of it. [GORDON *lights his own, and, as* FORBES *is about to turn for his light,* LEACH *protests amiably.*]

LEACH. I shall have to concentrate, and if there are any distractions—

DULCY [*hastily*]. There won't be any—tell us the name of it.

BILL. Ask him what it's called.

DULCY. Shut up, Willie!

LEACH [*waiting a moment until everyone is quiet*]. The name of the picture—

DULCY [*lifting an arm, and thus rattling her bracelets*]. Quiet, everybody!

LEACH. Is—*Sin*. [*This to the men.*] *Sin*. [*To the women.*]

DULCY [*Doing her bit*]. Sin. [VAN DYCK *starts the Rachmaninoff Prelude*. LEACH *steps up and stops him*.]

LEACH. Not yet. And when I'm ready, just a soft accompaniment. [*Starting with enthusiasm*.] This is really something quite new in films. I am going to show Sin—throughout the ages.

DULCY [*with anticipation*]. Well!

LEACH. In the beginning the picture is symbolic. I open with a quotation from Hawthorne— [*For the men's benefit*.] *Nathaniel* Hawthorne.

BILL [*raising his hand*]. Who's the director and the cameraman?

DULCY. Willie!

LEACH [*squelching him*]. The director is Frank Heming Stratton.

BILL. Oh! [BILL *prepares for as comfortable a nap as possible*.]

LEACH. It begins—with the setting out—of Noah's Ark. [LEACH *signals* VAN DYCK, *who stars "Sailing, Sailing."* LEACH *considers the music for a second, decides it will do, and continues*.] We see Noah, a man of advanced years. His wife, his sons, the animals—of each of its kind two. We see the Ark setting out upon its journey—we see the waters rise and rise and rise. For forty days it rains. [VAN DYCK *changes to "Rustle of Spring."*] Civilization is all but wiped out—it is kept alive—and SIN is kept alive—only in the Ark. [*At "Sin"* VAN DYCK *changes to "Kiss Me Again."*]

DULCY [*in hoarse whisper to* MRS. FORBES]. "Kiss Me Again."

LEACH. Then comes a calm— [VAN DYCK *changes to "Morning Mood" (Grieg).*] The dove is sent forth—it returns, unable to find a lighting place. [*Suiting action to the word*, FORBES *strikes a noisy match and lights his cigar, unmindful of* LEACH'S *glare*.] And then a second dove—and *it* returns—and then a third—and it does not return—for somewhere in the great beyond it had found LAND. [*A quick signal to* VAN DYCK.] LAND! [VAN DYCK *goes loudly into "My Country 'Tis of Thee."* DULCY *automatically rises, ever patriotic*. LEACH *is about to begin again, looks at her surprised*. DULCY *giggles her apology, then sits*. LEACH *continues as the curtain slowly falls*.] Many years pass—we are now at King Solomon's Court—his wives are bathing in the fountain— [*The curtain remains down for a few seconds to indicate the passing of thirty minutes. As the curtain rises,* LEACH, *somewhat dishevelled, is still talking.* BILL *is asleep in his chair,* STERRETT *asleep in his chair.* GORDON *has fallen asleep in a sitting posture as though he had attempted to be a perfect host but failed.* FORBES *is the one man wide-awake. He is chewing the stump of a cigar viciously, breathing heavily and seems to be wondering how many seconds he can stand it before he commits murder.* VAN DYCK, *at the piano, looks exhausted, and by this time is contributing only an occasional chord.* MRS. FORBES, ANGELA *and* DULCY *are still " eating it up."*]

LEACH [*talking as the curtain rises*]. Frances rushes to the edge of the cliff, and, looking over, sees an inert, lifeless form. The " Weasel " is dead. [LEACH *pantomimes his excuses hurriedly and takes a drink from a glass of water on the piano.* HENRY *enters to clear away the coffee cups.*]

DULCY. Not yet, Henry! How many times— [HENRY *departs with a shrug.*] Yes, Mr. Leach, the Weasel is dead—

LEACH [*picking up the story*]. And then—then the Zeppelin and Jack's automobile go into the final stretch neck and neck. On—on they speed! We get another close-up of Jack in the driver's seat! We see his face—tense—and putting into the car everything that he has, he forges—slowly—slowly ahead! Then more and more! The goal is nearer and nearer! Back in New York, Charley is seen leaving the Chinese Restaurant! On the corner he meets Fanny, who throws the money in his face. [*For emphasis he touches* FORBES' *arm.* FORBES *jumps.*] Then flash back to Jack—nearer and nearer— HE WINS. [BILL *is rudely awakened and springs up.*]

BILL. What?

LEACH [*explaining*]. He wins!! [BILL *returns to his chair and nap with the manner of a man annoyed at being called too early.* VAN DYCK *strikes a chord.*] Gradually he stops. The Zeppelin makes a landing. Coralie gets out of the dirigible and rushes to Jack to forgive him. Just as he takes her in his arms, her father arrives with the afternoon paper, which makes everything clear and vindicates Albert. Then the father clasps Jack's hand and apologizes to him for having thought *him* the thief. And, to keep the symbolism to the end, just as Jack kisses Coralie there in Chicago, Marc Antony is shown kissing Cleopatra in Ancient Egypt and George Washington kissing Martha Washington at Mt. Vernon. And so, at the end of the Dream Trail, we fade into a long shot of Jack and Coralie, once more in their South Sea bungalow, with the faithful old Toota Heva waiting to greet them in the sunset—and fade out. [VAN DYCK *finishes with a loud chord. The women rise.* LEACH *rushes to them, his hands outstretched, anticipating their congratulations. The women take his hands, chattering.* VAN DYCK *gets up, raising his arms and exercising his fingers.* BILL *awakes and rises, but finds his foot asleep. He gradually wakes himself up by some shakes and half-exercises, and awakens* GORDON, *who also has to exercise and stretch his legs and arms.* STERRETT *likewise awakes.* FORBES *has risen and holds his back.* HENRY *enters, clears the cups and saucers, and goes again.*]

DULCY [*when the excitement has died down a little*]. Oh, that was the most wonderful picture I ever saw! [*The women echo this.*] I mean heard! Eight marvelous reels!

BILL. What a picture! My God, what a picture! [*He slips away.*]

FORBES [*through his teeth*]. And now, Eleanor, they might enjoy hearing one of *your* scenarios. In fact, I'm going upstairs and get one!

MRS. FORBES. Charlie—you—you're not really going to get one of mine!

FORBES. So help me God! [*He starts up;* DULCY *stops him at the foot of the staircase.*]

DULCY. Mr. Forbes, wouldn't you like to play a game of billiards?

GORDON. Ah! Now, that's fine!

FORBES. Why, yes, I'm very, very fond of billiards!

DULCY. There, you see, Gordon, darling!

FORBES. I didn't know you had a billiard table.

DULCY. Why, yes, a wonderful one!

GORDON [*indicating the door*]. Downstairs.

VAN DYCK. That sounds interesting. May I look on? [GORDON *has gone to* DULCY *and squeezed her hand in appreciation.*]

GORDON [*at door*]. This way, Mr. Forbes.

FORBES. Good God, why didn't you mention billiards earlier! [VAN DYCK, GORDON, *and* FORBES *depart.*]

DULCY [*to* MRS. FORBES]. I think it's good for the men to get off by themselves once in a while—they seem to like it. Besides, I wanted to talk to you. Angela dear, why don't you and Mr. Leach go out for a stroll in the moonlight? It's a wonderful night, in the moonlight.

ANGELA. Yes, let's!

LEACH. The moonlight! I would adore it!

MRS. FORBES. You'd better put on a wrap, Angela.

ANGELA. Oh, mother, it isn't cold. [ANGELA *and* LEACH *stroll off, arm in arm.*]

STERRETT [*taking the pretty rough hint*]. I guess I'll watch the billiard game. [*He goes. The two women sit down.* DULCY *takes the box of candy from the piano and puts it on a stool between them. They eat and talk.*]

DULCY. Isn't everything going beautifully?

MRS. FORBES. Ah—yes.

DULCY. I think Mr. Forbes is beginning to like Vincent, too.

MRS. FORBES. Do you?

DULCY. Don't you? Didn't you see his face—so tense and excited while Mr. Leach was telling his story? Wasn't it nice, with Mr. Van Dyck playing the piano?

MRS. FORBES. He plays awfully well.

DULCY. Has he said anything to you?

MRS. FORBES. Who?

DULCY. Mr. Van Dyck, of course. Anybody can see he's attracted to you—he's an awfully nice man, and he's one of *the* Van Dycks of Newport—if you ever want to go there.

MRS. FORBES. Oh, *is* he?

DULCY. Yes, I could fix it for you. [GORDON *and* FORBES *return. They have removed their coats.*]

GORDON. Dulcy, dear, where did you put those billiard balls?

DULCY. The what? [VAN DYCK *comes back.*]

FORBES. The—billiard balls! It's—a little difficult to play billiards without them.

DULCY. Oh, the billiard balls!

GORDON. Yes.

DULCY. Did you look in the pockets?

GORDON [*sadly*]. There are no pockets on a billiard table.

FORBES [*willing to let the whole world go hang*]. What's the difference—what's the difference?

DULCY. Maybe I did put them some place—now, wait—I wonder if I could have—no—I put the curtains there. [*A pause.*] I'll come right away and look for them. I think I know where they are. Gordie, you and Mr. Forbes come with me. [VAN DYCK *starts to improvise on the piano.*] That's right, Mr. Van Dyck—you keep *Mrs.* Forbes company. [*To* FORBES.] I'm awfully sorry about those balls. You know, sometimes I think I'd lose my head if it wasn't fastened on. [*She goes, carrying* FORBES *and her husband with her.*]

MRS. FORBES. We can go along and watch them play, if you like.

VAN DYCK [*still playing*]. Do you want to?

MRS. FORBES. Not particularly.

VAN DYCK. Then let's don't.

MRS. FORBES [*listening to the music*]. That's pretty.

VAN DYCK. I would much rather talk to you.

MRS. FORBES. A clever man can do both.

VAN DYCK. But I'm not clever.

MRS. FORBES. You're at least modest.

VAN DYCK [*playing all through this speech*]. No—I'm not even that. The downright truth is—I'm embarrassed by opportunities. Here I have a moment alone with you—you're perfectly willing to be entertained. If I could play at all well —which I can't—I should dash off something brilliant—now. And if I could talk well, which I can't, I should simply scintillate—for you. But, you see—I'm just mediocre. [*A pause. He continues to play.*] Perhaps I wouldn't be quite so annoyed with myself if it weren't for you.

MRS. FORBES. But you're doing splendidly. You have a most respectful audience.

VAN DYCK [*stopping playing abruptly*]. Oh, please, not that! You know you're—charming.

MRS. FORBES. And just what is—a charming woman?

VAN DYCK. A charming woman? She's the one I never meet until she's married someone else.

MRS. FORBES. You're incorrigible. Play something more.

VAN DYCK. Oh, no. [*He rises.*] I don't feel like playing. What do you say to a stroll?

MRS. FORBES. I'd like it. I've not been out since dinner.

VAN DYCK. It's pleasant here, isn't it?

MRS. FORBES. Yes, isn't it?

VAN DYCK. I have a little place like this in the East—in Abyssinia. The moonlight comes down through the trees— have you ever been in Africa?

MRS. FORBES. No. [*They start out through the windows.*]

VAN DYCK. You should go to Africa. I have some diamond interests— [*They stroll out.* HENRY *enters, takes a glance around the room, and arranges the cushions on the divan. As he is replacing the one on the end his eyes fall upon something in the easy chair. He picks up* ANGELA'S *necklace, which* FORBES *had dropped, thinking he was putting it in his pocket.* HENRY, *in a matter-of-fact way, puts it in his own pocket and goes up the stairs.* ANGELA *and* LEACH *enter through the windows.* ANGELA *is considerably excited.*]

ANGELA. It *was* cool, wasn't it?

LEACH. Was it?

ANGELA. Weren't you?

LEACH. No—I was—afire—afire with love for you, Angela.

ANGELA. Why, what are you saying?

LEACH. Oh, those deep burning eyes! The mystery of your hair! Angela, you're wonderful! I love you! Almost from the first moment I saw you, I've loved you—wanted you —longed for you! Why, I patterned my newest heroine just after you! To be with you is to breathe the perfume of exaltation! Angela!

ANGELA [*breathlessly*]. Vincent!

LEACH. I am offering you myself—everything that I am— Oh, it's true that I've knocked about some— [*Modestly.*] A good many girls have loved me, but I have never loved any but you, dearest. [*He kneels.*] Say that you love me—a little—even though that love is now no greater than the glow of a single firefly in the fading day!

ANGELA [*rising*]. Oh, Vincent—my genius!

LEACH. My sweetheart! [*He kisses her and then holds her off, looking at her.*] My wonder girl! Will you marry me? [ANGELA'S *head drops in assent.*] And the day? [*Embracing her again.*] Love cries for its own!

ANGELA. Whenever you say—Vincent.

LEACH [*getting an idea*]. Why not—ah—but you wouldn't!

ANGELA. What?

LEACH. Why not now—to-day—to-night?

ANGELA. To-night?

LEACH. Yes—why not—elope!

ANGELA [*pleased*]. Elope! [*Sober.*] Oh, but mother and father—

LEACH. I am thinking of them. Your father would not understand.

ANGELA. Don't you think so?

LEACH. No! He doesn't know how our hearts cry for each other!

ANGELA. But he might never—

LEACH. Darling, since the beginning of Time hearts have been broken because they were not brave. And think how romantic it would be—you and I stealing away in the night—just we two—together. [*He draws her to him, they embrace again.*]

ANGELA. Oh, Vincent!

LEACH. Angela, dear!

ANGELA. And we'd not tell anybody? [*Withdrawing a bit from him.*] Oh, Vincent, I'd have to! Mother and—

LEACH [*quickly*]. But not your father!

ANGELA [*hesitant*]. No, I shan't tell father. But, mother—and Mrs. Smith. We'll need her.

LEACH. Just think of it, Angela—you and I eloping! [*They embrace again.*] Won't the world be surprised! [*Enter DULCY.*]

DULCY. Oh, excuse me. [*They break—embarrassed.*] I haven't interrupted anything, have I? [*Hoping to God she has.*]

LEACH. Why—no.

ANGELA [*speaking simultaneously with LEACH*]. Why—yes.

DULCY. Can I guess it? [*ANGELA nods, too full to speak.*] Angela, oh, Angela— [*She goes to her, embracing her.*] Oh, if this isn't the most wonderful thing I've ever heard! It's—it's—it's—it's—wonderful, that's all I can say! I'm so happy I could cry! Good news affects me that way.

[*She turns and takes* VINCENT'S *hand, which he has been holding out expectantly.*] Vincent! I may call you Vincent now, mayn't I?

LEACH. Of course!

ANGELA. Mrs. Smith—we're going to need your help.

DULCY. Yes, darling, of course.

ANGELA. Now, it's a secret, and you must promise that you won't tell anyone.

DULCY. Why, no—I wouldn't tell a soul.

ANGELA [*after an assenting signal from* LEACH]. Well—Vincent and I—are going to elope.

DULCY. E-elope?

ANGELA. To-night.

DULCY. T-t-to-night? You mean—run away and get married? [ANGELA *nods her head.*] Why—why—why—why—that's wonderful—[*she grows incoherent*]—that's just marvelous! I never heard of anything like that! It's—it's—why, it's—

ANGELA. Now, remember—you're not to tell a soul!

DULCY. Oh, no, I wouldn't tell anybody, no— How soon are you going?

ANGELA. Just as soon as we can—aren't we, Vincent?

LEACH. Yes! If we can get away.

ANGELA. We want you to help us!

DULCY. Of course. You—you—you—should tell your mother. She'll be crazy to know about it.

ANGELA. Oh, yes.

DULCY [*indicates windows*]. I guess she must have gone out there. My, I'm so excited I don't know what to do next! I just feel like jumping up and down! [*Enter* BILL. DULCY *rushes to him.*] Willie, what do you think! [LEACH *and* ANGELA *try to stop her, but she's too fast for them.*] Vincent and Angela are going to elope!

ANGELA. Oh! And you promised—

LEACH. Now you've—

DULCY. Well, it—it just came out before I could help it. But—but Willie won't tell anybody. You won't tell anybody, will you, Willie?

BILL [*slowly to* ANGELA]. You're going to elope? With Mr. Leach?

ANGELA [*not quite meeting his eye*]. Yes. [BILL *looks from* ANGELA *to* DULCY, *then back.*]

BILL. I won't tell a soul.

DULCY [*vindicated*]. See?

ANGELA. Thank you.

BILL. Where are you going to elope to?

ANGELA. Why—where were we, Vincent?

LEACH. I hadn't thought about it just yet.

DULCY. There are lots of places—

BILL [*after a glance at* DULCY]. How about a marriage license?

ANGELA. Why, I don't know—Vincent? [*She turns to him.*]

LEACH [*weakly*]. Well, I thought we might find some place—

BILL. Going to take your father's car?

ANGELA [*who had not thought about it before*]. Yes!

DULCY. You could have had mine—but I broke it.

BILL [*to* DULCY]. I suppose this was your idea.

DULCY. Well, I helped.

BILL. Yes, I could tell. [*Again to* ANGELA.] Well, after you get this license and find a minister—

DULCY. Willie, you could help them some way, couldn't you? You know where to get a license and everything.

LEACH. Do you?

BILL [*a pause*]. Why—yes.

DULCY. See, that's why I told him!

BILL. I live in—Bronxville, and I know the borough clerk. We could go to his house and get a license.

DULCY. Oh, that would be lovely!

ANGELA [*weakly*]. Yes.

LEACH [*dubiously*]. Yes.

BILL. Yes. Then I could drive you wherever you wanted to go, and bring the car back—that is, if Mr. Leach wants it brought back.

DULCY. You see! Everything is working out splendidly! Now I'll tell you what we'll do! We'll—ah—we'll—ah—what do you suggest, Willie?

BILL. Is everything ready?

ANGELA. We just have to get our bags.

DULCY. They just have to get their bags. Vincent, now you go out and find Mrs. Forbes and tell her; then we'll all meet in the garage in ten minutes. I'll go up and get Angela's things for her. [*She starts up, then turns to consider.*] Now let me see— [*Enter* STERRETT.]

STERRETT [*coming forward with attempted carelessness*]. Oh, hello!

DULCY [*weakly*]. Hello.

ANGELA [*also weakly*]. Hello, Tom. [*An awkward pause.* STERRETT *sees that there's something in the wind and that he's not part of it.*]

DULCY [*coming to the rescue*]. There's nothing the matter.

STERRETT. Oh—excuse me! [*He turns on his heel and goes.*]

ANGELA. You don't think he suspected?

DULCY. Of course not. I told him there was nothing the matter. Now let's see—Vincent—you go out and find Mrs. Forbes, and then go to the garage and wait for us there. Now, quick, quick! Go right through the tomatoes!

LEACH [*with his eye on* BILL]. Yes, but you know, I can drive a car, too, for that matter.

DULCY. Hurry up! The less speed the more haste, or something!

LEACH. All right. [*To* ANGELA.] My dream woman! [*He is gone.*]

DULCY. Oh—well, now that's settled. I'll go up and get the things, and we'll all meet in the garage in ten minutes!

ANGELA. I'll go with you!

DULCY. No, I'll bring everything out to the garage. If anybody sees me they won't suspect. You know, I'm so excited! Now you two hurry right out! Vincent will meet you there! My, it's—it's just like times of old when knights were bold! [*She gallops up the stairs.* ANGELA *looks uncertainly at* BILL, *starts out quickly, then pauses—to face whatever he may have to say.* BILL *turns and speaks quietly.*]

BILL. All ready for the elopement?

ANGELA. I think—I think you're just horrid.

BILL. Speaking to me?

ANGELA. You know very well I am.

BILL. But of course you don't mean it. I'm really being very good to you—helping you out in this way.

ANGELA. Well—well—you don't have to be so happy about it. After all we—we *are* old friends!

BILL. But that's why I'm glad. You're glad, aren't you?

ANGELA. That has nothing to do with it! [*A pause.*] Of course I am! [*Another pause.*] You're just—just impossible!

BILL. Angela, you told me once that I would never change. You were right—I never *have* changed.

ANGELA [*almost in tears*]. Oh, I don't care whether you have or not! I think you're positively hopeless! [*She flounces out through the French windows.* BILL, *left alone, looks after her a moment, then starts out, but seeing someone coming downstairs, he pauses at the window. It is* HENRY *on the stairs. He wears a sack coat and is carrying a derby. He seems hurried and nervous. As he turns to go,* BILL *touches him on the shoulder.* HENRY *starts.*]

BILL. Hello, Henry!

HENRY [*collecting himself*]. Yes, sir.

BILL. What seems to be the trouble?

HENRY [*nervous*]. Trouble, sir?

BILL. Yes.

HENRY. Oh, no trouble, sir. Have you the time, sir? [BILL *takes out watch, somewhat absent-mindedly holding it too closely to* HENRY—*then, realizing this mistake, turns away to consult it.*]

BILL. Sixteen minutes after ten.

HENRY. Thank you, sir. Excuse me, sir. [*He hurries out.* BILL *stands a moment, undecided whether to investigate* HENRY, *then turns and goes out through windows. Enter* GORDON *and* FORBES.]

GORDON. I'm—I'm sorry, but Dulcy—my wife—must have had the table moved for some reason, and then didn't get it quite level when it was put back.

FORBES. Oh, that's all right—that's all right. In fact, it was rather novel—playing billiards up and down hill.

GORDON. Probably I can have it fixed before you go home, and then—

FORBES. Doesn't matter, I assure you. I—ah—I—don't care very much for billiards, anyhow.

GORDON [*growing desperate*]. Some other time, then. Maybe you'd like to—to look at some new golf clubs I just got?

FORBES. What? [MRS. FORBES *comes through the windows. She is in a state of suppressed excitement, which becomes more suppressed when she finds her husband present.*]

MRS. FORBES. Oh, hello, dear!

FORBES [*sourly*]. Hello.

MRS. FORBES [*fencing*]. Who won the billiard game?

FORBES [*violently*]. Mrs. Smith!

MRS. FORBES. Have you—seen anybody?

FORBES. Have I *what?*

GORDON [*anxious to get away*]. Suppose I—go and lay out those golf clubs awhile, and—then you can come—later.

FORBES [*almost viciously*]. Yes—suppose you do.

GORDON. Yes, yes. All right—all right. [*He wipes his forehead nervously as he goes out.*]

MRS. FORBES [*casting apprehensive glances up the stairs and out the windows*]. What's the matter, dear?

FORBES. What's the matter? Why—why—good Heavens, the—the—

MRS. FORBES [*half fearful that he has learned about the elopement*]. Nothing has happened, has it?

FORBES. Happened? I should say it has!

MRS. FORBES [*alarmed*]. What?

FORBES. I go in here to play a game of—[*viciously*]—billiards. I think finally that I'm going to get ten minutes of pleasure out of this week-end, and—and—what do I find?

MRS. FORBES [*sweetly*]. Well?

FORBES [*yelling*]. What's the difference? [*A pause.*] You don't give a darn—you just go ahead carrying on with that fellow Van Dyck.

MRS. FORBES. But, sweetheart—

FORBES. Oh, I saw the way that woman fixed it up for you! And Angela—where's Angela?

MRS. FORBES [*nervously*]. I don't know, dear. [DULCY, *carrying two suitcases, comes tiptoeing down the stairs.* MRS. FORBES *sees her and* DULCY *wigwags to her to be quiet.* FORBES *is well down stage, with his back to* DULCY.]

FORBES. Out gallivanting with that moving picture nincompoop, I suppose. More of that woman's work!

MRS. FORBES. Mr. Leach—do you mean?

FORBES. Yes, Mr. Leach I mean! [DULCY *has reached the windows;* MRS. FORBES *is signaling to her.*] Just imagine having a fellow like that in the family—telling you—outlines. And the idea of you standing idly by while he and Angela— [*He sees* MRS. FORBES' *signals.*] What the devil's the matter with you? [DULCY *slips through the windows.*]

MRS. FORBES. Why, nothing, dear.

FORBES. Then stand still! And listen to me. If I find this Leach person actually making love to Angela, why, I'm— I'm going to raise hell, that's all. It's been nothing but a series of aggravations—annoyances—ever since I came into this house. Eleanor, I can truthfully say that in all my fifty-three years I have never spent an unhappier evening.

MRS. FORBES. Oh, Charlie!

FORBES. But I am not going to spend another! I am not going to stay here and ride golf and play horse-back!

MRS. FORBES. What are you going to do?

FORBES. I am going—home!

MRS. FORBES. Charlie!

FORBES. I'm going upstairs and pack! I promised Sterrett I'd drive him in to-night, and I'm not coming back! There's another thing! The way they're treating Sterrett! [*Starting up the stairs.*] Good *night!*

MRS. FORBES. Charlie—you can't do that!

FORBES. Maybe I can't, but I'm going to! You can stay here with Van Dyck and watch Angela carrying on with that Leach person if you want to. BUT—mark my words—if anything comes out of this—if Angela and that fool *are* infatuated with each other, and try to do anything silly—I don't ever want to see *you* or *her* again! That—is all! [*He storms up the stairs.* MRS. FORBES *looks after him a minute.* DULCY *enters through the windows and romps over to* MRS. FORBES.]

DULCY [*gleefully*]. Well, they're gone!

MRS. FORBES. Oh, I'm scared! Can't you call them back?

DULCY. Huh? Why, it's lovely!

MRS. FORBES. No—no! I've got to tell him! If I don't he'll—he'll never let me come back to him! He means it—I know him!

DULCY. Vincent and Angela have eloped and everything's fine!

MRS. FORBES. Fine? But—but—oh, it was all *your* doing! That and—Mr. Van Dyck, and—everything! Charles

would never have talked to me like that if it hadn't been for
you. [*Sobbing.*] He never talked to me like that before.

DULCY. Why, Mrs. Forbes, dear, you're tired.

MRS. FORBES. No, I'm not! I'm just mad, that's all—
mad at you! It's all your fault! If my husband ever knows
that—that I knew they were eloping, and didn't stop it, why,
he'll—he'll—oh, I don't know what he'll do! [*She breaks
down, sobbing.*]

DULCY [*wanting to pat her and not quite daring to*].
There, there, dear. Why, he won't do anything. He'll be the
first to congratulate— [*Enter* GORDON.]

GORDON [*coming toward them*]. Good Heavens, what's
all this about? What's the matter?

DULCY. It's nothing at all, darling. Just—just—
[FORBES *comes down the stairs. He is wearing a duster and
carrying his hat and suitcase.*]

GORDON. Why, Mr. Forbes!

MRS. FORBES. Charlie!

FORBES [*still boiling within*]. Mr. Smith—I—I am returning to New York—important business. My—ah—wife
and my daughter will remain here, I *believe*. I don't *know*
anything about them.

GORDON. But, Mr. Forbes, I don't understand.

FORBES. So far as our little deal is concerned, I—I haven't
made up my mind yet whether to go ahead with it or not.

GORDON. My dear sir—

MRS. FORBES. Oh, Charlie—Charlie—I want to tell you
something! [*She starts towards him, but* DULCY *stops her.*]

DULCY. Now, Mr. Forbes, you don't really mean what
you are saying. When in anger, you should always count ten.

GORDON [*sternly*]. What is this all about? [*Everybody
starts to tell him at once and all are talking as* VAN DYCK
enters through the windows.]

VAN DYCK. I've got it! [*Seats himself at piano.*] I just
thought of it!

DULCY. Ah—ah—huh?

VAN DYCK. You know, that little thing I couldn't remember. It was a little Sicilian love song—it went like this. [*He
launches into a pretty little thing.*]

FORBES [*after a few bars have been played, in great indignation*]. Oh!! [*He stalks out through windows.*]

GORDON. Mr. Forbes—Mr. Forbes! [*He follows him out.*]

MRS. FORBES. Charlie—Charlie! [*She follows.*]

DULCY. Oh, Mr. Van Dyck!

VAN DYCK. Do tell me, what's the trouble? Is Mrs. Forbes—

DULCY [*shaking her head*]. It's—it's Mr. Forbes.

VAN DYCK. Mr. Forbes?

DULCY. He just got angry—for no reason at all, and now he's going back home in his car. . . . [*She remembers that the car is gone.*] He thinks.

VAN DYCK. Dear me!

DULCY. But the worst of it is—he's awfully angry at Gordon, and—he won't go ahead with the business thing.

VAN DYCK. Business thing? Is that the—now, I don't want to seem inquisitive, but is that the jewelry merger I've heard discussed?

DULCY. Yes. Didn't you know? Well, Mr. Forbes was getting up one, and he was going to give my Gordie some of it. [*Her mood changes.*] I hope it *is* all off—only sixteen and two-thirds per cent.

VAN DYCK. Just a minute. As I understand, it was a combination which would have taken in about fifty per cent of the jewelry trade.

DULCY [*approaching tears*]. Yes, I think so.

VAN DYCK. And now Mr. Forbes is leaving your husband out of it? Is that right?

DULCY. Yes. [VAN DYCK *considers very seriously.*] Why? Oh, dear, maybe I shouldn't have told you. [VAN DYCK *in deep thought.*] Oh, oh, I wish I hadn't told you. [VAN DYCK *wheels with decision.*]

VAN DYCK. Mrs. Smith!

DULCY. Well?

VAN DYCK. Mrs. Smith, I like your husband very much.

DULCY [*greatly pleased*]. Oh, do you?

VAN DYCK. Would he be willing to get up his own merger, one bigger than Mr. Forbes ever dreamt of?

DULCY. Why—what do you mean?

VAN DYCK. Why doesn't he beat Mr. Forbes at his own game?

DULCY. Why—why—I never thought of that. But Mr. Forbes has all the money—and—and Gordie hasn't any.

VAN DYCK. That's it exactly! Now, I've always wanted to take a little flier in the jewelry business. Suppose I financed Mr. Smith—suppose he and I set out to beat Mr. Forbes together? How would that be?

DULCY [*incoherent*]. Be? Be? Why, it would be increditable—unbelievable! [*Tearfully.*] You—do you really mean it?

VAN DYCK. I do. I'll put up my check the moment your husband says the word.

DULCY [*crying with joy*]. Oh, Mr. Van Dyck, you've—you've made me the proudest woman in all the world! You let me break the news to him, won't you?

VAN DYCK. Why—of course, if you wish it.

DULCY. And to think I introduced you to him! Now, what will he think of me! [*Excited voices are heard off.*]

VAN DYCK. It's Mr. Forbes again!

DULCY. Is it?

VAN DYCK [*at the door*]. Perhaps I'd better go. My golf things are fearfully rumpled. Will I find your man Henry through here?

DULCY [*her mind on other matters*]. He's around somewhere. [VAN DYCK *goes.* DULCY *is almost hysterical with happiness. The voices outside become definite.*]

MRS. FORBES. But, Charlie dear, calm down a little, and don't fly off the handle!

FORBES. Handle! Handle, madam! Do you realize what has happened? [*He enters during this speech, wearing his coat and hat, and still carrying the suitcase. Stops short at sight of* DULCY; *then walks to her with terrible calm.*] Mrs. Smith. [*He pauses.*] Mrs. Smith, upon going to your garage, I first discovered that my car was gone.

DULCY. Oh, but that's nothing— [GORDON *appears in the windows.*]

FORBES. Just a moment, please! My wife thereupon informed me that you had told her that my daughter and Mr. Leach—have eloped! [*He is throwing a terrific emphasis on every word.*]

GORDON. What!

FORBES. Is—this—true?

DULCY [*quaking, but trying to be gay about it*]. Yes—yes! You see—

MRS. FORBES. It wasn't my fault, Charlie—honestly! [FORBES *silences her with a gesture, his eyes not leaving* DULCY.]

FORBES. Mrs. Smith— [*turning*] and Mr. Smith. I am measuring my words very carefully. Since—my car—is gone —and the last train—is gone, it seems that I shall be compelled to remain in this house—over night. [*He pauses—his eyes find* DULCY.] I shall—endeavor not to commit a murder.

GORDON. My dear Mr. Forbes, I'm sure this can be fixed up in some way.

DULCY. Yes. Of course it can. [*The old* DULCY *for a second.*] You know, an angry word spoken in haste—

FORBES. Please! [*He turns to* GORDON.] Mr. Smith, in the circumstances I don't see how we can possibly get on in business together. I don't like your methods!

GORDON. But, Mr. Forbes—

FORBES. I shall not call the matter off entirely, but any arrangement which we might eventually make would necessarily differ from our tentative discussions as to percentage. [GORDON *starts to speak.*] I'm sorry, but that's my decision! [STERRETT *comes running on through the windows.*]

STERRETT. Mr. Forbes, Mr. Forbes— [*He comes between* FORBES *and* GORDON.]

FORBES [*snapping at him*]. Well, what now?

STERRETT. *Your car is not in the garage!*

FORBES. You don't say so!

STERRETT. Leach and Angela were acting awfully funny! If you ask me, I think they've eloped in it!

FORBES. I was not aware that I *had* asked *you!*

STERRETT. But—how am *I* going to get back to town to-night?

FORBES. *You—might—try—skipping!* [STERRETT *tries to pass this off as a laugh, but a look from* FORBES *squelches him. He arranges an exit for himself.*]

STERRETT. Ah—well—I'll see if I can find them. [*He goes—somewhat precipitately.*]

FORBES [*to* GORDON]. I repeat—the percentage would have to be adjusted. And now I wish you good night! [*He makes for the stairs.*]

MRS. FORBES. Oh, Charlie, mayn't I come with you?

FORBES. It is a matter of utter indifference to me *where* you go!

MRS. FORBES. Oh, but, Charlie, it wasn't my fault—really it wasn't! I didn't know anything about it until after they eloped! [MRS. FORBES *follows her husband upstairs.*]

DULCY [*gleefully*]. Gordie!

GORDON [*turning and looking at her*]. My God, are you smiling?

DULCY. I've got the most wonderful news for you!

GORDON [*his anger rising*]. Is it a surprise? [*A pause.*] Dulcy—Dulcy, how could you?

DULCY. How could I what?

GORDON. You've ruined me—that's all. Ruined me. Dulcy, I'm afraid we don't hit it off very well—you and I. This thing is too big. Say what we may, it's come between us.

DULCY. Oh, no, it hasn't, darling. Wait till you hear.

GORDON. Hear? Hear what?

DULCY [*rising and approaching him*]. How would you like—to have Schuyler Van Dyck for a partner?

GORDON. A—partner? [*Going mad.*] More golf?

DULCY. Business.

GORDON. Huh?

DULCY [*with great excitement*]. How would you like to go in business with him, and have Taylor and Robbins and Spelvin and all those other people with you, and leave Mr. Forbes out of it? Get up—a—a—bigger merger than Mr. Forbes ever thought about, because—because you'd have all the money you wanted! Mr. Van Dyck said so!

GORDON [*dazed*]. He—says so?

DULCY. Yes! Think of that!

GORDON. Here! Wait a minute! You've—you've been talking to Van Dyck?

DULCY. Yes—just now!

GORDON. And he said that he'd finance a combination to beat Forbes and his crowd—with me at the head of it?

DULCY. He's just waiting for you to say the word, darling!

GORDON. I—I—I—can't believe it.

DULCY [*caressing him as if to restore his senses*]. But it's true—it *is,* dear.

GORDON. Why, it's—it's too good to be true. I—I could be rid of Forbes and put the business in for what it's worth. I—I could—

DULCY [*excited*]. Yes—oh, Gordon!

GORDON. I—I can really do big things! Why— [FORBES *comes downstairs.*]

FORBES. Excuse me. [DULCY *and* GORDON *break.* FORBES *is the pathetic sight of a strong man reduced to tears.*] I am sorry—to be compelled to make—another statement. I merely wish to announce—on top of everything else—that my daughter's pearl necklace has disappeared.

DULCY. Disappeared?

GORDON. What's that?

FORBES. In view of the fact that it took place in this house, I thought you might have a sentimental interest. I put it in my pocket not three-quarters of an hour ago, and now— [*Enter* VAN DYCK, *speaking as he comes in.*]

VAN DYCK. I'm sorry, but I've been all over the house and I can't find Henry any place. [VAN DYCK *senses that he faces a situation of some sort.*] He must have gone out. [GORDON *and* DULCY *exchange terrible looks.* DULCY *is the first to recover.*]

DULCY. Henry!

GORDON. Well, I'll be—

FORBES. What's that? Who's Henry? What's he got to do with it?

VAN DYCK. I'll look again, but I'm certain he's not here. [*He is about to start out.*]

GORDON [*stopping him*]. Before you go, Mr. Van Dyck— [VAN DYCK *halts.*] And just a second, Mr. Forbes— [*Stopping* FORBES.] We'll straighten out about the necklace later. Mr. Van Dyck, I understand that you have offered to back me with unlimited capital in an independent jewelry merger? [DULCY *sits, enjoying the situation.*]

FORBES. WHAT?

GORDON. Am I correct?

VAN DYCK. You are! Mrs. Smith has interested me very much in this matter. I'll put up the necessary capital, provided, of course, we can agree on the details.

GORDON [*willing to agree to anything*]. Oh, there'll be no difficulty about that. [*With dignity.*] I accept your offer. Mr. Forbes, you said a minute ago that you were not certain whether or not our deal was off. Well, I've decided! It *is* off! I am going to line up with Van Dyck and fight you— fight you till one of us is forced to the wall. But before I do it, I'm going to tell you *why* I'm fighting you! I'm fighting you because you tried to take advantage of me!

FORBES. Advantage?

GORDON. Yes, advantage! By offering me less than you knew my business was worth! You knew I was in a hole, and now you're going to get just what you deserve! You're going to get a first rate licking!

DULCY. Oh, Gordie!

VAN DYCK [*anxious to get away*]. I—I'll see if I can *find* Henry, but I'm afraid he's gone. [*He slips out.*]

FORBES. All right. Make your fine speeches, but when you talk about fighting, don't forget that I can fight, too. And before you win, you're going to know that you've been in a *real fight!* Remember that! [*He goes upstairs.*]

DULCY [*rising and going to* GORDON]. Gordie, darling, you were wonderful! [*Embraces him.*] But the necklace! Do you think Henry—

GORDON [*impatiently*]. What's the difference whether he did or not? I feel like a new man.

DULCY. Gordie, you see—I *was* of some use after all.

GORDON. Use! You were wonderful! [*Taking her in his arms.*] The best—the finest little wife in the world. [*He kisses her.*] I'm going to beat Forbes, dear—I'm going to succeed—and I'll owe it all to you.

DULCY. Wasn't it lucky, my finding Mr. Van Dyck?

GORDON. Lucky! It was an inspiration!

DULCY. And I *am* a real helpmate?

GORDON. My darling! [*She is again in his arms.*]

DULCY. My Gordie! [*The door bell rings.*] That's the door bell. You'll have to answer it, darling, since Henry isn't here.

GORDON. One of the neighbors, probably. [*He goes out, leaving the door open.*]

DULCY. Oh, Henry! [*Voices are heard off stage.*]

PATTERSON. Is this Mr. Smith's house?

GORDON. I am Mr. Smith.

PATTERSON. Can I speak to you a moment on a rather important matter?

GORDON. Won't you step in? [*Enter* BLAIR PATTERSON. *A man somewhat under middle-age, well groomed, and with quite an air of authority. He makes a good impression.* GORDON *follows him on, closing the door.*] Ah—my wife.

PATTERSON. How do you do, Mrs. Smith? I must apologize for calling at this hour. My name is Patterson—Blair Patterson.

GORDON. The attorney!

PATTERSON. Yes. I was referred to you by Mrs. Kennedy.

DULCY. Oh, across the street?

PATTERSON. Ah—yes. She said you had—guests. I just wondered if—among them—there is a Mr.—Morgan? Can you tell me?

GORDON. Morgan? Why, no.

DULCY. No.

PATTERSON. Well—is there a Mr. Ford?

GORDON. No. He's not here either.

PATTERSON. Mr.—Vanderbilt?

GORDON [*somewhat flattered*]. Vanderbilt? No.

PATTERSON. Mr.—Astor?

GORDON [*more flattered and somewhat surprised*]. No. I don't understand.

PATTERSON. H'm. Well, let me ask you—is one of your guests—tall, good-looking, plays the piano, interested in various —ah—investments—?

DULCY [*proudly*]. Oh, you mean Schuyler Van Dyck?

PATTERSON [*thoughtfully*]. Schuyler—Van Dyck.

DULCY. *He's* here.

PATTERSON [*slowly*]. Yes, I think I do mean Schuyler Van Dyck. I'm his cousin. [GORDON *and* DULCY *are cordiality itself.*] I—I've come for him.

DULCY. Come for him?

PATTERSON. Yes. His real name is Patterson—Horace Patterson. He has an hallucination that he's a millionaire. Goes round forming big companies— But I assure you he's perfectly harmless. [*He taps his head significantly as*

[THE CURTAIN FALLS.]

ACT III

*The scene is the same; the time is the following morning.
The windows are open and bright morning sunlight is
pouring into the room.*

[*The curtain rises on a bare stage and after a second* FORBES
*comes downstairs. He is utterly broken. After throwing
a hard look toward the easy chair he sits stiff and upright
in the side chair, groaning as he sits. He takes out his
cigar case; it is empty; with a growl he rises and looks
in humidor on table. There is nothing there. He sits
again in the same chair.*

STERRETT *comes tripping down the stairs.*

STERRETT [*blithely*]. Good morning, Chief!

FORBES. Got anything to smoke?

STERRETT. Oh, sure. [STERRETT *hauls out his cigarette
case and opens it.*]

FORBES. I meant a cigar.

STERRETT. Oh—just a minute. [*He goes for humidor.*]

FORBES. There's none there. None any place. Mrs.
Smith probably discovered that I *like* cigars.

STERRETT. Haven't you any in your room?

FORBES. Yes, but—ah—I don't want to disturb Mrs.
Forbes.

STERRETT. Oh, I thought you had separate rooms.

FORBES [*viciously*]. No. We have the bridal suite.

STERRETT. Well, Mrs. Forbes must be up by this time.
Why don't you go up and—

FORBES [*rising*]. Sterrett.

STERRETT. Yes, Chief.

FORBES. I don't want this to go any further—but I did
not sleep in the bridal suite last night. I—took a walk until
rather late and when I returned everyone had gone to bed.
I didn't know just which rooms were unoccupied, so I slept
on a couch in the hall.

STERRETT. All night?

FORBES. Now and then. I tiptoed into my room about four o'clock this morning to get this— [*Indicating his business suit.*] Did you ever try to get a suit of clothes out of a closet in the dark, without making any noise?

STERRETT. Why, no.

FORBES [*putting hand to his head*]. Oh, dear.

STERRETT. You're not ill, Chief?

FORBES [*sitting*]. I wouldn't be surprised. It would be too much to expect to get out of this with just a *mental* breakdown and a celluloid son-in-law.

STERRETT. Nothing new on—the necklace, I suppose?

FORBES. Oh, yes. It was brought back and I'm wearing it.

STERRETT. You're what?

FORBES. Don't you see it? [STERRETT *makes a weak attempt at a laugh.*]

STERRETT. Oh, Chief—Chief—you certainly have a sense of humor.

FORBES [*grimly*]. Yes, and at this time of the morning I'm at my best.

STERRETT. But—ah—I meant the police.

FORBES. Huh?

STERRETT. The police were sent for, weren't they?

FORBES. Probably. I asked Mrs. Smith *not* to send for them, so I suppose she did.

STERRETT. Well, if I were you, I'd put them right on it.

FORBES. It may seem impossible to *you,* Sterrett, but there are times when it does *not* pay to advertise. You may recall that my daughter eloped last night.

STERRETT. It has been a very painful experience for me, Chief.

FORBES. Well, damn it, you don't think it's been any diversion for me?

STERRETT [*hastily*]. Oh, of course not. [*Trying to say something comforting.*] As her father I can keenly appreciate how you're going to suffer.

FORBES [*giving him a look*]. Thank you. The reason I don't want the police sent for is that I'm not anxious to have my daughter's elopement become public.

STERRETT. Oh!

FORBES. I can see the newspaper headlines now. "Daughter of C. Rogers Forbes Elopes With Nut." [*A pause.*] I'm going to have it annulled—quietly.

STERRETT [*an idea dawning*]. Maybe they didn't get married!

FORBES. What?

STERRETT. Maybe they're not married yet! They couldn't get a license last night! I'll telephone—

FORBES. They made special arrangements to get a license. Mrs. Smith's brother saw to that. H'm. I rather liked him. I wondered what *he'd* do.

STERRETT. I never trusted him.

FORBES. And on top of everything else, the third member of the family gets the Van Dyck money behind him and practically tells me to go to hell.

STERRETT. Certainly is an unlucky house. What time are we going back to town? [GORDON *comes downstairs.*]

FORBES. Just as soon as possible.

GORDON [*who hasn't slept either. Meekly*]. Good morning.

STERRETT [*right back at him*]. Good morning.

FORBES [*after hesitating*]. Good morning. [*Looks away.*]

GORDON. Breakfast will be ready in a minute, if the cook is still here. [GORDON *goes out,* FORBES *not noticing that he has left the room.* MRS. FORBES *comes downstairs.*]

FORBES. Mr. Smith— [*Rises.*] After taking into consideration everything that has happened here since my arrival— [FORBES *turns at this point and notices* GORDON *is not in the room, but sees* MRS. FORBES.]

MRS. FORBES [*to* FORBES]. Good morning— [*Finishing it to* STERRETT.] Mr. Sterrett.

STERRETT. Good morning, Mrs. Forbes.

MRS. FORBES. Aren't you—going to speak to me—Charlie?

FORBES. I'm speaking to no one. [GORDON *returns.*] I will take up our affairs when I get back to the city—if I ever do. [*He sees* GORDON.] Mr. Smith, I was about to say, when you walked away a minute ago— [DULCY *comes downstairs. She is wearing bright sport clothes and is ready for a busy day, but is somewhat subdued.*]

DULCY. Good morning, everybody. All ready for breakfast? It's a lovely day, isn't it? Has anyone been out? The sun is shining; it's just good to be alive. How do you feel this morning, Mrs. Forbes?

MRS. FORBES. I'm rather depressed.

DULCY. Depressed? Well, you mustn't be. I have some wonderful news for you. It's a surprise. Who do you think will be here inside an hour?

FORBES. A couple dozen reporters, I suppose.

DULCY [almost singing it]. A bridal party.

FORBES. So they are married!

DULCY. Yes. Willie phoned me just now. He said they had trouble getting in touch with the license clerk. I suppose all those people are like policemen—when you want one you never can find one. Anyway, they got him up at last and they were married at midnight.

FORBES. By a Justice of the Peace?

DULCY. No, indeed. By Dr. Carmichael—he's one of the finest ministers in Westchester. Willie knows him awfully well, so I suppose he did it as a special favor. Wasn't it nice of him?

FORBES. Yes, I appreciate it.

DULCY. So now you have a genius in the family, Mr. Forbes.

FORBES. Is he returning the car?

DULCY. Oh, of course—they'll be here any minute now—the happy couple.

FORBES. You can give them—the bridal suite.

DULCY. But where will you sleep?

FORBES. I shall be returning to town as soon as the car arrives. [To GORDON.] Mr. Smith, I hope we can have a little talk before I go.

GORDON [meekly]. Just as you say, Mr. Forbes.

DULCY. Now, now, no business before breakfast. Come along—let's all go in before the grape fruit gets cold. [She returns to FORBES and takes his arm.] Mr. Forbes. You come in with me.

FORBES [disengaging himself]. No, thank you. I'm afraid I must be excused. I'm not very hungry this morning. [He goes up into windows.]

DULCY [feeling the rebuff]. Mr. Sterrett, you'll eat some breakfast, won't you?

STERRETT [always willing]. Why, surely.

MRS. FORBES [*stepping toward her husband*]. There isn't —anything—the matter, is there, Charlie?

FORBES. The matter? Oh, no! I'm just too happy to eat. [*He stamps through the windows.*]

DULCY. Gordon, darling, you must eat some breakfast. Come along.

GORDON. Dulcy, will you go ahead and leave me alone?

DULCY [*persistent*]. Mrs. Forbes, you'll have some breakfast? [MRS. FORBES *nods.*] Ah! [*Victorious.*] You know, I'm never myself until I've had a cup of coffee in the morning. [STERRETT *opens the door for them.*] Of course, we're all depressed now, but maybe after breakfast I'll think of something to cheer us up. [*All but* GORDON *depart;* BLAIR PATTERSON *comes downstairs.*]

PATTERSON. Good morning, Mr. Smith.

GORDON. Oh, good morning, Mr. Patterson. *You*—slept well, I trust.

PATTERSON. Thank you—yes. [*Earnestly.*] I'm very sorry to have caused you this trouble.

GORDON [*dejectedly*]. Oh, that's all right. Ready for breakfast?

PATTERSON. Thank you. I'll take Mr. Patterson home with me just as soon as he can get his things together.

GORDON. There's no hurry—any more. Have you—told him?

PATTERSON. No, he hasn't seen me yet. I'll not have any difficulty; it's happened before.

GORDON. He's—a cousin, I believe you said?

PATTERSON. A distant cousin—it's really too bad. Brilliant chap—agreeable—obliging—

GORDON. He certainly is.

PATTERSON. Quite all right. Lives on Long Island with his mother and sister. Just this one hallucination.

GORDON. That's all he has?

PATTERSON. Oh, yes. Now and then he wanders off alone like this, but happily he never causes any real trouble.

GORDON. He doesn't, eh? That's fine.

PATTERSON. It's a little hard on *me*—being compelled to round him up at intervals. I have to divide my activities as a lawyer with those of a truant officer.

GORDON. Yes, it must be hard on you.

PATTERSON [*looking about and approaching* GORDON]. Ah—if I might ask a small favor?

GORDON. Certainly.

PATTERSON. I hope none of your guests has learned about my cousin's—weakness?

GORDON. I don't think so. [*With a look toward the windows.*] I hope not.

PATTERSON. If I may suggest it, it might be better to wait until I've taken him home, in case you wish to explain to anyone. It will save embarrassment. [VAN DYCK *comes downstairs.*]

GORDON. I won't say anything.

PATTERSON. Thank you.

VAN DYCK [*noticing* GORDON *only*]. Good morning.

GORDON. Good morning. [*He indicates* PATTERSON.] Here's a—friend of yours. [*Exit* GORDON *through windows.*]

PATTERSON [*turning*]. Hello, Horace.

VAN DYCK. Blair! Why, what in the world are you doing here?

PATTERSON. Oh, just dropped in to say hello.

VAN DYCK. You can't fool me. You've come to make me leave—that's what you've done.

PATTERSON. Oh, no—that is—unless you really want to.

VAN DYCK [*aggrieved*]. It's very—embarrassing.

PATTERSON [*annoyed*]. Well, if it's embarrassing for you, what do you think it is for me? I've a law practice to attend to. I'm getting a little tired of—these—excursions.

VAN DYCK. Well, I wish you'd leave me alone. At least half a dozen times during the past few years you've interrupted me in business negotiations that were exceedingly interesting.

PATTERSON [*suddenly suspicious*]. Have you been—putting through—something—here?

VAN DYCK. Well, yes—I've been representing my Van Dyck interests. We had all sorts of wonderful things planned. My share alone would have been eight and a half millions. Besides, we were going to play golf.

PATTERSON. Horace, haven't I told you repeatedly that I represent the Van Dyck interests? Now, you must let me handle it. You come back to town with me and we'll talk it over.

VAN DYCK [*protesting*]. But I can't leave *now*. If I do—

PATTERSON. I'm sorry, Horace, but you know our agreement. Unless you do as I say, I'll never go through with that two hundred million dollar aeroplane company of ours.

VAN DYCK [*appeased and smiling*]. Oh, all right. [*Enter* DULCY. *Coming face to face with* VAN DYCK, *she is startled and uncertain as to how to greet him.*]

DULCY. Oh, good morning. [*Timorously.*] How do you —feel this morning?

VAN DYCK. Very melancholy. [DULCY *sidles away from him.*] I'm afraid I must go back to town.

DULCY. Ah—! [*The height of sympathy.*]

VAN DYCK. You don't know how I wish I could stay.

DULCY. Ah . . . ! Well, that's too bad. Still, it's all for the best. You—you must have some breakfast first.

VAN DYCK. Oh, thank you.

DULCY [*in a whisper to* PATTERSON]. He can eat breakfast, can't he? [GORDON *comes back.*]

PATTERSON. Oh, yes.

VAN DYCK. I hope we're not the last.

DULCY. Oh, that's all right. The last shall be first and— everything. [VAN DYCK *goes. To* PATTERSON.] I had some soft boiled eggs prepared for him, and some soft milk toast—all very soft, you know. Is that all right? [PATTERSON, *with a nod, goes in for breakfast.* DULCY *is about to follow.*]

GORDON [*sharply*]. Dulcy!

DULCY [*turning nervously*]. Yes—dear.

GORDON [*very seriously*]. Dulcy, come here, please.

DULCY [*prattling on to cover her nervousness*]. I—I was just seeing about Mr. Van Dyck's breakfast—Mr.—Mr. Patterson's—I mean. He's—he's all right, really. I mean, of course, he isn't—*exactly* all right, but he's—he's all right for— for what he is—and—I mean—everything *could* be much worse—couldn't it, darling? [*She finishes rather weakly, going to* GORDON.]

GORDON. Dulcy—do you realize—exactly what has happened?

DULCY. Well, I—I don't know—I think so. Oh, Gordie, I didn't mean to—

GORDON [*simply and kindly*]. You must listen quietly, dear, until I finish.

DULCY [*momentarily subdued*]. Yes, darling.

GORDON. The time has come when—I must speak—frankly. [*A pause.*] Do you know what Mr. Forbes is going to say to me when he learns who Van Dyck really is? [DULCY *shakes her head; she cannot speak at the moment.*] He is going to tell me that my factory and my services are of no use to him. Mr. Forbes thinks—that he has been made a fool of, and—he's right. Our future success—depended entirely on him.

DULCY. But—but—we haven't really done anything to him. Just because we—we asked for more.

GORDON. It wasn't—our asking for more.

DULCY. Oh, you mean the elopement? [*She considers.*] He doesn't like pictures.

GORDON. That was the crowning mistake.

DULCY. It was me again. It was me as usual. Oh, dear —how will it all end! [*She sinks onto the sofa.*]

GORDON [*slowly*]. Forbes will probably force me out of business. Then I'll have to start in all over again without— [*He glances around the room.*] Without—this.

DULCY [*forcing herself to say it*]. And without me?

GORDON [*dispassionately*]. Dulcy, I love you. I shall always love you. I don't know whether it's because you have the soul of a child, or in spite of the fact that you act like one. [*He turns away.*] I don't know what the future is going to do to us. You mean well, but you just don't stop to think.

DULCY. I guess I don't think—I just think I think. [*Rising and speaking bravely.*] I'll let you go, darling—if you want me to. I'm just—all wrong. I'm—a false note. I always wondered how I'd be able to make a man like you care for me—it seems so absurd for a man like you ever to love— a false note. And now—we're finding out—he can't.

GORDON [*carried away for a second*]. Dulcy, we can't end everything like this! You're not a false note—you're a melody —a whole tune. [*A pause. He reverts to his previous mood.*] But I don't know what to do.

DULCY [*sadly*]. I don't think I can reform.

GORDON. No—I suppose not.

DULCY [*a bit hopefully*]. I could make out a kind of

budget of things not to do—you know, like the one we did for the household expenses.

GORDON. I'm afraid—that wouldn't do much good.

DULCY [*realizing that it's old stuff but hopefully trying it anyhow*]. I could make another promise. One that would take in everything.

GORDON. Oh, I know you'd try to keep it, but—

DULCY [*with tears in her voice*]. Oh, but I *would* keep this one! Dearest, if you'll let me, I'll promise that I'll never interfere with your business affairs again.

GORDON. But you practically promised that once, and—

DULCY. I mean in any way whatever! Inviting people to parties, and everything! I'll—I'll revolutionize myself.

GORDON [*turning sharply*]. Dulcy, I don't want you to change yourself a bit. I love you just as you are. [*With desperate earnestness.*] I simply want you to let me handle my own affairs. Promise me that you won't even suggest helping me in business.

DULCY [*hysterically*]. All right, I'll promise! And I'll keep it! I will!

GORDON [*embracing her*]. I'm sure you will!

DULCY. I will, I will! And furthermore, I'll do everything in my power to repair the damage I've done.

GORDON [*thoroughly frightened*]. Repair it?

DULCY. Yes—about Mr. Forbes. I'll go to him and tell him how sorry I am, and see if there isn't something I can do— [FORBES *comes striding in through the windows.*]

FORBES. I beg your pardon, but it is extremely necessary that I get back to town immediately. Can I get a car anywhere in the village?

GORDON. Oh, but, surely—you're not going before we have our little talk?

FORBES. I regret that I must.

GORDON [*evidently conspiring to keep him there*]. But—I'm afraid you can't get in—this morning. There are no cars to be had out there—so, if you'll just make yourself comfortable—

DULCY [*spilling the beans*]. Oh, yes, he can get a car, darling— [*Starting off.*] He can get one right away. I'll phone Kelly. Kelly always has a car.

GORDON [*following her*]. But, Dulcy—

FORBES. Thank you very much, Mrs. Smith.

GORDON. But, Dulcy—Dulcy— [*Turning back to* FORBES *hastily.*] I'll be back. Dulcy! [*He races out after her.* FORBES *takes a turn around the room, automatically reaching for his cigar case, which he opens and finds empty. Enter* BLAIR PATTERSON.]

FORBES. Why, Mr. Patterson—

PATTERSON. Oh, it's—ah—

FORBES. Forbes. C. Roger Forbes.

PATTERSON. Oh, of course. [*He shakes his hand.*]

FORBES [*puzzled and suspicious*]. I—ah—I didn't know you were a friend of Mr. Smith's?

PATTERSON. Well—ah—no—that is, yes—I—

FORBES. H'm. Came down—this morning, did you?

PATTERSON. Ah—yes, yes. Just—got in. Beautiful country.

FORBES. Isn't it? [*A pause.*] The Van Dyck interests seem to keep you quite busy.

PATTERSON. Ah—yes, yes.

FORBES. I was just—wondering what had brought you, and—

PATTERSON [*in a corner*]. Yes.

FORBES. H'm. [*Lightly.*] Must be—something pretty important—for him to send for *you* at—this hour?

PATTERSON. Well, ah—just a little matter of business, which he thought—advisable— [*He finishes with a cough.*]

FORBES. I see. What I was about to say was—of course, I don't know just what Mr. Van Dyck is thinking of going into, but—ah—if I had a client who was—thinking of *going* into it, why, I'd look into it pretty thoroughly myself. Now I can give you a good deal of facts about— [*Enter* STERRETT *and* VAN DYCK.]

STERRETT [*as they enter*]. Well, that's certainly very interesting to me.

VAN DYCK. Yes, I—I hoped that it would be.

STERRETT. Well, Mr. Forbes, if you want *me* to handle your advertising after this you'll have to bring it to a different office.

PATTERSON [*suddenly suspicious*]. What was that?

STERRETT. I've just fixed up a little deal with Mr. Van Dyck. I'm to head his new advertising agency!

FORBES. You don't say so?

PATTERSON [*with a side glance at* VAN DYCK]. Well!

FORBES. That's splendid! Anyone who can join hands with Mr. Van Dyck is a very fortunate person.

PATTERSON. Ah—would you care to finish your packing, Mr. Van Dyck?

VAN DYCK. All right, Blair. In a minute.

PATTERSON [*going up to the staircase*]. Well, whenever you're ready—Schuyler. [*This informality of address registers strongly with* FORBES.]

FORBES. Ah—now that we've met, Mr. Van Dyck, I hope we can see something of each other in town.

VAN DYCK. I trust so. As a matter of fact, there are several things I would be interested in going over with you.

FORBES [*eagerly*]. That so? What are they?

PATTERSON [*warningly*]. Ah—don't forget—Schuyler—your packing—

VAN DYCK [*airily*]. Oh, that's all right, Blair.

FORBES. You were saying, Mr. Van Dyck—

VAN DYCK. Well, it just occurred to me that we might have interests which—ah—

FORBES. Yes?

VAN DYCK. Which we might pool to advantage.

FORBES. Indeed, yes. Something of that kind has been in my mind for a long time. Of course I hesitated to suggest it to *you*.

PATTERSON. Don't you think that we'd better be—

STERRETT. Now, there's something I'd like to ask you, Mr. Van Dyck—and I hope you won't mind my—presuming. Ah —do you—that is, what is your attitude—just at present—on the market? Do you look for further declines, or— [*He pauses.*]

VAN DYCK [*importantly*]. No, sir.

FORBES. Ah!

STERRETT. That's very interesting.

VAN DYCK. As a matter of fact, I look for a sharp rise throughout the list.

FORBES. Indeed?

STERRETT. What do you base that on, Mr. Van Dyck? [*Quickly.*] If I may ask?

PATTERSON. I hardly think you have time to go into that now, Schuyler—

VAN DYCK. It'll just take a second. [*Pompously.*] The reason that I look for a rising market, Mr. Forbes—is—

FORBES. Yes?

VAN DYCK. Is that a war with Spain is now inevitable!

FORBES. A war with—Spain?

VAN DYCK. Exactly.

PATTERSON. Schuyler!

STERRETT. A war between—Spain and—this country?

VAN DYCK. Oh, no! That's it, exactly. Spain and— Abyssinia!

FORBES. What's that?

STERRETT. But I don't—

PATTERSON [*reaching across* STERRETT *and leading* VAN DYCK *away*]. Come, come. I really must get back to town, Mr. Van Dyck. There's a train that goes almost immediately. [*To* VAN DYCK, *confidentially.*] It's a matter of two hundred millions. [STERRETT *and* FORBES *exchange a glance.*] Sorry to take Mr. Van Dyck away from you, Mr. Forbes— Mr. Sterrett—but you know how it is. We'll see you presently.

FORBES. Certainly.

PATTERSON. Come along, Schuyler. [*He starts up with* VAN DYCK.]

STERRETT [*following*]. Mr. Patterson, you don't mind if I go up—along with Mr. Van Dyck, do you?

VAN DYCK [*turning back to him*]. Come right along, Mr. Sterrett. I haven't finished with you yet. [PATTERSON *is now on the stairs. The other two work their way up the stairs as they speak.*]

STERRETT. No, I didn't think you had. Now, if that April 1st date is O. K. with you—

VAN DYCK. Yes, and I'll tell you what else you can do for me. I have some copper interests out in Montana— [VAN DYCK, STERRETT *and* PATTERSON *go up the stairs.* FORBES *follows up to the foot of the stairs, looking after them. Enter* MRS. FORBES.]

MRS. FORBES. Oh—Charlie—

FORBES. Oh, it's you.

MRS. FORBES [*approaching*]. Charlie, it wasn't my fault—Angela, I mean. [FORBES *listens in stony silence.*] Honestly it wasn't, Charlie. [*She makes up her mind to stretch the truth just a little.*] I didn't know anything about it until after they'd eloped. Really I didn't!

FORBES. Well, I—I've no wish to be unjust, Eleanor.

MRS. FORBES. Then you'll—forgive me?

FORBES. You—you're telling me the truth? You didn't know anything about the elopement until—

MRS. FORBES. Until after Mrs. Smith told me.

FORBES. That woman!

MRS. FORBES. Then you will—take me back? [FORBES *looks at her, pinches her cheeks, then embraces her awkwardly.*]

FORBES. Eleanor, dear—my little widgie!

MRS. FORBES [*sinking into his embrace*]. Oh, Charlie, I'm so happy!

FORBES. My dear, this has been a most unfortunate visit.

MRS. FORBES. Yes, dearest.

FORBES. But it has done—one thing for me. I didn't know until I saw you with Mr. Van Dyck how much I really cared for you.

MRS. FORBES. Oh, Charlie—do you honestly? Say it again!

FORBES. I was actually—jealous.

MRS. FORBES [*embracing him*]. Charlie—how wonderful! I'll never talk to Mr. Van Dyck again, and I'll even give up the Smiths if you insist.

FORBES [*quickly*]. Oh, no, no, no. You must stay friendly with the Smiths no matter what happens. Smith's factory equipment couldn't be duplicated right now for any amount. I've got to have it.

MRS. FORBES. But, Charlie—

FORBES. Now don't go and tell him.

MRS. FORBES. Oh, I wouldn't.

FORBES. I just wanted to be sure. [*Enter* DULCY.]

DULCY. Oh, Mr. Forbes, they haven't any automobiles—just now. They said—maybe they'd have one later.

FORBES. To-morrow, perhaps?

DULCY. Oh, Mr. Forbes—I'm sorry— [*She pauses a*

second.] Sorry about—the elopement, I mean— [*There is no response from* FORBES.] And everything.

FORBES [*annoyed*]. It's quite all right, Mrs. Smith— quite all right.

DULCY. And I'm sorry about the business deal, too. But it's going to come out all right.

FORBES. What's that?

DULCY. I say the business deal between you and Gordie is going to come out all right.

FORBES. Oh, is it?

DULCY. Yes. Gordie will go in with you after all. Because Mr. Van Dyck isn't Mr. Van Dyck at all.

MRS. FORBES. What?

FORBES. What's that?

DULCY. No—he has something wrong up here. [*She taps her head.*] He only *thinks* he's a millionaire.

MRS. FORBES. Good heavens!

FORBES [*keeping calm*]. Oh—so Mr. Van Dyck is—not Mr. Van Dyck!

DULCY. No.

FORBES. I see.

DULCY [*after a pause*]. So everything's all right now, isn't it?

FORBES. Oh, yes. Splendid!

DULCY. And it's all right between you and Mrs. Forbes, too? [MRS. FORBES *smilingly puts her arm around him. He smiles at her.* DULCY *gurgles with joy.*] Ah—! H'm—! It was sweet of you to forgive her for helping with the elopement.

MRS. FORBES [*drawing back with an involuntary exclamation*]. Oh!

FORBES. For—helping with the elopement! [*To his wife.*] Then you—*did* know about it? You *helped!* [*He turns to* DULCY, *who has crept a few steps away, as if to escape.*] Did she? [*Enter* GORDON. DULCY *sees escape is hopeless.*]

DULCY. I—I—

FORBES [*to* MRS. FORBES]. And you told me you didn't!

MRS. FORBES [*sobbing*]. Oh, Charlie, Charlie—I didn't very much! And I was sorry I did, right away. [*She tries to embrace him; he puts her off.*]

FORBES. I don't care to hear anything about it!

MRS. FORBES. Oh, but, Charlie—

DULCY. Ah! Ah! [*She crosses to her.*] There! there!

MRS. FORBES. I feel faint.

DULCY. She feels faint! Come out into the garden and get some fresh air. [*Leading her into the windows and out.*] Breathe deeply, dear. Ten times. One—two—three— [*They are out of sight and hearing.*]

GORDON. I'm sorry. Sorrier than I can tell you—about all of it.

FORBES [*after a pause*]. Oh, Mr. Smith—I've just been hearing something from Mrs. Smith about Mr. Van Dyck.

GORDON [*scared*]. You—have?

FORBES. Yes.

GORDON [*he grits his teeth*]. Well, then of course you know that—

FORBES. Yes, I know. [*A pause*]. But it won't work, Mr. Smith.

GORDON. What's that?

FORBES. I'll admit that Mrs. Smith is a clever woman— a very clever woman. [GORDON *looks at him wonderingly.*] But it won't work. [*A pause.*] Van Dyck *not* Van Dyck. Hah! [GORDON *laughs nervously.*] I might have believed it—if I hadn't happened to meet Blair Patterson down here. No, Mr. Smith! I know Patterson, and I know that he represents the Van Dyck interests. A man like Patterson doesn't suddenly pop up in Westchester to talk business with a man with hallucinations!

GORDON [*not knowing just what to do*]. Oh! Well, of course you know—

FORBES. You bet I do! I saw it all! You began to be sorry you'd told me about the Van Dyck merger, and wanted to throw me off the trail—eh? Well, you can't do it. I know what's in the wind, and I'm going to hold you to your agreement.

GORDON. Agreement?

FORBES. Well, it was a verbal agreement. As a gentleman you agreed to come in with me and take sixteen and two-thirds per cent, and you've got to do it.

GORDON [*having difficulty in not betraying himself*]. But, Mr. Forbes—

FORBES. You've not signed anything with Van Dyck yet and it was just as good as settled with me. Now, if you don't— [ANGELA *bursts through the windows—still in her evening dress.* MRS. FORBES *and* DULCY *follow her.*]

ANGELA. Father!

DULCY. Well, here she is!

FORBES. Angela!

MRS. FORBES [*quaveringly, her hands on* ANGELA'S *arms*]. Angela, oh, Angela!

ANGELA. Oh, mother—father!

DULCY [*expectantly, as though awaiting a speech of forgiveness from* FORBES]. Well—?

FORBES [*as all eyes go towards him—a short pause*]. Are you—married?

ANGELA. Yes, father.

MRS. FORBES. Oh, she's married! [*She takes* ANGELA *into her arms.*]

DULCY. She's married!

FORBES. Well—where is your husband? [ANGELA *looks up at him, then buries her face in her mother's shoulder.*] Answer me, Angela! [*Enter* BILL. *He still wears his dinner clothes.*]

BILL [*quietly*]. Good morning, everybody.

GORDON [*casually*]. Hello, Bill.

DULCY [*carelessly*]. Oh, hello, Willie.

FORBES. Where is Leach?

ANGELA [*with a half smile*]. I don't know, father.

FORBES. You—don't know? [*To* BILL.] Well, perhaps you can tell us!

BILL [*shaking his head*]. I'm sorry.

FORBES. Didn't you help to arrange this wedding?

BILL. Why—yes.

FORBES. Well, don't you know where the groom is?

BILL. Sure—I'm the groom.

FORBES [*staggering*]. You're—wh-wh-what's that?

DULCY. Gr-gr-groom—Willie!

GORDON. What?

MRS. FORBES. Why—why—Angela— [*They all come together—there is a burst of excitement.* MRS. FORBES *embraces* ANGELA *again,* DULCY *embraces* WILLIE. FORBES *and* GORDON *exchange looks. Slowly the excitement dies down.*]

DULCY. Well—well, tell us about it! Good heavens! Willie! Just think!

ANGELA [*breaking from her mother's embrace*]. It was just the most romantic thing that ever happened in the world! William—William just kidnapped me, that's all! Oh, William! [*She goes into his arms.* DULCY *laughs ecstatically.*]

FORBES [*to* BILL]. Are you a—genius?

BILL. I should say not. [*They shake hands.*]

DULCY [*to* FORBES]. He's a broker! Isn't it wonderful?

MRS. FORBES. Oh, Charlie!

GORDON. Well, what about Leach—where is he?

BILL. I don't know.

DULCY. Don't know?

BILL. We started from here together all right last night—but—ah—down the road a piece I suddenly thought my tail-light was out. Mr. Leach was kind enough to get out and see that everything was all right; suddenly the darned thing started. I tossed his suit-case out to him—I don't think you'll ever see him again.

FORBES [*after a laugh—slapping* BILL'S *back*]. You're pretty damn clever.

DULCY. I introduced them!

FORBES [*to* DULCY]. Oh, so this was what you were working for, underneath that Leach business?

DULCY [*suddenly seeing a chance to claim the credit*]. Yes. [*She meets* BILL'S *eye.*] And no— [*She evades the issue.*] You don't understand women very well, Mr. Forbes. [*Enter* HENRY *with the morning papers.*]

GORDON [*taken off his feet.*] Henry!

HENRY [*as though it were all part of his duties*]. Good morning, sir.

DULCY [*to* GORDON]. Aren't you glad he's back?

GORDON. But—but—what's this mean?

DULCY. Oh, I forgot to tell you. Henry had to go to town last night— [*She lowers her voice.*] You know—to report to the Probation Officer. Every week.

GORDON. But—but—the necklace?

FORBES. Yes, the necklace.

DULCY. Oh, I forgot to tell you that, too. Henry found it last night and took it for safe-keeping. He gave it to me back this morning.

GORDON. He did?

HENRY. Yes, sir, I found it lying about, so I thought I'd better take charge of it, with so many people in the house. [*He departs.*]

DULCY [*takes her place between* BILL *and* ANGELA, *an arm around each*]. It's upstairs for you, Angie, dear. Think of Angie being a married woman, and Willie a married man! Now, Mr. Forbes, you know sixteen and two-thirds per cent isn't very much—for a relation, a brother-in-law.

FORBES. Well, I wasn't very generous about that deal of ours, or very just. Smith—

GORDON. Yes, sir.

FORBES. What do you say to coming in with me for twenty per cent?

DULCY. Twenty!

FORBES [*anticipating further objections*]. Well, then, twenty-five.

DULCY. Twenty-five!

GORDON. Dulcinea, that satisfies *me!*

DULCY. Does it? Well, if it satisfies Gordon— [*She turns to him.*] I didn't mean to interfere, dear. I never will again. You can rely on me. A burnt child dreads the fire. Once bitten— [GORDON *is embracing her and stops her with a kiss, as*

[THE CURTAIN FALLS.]

THE INTIMATE STRANGERS *

By

BOOTH TARKINGTON

Dramatic reviewing in America is usually supposed by historians of American literature to have begun with Pierre Irving and a group of his young friends in the early years of the nineteenth century in New York. Since those days there has been a succession of intelligent and independent play critics. In the weekly and in the monthly journals, some of the prominent names have been Laurence Hutton, William Winter, H. A. Clapp, John Corbin, Norman Hapgood, Clayton Hamilton, Walter Pritchard Eaton, Ludwig Lewisohn, and Stark Young. At the present moment in New York J. Ranken Towse is writing dramatic criticisms for *The New York Evening Post*. Alexander Woolcott, following the practice of the great French critic, Francisque Sarcey, adds to the tale of his day-to-day reactions in *The New York Times* a thoughtful essay on the current theatre which appears every Sunday under the heading "Second Thoughts on First Nights." Kenneth Macgowan is the dramatic critic of *The Globe* and a regular contributor to *Vanity Fair* on subjects connected with the drama. On *The Sun* the dramatic reviewer is Stephen Rathbun, on *The New York Herald,* Lawrence Reamer, on *The New York Mail,* Burns Mantle, and on the *Evening Telegram,* Robert Gilbert Welsh. Heywood Broun has recently migrated from *The Tribune* to *The World,* and his place on *The Tribune* has been taken by Percy Hammond, who made his first success as a play reviewer in Chicago.

It is Percy Hammond's criticism of Booth Tarkington's [1] play that has been chosen as a sympathetic introduction to *The Intimate Strangers:*

"For a while, in the course of *The Intimate Strangers,* you share with middle-aged Mr. Ames (Alfred Lunt) the perplexities of sex in which he finds himself involved by Mr. Tarkington. You know, as well as he does, that the mannerly Aunt Isabel (Miss Billie Burke) is a woman far superior to her rambunctious young niece (Miss Frances Howard). Yet, though you are in love with the older lady

[1] See for biographical sketch the same editor's *One-Act Plays by Modern Authors,* New York, 1921, p. 3.

(having just met her a few hours before) you feel an urge toward the vociferous woman-child as she plies you with the blunt seductions of her type. Though you are censorious of her perturbing demerits, you wish, when she is off the scene, that she would hurry back again. She is the kind of horsey nineteen-year-old that you think you abhor, but still, in the lingo of the maiden herself, she 'intrigues' you. . . . You discover, to your distress, that her bad habits are as interesting as are the good ones of her attractive aunt, to whom you are almost engaged.

This, of course, does not disparage the delightful impersonation by Miss Burke of the pretty and cunning spinster. That effort is a fine embodiment of adult charm, humor and beauty, helped or hindered, as you may be inclined to believe, by the player's judicious mannerisms. You divide your allegiance simply because you are weak and a man. You are indulging a man's prerogative for occasional bad taste in women. Mr. Tarkington ascribes this clumsy male attitude to the call of youth—the lure of 'breath all incense and cheek all bloom,' to the heedless laughter of the nineteen-year-old who thinks she is eternity's pal and that age exists only for others. She believes that maturity is antique and funny. 'Why is Aunt Isabel ashamed of how old she is?' this flapper shouts. 'I'm nineteen!' It might be interesting for you to analyze, if you are over thirty, your emotions in the matter, in the event that you have not already done so.

All is propitious in the romance of Mr. Ames and Aunt Isabel until the gusty advent of the virgin mænad. Having been castaways for ten hours in a desolate railway station in upper New York State, they quarrel over food and fall in love. Incidental to his soft avowals Mr. Ames announces his displeasure with the new generation of women. He has remained a bachelor because of his loathing for the loud, slangy, cigarette-smoking, gin-drinking, breeches-wearing ingenue of the day. He likes quiet women of gentle breeding, like Aunt Isabel, and he assures her that he will not care for her obstreperous kinswoman. In one of the most sweetly sophisticated interludes of Mr. Tarkington's achievements as a playwright, Mr. Ames and Aunt Isabel go to sleep on two benches in the desolate depot, almost engaged to be married. At least, they are tenderly solicitous about each other's comfort; and after sentimental negotiations they decide that both may be allowed to say 'Good night . . . dear!'

But arriving with the morning is the brisk flapper in breeches and bobbed hair, affronting the rural silences with ribald jocularities about the compromising position in which she finds her decorous aunt. She thinks it might be subject to interpretations . . . observing, meantime, that, by golly, he [Mr. Ames] isn't bad looking. 'Old,' of course, but still a prospect. 'Ab-so-lutely!' Dazed by her fascinations, he slips into her spell, and it is he who sits beside her as she drives the forty miles to the home of her and her aunt.

There it is that the two ladies strive each to win the visitor's admiration, the breezy virgin with the sex's most ancient tricks, the sedate spinster with its most modern ones. The niece talks to him with the obviously dishonest candors of her kind, telling him that he sure is a 'fast worker' and operating the eyes and the arms in the platitudinous gestures of the baby-wanton. Her favorite device is the prehistoric expedient of causing him every now and then to fasten or unfasten her slippers. All of which causes her youthful suitor (Mr. Glenn Hunter) to brood in bitter disapprobation and to make wise and cutting comment. Mr. Tarkington was never more humorous than he is in this character, and neither was Mr. Hunter.

Aunt Isabel, however, performs the oldest wiles in the newest ways. Knowing that Mr. Ames suspects her to be aged, because she is the great-aunt of the terrible infant, she feigns years and their infirmities, planning at the end to surprise him with her comparative youth. She acquires rheumatism, wears a shawl and woolen slippers, and talks to him (smiling to herself) of the World's Fair and President Harrison. When finally, after winning him, she offers him the family Bible so that he may calculate her age therefrom, he foregoes the information, and takes her in his arms.

Miss Burke's performance of Aunt Isabel is, to my mind, rather a noteworthy endeavor in comedy, embracing, as it does, in skillful fashion, the varying moods of the character—its twinkling pathos, its sagacities, its mockery and banter. It causes one to wonder why, as it is suspected, her reputation as a comedienne is less than her achievements entitle it to be. I recall few if any ill deeds in her stage career, and I remember one impersonation that was a masterpiece—that of Pinero's *Mind-the-Paint Girl*. *The Intimate Strangers*, by the way, was written by Mr. Tarkington for Miss Maude Adams who, wisely, I think, refrained from playing it." [1]

The Intimate Strangers is one of a lengthening list of Mr. Tarkington's plays. With Harry Leon Wilson he wrote *The Man from Home* (1907), *Cameo Kirby* (1908), *Foreign Exchange* (1909), *If I Had Money,* subsequently known as *Mrs. Jim,* and *Getting a Polish* (1909), *Your Humble Servant* (1909), *Springtime* (1909), *Up from Nowhere* (1919), and *The Gibson Upright* (1919). In 1917, Mr. Tarkington collaborated with Julian Street in *The Country Cousin.* He had Evelyn Greenleaf Sutherland as his collaborator in the dramatization of his *Monsieur Beaucaire,* known as *Beaucaire* (1901), in which Richard Mansfield is so happily remembered.

Other plays by Mr. Tarkington include *A Man on Horseback* (1912), *Beauty and the Jacobin* (1912), *Mister Antonio* (1916), in which Otis Skinner starred, *Clarence* (1919), *Poldekin* (1920), in which George Arliss took the principal rôle, and *The Wren* (1921). At least three

---

[1] Printed by courteous permission of Percy Hammond.

of Mr. Tarkington's stories have been dramatized by playwrights other than himself. *The Man from Indiana, Seventeen,* and *Penrod* have all made stage appearances.

The Intimate Strangers is Mr. Tarkington's contribution to the controversy which is now being waged on the subject of the manners and morals of the younger generation; not that *The Intimate Strangers* is a polemic—far from it. It is infinitely less doctrinaire in its attitude than Rachel Crothers's *Nice People,* produced also in the year 1921. Miss Crothers drew a lurid picture of the invasion of the social sanctities by the youths and maidens of to-day.

Booth Tarkington gets his verdict by means of the most delicate of satirical touches. His rapier wit does not hurt, for the button is on the foil. It is doubtful, indeed, whether since the days of Mark Twain there has arisen among our American writers of the first rank a man who so thoroughly understands the way young people reason and feel as Booth Tarkington. He knows the tastes of youth, the heart of youth, and the soul of youth; and so as a novelist and as a playwright, he is the possessor of a golden gift.

THE INTIMATE STRANGERS

CHARACTERS

(In the order of their appearance)

THE STATION-MASTER.
WILLIAM AMES.
ISABEL STUART.
FLORENCE.
JOHNNIE WHITE.
HENRY.
AUNT ELLEN.
MATTIE.

Produced by Erlanger, Dillingham, and Ziegfeld at the New National Theatre, Washington, D. C., October 31, 1921, with the following cast:

THE STATION-MASTER.............*Charles Abbe*
AMES ....*Alfred Lunt*
ISABEL ....*Miss Burke*
FLORENCE ....*Frances Howard*
JOHNNIE WHITE................*Glenn Hunter*
HENRY ....*Frank J. Kirk*
AUNT ELLEN ....*Elizabeth Patterson*
MATTIE ....*Clare Weldon*

SYNOPSIS OF SCENES

ACT I

*A railway station. A night in April. During Act I the cur-
tain is lowered to denote a lapse of a few hours.*

ACT II

The living-room at ISABEL'S. *The next morning.*

ACT III

The same. That evening.

ACT I

Scene

The rise of the curtain discloses a darkness complete except for an oblong of faintly luminous blue; this is a large window; and one or two stars are seen through the upper panes. After a moment a door up right is opened and a man enters carrying a lantern. He pushes a switch button near the door and two bulbs, shaded by green painted tin, come to life, right center, two other bulbs, left center, take on similar life simultaneously. These lights hang by wires from the ceiling.

The interior revealed is that of a small railway station, a "way station" at an obscure junction in the country. The walls are wainscoted in wood to a height of four feet; above that is plaster painted a tan brown. In the right wall (half way up) is the ticket window, with a little shelf; the up-and-down sliding inner panel of the window closed. Up to this, in right wall, is a door. In the back wall up right is another door, that which has admitted the man with the lantern. Center in the rear wall is the window. There is a stove, left, with a pipe running to the left wall. The only decorations are some printed posters giving notice of changes in train schedules, a Navy Recruiting poster, a "warning" concerning forest fires, a penny-in-the-slot weighing machine against the rear wall, and "No Smoking." There is a clock on right wall; it has stopped at seventeen minutes after six. The furniture consists of four or five wooden benches, with iron legs, the feet screwed to the floor; these benches are set in rigid rows, facing front; one straight behind the other. Upon the front one is seen a knowing, small lunch basket, closed but not strapped, and a very small thermos bottle. Several traveling bags, a couple of guns in cases and a trout-fishing outfit are there also.

*The man with the lantern is the station-master, ticket-agent,
telegraph operator, baggage-man, and janitor; but he wears
no uniform except a cap. He is elderly and smooth-shaven;
his clothes are elderly, too; though not shabby. A dark
old overcoat with the collar turned up; his rubber boots
are heavy with mudded clay, and his trousers are tucked
into the bottoms of them.*

*He goes casually near the clock; looks at it; grunts thought-
fully; goes out right, returns with a plain, wooden-seated
chair, once painted yellow; places it under the clock. He
moves the hands around to ten-twenty-four, consulting his
watch as he does so. Then he winds the clock.*

*As the winding begins, there is the sound of an annoyed yawn
from the apparently empty benches. A man has been lying
at full length on the bench second from front, and until
now, as he slowly " sits up," has been invisible.*

*He is " somewhere in the early forties"—but not yet " well-
preserved" looking. People of sixty would speak of him as
" a young man"; people of sixteen would of course think
him of an advanced age. He is urban, intelligent looking—a " man of the world"; very " attractive." His
clothes are of an imported texture, pleasant for travel, and
he has on a soft hat and a light-weight overcoat.*

The STATION-MASTER, *having wound the clock, looks at him.*

STATION-MASTER [*casually*]. Been asleep, I expect. [*Gets
down from chair.*]

AMES [*passing a gloved hand over his eyes*]. I have not.
[*He looks at the* STATION-MASTER *drowsily.*] You aren't the
same one, are you. [*He states this as an interesting dis-
covery; it is not a question.*]

STATION-MASTER. I'm not the same one *what?*

AMES. You aren't the same Station-Master that was here
this afternoon.

STATION-MASTER. He ain't no Station-Master; he's my
brother-in-law. [*Starts with chair.*]

AMES. Oh!

STATION-MASTER. He jes' *spelled* me to-day; I was
teamin'.

AMES. I *thought* he seemed to be an amateur.

STATION-MASTER [*moving right with the chair to return it*

to the room off right]. How? [*He means " What did you say?"*]

AMES. He seemed bashful. About giving any information, I mean.

STATION-MASTER. Information? He ain't got no infamation to *give*. Never *did* have.

AMES. He struck *me* in that light—particularly about trains.

STATION-MASTER. Well, right *to-night,* I ain't much better, myself. The wires are all down after them storms; the bridge at Millersville washed out on one road and they was a big freight smash on the other one. My brother-in-law says he told you *that* much.

AMES [*gloomily*]. Yes; he did tell me that much.

STATION-MASTER. Well, the Lord A'Mighty couldn't tell you no more till them wires start workin' again. [*He moves to go off right with the chair, then turns back.*] Where'd you say you was aimin' to git to?

AMES. Well, New York—eventually! [*Plaintively.*] I have a place there with a bed in it—and food.

STATION-MASTER [*reflectively*]. New York. You got to git from here down to Uticky first—then change for Albany.

AMES [*drearily*]. Yes, I know, I know. I made a mistake in coming round by this junction . . . I ought to have walked.

STATION-MASTER [*with a short laugh*]. I reckon! You'd a-got there pretty near as soon, mebbe. These here hurry-canes [*he means hurricanes*] got train service in this whole section jest about disorganized. They say it's sun-spots—*I* dunno if *'tis* or not, though. [*Exits right with his chair.* AMES *rises and goes to the window, he looks out toward off left. After a moment he goes to the door up right, opens it. Steps just outside the door, but remains in view. Then speaks to some-one invisible and apparently at a little distance off left.*]

AMES [*hesitating*]. Ah—don't you think this is pretty fool-ish? [*He waits a moment for an answer. None is heard; he speaks louder.*] I say, I think this is—ah—don't you think, yourself, this is pretty foolish? Ah—I'm sure you can *hear* me, you know! [*He waits again.*] Ah— [*He seems about to address further remarks to the invisible person; but decides not to do so, and with a somewhat baffled and puzzled air, comes in, closes the door, sits on first bench, murmuring rather crossly:*] Well, *all* right! [*Moves lunch basket a little center of bench. The* STATION-MASTER *returns from the room off right. He speaks as he enters.*]

STATION-MASTER. Nary a single click from my telegraph instament. [*He refers to room off right, then he comes over and looks at the luggage on the front bench.*] See you been gunnun. [*He means gunning.*]

AMES. What?

STATION-MASTER. See you been fishun and gunnun up in the woods.

AMES. Yes, I have been up at a lodge in the woods, that's how I happen to be here;—getting out of the *woods*.

STATION-MASTER [*examining the guns*]. Have any luck?

AMES [*abysmal*]. No.

STATION-MASTER. If you'd a-shot anything or caught any fish you'd a-done well by yourself to bring it along; you c'd a-built a fire and cooked it, anyways.

AMES [*roused to earnestness*]. See here; your brother-in-law told me there was absolutely *no food* in this neighborhood.

STATION-MASTER. He was right. They ain't.

AMES. But, my Lord, the people in this neighborhood have to live on *something!*

STATION-MASTER. Ain't no people in this neighborhood 'cept me and my brother-in-law's fam'lies.

AMES. Well, even you and your brother-in-law have to *eat*, don't you?

STATION-MASTER. My hens ain't layin'. [*Sits on front bench, center.*] We got jest three eggs in two days from seventeen hens.

AMES [*pessimistically*]. I suppose you used all three eggs.

STATION-MASTER [*with a dry laugh*]. I s'pose we did, among seven childern. We had nine potatoes left and about four slices o' bacon. That's all we had fer supper, and we won't have no breakfast at all unless the north-bound train gits through. April's an awful scanty month in the country, and I expected supplies to-day myself. You ain't the only one them sun-spots's been foolin' with.

AMES. I suppose that's as good an explanation as any for a train over eleven hours late—sun-spots!

STATION-MASTER [*looking in the lunch basket*]. Why, *you* got food here, right now. *Good* food!

AMES.   One chicken sandwich and one hard-boiled egg; left over from a light lunch—a *very* light lunch.

STATION-MASTER.   Well, why don't you eat it?

AMES [*shortly*].   It isn't mine.   [*Pushes basket to* STATION-MASTER.]

STATION-MASTER [*surprised*].   Oh!   [*He nods; glances up off left, and nods again, as if understanding.*]   Well, waitin' fer trains does git people kind of pettish with each other.   [*Rises and moves right.   Glances off left.*]   I noticed your wife's still a-settin' on that baggage-truck out yonder.

AMES [*shortly*].   She isn't my wife!

STATION-MASTER.   Oh!   Your lady, I mean.   She's still settin' out yonder, I see.

AMES [*rather bothered, shakes his head, mutters*].   She isn't my lady.   [*He gets up and goes to the window.*]

STATION-MASTER.   Well, excuse me.   My brother-in-law, he took her and you fer married.   [AMES *comes down left.*]   He told me you and her had kind of a spat, jest before he left here, this evenin'.   But of course a man's got a right to quarrel with other women's well's his wife.

AMES [*slightly annoyed with himself for being annoyed by this report of the* STATION-MASTER'S *brother-in-law*].   The— ah—lady and I were hardly—ah—quarreling.

STATION-MASTER [*placatively*].   To tell the truth . . . [*Crosses left.*]   My brother-in-law ain't hardly got sense enough to tell the difference between a couple that's quarrelin' and a couple that's jest kind of startin' to make *up* to each other like. [*Sits left end of front bench.*]

AMES [*more annoyed*].   This lady and I weren't doing either.   I never saw her before I got on the train this morning.

STATION-MASTER.   Well, that often happens.   I've knowed plenty of perfeckly respectable people to do it, too.   You might say it's *nature*.

AMES.   What is?

STATION-MASTER.   Why, fer strange couples to git to talkin' to each other—and all *so* on—on a train.

AMES [*rather crossly*].   I didn't speak to this lady on the train.   [*He goes up left and comes right down again.*]   In fact, we didn't speak to each other till we'd been moping about this God-forsaken station for an hour.   Then, as there wasn't anything else in the world in sight but mud—and your brother-in-law—and she didn't need to guess very hard to guess I was hungry—she offered to share her lunch basket with me, and we naturally got to talking.

STATION-MASTER. Well, sir, a person can git mighty well acquainted with anybody in about ten hours' talkin'.

AMES [crossly]. We haven't been talking for the *last* two hours.

STATION-MASTER. Got acquainted at noon and quit speakin' *already!* [Rises. Chuckles.]

AMES. Oh, no. She still speaks—at least she nodded to show that she heard me, the last time I spoke to *her*. [He is grimly humorous here, but does not smile.]

STATION-MASTER. Well, sir; it's funny, some people don't more'n say howdy-do, they can't neither of 'em hardly stand a word the other one says. [Crosses right.] I sh'd think she'd be *chilly* out there, by *this* time, though.

AMES [looks at the STATION-MASTER earnestly]. You seem to be a man of unusual experience. [Crosses center.]

STATION-MASTER. Unusual? I guess if you think that, you ain't married.

AMES [muttering]. No, and not likely to be.

STATION-MASTER. Look out, mister! *No* man in a spat with a lady ain't *safe!* Where's she bound fer?

AMES. I think she said a station about thirty or forty miles from here—Amity.

STATION-MASTER. Amity? She's worse off'n what *you* are!

AMES. No, that's impossible!

STATION-MASTER. Amity's on the *branch* line. *Everything's* blowed to hell down *that* way; creeks over the rails and all.

AMES. Isn't there *any* way of getting a motor car? [Rises.]

STATION-MASTER. Not with the telephone lines down like they are. I don't reckon no car could git through these roads, neither.

AMES [gloomily]. Yes; so your brother-in-law said. [A clicking is heard off right.] Isn't that your telegraph instrument? [Indicating right.]

STATION-MASTER [jumping up]. So 'tis. [Going right.] That means they got the wire up again at Logan's station.

Well, *now* we'll see what's what, mebbe! [*Exits right, leaving the door open. The telegraph instrument can be heard clicking.* AMES *listens at the open door, right, a moment; then he goes to the door up right, opens it, and speaks off; as before.*]

AMES. I think you'd better come in now, Miss Stuart. [*In response, a thrillingly lovely voice is heard, though the words are not necessarily discernible. However, what* MISS STUART *says is,* "*I'm quite comfortable here, thank you.*"] I really think you'd better come in. There may be some news of your train—or mine! [*This seems to mean more to* MISS STUART *than have his previous appeals. Her voice is heard again,* "*Oh!*" *She is evidently approaching.* AMES, *seriously.*] That's better. Do come in and be sensible. [*Her voice is heard once more before she appears. A faint amusement and protest are audible in it:* "*Sensible? My dear sir!*" *He holds the door open for her as she appears and comes down. Then he follows. She is of a lovely and charming presence; one is aware of that instantly though she is pretty thoroughly muffled in furs and veils; and one becomes even more aware of it as she pushes up the veil from her face as she comes in. A muff is held in her left hand.*]

MISS STUART. My dear sir, I think maybe I could be more sensible if the news turns out to be of *my* train. Could you stand its being about my train instead of yours, Mr. Ames? [*Comes down right. She has gone toward the lunch basket.*]

AMES [*a little stiffly*]. If mine came first you'd be relieved of *me*. [*At upper end of benches, left.*]

MISS STUART. Yes; so I should. [*She lifts the lid of the lunch basket, closed by the* STATION-MASTER.] Oh, you haven't eaten the sandwich—nor the egg either! [*As if in reproachful surprise.*]

AMES [*stiffly*]. Certainly not. [*Comes down left.*]

MISS STUART [*lifting a hard-boiled egg from the basket daintily, in a gloved hand*]. Didn't you even *nibble* at it? [*She looks at him, not at the egg.*]

AMES [*stiffly*]. I did not.

MISS STUART. Are you sure?

AMES [*indignantly*]. I'm not in the habit of "nibbling" things.

MISS STUART [*with a hint of suspicion and severity*]. You're *sure*? I knew a Bishop once who used to steal little bits of icing off of icing cakes. He'd slip out in the kitchen on baking days when no one was looking—and then he'd deny it!

AMES [*coldly, interrupting her*]. I'm not a Bishop, please.

MISS STUART [*reasonably*]. How could I tell? I've only known you— [*She glances at the clock.*] Ten hours and thirty-some minutes, and this is the first time you've *mentioned* that you're not a Bishop. [*With an increase of severity.*] *Why* didn't you eat this egg?

AMES [*coldly*]. You know perfectly well why I didn't.

MISS STUART. But I thought you *would,* if I left you alone with it. I've left you alone with it on purpose—two hours. I'm afraid you're stubborn.

AMES. *More* personalities?

MISS STUART. Well, doesn't a question of what one eats *have* to be rather personal?

AMES. I think you *made* it personal when you lost your temper.

MISS STUART [*interrupting*]. When I lost *my* temper? Oh, oh!

AMES. But you did! [*Coming towards her.*] You lost your temper and declined to sit in the same room with me. Rather than do that you went out in the night air and sat two hours on a baggage truck! [*Turns away to left.*]

MISS STUART [*hurriedly*]. Please listen, Mr. Ames—your name *is* Ames, isn't it? [*There is a stronger hint of humor in her voice.*]

AMES. You seemed to have no doubt of it before you lost your—

MISS STUART [*interrupting*]. Mr. Ames, let's put it this way: I lost—*your* temper; as for *me,* it seems at least you ought to distinguish between a loss of temper and a sense of injury.

AMES [*quickly*]. Yes, I had the sense of injury.

MISS STUART. When we found there was only one egg and one sandwich left for *dinner,* and no other food in reach, I said—

AMES [*interrupting*]. You distinctly said it wouldn't be enough for *two.*

MISS STUART. Yes. That's what I " distinctly " said. It really isn't enough for *one,* is it?

AMES. Need I explain again, I had no intention of asking to share it with you?

MISS STUART. *No. Don't* explain again. When I said there wasn't enough for two I meant—

AMES [*interrupting*]. It was yours, and you meant you wanted it all, naturally.

MISS STUART [*indignantly*]. Oh!

AMES. What *I* minded was your thinking I *expected* any of it.

MISS STUART. When I said there wasn't enough for two I meant *I* expected to eat *all* of it, did I?

AMES. Why, of course.

MISS STUART [*after drawing an indignant breath. Puts egg in basket*]. Now, before I go out for two hours more on the baggage-truck, will you please ask that man if there *is* any news of my train?

AMES [*stiffly*]. Certainly.

MISS STUART. Thank you.

AMES. Don't mention it. [*Goes to door, right, and speaks off.*] What do they wire you about . . .

STATION-MASTER [*voice off right*]. Nothin' yet about *no* passenger traffic.

AMES [*turning toward* MISS STUART]. He says there's nothing yet.

MISS STUART [*sinking upon the front bench*]. Oh! [*She sighs with exasperation, sits on front bench.*] You said there was news.

AMES. There will be in a few minutes, now the wire's working.

MISS STUART. Well, do you still pretend not to understand?

AMES. Understand what? [*Comes down right.*]

MISS STUART. That of *course* I meant men need more sustenance than women, and of *course* when I said there wasn't enough food for two I meant *I* didn't want *any*—that is, I did *want* it, certainly, but I wouldn't touch it because—because you're a man and *ought*—to have it *all*.

AMES [*in an earnestly interested voice*]. Do you honestly mean that? [*He sits on the bench, right of* MISS STUART, *looking at her with great earnestness.*]

MISS STUART. Why, of course.

AMES. Are you serious?

MISS STUART. Why, of *course* I'm serious.

AMES. You really wanted me to eat it *all?*

MISS STUART. Certainly.

AMES [*remorsefully*]. I thought you were warning me your hospitality was over when it came to one egg and one sandwich.

MISS STUART [*glancing at the clock*]. Ten hours and thirty-seven minutes. You certainly ought to know me well enough to understand better than that!

AMES. You honestly mean I ought to eat it all because I'm a man.

MISS STUART. Of course. It hurts a man a great deal more not to indulge himself than it does a woman. When there's only a little of anything, it ought always to be given to the man.

AMES. Because he's the more selfish?

MISS STUART. No. Because he *has* to have *his* strength. A *woman* can live " on her nerves."

AMES. So you think the woman *ought* to give up the food to the man. [*This is serious on his part, and appears to be serious on hers; though one cannot always be sure when she is serious. There is a mysteriousness about her; we won't really know her for a considerable time.*]

MISS STUART. I think she'd *better*. If she didn't she might be mistreated!

AMES [*frowning*]. So! Her unselfishness is only self-preservation, is it?

MISS STUART [*with a twinkle*]. No. She wants to preserve them both. If the Indians come the man will have to do most of the fighting; if the waters rise he'll have to build a raft. If it gets *very* chilly [*she glances at the stove*] he'll have to build a fire.

AMES [*following her glance*]. It *is* very chilly. I wonder— [*He rises and goes to the door right, calls off.*] How about a fire in that stove?

STATION-MASTER [*off right*]. It's fixed, if you want to light it.

AMES. All right. [*He crosses to the stove, producing a match which he lights and places within the door of the stove. In a moment a rosy glow comes from the door of the stove, which opens toward right. He watches it and the lady inscrutably watches him.*]

MISS STUART. It *is* a new experience. [*She loosens her furs as the glow grows stronger from the stove.*]

AMES. My lighting a fire for you?

MISS STUART [*indicating the lunch basket*]. No. To see a man making such a fuss about eating when he's starving.

AMES [*returning to her, he smiles*]. Suppose we divide it.

MISS STUART. You might have thought of that before.

AMES. *I* might? Why, it was you that said—

MISS STUART. Have you a pocket-knife—with a very clean blade? [*He hands his knife to her with a blade open.*] Yes, I *thought* you looked like a man who *would* have. I'll do the dividing, and you'll do the choosing— [*He sits end of bench. She cuts the egg so that the two parts are anything but equal; the smaller part is about a fifth of the egg. She cuts the sandwich in the same uneven way.*] There. Choose.

AMES. Thanks. [*He takes the small bit of egg and the tiny fragment of the sandwich.*]

MISS STUART. Well, eat them. [*He does so. His portions vanish as if hardly realized as they pass. Meanwhile she is cutting the egg and the sandwich again.*]

AMES [*as he swallows the two small bits together*]. Thanks. Aren't you—

MISS STUART. Oh, yes, I'm only— [*She offers the newly divided portions.*] Here.

AMES. Oh, no. I've had my share.

MISS STUART [*laughing a little*]. That was a test, to see how you'd choose. *Now* it's a *fair* division.

AMES. No. I really— [*He takes off his overcoat and sits on the bench, near her.*]

MISS STUART. Don't let's be ridiculous any more. I imagine *neither* of us has much right to behave like a child of ten—or nineteen for that matter. Here! [*She insists upon his taking what she offers.*]

AMES. It doesn't seem fair. [*He accepts what is offered and eats.*] *Murder*, but I *am* hungry!

MISS STUART. And there's still some coffee in the thermos. Didn't you know it? [*She pours it in the cap-cup of the bottle as she speaks, turning the bottle upside down to get the last.*]

AMES. No! *Is* there some coffee left? My, my! [*She puts the cup in his hand.*] Coffee!

MISS STUART. Yes, that *is* lucky. [*She puts the remaining bit of egg upon the remaining bit of sandwich.*] Here, this is yours, too, to go with the coffee. *Eat* it! [*He does so before he thinks.*] That's it!

AMES. Oh, lovely! A whole mouthful at once! [*He finishes the coffee in a gulp; then starts.*] That was *yours!* [*Rises.*]

MISS STUART. No, no, it wasn't.

AMES. Why, it *was!* [*He goes back of bench to center.*] Have you given me all the coffee, too? [*He shakes the thermos bottle and turns it upside down.*] Well, by George! Did you do that to escape mistreatment?

MISS STUART. No. It was just the way I was brought up. [*Goes left and throws paper napkins, etc., into stove.*]

AMES. You were brought up to make a man be selfish?

MISS STUART. About food and when he thinks he's sick, yes. That was the old-fashioned way of bringing girls up, wasn't it?

AMES. I thought that went out a *long* time ago.

MISS STUART. It prevailed in *my* girlhood, you see.

AMES [*seriously, quickly*]. Well, *that* couldn't have been very long ago.

MISS STUART [*putting the thermos bottle in the basket and closing the lid, she smiles faintly*]. No? Hasn't the Station-Master any news for us yet? [*The* STATION-MASTER *answers for himself. Enters right as she speaks, carrying his lantern and a bucket of coal. Goes left back of benches and down to stove.*]

STATION-MASTER. Not very good, I reckon. . . . Least not as *you'd* think. You won't git no train fer Amity to-night.

MISS STUART [*disturbed, but she has usually somewhere a little humor left for her own misfortune*]. Not *to-night!*

STATION-MASTER. No'm; an' so fur as *I* know, not before noon, or mebbe three—four—five o'clock in the afternoon to-morrow.

MISS STUART [*weakly*]. Will there be any *food* in this part of America to-morrow?

STATION-MASTER [*pouring some coal into the stove*]. Not as I know of now.

MISS STUART. Good gracious!

AMES [*huskily*]. How about *my* train?

STATION-MASTER. Number Twenty-one? If she don't git no later she'll be due by eight or nine in the morning.

AMES [*quickly*]. Is there a diner on her?

STATION-MASTER. On Number Twenty-one? A diner? My gosh! [*He sets the coal bucket down by the stove with a bang, and puts shovel full of coal in stove.*]

AMES. Isn't there a buffet?

STATION-MASTER. Mister, they's a caboose; that's all.

AMES. *Oh,* my!

STATION-MASTER [*buttoning his overcoat and moving toward right*]. They's more coal in yonder, if you need it.

MISS STUART [*looking at him incredulously*]. Where are you *going?* [*She jumps up, continuing instantly.*] Mr. Ames, you'd better ask him where he's going.

STATION-MASTER [*easily*]. Me? Why you ast me yourself. Where you think I'm goin'? I'm goin' home to bed.

MISS STUART [*gravely, quickly*]. You are? [*Rises.*]

STATION-MASTER. Yes'm. I got to sleep same as anybody.

AMES. What? Why, you *can't!*

STATION-MASTER. Why, *I* ain't got anything more to do around here till jest before Twenty-one's due. [*Then, reassuringly.*] I'll be back by seven-thirty in the morning, though.

AMES. But this *lady*—where's she going to *sleep?*

STATION-MASTER [*disclaiming responsibility*]. I couldn't tell you.

AMES. What about your house? Can't she . . .

STATION-MASTER [*looking at* MISS STUART]. In the first place, how would she git through the mud? [*Shows his boots, dried mud to the knee.*]

AMES. Why—why, we could take her on the baggage-truck. [*This, he thinks, is a real idea.*]

MISS STUART [*graciously*]. No, thank you.

STATION-MASTER. No room for her if she *got* there. No way to *make* none, either.

AMES. What about your brother-in-law's house?

STATION-MASTER. 'Bout same as me. Him and his wife and two childern's in one room and the other five childern's in the other.

MISS STUART. No, thank you.

AMES. Well, but, good heavens . . .

MISS STUART [*soothingly*]. Never mind. It's all right.

AMES [*turning back to the* STATION-MASTER]. Well, but look *here*—

STATION-MASTER. Mister, you can make yourself comfatble enough; it's nice and warm here now; and night-duty when they ain't no trains runnin', why that ain't part o' my job. I got a heavy day to-morrow, and I need sleep. *Good* night, lady! [*He goes out briskly up right.* MISS STUART *goes to stove, left.*]

AMES. Well, good heavens— [*He goes up nervously, opens the door, steps out and calls after the* STATION-MASTER.] Listen—*you!* See *here!*

STATION-MASTER [*outside*]. Good night!

AMES. But see *here*— [*There is no response, and after a few moments* AMES *closes the door, much disturbed.* MISS STUART *stands near the stove, observes him; then laughs faintly.*]

MISS STUART. Don't worry about me; I'm an old traveler. We can be comfortable enough; it *is* warm now!

AMES. I'll—I'll go take a nap—later—on the baggage-truck. [*Jerks his head toward up left.*]

MISS STUART. How absurd! I nearly froze out there, even in these. [*Her furs.*]

AMES [*almost pathetically*]. But what's to be *done?*

MISS STUART. Nothing. When railroads break down passengers can't travel, can they?

AMES. I ought to be able to think of *something* to do. [*Comes down right.*]

MISS STUART. Well, for one thing, now that all the officials have gone, I don't think you need to bother about that sign any longer. [*She points to "No Smoking."*] Don't you usually smoke—after dinner? [*She laughs on the word "dinner" with a glance at the lunch basket, and then sits again, throwing back her fur coat.*]

AMES [*a little awkwardly*]. Oh, thanks. [*Comes down right. He brings forth a cigarette-case.*] But that won't be of much *use*, will it?

MISS STUART. Well, what else *useful* can *you* think of?

AMES. I can't think of a thing.

MISS STUART. Neither can I. So—[*she laughs faintly, crosses to left center, and sits on front bench*]—so where are your matches?

AMES [*produces a box of matches, then makes a gesture as if to offer her his cigarette-case*]. Ah—do you—?

MISS STUART [*shaking her head*]. No; I still stick to the way I was brought up. [*She takes off her heavy coat. Not rising.*]

AMES [*seriously*]. No! Is there still an old-fashioned woman left in America?

MISS STUART. Yes. "Left" is the word. Left over!

AMES. How "left over"?

MISS STUART. Old maids *are,* aren't they?

AMES. Old bachelors are! That's what *I* am. [*Lights his cigarette, adding grimly:*] An old bachelor, and perhaps an older one than I look, too! A *little,* that is.

MISS STUART [*wistfully*]. What's it matter how many times you've seen the earth go round the sun? That's all we mean when we say "a year," isn't it? Our ages ought to be reckoned another way; not in these foolish "years."

AMES. What other way do you suggest?

MISS STUART. Well, let's call a man as old as he behaves —toward a woman!

AMES. Then how old will you call a woman?

MISS STUART. As old as she makes men behave toward her.

AMES [*with a little laugh*]. Well, if *I'm* as old as I behave now-a-days toward women, I'm dead.

MISS STUART [*smiling*]. But what's the *matter* with the women you know?

AMES [*laughs ruefully, and walks about as he speaks*]. Well, most of those I *did* know are so married and raising children I hardly ever see 'em at all. And I just can't stand the new generation.

MISS STUART [*thoughtfully*]. Yes—there *is* a new American girl. I've got one myself.

AMES [*staring*]. *You* have?

MISS STUART. I'm bringing up an orphan niece—or she's bringing me up; it's hard to say which. In fact, I'm bringing up two orphan nieces. [*She smiles at a thought.*] Only one of 'em belongs to the new generation, though. You don't like these new young things then?

AMES. Great Lord, no! They smoke and drink and wear men's clothes and short hair—

MISS STUART. Well, boys' clothes are better for the outdoor things they *do* nowadays, aren't they?

AMES. That may be, but they've given up a great thing to get this new *liberty* I hear they talk about.

MISS STUART. What great thing did they give up?

AMES [*emphatically*]. Charm!

MISS STUART. You haven't met a charming one?

AMES. There *aren't* any. How can a brazen little hussy in breeches with a flask of home-made gin in her hip pocket have any *charm?*

MISS STUART. Ah—but she can, because she has youth, and youth is charm. *Don't* you *care* for the youth you see in a young girl?

AMES [*sitting down by her*]. *I'll* tell you what I care for. I care for the *graces I used* to see in the girls I grew up with.

MISS STUART. You're sure it wasn't really their youth that *gave* them the graces?

AMES. I can *show* you what I care for! [*Very earnestly and decisively.*] To-morrow we'll be moving miles and miles apart. . . .

MISS STUART. Will we? I'm afraid you think more of this railroad system than I do.

AMES. I'm serious. Probably after to-morrow morning we'll never see each other again.

MISS STUART. Why, I feel as if you were my most intimate friend! Life-long! After we finished Italy, wasn't it *two* hours you talked about religion?

AMES. What I'm trying to *show* you—

MISS STUART. Yes; I forgot.

AMES. I had a temptation to tell you something that *would* show you.

MISS STUART [*gaily*]. Why, you could tell me anything. I couldn't stop you. [*Her gesture indicates the surrounding isolation.*]

AMES. Then I will. I'll tell you what I thought about you when I got on that little junk-line train this morning. I hadn't expected to see anybody looking like *you* getting on at one of these way stations—

MISS STUART. I'm a farmer, you know. I have a farm

down near Amity. I've been away to see about a new tenant for part of the land! [*Then abruptly.*] Oh, I don't mean to stop you! *Go* on!

AMES. When you got on the train I thought: "There! There's a lady!" When these *new*-generation girls get on a train I usually think: "There! There's a rowdy!"

MISS STUART. You must have met some strange ones!

AMES. I haven't *met any*. Just hearing and looking at 'em's enough for *me!* But when I looked at you—well, I'm going to talk as sentimentally as I *feel,* just for once in my life—when I looked at you I caught a—a perfume of sweeter days—yes, *better* days than this! And I'll go ahead, now I'm started; I'm hungry as a bear, in spite of your giving me all your lunch, and I *did* feel really cross, during our quarrel, but I'm glad the sun-spots—*he* thought it was the sun-spots—I'm *glad* they've given me this chance to know you.

MISS STUART. My dear man, you don't know an earthly thing about me!

AMES. Oh, yes, I do. There are some people you know all about in a little while.

MISS STUART. "All about?" Good gracious!

AMES. No; not all. You don't know all the *lovely* things about 'em, but you do know there aren't any things that *aren't* lovely; you're one of those transparently perfect things, Miss Stuart.

MISS STUART. What?

AMES [*rises and goes a little to the right*]. You are. And that's all there is to it!

MISS STUART. And only to think of it!

AMES [*turning to her, rather sharply*]. To think of what?

MISS STUART. So much praise—bought by one hard-boiled egg and a sandwich!

AMES [*rather brusquely*]. Well, some of it *is* for that, if you want to know it! It seemed a little thing; but it showed that when you were hungry yourself you'd force your last bit of food on a stranger.

MISS STUART. A "stranger"? Why, by this time I know you *better* than I do my most intimate friend, Mr. Ames!

AMES [*sits. Then pacing up and down and going on with his thought.*] I kept looking at you on the train, though you didn't know it—

MISS STUART. I was brought up always not to know it.

AMES [*continuing*]. I kept looking at you, and I—

MISS STUART [*quoting him*]. " I said to myself, ' There's a woman I'd hate to be cast away in a desert junction with! ' "

AMES. I said to myself, " There's the first woman I've seen in a long time I'd like to know! "

MISS STUART. *How* long a time?

AMES. Well, since this *new* type came in.

MISS STUART [*thoughtfully*]. I'm afraid you wouldn't approve of my niece!

AMES. If *you're* bringing her up I don't believe she'd be the new type.

MISS STUART. Oh, yes, she is! It doesn't matter *who* brings 'em up; they get it from one another.

AMES. Well, let's forget the new type just now.

MISS STUART [*smiling*]. All right.

AMES. I'd rather keep to what I feel about you.

MISS STUART [*nodding smilingly*]. Well, *keep* to it—it began promisingly.

AMES [*coming toward her a little way*]. I will. I'll speak out! As a man gets older most of his friends marry off—or they die off—it's the same thing so far as *he's* concerned!

MISS STUART [*gravely*]. Yes; I know it is!

AMES. Well, a man gets pretty lonely.

MISS STUART. *Men* always seem to think that's so singular!

AMES [*quietly*]. All I meant to say is [*she yawns*] it's been a great thing for me to have a woman's companionship for a day.

MISS STUART. Well, it still seems to be going on.

AMES. I wish . . .

MISS STUART. Yes? [*She conceals a yawn by turning away quickly. She doesn't wish to yawn, she is interested; but she is beginning to be really threatened by drowsiness. He does not perceive this, and the symptoms are, so far, very slight.*]

AMES [*thoughtfully*]. Of course you don't know anything about me—except to-day—

MISS STUART. I do, a little.

AMES [*surprised*]. How?

MISS STUART. Why, you said your name was William Ames: I supposed you were the William Berry Ames that the papers say is so remarkable. "Remarkable's" the word they always use.

AMES [*frowning*]. I'm not much in newspapers—and isn't it obvious I'm not remarkable?

MISS STUART. Oh, yes; I've seen it any number of times: "Mr. William Berry Ames, *still* playing remarkable polo."

AMES [*sharply*]. That's my *uncle!* [*Rises.*] It's "*still* remarkable that he plays polo at *sixty-six!*" "Remarkable" because he's sixty-six! They always use the word remarkable about elderly people. And you thought . . .

MISS STUART [*a little disturbed, hastily*]. I'm so sorry!

AMES [*somewhat upset*]. You thought I was that old man!

MISS STUART [*quickly*]. Oh, I never heard he was quite sixty-six.

AMES. So! You didn't see how I could be quite sixty-six!

MISS STUART [*hastily, with apparent seriousness in placating him*]. But wouldn't it be *wonderful* if you *were!* To be sixty-six and look only—

AMES [*interrupting*]. What age do I look?

MISS STUART. Ah, let's not go into that. It might become mutual!

AMES. I can't get over it: you thought I was my uncle!

MISS STUART. You must *tell* him about it. And then tell *me* sometime if it upsets him too.

AMES [*mollified; his tone changes*]. "Sometime." You think we *might* see each other again after to-morrow?

MISS STUART. Why not, if you think it would be pleasant? I should be— [*She is caught by a yawn and conceals it imperfectly.*] I should be—very glad—

AMES [*sadly*]. Oh, you're sleepy.

MISS STUART. I'm not. I'm interested. I'm interested in everything you've been saying. I was never more interested in my life.

AMES. Honestly? [*Sits.*]

MISS STUART. At least, it's been quite a time since I've had as cheering things said to me as you've been saying. I like it.

AMES. Could you stand some more?

MISS STUART. I—think so.

AMES. Then, *do* let me see you again after to-morrow, will you?

MISS STUART [*after a moment*].   Yes.

AMES.   Could I come to Amity to see you—sometime?

MISS STUART.   Why, I think so.

AMES.   Could I come—before long?

MISS STUART.   If—you like.

AMES [*huskily, gravely, quickly*].   I think I should like it more than I've ever liked anything in my life.

MISS STUART [*rather startled*].   Why, that's—that's saying quite a great deal—isn't it?

AMES.   I can't help it.   It's the way I feel.

MISS STUART.   Yes, but at these pleasant quieter years, you say you have arrived at—haven't you learned more caution?

AMES.   More caution than what?

MISS STUART.   Than to say quite so much as you just did— and to an unknown woman!

AMES [*quickly, with feeling that increases*].   I tell you you're not unknown.   You've shown me—yes, just in the way you *fed* me, if you like—yes, and in the dear, pretty way you took this being " cast away " with me here, you've shown me you *are* the old-fashioned, *perfect* kind of woman—I thought had disappeared.   Well, I've found you—I don't want to let you go!   My life has been getting so confoundedly lonely—I— well, why not?

MISS STUART [*gently*].   I don't know—you're a *little* indefinite, perhaps?

AMES.   It's a long time since I felt like this—and the reason I'm lonely's because fifteen or so years ago I didn't *speak* when something like this came over me.   Instead, I went away to think it over, and another man spoke first.

MISS STUART [*with a humor that fights with drowsiness and an inclination to take him seriously*].   You needn't be afraid of that now.   Farming means a very retired life, with me.   No one else will " speak " while you retire to think it over.   [*She closes her eyes for a moment.*]

AMES.   I don't want to think it over at all!   Listen.   Do I seem to you the sort of man you could like pretty well?

MISS STUART [*looking up quickly*].   Oh, I think so.   [*She closes her eyes for a moment again.*]

AMES [*so impulsively as to be almost explosive*].   Well, if you'll let me hope something might come of it, I'll be any kind of man you *want* me to be!

MISS STUART [*opening her eyes quickly*]. Aren't you a little susceptible, Mr. Ames?

AMES. Does it look like it; to still be a bachelor at my age?

MISS STUART. But it struck me you were—almost—proposing to me just then.

AMES [*with great feeling*]. Well, I was. I *am!*

MISS STUART. Almost.

AMES. Almost or quite—just as you like, Miss Stuart.

MISS STUART [*smiling a little*]. Perhaps it had better be " almost."

AMES [*with feeling*]. If it's to be that way—almost a proposal—is there any chance of your—almost—thinking of it?

MISS STUART [*gently and smiling*]. Why—I might *almost*—think of it—sometime. [*Again the symptoms of drowsiness overtake her.*]

AMES [*remorsefully*]. You *are* sleepy!

MISS STUART [*with feeble insistence*]. I'm not!

AMES [*ruefully humorous, rising*]. I ought to be ashamed trying to keep you awake with a proposal of marriage! [*As he speaks he places a satchel on the end of bench and rolls his overcoat over it for a pillow.*]

MISS STUART. Was that all you made it for—to keep me awake?

AMES. You know better. Here; lie down. I'll cover you over.

MISS STUART. I won't take your overcoat. You'll need it. The satchel's a good enough pillow.

AMES. No. It isn't. Lie down.

MISS STUART. Take your overcoat away or I'll sit up all night. I will. Take it away.

AMES [*submitting*]. All right.

MISS STUART. When you lie down yourself, put your overcoat over you. Will you?

AMES. If I need it.

MISS STUART [*in a matter-of-fact voice*]. No. Promise me.

AMES. I will.

MISS STUART [*lying down with her cheek against the satchel*]. Ah, that's—ah! [*She sighs with satisfaction.*]

AMES [*gently covers her over with her fur coat and stole.*

Then he discovers her muff]. Here. This is a better pillow.
[*He places it under her head.*]

MISS STUART. Thank you. You're very kind. [*She is
silent; then says sleepily:*] I knew you were.

AMES. Knew I was what?

MISS STUART [*contentedly*]. Kind.

AMES [*muttering*]. Who *wouldn't* be? [*He goes to the
stove.*]

MISS STUART [*with her eyes shut*]. I had to be up at four
o'clock and drive seventeen miles to get my train. I'd *rather*
stay awake and listen to you—you'll forgive me for being—so
sleepy—won't you? [AMES *turns the damper on stove.*]

AMES [*smiling, as he looks round*]. Yes. I'll forgive you!
[*He takes his overcoat and spreads it on the second bench; puts
a "suit-case" for a pillow.*]

MISS STUART [*in a sweet drowsy voice, with her eyes
closed*]. It certainly didn't seem—appreciative—going almost
to sleep—when you were almost proposing—but I do appreciate
it—very much—

AMES [*with feeling*]. You dear thing! I wasn't "almost
proposing—" I was *all* proposing and you know it.

MISS STUART. Well, it's very nice of you. I think I'm
glad—you were. But—

AMES. But what?

MISS STUART. We don't need the light, do we? If you
leave the stove door open—

AMES [*goes up and snaps off the switch*]. There! [*A rosy
glow from the stove door crosses the benches, falling upon the
recumbent lady.*]

MISS STUART [*cosily*]. There. That's better. [AMES
goes to the second bench.] You'll put your overcoat over you?

AMES. Yes.

MISS STUART. What have you got for a pillow?

AMES. It's all right.

MISS STUART. A suit-case?

AMES. It's plenty. [MISS STUART, *without opening her
eyes or lifting her head, pulls the muff from beneath her cheek
and lets her cheek rest on the satchel. Then, not otherwise
moving, she swings the muff behind her to him.*]

AMES. What's that for?

MISS STUART. Your pillow. Take it.

AMES. I won't.

MISS STUART. You will.

AMES. Of course I won't.

MISS STUART [*gently and confidently*]. You will.

AMES. You do make me selfish! [*He takes the pillow, places it, and sits on the second bench, preparing to lie down and pull his overcoat over him.*]

MISS STUART [*in a very sleepy murmur*]. I'm sorry I thought you were your uncle. [*She is lying on her right side, and she lifts her left hand over the back of the bench to him, the rest of her not moving. He takes it reverently, kisses it lightly; she brings the hand back and puts it under her cheek. She speaks disjointedly and very drowsily.*] I only thought so because the papers said he was so remarkable.

AMES [*gently*]. I don't mind that now. [*Lies down on second bench.*]

MISS STUART. It would be too bad if you met some pretty, very young thing after—after it was too late. Most men care more for early youth than they do for— [*A little yawn interrupts her.*]

AMES [*gently*]. Than they do for what?

MISS STUART. Than they do for anything. Is the muff all right for a pillow?

AMES [*gently*]. I never had such a pillow before.

MISS STUART. Aren't you sleepy, too?

AMES. Yes; the truth is, I am. It seems strange, when I feel so much that's *new* to me—to be sleepy—

MISS STUART. Oh, no. We *aren't* a young couple at a college dance—getting engaged.

AMES. No—of course not—but aren't we—almost— [*Rises and looks at her over the back of bench.*]

MISS STUART. I think—you must go to sleep now.

AMES. Yes, I will. [*He stretches himself on the bench.*]

MISS STUART. Are you at all—sure?

AMES. Yes, I am.

MISS STUART. I know what I say *sounds* very sleepy, and I *am* almost asleep, but my *mind,* you know—

AMES. Yes?

MISS STUART [*more sleepily than ever*]. My *mind's* working just as clearly as ever, and I keep thinking you've said all this—so suddenly—perhaps you *are* a little susceptible—perhaps when you see some pretty young thing—you'll—you'll—

AMES [*decisively*]. No, I won't.

MISS STUART [*dreamily, in a soft, almost contented voice, and smiling a little*]. Perhaps not.

AMES. May I say just one last thing to you? It seems foolish—but it would be pretty lovely to me if you'd let me say it.

MISS STUART. Say what?

AMES. May I say to you, " Good night, dear " ?

MISS STUART. I believe you might. Say it.

AMES [*gently*]. Good night, dear. [*Her left hand goes up again, his own hand is seen above the back of the bench, clasping it; then she returns it to her cheek.*]

MISS STUART. Good night, dear. [*There is quiet. The Act Drop descends for a few seconds, and rises. Everything is as it was, except that the rosy glow from the stove has paled, and a gray light shows outside the window. The clock marks 5:45. The light outside the window grows a little stronger; distant trees just coming into new leaf on muddy hills are revealed there—an April landscape. The light continually grows stronger throughout the whole scene. A GIRL'S voice is barely heard, shouting in the distance, " Hello there!" "Hell-ooo there!" Then after a pause, a stamping is heard on the platform outside, as though someone stamped mud from his shoes. A quick, sharp tread is heard; the knob of the door up right is fumbled—then the door is opened and a GIRL of nineteen enters. She is distractingly pretty, in spite of—or it may be partly because of—her general style and costume. She wears a soft "sport" hat, beneath which her thick "bobbed" hair is additionally coquettish. She has on a short overcoat, knickerbockers, green stockings and high-laced shoes; the latter covered with mud which has also splashed her stockings. She comes in briskly and goes down left, then halts short with a breathed exclamation as she sees the two sleepers, "Well, for the love o' Mike!" This is in a husky whisper. She stares. A light snoring comes from the second bench. She looks long at the first bench, smiles; then controls a tendency to laughter. Then she moves back to the second bench and looks at AMES. After this contemplation she speaks again in the husky whisper: "Pretty good-lookin' ole bird, if you do snore!" The snoring*] *stops with a little snort.* AMES *coughs, waking himself. Suddenly he sits up, dazed, and stares at the girl. She chokes down an increasing tendency to mirth during their scene.*]

AMES [*confused*]. Oh—ah, how d'ya do.

THE GIRL (FLORENCE). Sh! Don't wake Aunt Isabel. [*After this they both speak in husky whispers.*]

AMES. Who?

THE GIRL. My *aunt*. [*She gestures widely to* MISS STUART.] My Aunt *Isabel!* Don't you *know* her?

AMES [*rises and looks at* MISS STUART]. Yes, indeed!

THE GIRL. Well, I should *think* so! I'm her niece, Florence.

AMES [*conventionally but in a whisper*]. I'm glad to uh— [*Shakes hands.*]

FLORENCE. A man and I've been all night tryin' to get here in a car. He's back in the woods with it now, tryin' to get it out of a mud-hole. We've had a hell of a night!

AMES. I beg your pardon?

FLORENCE. It really was. Are you an old friend of hers?

AMES. I—hope to be. [*Rubbing his face and eyes with his hands.*]

FLORENCE. We'll take you with us when he gets the car out the mud. No use to wake *her* up till it comes.

AMES. No. It's cold, isn't it?

FLORENCE [*pointing to the stove*]. You might make the fire up if you can do it without waking her.

AMES. I only need to turn the draft. I got up about two o'clock and put on some coal.

FLORENCE [*as he moves toward the stove*]. Cigarette?

AMES. What?

FLORENCE. Got a cigarette?

AMES. Oh! [*He hands her his case; she takes one.*]

FLORENCE. Light? [*He lights a match and holds it for her. She smiles at him with brazen coquetry, her hand on his as she lights the cigarette from the match*]. She makes a *fuss* about my smoking. Don't tell her, will you? [*She smiles again, her face not far from his; he looks thoughtful.*]

AMES. No. [*The fire begins to pick up.* FLORENCE *turns to* AMES *suddenly.*]

FLORENCE. How long you known her?

AMES. What?

FLORENCE [*emphasizing her whisper*]. How *long* have you known my Aunt *Isabel?*

AMES. Yesterday!

FLORENCE [*she is suddenly overcome with mirth. She lifts both hands in a gesture of " Oh, go 'way!" and choking with laughter, slaps him with her two palms upon the shoulders. She is unable to control herself; she convulses, leaning against him, then clapping both hands over her mouth, runs spluttering to up right. At the door she checks herself, speaks back to him huskily*]. I'll see if he's got the car out the *mud!* [*Laughter breaks from her as she runs out of the door, up right.* AMES *is bothered and a little fascinated. He glances at* ISABEL, *then goes slowly to the door up right; looks out. He comes down; goes near the stove and stands, frowning thoughtfully.* ISABEL *murmurs, she opens her eyes; they fall upon* AMES *without expression. Then she smiles slowly and speaks.*]

ISABEL. I'm awake.

AMES [*starts*]. Good morning!

ISABEL. Good morning. What time is it?

AMES. It's daylight. Did you—ah—sleep well?

ISABEL. Yes. Did you?

AMES. Yes. I did.

ISABEL. I was trying to stay asleep, but I thought— Was the Station-Master here just now?

AMES. No; it was your niece.

ISABEL. What? [*She stretches her hand to him; he comes quickly and takes her hand. She rises.*] You don't mean it!

AMES. Somehow she found you were here. She's been all night trying to get a car here, she said.

ISABEL. Why, the dear thing! Where'd she go?

AMES [*moving toward the door up right with her*]. She went to see if— [*The door is flung open by* FLORENCE, *returning.*]

FLORENCE. It's coming! [*Comes down right.*]

ISABEL. *Florence!* How'd you *find* me? [*They go to each other and embrace.*]

FLORENCE. We telephoned all over the world, where the wires weren't down, and this was the only place you *could* be!

ISABEL. Florence, this is Mr. Ames.

FLORENCE [*gaily*]. Right-o! We've had *quite* a chat!

We'd better take him home with us, hadn't we? [*Goes back of first bench to center.*]

ISABEL [*turning to* AMES *with a little tremulous self-consciousness at which she smiles herself*]. Will you?

AMES [*embarrassed*]. Ah—you're very kind—I—

FLORENCE [*breezily*]. Why, of *course* we're not going to leave you *here!* It's only a forty mile drive and we won't get stuck by daylight. You'll never see breakfast in *this* hole!

AMES. Well, as you're so kind—

FLORENCE. Of *course* you're coming! *We'll* make him, won't we, Aunt Isabel?

ISABEL [*a little coldly*]. I hope so.

AMES [*awkwardly, to* FLORENCE]. Well, since you're so hospitable—

FLORENCE [*she slaps him on shoulder*]. Hospitable nothing; we don't see a new man-person twice a year in our neck o' the woods, except Johnnie White, and we're *used* to him! I made the poor kid drive me, Aunt Isabel. [*She runs to the door and calls out, "Yay, Johnnie!"*]

ISABEL. "Brazen hussies in boys' breeches"—wasn't that what you called them?

AMES [*nervously*]. Oh, but she's different—she's *your* niece.

ISABEL. Yes, my *great*-niece.

AMES. What? I beg your pardon—

ISABEL [*calmly*]. I forgot to tell you, she isn't my niece precisely—she's my *great*-niece. Florence's father wasn't—

AMES [*rather dazed, but trying to conceal it*]. Your—she's your *great*-niece? Oh, yes— [*A young man appears in the doorway with* FLORENCE. FLORENCE *enters first and goes back of first bench to center, looking at* AMES.]

ISABEL. Come in, Johnnie! [*He does so. He is a boy of about twenty, dressed for motoring and heavily stained with mud and grease; he carries a woman's fur coat over his arm. He smiles vaguely as he comes to take* ISABEL'S *hand. She goes on.*] It was lovely of you to drive all night through the mud to find me.

JOHNNIE [*grinning vaguely*]. Well, Florence wanted me to—

ISABEL. And we all do what Florence wants; yes. This is Mr. Ames, Mr. White. [JOHNNIE *goes to center behind first bench, tosses coat to* FLORENCE, *and shakes hands as she goes on.*] If you'll help us get our bags in the car—

JOHNNIE. Yes, indeed. [*He picks up the bags, getting both arms full.* FLORENCE, *with a sweet smile, gives the coat to* AMES *to hold for her.*]

ISABEL [*continuing smilingly*]. We ought to be home by seven; and there'll be *food*, Mr. Ames! Won't that be— [*She checks herself as she sees the care with which he is putting* FLORENCE *into her coat, and goes to* JOHNNIE, *left center. She hands him her own coat, still smiling.*] Johnnie, dear, if you'll— [JOHNNIE *drops bags and holds coat for* ISABEL.]

JOHNNIE [*politely*]. Yes, indeed, Miss Stuart.

FLORENCE [*to* AMES, *right center*]. I think you're a rogue!

AMES [*laughing consciously and rather uncomfortable*]. What nonsense!

ISABEL. Now if we can get the things into the car— [JOHNNIE *and* AMES *pick up the bags and lunch basket;* AMES *gets into his overcoat.* ISABEL *goes on.*] I think you'll have to let me sit by you, Johnnie, going home. I think you'll drive better.

JOHNNIE [*a little blankly*]. Yes'm. Glad to have you.

ISABEL. Are we all ready?

JOHNNIE [*going out up right with bags*]. Yes'm.

FLORENCE [*to* AMES]. D'you think you can entertain me for forty miles? *I* do! [*She runs out.*]

AMES [*right center*]. This is *very* kind of you to take me *in*, this way—I—ah, are you coming?

ISABEL [*left center, starts as if to go out, then stops and looks about her wistfully, yet smiling a little*]. I just wanted to remember what this room looks like—by daylight. Things change so then. [*She takes his arm and starts up left.*] I'll take your arm just till we get to the car; then you'll have Florence. [*As they go slowly up she continues cheerfully:*] Yes—I forgot to mention it last night; yes, she's my *great*-niece. It wasn't her *father* who was my brother, you see—

AMES [*feebly*]. It wasn't?

ISABEL [*cheerfully, as they reach a point near the door and pause*]. No. It was her *grand*father. [ISABEL *takes a last rather wistfully smiling look about the room as she speaks—a little absently.*]

AMES [*trying not to speak feebly*]. Her grandfather was?

FLORENCE [*enters door. Takes* AMES' *arm with both of her hands*]. Aren't you coming? You're going to sit with me, you know.

AMES. Well, I— [*He is rather bewildered and* FLORENCE *pulls him out through door.* JOHNNIE *enters door and offers his arm to* ISABEL.]

ISABEL. Thank you, Johnnie. [*Both exit.*]

[CURTAIN.]

ACT II

*An interior—a "living room" and "sun-room" combined—of
the house at* MISS STUART'S *farm. It is a cheerful apart-
ment in imaginative but quiet taste.*

*The sun-room does not so much open out of the living-room as
form a part of it—the upper part—as an ample sort of
alcove. Very simple pilasters against the living-room wall,
up right and up left, mark the lower corners of the sun-
room, giving the opening somewhat the effect of a very
wide doorway or entrance. From each of these, the sun-
room walls (which consist principally of French windows)
extend a little distance up; and the living-room walls extend to right and to left, thence down to front. Two of
the French windows of the sun-room are practicable doors,
one up right and one up left. The back of the sun-room
consists mainly of three French windows, through which
there is a glimpse of trees just coming into young April
leaf. This is only a glimpse, however, as the windows
(which are all oblong, and without "half-moons" or
arches at the top) are prettily curtained with figured or
embroidered linen. The woodwork of the sun-room is
apple green.*

*The living-room walls are done in a rather warm shade of tan;
there is a fire-place with a Todhunter type of simple mantel, right center; and over it on the wall, a large old-
fashioned mirror with gilt frame. Opposite the fire-place,
left, are double doors. There is a phonograph in the sun-
room, up right, the view of which is obscured by plants
and there is a "baby-grand" piano in the corner of the
living-room up left, a closed cabinet stands against the up
right wall of the living-room, opposite the piano. The
furniture is all comfortable, pleasant to the eye and not
new; blue-figured chintzes and easy upholstery. There is
a short blue velvet "davenport" or sofa, right center, near
the fireplace, and at its right elbow a very dark green console table.*

287

There is a wire flower stand with potted flowers up center in
the sun-room, two old-fashioned chairs, and a rag carpet
medallion on the floor. There are side-lights, in both
living-room and sun-room, with shaded bulbs. There
are some sprays of apple-blossoms in a jar on the piano.

The morning sunshine is bright outside the sun-room windows,
and the place is cheerful, but not eye-murdering, with
light. The fire is burning, left, and facing it is an " old
lady," for she is undeniably both; and with her cap, and
old-fashioned gown, rather suggests Whistler's portrait of
his mother. She is dainty, but rather fretful. A youngish
middle-aged man, on his knees, is rubbing the hearth and
brass fender with a rag. He is a house-servant in work-
ing-clothes; wearing a great old blue apron, his dark
trousers and waistcoat; his shirt-sleeves are rolled up and
he has omitted a collar and tie. The old lady is FLOR-
ENCE'S *aunt,* ELLEN.

AUNT ELLEN [*in armchair by fireplace. Wishing him to*
continue a narration]. Well, and then, *after* they had their
breakfast—

HENRY. Well, he went to sleep leanin' on the mantelpiece,
and then she had me take him up to bed in the *big* room.

AUNT ELLEN. Our having a gentleman visitor, it's quite
exciting.

HENRY. Yes'm.

AUNT ELLEN. Is he going to stay over to-night with us?

HENRY. No'm. He said he had to get the noon train at
Clinton on the main line. I got to drive him over, she says.

AUNT ELLEN. Would you consider him a very nice looking
gentleman, Henry?

HENRY [*judicially*]. Well, to *me* he looks more like a man
that's kind o' got somep'm layin' heavy on his *mind*—like.

AUNT ELLEN. I should think *she'd* have been *dead.*

HENRY. No'm; she went over to the empty tenant's house
in the buckboard.

AUNT ELLEN. She's a very remarkable woman, Henry.
[*She says this slowly and with a kind of placid emphasis, as if*
she has said it, to the same listener, many times before.]

HENRY [*placidly*]. Yes, Miss Ellen. [FLORENCE *is*
heard outside, off up right.]

FLORENCE [*off*]. Henry! Hen-er-y! *Whoa,* there!

HENRY [*crosses to center*]. It's Miss Florence; *she* went off horseback for *her* sleep. [FLORENCE *enters up right. She is dressed in riding-clothes: breeches, boots, waist, a short coat, and a dark straw hat; she has a riding crop in her hand. Yet there is a daintiness about her.*]

FLORENCE [*as she enters*]. Henry, don't you want to ride Tim down to the barn for me?

HENRY [*going up obediently*]. Yes'm.

FLORENCE [*coming down*]. H'lo, Aunt Ellen! [HENRY *exits up right.*] Had your breakfast? *Where's* Mr. Ames? [*She flings herself in a chair right of table left with one knee over its arm.*]

AUNT ELLEN [*frowning at the posture*]. I haven't met him. Henry tells me he's resting.

FLORENCE. Poor thing! He's a right *natty* ole berry, though, Aunt Ellen.

AUNT ELLEN [*shuddering slightly*]. Won't you *sometime* speak English, Florence?

FLORENCE [*lightly*]. None o' my friends 'd understand me if I did. [FLORENCE *is always lighter than she is rough; and her tone of voice is prettier than the words she says. An electric bell rings faintly off left.*] That's Johnnie; I told him to clean up and come over and shoot some tennis.

AUNT ELLEN [*frowning*]. When were you last in bed, Florence?

FLORENCE. When d'you think I was? Why, night before last. [*She giggles.*] Same as Aunt Isabel!

AUNT ELLEN [*coldly*]. We won't discuss—

FLORENCE [*with a suppressed chuckle*]. No; I guess we better not!

AUNT ELLEN. But *you*, after being out in an automobile all night with this young Mr. White—

FLORENCE [*severely*]. Hunting Aunt Isabel! [*She goes on at once with amused slyness.*] What do you *think* of Aunt Isabel's conduct, Aunt Ellen?

AUNT ELLEN [*primly*]. I've told you I never discuss Aunt Isabel. [*One of the double doors, left, opens and a middle-aged woman steps in. She is neat and responsible looking; but more of the housekeeper type than a "maid"; her name is* MATTIE. *She speaks immediately.*]

MATTIE. It's Mr. White.

FLORENCE [*not rising, turns her head and calls loudly toward the door*]. Come on in, Johnnie!

AUNT ELLEN [*annoyed*]. Florence, please!

FLORENCE. If Aunt Isabel can't reform me, *you* can't, Aunt Ellen. [*Calling again*]. Johnnie! Come ahead *in!* [JOHNNIE *enters left, passing* MATTIE, *who goes out left at once, closing the door.* JOHNNIE *wears an old Norfolk jacket, a flannel shirt, white flannel trousers, and tennis shoes. He carries a racket in a shabby case under his arm and has a cap in his hand. He speaks in a grieved tone as he enters.*]

JOHNNIE. You said you'd be ready for— Howdy do, Miss Ellen— [*This is a brief parenthesis to* AUNT ELLEN, *and he goes on immediately to* FLORENCE.] You expect to shoot tennis in boots?

FLORENCE [*rising*]. Oh, I'll change. You pretty near dead for sleep?

JOHNNIE [*incredulously*]. Me? Bet *you* are!

FLORENCE [*carelessly*]. I'll bet you ten dollars I can go till day after to-morrow!

JOHNNIE. Never close your eyes?

FLORENCE. Yes, nor my mouth, either! [*Goes up center.*]

JOHNNIE [*grimly*]. *I* lose!

FLORENCE. I'll show you how sleepy *I* am! [*She is at the victrola in the sun-room and as she speaks she releases a lively dance record, and turns down, extending her arms.*]

AUNT ELLEN [*crossly*]. Florence! Do you have to dance *all* the time?

FLORENCE [*seizing upon* JOHNNIE]. Absolutely! Come on! [*They begin to dance a very modern dance.*]

AUNT ELLEN. And that poor gentleman trying to get some rest upstairs!

FLORENCE. It's time for the ole kid to come down. I want to *talk* some more to *him!*

JOHNNIE [*as they go on dancing*]. Done up, was he? Well, take men that age, they can't do as much as if—

FLORENCE. No! Think he's some three-year-old? That was a pretty rough trip we brought him.

JOHNNIE. Hark! I believe you'd flirt with George Washington if you got a chance!

FLORENCE. Hush up and get off my foot! [AUNT ELLEN *shudders.*]

JOHNNIE [*plaintive*]. Your Aunt Isabel was listenin' to you the whole way too! She didn't look to me as if she thought much of your style, either!

FLORENCE. Can't you dance without talkin'? What you think this is: a Chautauqua?

AUNT ELLEN [*she has put on a pince-nez and looks at them sourly over her shoulder*]. It certainly isn't *dancing,* is it? [*She is plaintively severe.*]

FLORENCE. I never *could* remember, Aunt Ellen: Was it you or grandma that walked a minuet with Alexander Hamilton?

AUNT ELLEN [*angrily*]. It was my great-grandmother!

FLORENCE. I guess *she'd* have been shocked enough if she'd ever seen *you* dancing when *you* were young?

AUNT ELLEN [*rising angrily*]. Shocked at *my* dancing? At the *waltz?* The polka! The *schottische?*

FLORENCE. Oh, don't get so upset! [*She is a little irritated and speaks flippantly, but she keeps on dancing.*]

AUNT ELLEN [*sharply*]. Shame on you!

FLORENCE [*hotly*]. What for?

AUNT ELLEN [*rapidly*]. To dance, yourself, in *that* manner and say anyone would be shocked at *my* dancing, and for saying I might have danced with Alexander Hamilton!

FLORENCE [*giggling*]. Why? Wasn't he nice?

AUNT ELLEN. Shame!

FLORENCE. Oh, *do* sit down! [*It is a tiff, and they speak sharply and quickly.*]

AUNT ELLEN [*trembling*]. Indeed, I shall not!

FLORENCE. Stand up, then! Gosh!

AUNT ELLEN. I will retire from the room! [*Going left.*]

FLORENCE. Oh, *I* apologize. Golly! [HENRY *enters up right, leaving the door open.*]

HENRY [*as he enters*]. She's back.

FLORENCE [*with gloomy scorn, to* AUNT ELLEN]. Now I s'pose you'll tell her all about it!

AUNT ELLEN [*quickly, but with over-dignity*]. I shall not. Excuse me! [*Exits left.*]

FLORENCE. Oh, my! [*She flings herself in a chair right of table left.*] I wish—

JOHNNIE [*looking off up right and gloomily nodding in that direction to check* FLORENCE, *who is about to continue speaking*]. Hark! You better hush up 'f you don't want *her* to— [*He means: if* FLORENCE *doesn't want* ISABEL *to perceive that there's been a row.* FLORENCE *checks herself.* JOHNNIE *goes to left of table.*]

ISABEL [*outside, up right*]. Henry?

HENRY [*right center*]. I'm waitin'. [ISABEL *enters cheerfully up right in the sun-room. She wears a driving-coat over her dress, driving-gloves, and a "pretty little hat." As she comes in, her air is brisk, as of one fresh from driving on a cool morning, and she speaks as she comes down.*]

ISABEL [*center. Beginning to* HENRY, *interrupting herself to greet* JOHNNIE, *and then reverting to* HENRY]. Henry— howdy do, Johnnie White—Henry, I want *you* to drive Mr. Ames to the train.

HENRY. *Yes'm,* you awready told me.

ISABEL. Let him know in plenty of time to start—but— well, not too *much* time. Not so that he'll have to *wait a long while at the station.* [*With a significance in her own thought that* AMES *has had a great deal of station waiting lately.*]

HENRY. No'm. [*Exit up left.*]

ISABEL [*she turns to* FLORENCE *as* HENRY *goes out up right.* FLORENCE'S *attitude and look are of a brooding sort.* ISABEL'S *glance rests momentarily upon her, but she speaks to* JOHNNIE]. Johnnie White, why is this lady so gloomy? [JOHNNIE *shakes his head briefly.*] What's the matter? [*To* FLORENCE.] Where's your Aunt Ellen? Hasn't she come down yet?

FLORENCE [*with rueful sulkiness*]. Oh, yes; she was here!

ISABEL [*comprehending cheerfully*]. Oh, I see. What was it about?

FLORENCE. She didn't like it because— Why, I was only makin' fun of *old*-fashioned dancing. Everything old-fashioned is so funny.

ISABEL [*center*]. Isn't it! I used to say that to my grandmother. Did you apologize?

FLORENCE. Yes. I did.

ISABEL. Did you say, " I apologize golly "?

JOHNNIE [*surprised*]. Why, Miss Stuart! How'd you guess Florence said that?

ISABEL [*back of* FLORENCE]. When you live with 'em, Johnnie, you get to know their habits. Do you know what she's thinking now? [*She puts her hand on* FLORENCE'S *shoulder,* FLORENCE *still being seated.*]

JOHNNIE [*shaking his head*]. No'm; I certainly don't.

ISABEL. She's wondering why people are always so *queer* when they get older.

JOHNNIE [*with slightly sour significance*]. Well, she might ask Mr. *Ames* about that. He must be anyway pretty near something way long over thirty or something, isn't he, Miss Stuart?

ISABEL. Yes, I'm afraid he must be almost that near the end! But still I rather doubt if she *will* ask Mr. Ames about it, Johnnie. No; hardly. [*Crosses center. Smiling to him as he grins in rueful comprehension.*]

FLORENCE. Oh, I *like* old *men*. [*She comes out of her brooding fit as she rises.*] Don't you think Mr. Ames is terribly *intriguing?* [*Seriously and quickly.*]

ISABEL. "Intriguing"? No, I think he seems honest— well, *quite* honest, at least!

FLORENCE. But he has such a distinguished looking *face*.

ISABEL. Well, he has an *uncle* who's distinguished; that is, he's always spoken of as *remarkable* because he plays polo at sixty-six. The uncle, I mean, Florence, of course.

FLORENCE. This man's a man that really interests me. I think from his looks he has the power to think. [*Severely.*] Very few people have the power to think in this world, you know, Aunt Isabel.

ISABEL [*back of table*]. Oh, yes; fewer and fewer every day! It's quite natural for— [*Turning unexpectedly to* JOHNNIE.] Have *you* the power to think, Johnnie White?

JOHNNIE. No'm. You know what she means, don't you?

FLORENCE [*coldly, absently*]. Never mind.

ISABEL [*in an impressed whisper, to* JOHNNIE]. She's thinking. [*Crosses center.*]

FLORENCE. Aunt Isabel, I really *would* like him to stay over a day or so.

ISABEL. He said he had to go on to New York at noon. I'm afraid he made quite a point of it.

FLORENCE [*rises and crosses center*]. Oh, well, you know men always *can* stay if they want to.

ISABEL. That's why it's better not to urge them; they may only make it clearer they don't want to.

FLORENCE [*at the door*]. Oh, Mr. Ames might change his mind—later. [*Crosses to door, left.*]

ISABEL. Before you begin with *that,* dear, could you please first go and apologize to your Aunt Ellen?

FLORENCE. Oh, all right. [*Moodily.*]

ISABEL [*by the fireplace*]. Try it without a golly!

FLORENCE. All right, I'll go and kid her to death. [*Exit left.*]

ISABEL [*turns to* JOHNNIE, *sitting on sofa, right*]. Don't *you* seem to " intrigue " Florence at *all,* Johnnie?

JOHNNIE. No'm. She just takes a notion. [*Crosses to center.*]

ISABEL. You mean she just *gets* this way.

JOHNNIE. Yes'm; when there's somebody around she's fixin' to make 'em get mush over her. *You*'ve noticed that, haven't you, Miss Stuart?

ISABEL. I fancy I may have, just possibly!

JOHNNIE. *Then* she rubs that power-to-think business all over *me,* because the faculty found out I wasn't intellectual or something, so I had to abandon my college career. [*He is very serious.*]

ISABEL [*sitting on the sofa and concealing a tendency to laugh*]. Come on. I see you want to say something more to me.

JOHNNIE [*swallowing. Sits on sofa left of* MISS STUART]. Yes'm. Miss Stuart, you're a woman that's had a good many men go mush over you; so with your experience, why, the truth is, I may not have all the brains in the world, but she hasn't, either, but she gets these fits when she *thinks* she has; and what I want to say is simply: why, *you* know how it is, when there's some *new* man around, she treats me more like some door-mat than a person.

ISABEL. I understand you perfectly, Johnnie. Go ahead.

JOHNNIE. I just wanted to say so because you've had prob'ly more experience of life than I've had, no doubt.

ISABEL. How long do you expect to feel this way about her, Johnnie?

JOHNNIE [*swallowing*]. Well, if everything turns out all *right*—though it don't look so much like it right now, but if it does, and she finds out I'm her—her—well, her *real* mate, as it were, why, I expect to go on and on with her—and on and on—and on and— [*He seems to be going on, though slowing down.*]

ISABEL. "On and on and on"—until you're just any age— oh, twenty-eight or even twenty-nine, maybe?

JOHNNIE. Yes'm. Indefinitely.

ISABEL. Suppose you were—past *thirty,* Johnnie. Suppose, like Mr. Ames, you were even—well, whatever age we'll say Mr. Ames is.

JOHNNIE [*slightly amused and incredulous*]. What age— me? I guess prob'ly I'd be sittin' around somewhere, if I was alive.

ISABEL. But you'd still like Florence to be about nineteen, wouldn't you?

JOHNNIE. Well, about the way she looks now, yes'm. That's a good deal why I like her: the way she looks.

ISABEL [*smiling*]. It isn't fair, is it?

JOHNNIE. Ma'am?

ISABEL. You see, when *you're* twenty you like us to be nineteen, and when you're fifty you're apt to like us to be nineteen! Well, we can't manage it, you see! We can't stay nineteen, much as we want to please you!

JOHNNIE [*smiles*]. Oh, well, I guess I'd feel just the same about Florence if she was a thousand.

ISABEL [*looking at him quickly*]. Would you? If she were a thousand?

JOHNNIE [*laughing a little ruefully*]. I guess I would! [*As if he'd prob'ly have to.*]

ISABEL. You *think* so?

JOHNNIE [*becoming serious*]. Well, if I did, I guess *then* she'd know what sort of a man I am.

ISABEL [*thoughtfully and rather slowly*]. Yes; she ought to!

JOHNNIE [*going on*]. And she'd see how I really feel about her.

ISABEL [*smiling quickly*]. Yes; so she would! It's quite an idea! [*Rises.*]

JOHNNIE [*rises*]. 'Course I don't *think* anything'll come o' the way she acts over this Mr. Ames. For one thing, I b'lieve *he'd* have too much sense.

ISABEL. Do you? You can never be sure of *that,* Johnnie!

JOHNNIE. Well, she begged him a lot to stay over till to-morrow and he said he couldn't; just like he did when you asked him, Miss Stuart.

ISABEL. Yes, that looks intelligent of him, if he sticks to it and goes.

JOHNNIE. And, anyhow, he only said one *personal* thing to her all the time, and *it* was kind of a joke.

ISABEL [*quickly*]. He *did* say a personal thing to her?

JOHNNIE. It was when you went to hurry the cook with breakfast. Mr. Ames asked Florence—oh, well, it wasn't so *frightful* " personal."

ISABEL. What was it, Johnnie?

JOHNNIE. Well, she said she s'posed she'd be as old as her grandfather before she got any breakfast and he asked her if she knew how old her grandfather was.

ISABEL. He did? He asked her that? What did she tell him?

JOHNNIE. She didn't know. [*Anxiously.*] Do you think that was pretty personal? I don't see—

ISABEL [*crosses center*]. Why, *yes;* I believe I *do.* I believe I think it was quite " personal " indeed—asking her how old her grandfather was! [MATTIE *enters, left.*]

ISABEL [*quickly on her entrance*]. What is it?

MATTIE. The gentleman. I heard him stirrin' round; you said to let you know.

ISABEL [*rather eagerly*]. Yes?

MATTIE. I think he's comin' down.

ISABEL [*going toward her quickly*]. Mattie, it seems to me you told me once you didn't think this was a becoming hat.

MATTIE. No'm. You *ast* me, and I says I never could like it on you, ma'am.

ISABEL. Good gracious! You might be right! [*She hurries away up through the sun-room and off up left.*]

JOHNNIE. Didn't hear Miss *Florence* stirrin' around or anything, did you?

MATTIE [*with a glance toward where* ISABEL *departed*]. Yes, sir. *She's* changin' *her* things—again—*too!* [*Going to exit left.*]

JOHNNIE [*rather sharply as she opens the door*]. Will you

ask her how long she thinks I— [*He is checked by an approach seen through the open door; mutters*] oh! [*and turns right.* AMES *enters right, passing* MATTIE, *who waits for him to pass; then exit right.* AMES *has changed his clothes for tweeds; he looks freshened but preoccupied.*]

AMES [*in greeting*]. Ah—Mr. White? Haven't you been to bed at all?

JOHNNIE [*smiling*]. No. J'you get rested up some? [*They shake hands.*]

AMES [*crossing to the fire, right*]. Oh, yes; quite a little. I suppose our two—ah—comrades—aren't down yet. Miss *Stuart* must be pretty much exhausted, I'm afraid.

JOHNNIE. She doesn't act like it. Right after you went up to bed she drove off to one of her farms on business. [*Sits right of table left.*]

AMES. She did?

JOHNNIE [*casually; not boasting for her*]. Drivin' herself in a buckboard.

AMES. Why, I declare!

JOHNNIE. Oh, Miss Stuart's considered a pretty remarkable woman, you know.

AMES [*struck by this, frowns somewhat thoughtfully*]. She is. She's considered—remarkable?

JOHNNIE [*shaking his head, seriously*]. Yes, *indeed!* She's the most remarkable of her family.

AMES [*thoughtful*]. I feel myself rather at a loss; I seem to be here so—so unexpectedly, as it were—and such a—a stranger. I'm rather—ah—confused about the family. Miss Stuart's father and mother, I take it, aren't living?

JOHNNIE. Golly, no! I dunno *when they* died!

AMES [*set back a little*]. A considerable time ago, I suppose.

JOHNNIE. Well, *yes! Must* 'a' been!

AMES [*rather wistfully, yet trying to sound careless and casual*]. You don't remember them, I take it.

JOHNNIE [*carelessly*]. Me? Golly, no!

AMES. Ah—the present family, then—

JOHNNIE. It's just Miss Stuart and Miss *Ellen* Stuart and Florence.

AMES. Miss *Ellen* Stuart I haven't met. [*Sits on sofa.*]

JOHNNIE. She's Florence's aunt.

AMES. Her aunt?

JOHNNIE. Yes, I always get mixed up on relations, too. [*He sits on the small of his back, crossing his legs; and decides to try a wicked shot.*] I don't know how old *my* grandfather was when he died, any more'n Florence did hers!

AMES [*unconscious of the effort just made*]. It seems to me that last night Miss Stuart spoke of *two* orphan nieces she was bringing up.

JOHNNIE. Bringin' up? Florence is one, but Miss Stuart couldn't 'a' meant she was bringin' Miss *Ellen* up. *She's* about a hundred—or a hundred and ten, maybe! Anyhow, she must be around sixty.

AMES. I must have been mistaken. Then there are just these three ladies in the family.

JOHNNIE. Three's all. They *do* need a man around.

AMES. Uh—yes. It would—ah—seem so. [*They look at each other with some coldness.* FLORENCE *is heard singing off left.*]

JOHNNIE. This un comin' needs more'n *one* the way she acts—lately! [FLORENCE *enters, left, singing till she gets into the room, then she stops suddenly. She wears a most becoming tennis costume, but accompanies it with white high-heeled slippers. She has a pair of white tennis shoes in one hand, and a racquet and a net bag of tennis balls in the other. There are five or six balls, not all new.* AMES *rises and goes a little to right.*]

FLORENCE [*crosses to center, back of table. To* AMES]. Oh! *You're* here, too!

JOHNNIE [*muttering ironically, not moving*]. So'm I here, too!

AMES [*gallantly*]. I'm glad you didn't know it, if that's why you kept on singing.

FLORENCE [*going over to him*]. I told you in the *car* you were a quick worker! [*She doesn't smile.*] I've taken a frightful fancy to *you!*

JOHNNIE [*before* AMES *can speak*]. One of the mail service aviators had to land in their back meadow here, last month. She pulled that on him before his wheels touched ground.

FLORENCE. I didn't!

JOHNNIE [*placidly stubborn*]. You did. You had to holler to make him hear it!

FLORENCE [*turning seriously to* AMES *for sympathy*]. These boys, nowadays, they think life's nothing but jazz. In this life people meet a girl, but so often they don't see she prob'ly has *thoughts* other people *couldn't think!* I have to lead two lives: one outdoors with mere adolescents, but the other: that's a life *apart*. *You* understand what I mean, don't you?

AMES [*smiling*]. I think so.

FLORENCE. I thought you would. That's why you intrigue me so. [*Softly*.] You're a great kid! [*She slaps him on arm*.]

JOHNNIE. Oh, listen! [FLORENCE *glances at him*.]

FLORENCE. Mr. Ames, don't you believe that very few people in this life have the power to really *think?*

JOHNNIE [*sliding to the floor from his chair*]. Oo-ooh, Mike!

FLORENCE [*annoyed, turning*]. Cut the rough stuff, you caterpillar. [*Her tone is severe but quiet*.]

JOHNNIE [*rising to his knees and seeming to paddle with his racquet at the tennis shoes in her hand*]. You goin' to wear four shoes at the same time, *centipede?*

FLORENCE [*sitting*]. I never can bear to put flat shoes on till the last minute. And then— [*She removes one slipper*.] It's so troublesome *gettin'* 'em on—

AMES. May I help you?

FLORENCE. Oh, if you *would*—

JOHNNIE [*embittered, up center*]. Oh! That's why you brought 'em! I *see!*

FLORENCE [*giving him a cold quick glance, but speaking to* AMES. *He kneels before her*]. It's outrageous of me to let you take so much trouble! [*Then leaning toward him, she speaks softly*.]

JOHNNIE. Oh, my! [*He goes out of the picture, stepping out up right*.]

FLORENCE [*softly*]. Mr. Ames, please stay over till tomorrow. *I* ask you to.

AMES. You're very kind. I couldn't let your aunt think I'm so vacillating. You see, I told her I had to be in New York this evening.

FLORENCE. But you just *said* you had to go, didn't you?—
because you wanted to be polite about making an unexpected
visit?

AMES [*laughing*]. Yes; something like that. But after
telling your aunt that I *couldn't* stay—

FLORENCE. But aren't there any reasons you'd *like* to stay?

AMES [*thoughtfully*]. Yes, there are.

FLORENCE. Then I'll fix it for you. I'll say you sent a
wire to New York letting 'em know you reached *here,* and I'll
write a message on one of our telegraph blanks to *you.* It'll
be the *answer* from New York telling you there isn't any reason
for you to leave. [*She is pleased with her idea.*]

AMES [*laughing, but a little nervous over her idea*]. Oh,
no!

FLORENCE. I *will!* I'll have a man bring it in. Don't
you spoil it.

AMES. I couldn't—

FLORENCE. Yes, you could! And when my telegram
comes, if you give me *away*— [*She is interrupted by* JOHN-
NIE'S *return.* JOHNNIE *has been just beyond the threshold
up right, looking off out doors, and now comes in and down
a few steps.*]

JOHNNIE. I got it!

FLORENCE [*she checks* AMES, *who is about to expound his
protest*]. Hush! [*To* JOHNNIE.] You got what?

JOHNNIE. Got a *wish* I just made. [*He points to door
up left, then claps his hand over his mouth as if undesirous the
lady entering should hear him; he is facing that way.* ISABEL
*enters up left in the sun-room. She has taken off her hat
and coat; is in a very pretty morning dress, and carries some
" work " in her hand; a " work bag." She comes in looking
at* JOHNNIE, *who has his hand over his mouth.*]

ISABEL. What's the matter, Johnnie White? [*He jerks
his head toward* AMES *and* FLORENCE, *who are down right
center. For an instant* ISABEL *lets it be seen that she is the
least bit taken aback.*] Oh! [*She immediately smiles, as if
pleased.*] Oh! [*She comes down as she speaks.*] Your shoes
are too—large again, dear? [*The slightest check before
" large."*]

AMES [*looking up at* ISABEL *with a little embarrassment*].
Ah—she—I was helping her to—ah—change.

ISABEL [*smiling*]. You were?

AMES. That is, I am. She mentioned some difficulty in—ah—doing it herself, and I—

ISABEL [*sunnily*]. I should think you would! Who wouldn't? And who wouldn't make it as long as possible, too! [*She turns to a chair, left center.*]

AMES [*rising*]. It's—ah—done. [*As he has taken off FLORENCE'S second slipper he has unconsciously put it under his arm, where it still is.*]

ISABEL. Is it? Already?

JOHNNIE [*sharply, to FLORENCE*]. C'm on, here!

FLORENCE. All right, I'm coming; what's the hurry?

JOHNNIE [*FLORENCE goes up as he speaks. JOHNNIE has gone down to the sofa she has occupied, and has picked up the bag of tennis balls. He immediately goes up, after FLORENCE. He calls out.*] Go ahead! [*All in a breath.*] Betcha dollar I beat you t' the tennis court! [*Both rush for the door up right. He swings her back up right. FLORENCE strikes at him with her racket.*]

FLORENCE [*giggling as she runs after him*]. No fair, you got a start. [*ISABEL is looking at AMES, who is standing, still in some embarrassment, near the fireplace, unconscious of the slipper under his arm; he is looking up at the departing couple. The other slipper is on the seat of FLORENCE'S chair.*]

ISABEL. Aren't they extraordinary, Mr. Ames? [*AMES turns.*] Aren't they extraordinary, these young things! Not tidy, though. She's left her slippers on the sofa. [*Glancing at the slipper, then again at him; she begins to sew some lace into cambric.*]

AMES [*still embarrassed and not catching this*]. It seems to me you're rather extraordinary yourself, my dear—[*he pauses an instant, then hastily adds*]—lady. [*So that his phrase is " my dear lady."*]

ISABEL [*as if a little suspiciously*]. I? Do you think so? In what *way*?

AMES. Sleeping a few hours on a wooden bench, motoring forty miles of mud hills, then driving off in a buckboard instead of collapsing!

ISABEL [*looking at him*]. Oh, a country life keeps people *quite* robust. It's—" remarkable!" [*Then looking at her work.*] As I *said*, though. I'm afraid Florence is untidy, sometimes. [*With a little gesture toward the slipper.*] You see where she's left that pair of slippers.

AMES [*glancing at it absently*]. Pair? Ah—there's only one.

ISABEL [*bending her head over her work*]. So? Could you find the other? [*Sits right of table left.*]

AMES. Oh, certainly. [*He glances absently about, then realizes, with a start, that the slipper is under his arm; she seems oblivious of everything except her lace-making. He hastily puts the slipper under the chair; straightens up and looks at her again. She seems as before. He stoops, looking about.*] Ah—I think it's under the— Oh, yes. Here it is. [*He puts it with the other one and comes to center.*]

ISABEL. Will you set them on the hearth, please?

AMES. Certainly.

ISABEL [*with a matter-of-fact amiability*]. Then it'll be easy to find them if she comes back soon to have them put on again.

AMES. Oh, ye— [*He begins to say " Oh, yes," but checks himself uncomfortably. He places shoes at fireplace, then goes to right center—and is conscious of them as rather damnatory; and a pause follows in which he glances back and down at them twice.*]

ISABEL. I'm sorry you felt you couldn't stay over till to-morrow, but since you insisted you *couldn't*— [*Inquiringly, as if giving him a chance to alter his mind.*]

AMES. I—I'm afraid I ought to get back.

ISABEL [*with a submissive nod, regretting*]. Very well. I've arranged for you to go.

AMES. Ah—thank you. [*Moving toward her.*] Ah— Is that lace you are making?

ISABEL. Do you like it?

AMES [*putting on a pair of glasses, rather hastily looking at the lace and, as hastily, slipping the glasses back into his waist-coat pocket again as he speaks*]. It's very lovely—yes. You must have *remarkable* eyes to do that.

ISABEL [*after a look at him*]. Yes, my eyes are *quite* good. [*Using " quite" to mean " rather" as elderly people speak of pleasant faculties still remaining.*]

AMES. Is it a—what they call a doyley?

ISABEL [*glancing at him thoughtfully*]. I wonder if I oughtn't to make a little—cap—of it.

AMES [*perplexed*]. A *cap?*

ISABEL. Don't you think it's a pretty fashion—a lace cap on the head?

AMES. You mean like the Breton peasant women?

ISABEL. No; I was thinking of our grandmothers

AMES. But—ah—

ISABEL [*letting it touch her hair a moment*]. Would you —like me in it? [*Her tone is entirely " natural," as if she considered the possibility seriously.*]

AMES [*trying not to be at all flustered*]. Of course I should —like you—in anything.

ISABEL. Are you sure you would?

AMES. Why, how can you ask me?

ISABEL [*working*]. As sure as you were last night?

AMES. Yes, indeed.

ISABEL. And you *would* like me in a cap?

AMES. Well, wouldn't it seem a little—

ISABEL. Do you mean you think it would seem a little— premature?

AMES. Decidedly, I— [*Breathlessly correcting himself.*] Of course it would. I meant— [*Goes back of table to left.*]

ISABEL. You mustn't flatter me too much.

AMES [*with almost plaintive inquiry*]. " Flatter " you?

ISABEL [*smiling*]. I'll keep off the cap as long as I *can*. Really, there's no excuse for caps now. I suppose women used to wear 'em because in those days there were so few supplies.

AMES [*blankly*]. Supplies?

ISABEL. Yes—like imports from Paris. And, besides, they didn't approve of 'em, poor things!

AMES. Pardon me. Who didn't approve of what?

ISABEL. Our grandmothers didn't approve of accomplishing marvels with cosmetics. You know the miracles they do to faces nowadays.

AMES. Miracles? [*Sits left of table.*]

ISABEL. It's—remarkable! No; there's no excuse for a woman to wear a cap these days—not till she has to just *absolutely* give up! [*Then at her work.*] Don't you think so?

AMES. Oh—oh, yes!

ISABEL. Oh, it's just struck me— [*Rises.*] I ought to be

entertaining you, oughtn't I? But we *haven't* any family photograph album.

AMES. What a lucky family!

ISABEL. I could show you some daguerreotypes, though. Yes—[*rising suddenly upon a thought*]—you *ought* to see some of our heirlooms. [*She gives him a fleeting faint smile, and leaving her work on the table, left center, goes to the closed cabinet against the wall up right; opens the doors, and brings forth an old mahogany case. She brings this down to the table, left center, opens it, takes out a folding daguerreotype.*]

AMES [*rather surprised*]. Daguerreotypes?

ISABEL [*stands back of table*]. Yes. We don't show them to *every* visitor, of course. Sit down. [*She hands him the daguerreotype.*] There. You like my father?

AMES [*rather touched, yet rather apprehensive*]. Is that your father? He must have been a very fine-looking man. Is that a—a stock he's wearing?

ISABEL. Yes. I did think stocks were so becoming, didn't you? [*Handing him another daguerreotype.*] That's my Aunt Margaret, father's sister, at ninety-one. We all live very long on my father's side.

AMES. Ah—very intelligent face.

ISABEL. Daguerreotypes *have* a charm, haven't they? I wonder people stopped taking them.

AMES [*becoming more preoccupied*]. I don't think I ever saw any daguerreotypes taken much after the Civil War.

ISABEL. No; I don't think I have, either. [*Handing him another.*] That's my Uncle Charles, in his uniform. He was a colonel.

AMES. In the—Civil War?

ISABEL. Oh, no, in the Mexican War.

AMES [*more disturbed, but concealing it fairly well*]. Ah— he must have been a very fine-looking man.

ISABEL. Yes, indeed! [*She smiles as she hands him another.*] Here's one of a little girl—that is, a young girl. Does anything about her strike you as—familiar?

AMES [*looking at her, not at the daguerreotype, and trying to conceal a foreboding*]. Familiar?

ISABEL. Yes. See if you don't guess who it is.

AMES [*vaguely*]. "Who is it?" [*He looks at it; then*

suddenly looks closer; starts slightly, draws his head back from it, staring incredulously.]

ISABEL. Can't you guess who it is?

AMES [*huskily*]. Why, it *can't*— [*He looks apprehensively to her and back again with painfully growing conviction.*]

ISABEL. Why can't it?

AMES. Isn't it your—*mother?*

ISABEL [*in a tone that smilingly chides him for being so slow*]. No-o—

AMES [*with some plaintiveness*]. Why, there weren't any taken after—why, it *couldn't* be—

ISABEL [*with a little archness*]. Oh, but this girl—you see, she was only a child, really.

AMES [*feebly trying to be hearty*]. Oh, yes; that's all she was. I see. She wasn't—

ISABEL [*sunnily*]. No. Not over sixteen or seventeen, no. Don't you see any resemblance?

AMES [*with a slight struggle*]. Well, it's charming enough to—

ISABEL. It's a sister of mine.

AMES. It is? Your sister?

ISABEL [*musingly*]. Yes, she was quite a lot older than I am and married a missionary and they were lost in a typhoon.

AMES. Oh—I'm sorry.

ISABEL [*reassuringly*]. Oh, it was *quite* a time ago. [*She smiles and puts the pictures back in the box.*] There! I just wanted to see if you'd see the resemblance: I won't put you through all the others. [*She takes up her work and sits again as she speaks.*]

AMES [*huskily*]. Thank you! [*Then hurriedly.*] Thank you for *showing* 'em to me! [*He rises, wipes his forehead hastily, and moves toward the fireplace, taking out his cigarette case.*] Thank you. May I smoke here? [*She nods.*] I— ah—I—ah— [*Crosses to console table, right center. Lights cigarette.*]

ISABEL [*cheerfully and working*]. Daguerreotypes and things like that bring back such dear old times to us, don't they?

AMES [*unguardedly*]. I suppose they— [*Hastily.*] They *do*, of course! [*He takes out two cigarettes.*] Yes, they do bring them back. [*She gives him a glance, and bends over her work. Seated right of table left.*]

ISABEL. "Where are the snows of yesteryear?" Yes, but where are the yesteryears themselves? "The wind has blown them all away!" Do you remember when all the young men made "New Year's Calls" and all the girls and their mothers kept "Open House"—those dear jolly old times?

AMES. Oh, yes, indeed. I've *heard* they—

ISABEL. Even politics seemed simpler then. It was easier when we let men do all that for us, though they *did* get so many things wrong, poor things!

AMES. Oh, I don't know; we elected Roosevelt, and—

ISABEL [*with a spiritedness, as of patriotic indignation*]. Yes, but if women had voted when Mr. Tilden ran against Hayes—and—Wheeler, you surely don't believe there'd have been all that excitement over the election, do you?

AMES. I—I—don't—

ISABEL [*earnestly*]. You *know* that was a terrible thing.

AMES. About Tilden and Hayes—and—Wheeler?

ISABEL. *Don't* you think it was?

AMES. Yes, I suppose it— [*He does not finish but hastily substitutes:*] Oh, yes; it *was*, of course.

ISABEL. My poor father used to get excited over that to the day of his death!

AMES [*relieved*]. Oh, your *father* did! [*Crosses right.*]

ISABEL. Well, I thought it was wrong, too. [*He stares at her, again perplexed; she sews.*]

AMES. You ah—

ISABEL [*casually*]. What?

AMES [*apologetically*]. Nothing. That is, I had nothing in mind to say. [*Goes up right.*]

ISABEL [*musing, smiling*]. I suppose my father felt it so much because he *knew* Mr. Tilden. *I* never *met* him. [*As if she had met others like him.*] But I *should* like to see Mr. Cleveland's expression if he could see women voting! Or General Harrison's!

AMES. General Harrison's expression? Do you mean Harrison who was *President*—in—ah—eighteen—ah— [*Goes to right center back of sofa.*]

ISABEL. Yes; President Benjamin Harrison. Good gracious! I didn't mean his *grandfather*, President William

Henry Harrison, who was President in eighteen-forty or something!

AMES [*hastily, laughing feebly*]. No, no. I knew you didn't mean *him!*

ISABEL. Well, no! [*She sews, and takes up the theme as if musing absently.*] *Most* of them used to be Generals before they ran for President, didn't they?

AMES. You mean like General Harrison?

ISABEL. Yes. General Harrison, General Garfield—

AMES. Oh—yes.

ISABEL. And most of *all,* General Grant.

AMES [*feebly*]. Yes, General Grant.

ISABEL [*laughing absently as she sews*]. *We'd* hardly remember *him*—of course. [*She looks up at him as if disquieted by a thought, though she smiles nervously.*] You—you never *did* see him, did you? [*As if diplomatically getting at his age.*]

AMES. General Grant? No.

ISABEL [*as if relieved, smiling a little, as if at an absurdity as she looks back at her work*]. Of course I supposed not.

AMES. No. I never did. [*She looks up at him innocently, carelessly, then seems to become aware of something unusual in his look at her.*]

ISABEL. What is it?

AMES. I—ah—nothing!

ISABEL. Oh, yes; I can tell: You're thinking about something that bothers you. At least you looked as if you were puzzling about something. Weren't you?

AMES [*hurriedly*]. Indeed, I wasn't; not at all!

ISABEL. I'm sure you *are* wondering about something.

AMES. No. I'm not. Not about anything at all. [*Crosses right to front of sofa.*]

ISABEL. Yes, but you are. I wonder if I know what you're wondering about.

AMES [*too quickly. Sits on sofa*]. No, you don't. That is, I meant to say you don't, because I'm *not,* so you couldn't.

ISABEL. But I think I do.

AMES. Indeed, you're mistaken. I'm not wondering about anything. Not about *anything!*

ISABEL. Aren't you even wondering anything—about *me?*

AMES. No, no; certainly not. [*Rises.*] Nothing at all.

That is, I'm not wondering. Of course I'm *thinking* about you—

ISABEL [*quickly*]. What are you thinking about me?

AMES. Nothing. Nothing at all.

ISABEL [*nodding*]. I see. You're thinking about me but you aren't thinking anything in *particular* about me.

AMES. Yes. No!

ISABEL. I understand perfectly.

AMES. No, but you don't.

ISABEL. Yes. You meant Yes *and* no. Didn't you?

AMES. Well, I— [*Crosses back of table to left.*]

ISABEL. Of course you did. That clears it all up, you see; " yes *and* no." [*Smiling.*] I'm glad you made it so plain.

AMES [*thoroughly confused and rather dismayed*]. But what? What was it I made plain?

ISABEL. What you were thinking about *me*. It's perfectly natural you *would* wonder a little about that, too.

AMES. But I didn't. I *assure* you I didn't wonder—

ISABEL [*interrupting*]. Now could you *help* wondering about what you're wondering about?

AMES. But I'm *not!* In*deed* I'm *not!*

ISABEL [*laughing*]. Why, of course you are! You're wondering *just how* romantic I am. That's what you're wondering!

AMES [*much relieved. Sits*]. Oh! Oh, well, perhaps I was wondering a little about *that!* Yes, I—I admit it. You *are* romantic, you say?

ISABEL. I was when I was a child.

AMES [*with some eagerness*]. What were you romantic about then?

ISABEL. When I was a child?

AMES. Yes. What did you find to be romantic about? What—uh—in a *general* way, I mean.

ISABEL [*lightly thoughtful*]. Oh—well, I suppose the same things *you* were being romantic about at the same time—that is, *about* the same time—I suppose. [*She does not smile and speaks without stress.*]

AMES [*smiling nervously, trying to be easy*]. Oh, yes.

ISABEL. I think there was a great romantic influence upon the whole country about that time, don't you?

AMES. Just about—then? [*Slight stress on " then."*]

ISABEL. Yes. I think what did it was the World's Fair.

AMES. You do? Well, there was the San Francisco Fair and the St. Louis one and the—the one at Buffalo and—and, yes, wasn't there one once in Chicago in—ah, in—

ISABEL. Yes, and one in Philadelphia in 1876.

AMES. But I meant: which one was the one you meant made everybody so romantic?

ISABEL [*easily as she sews again*]. I was speaking of the one when I was a child.

AMES. Oh, yes, *that* one. [*He is uncomfortably going on, if he can think what to say.*]

ISABEL [*looking up innocently*]. I know what you're trying to do.

AMES. Why, we were just talking along. I wasn't trying to—to—to—

ISABEL. Why, yes, you were.

AMES. No, no, I—

ISABEL. Yes. You keep on trying to find out how romantic I still *am!*

AMES. Oh! Oh, well—

ISABEL. Oh, I don't mean that I'm as romantic as *you* are, Mr. Ames! The *most* romantic woman isn't so romantic as the *least* romantic man.

AMES. What?

ISABEL. It's very simple. You see, men don't get older.

AMES. Men don't?

ISABEL. No, they don't. They don't get older and they stay young and romantic.

FLORENCE [*outside*]. Mr. Ames! Mr. Ames!

ISABEL. Don't they? Stay romantic?

AMES. Well, I—I—

ISABEL. For instance, when you're interested in anyone, don't you prefer to be alone with them?

AMES. Yes, I do—I am—we are—

FLORENCE [*outside*]. Mr. Ames! Mr. Ames!

ISABEL. Doesn't she mean you?

AMES. Oh, yes, your charming little niece.

ISABEL. Charming! Yes!

AMES. Oh, that doesn't mean that I like all of them. I believe I mentioned last night.

ISABEL. Yes, I believe you did.

AMES. But there is something about this one that—

ISABEL. Yes!

AMES. Yes, indeed! She's your—

FLORENCE [outside]. Mr. Ames! Mr. Ames!

ISABEL. She's calling you, isn't she?

AMES. So it seems.

ISABEL. Hadn't you better—

AMES. Yes. I'll just tell her—perhaps I'd better.

ISABEL. Yes, do.

AMES. Yes, yes, I— [Goes up center, looking off right.]

FLORENCE [outside]. Mr. Ames! [ISABEL rises and goes to left center, listens for a second, and then crosses to door, left.]

AMES. Just a moment! Your aunt and I—oh, have you finished your game? [ISABEL exits door, left.]

FLORENCE [outside]. I'm coming.

AMES. She's coming. [Turns and stares at ISABEL's vacant chair. Goes up center, looks off left. Goes to door down left and looks off.] Well, I— [FLORENCE enters up right.]

FLORENCE [has her racquet but not the net of balls]. I knocked all the balls as far as I could in the shrubbery. He has to hunt till he finds 'em. [Comes down left center.] Then I ran and fixed about that telegram.

AMES [apprehensively]. Oh, no. I really can't—

FLORENCE [lightly]. Don't worry! If you don't like it when it comes, you can just say it isn't important and tear it up, can't you?

AMES. I suppose so. [Disturbed.]

FLORENCE. Attaboy! [Crosses right.]

AMES [nervously, pacing up and down left]. But I—

FLORENCE [seriously]. Is anything bothering you? [She sits on sofa, right.]

AMES [with a rather hurried laugh]. Why, of course not!

FLORENCE. Did Aunt Isabel say—

AMES. She said—she said—I understood her to say that she wasn't your aunt exactly—

FLORENCE [carelessly]. No, she's my great-aunt.

AMES. Yes; so she said.

FLORENCE. Why?

AMES. Of course there are a great many young great-aunts.

FLORENCE [*carelessly*]. Young *great*-aunts? I don't see how they *could* be.

AMES [*looking at her plaintively*]. Oh, I meant comparatively, like your Aunt Isabel.

FLORENCE. Oh, I s'pose Aunt Ellen knows how old Aunt Isabel is, but you know how some women are.

AMES [*hurriedly*]. You mean these miracles?

FLORENCE. No; I mean they don't usually *tell*. I don't see why people get so sensitive about things like that; I'll tell anybody that wants to know, what *I* am; I'm nineteen; *I* don't care! Golly!

AMES [*right*]. Well, it's a subject I'm interested in; always been interested in, I mean. I mean in a *general* way, of course.

FLORENCE. What you gettin' at? Do you always do this when you're alone with people; talk about other women and their ages?

AMES [*hastily*]. No! No, indeed, I don't!

FLORENCE [*coldly*]. If you're so anxious about it, why, I'm on right confidential terms with Aunt Isabel and I *could* ask her right out how—

AMES [*vehemently*]. No! You mustn't think of such a thing. You really mustn't!

FLORENCE. I won't. That is, I won't if you're nice to me. Don't *I* intrigue you *any?*

AMES. You do! Don't you see how much you do?

FLORENCE. I never have had a chance at a man of experience. You wouldn't ever think that I *suffer* terribly, would you?

AMES. *You* do? [*Sits on sofa left of* FLORENCE.]

FLORENCE. I suffer *fearfully!*

AMES. What from?

FLORENCE. Well, from thoughts. I suffer because nobody understands 'em and so I can't tell 'em. I don't know what makes me tell *you* all these things, like this—[*smiles at him trustingly*]—but it's nice, our getting intimate this way, isn't it? [*Going almost straight on.*] Do you remember where you left my slippers?

AMES [*with secret alarm*]. Your slippers?

FLORENCE. Will you see, please? I thought maybe you'd
be so awfully kind as to— [*She sweetly lets the inference be
made as she projects a foot.*]

AMES [*uneasily*]. I rather think your aunt said she was
coming back.

FLORENCE. Don't you remember what you did with 'em?
[*A sweet, slight reproach.*]

AMES. I think I put them—

FLORENCE [*looking about*]. They haven't been taken *out,*
have they?

AMES [*right center*]. I don't *think* so. I didn't see anyone—

FLORENCE. Why, there they are on the hearth!

AMES. Oh, yes, so they are!

FLORENCE. Would it be too outrageous of me to—

AMES. Oh, no, indeed! [*Rises and starts left.*]

FLORENCE. No, over there. [AMES *crosses to fireplace.
Gets slippers.*]

AMES [*glancing apprehensively left*]. I'll be only too delighted! [*He kneels.*]

FLORENCE [*as he helps her to exchange the tennis shoes for
the slippers*]. *My,* it's a relief to be with a man that understands the *deeper* side of life a few *minutes* now and then!
[*None of* FLORENCE'S *speeches should be exaggerated in manner or " pointed."*]

AMES [*nervously*]. I'm glad you like it.

FLORENCE. Is that all? Couldn't you make it any
stronger? Don't you think I'm a *grand* little thing? [*She
bends toward him, apparently earnest.*]

AMES [*smiling wanly but speaking with warmth*]. I do.

FLORENCE. You do—what?

AMES. I do—indeed! [JOHNNIE *enters up right with the
net of tennis balls.*]

FLORENCE [*earnestly*]. Attaboy! You're *sure* you " do indeed "?

JOHNNIE [*up right center, speaking all in a breath*]. Why
don't you try the lady with a pair o' nines, Mr. Ames; we got
a *good* stock o' nine-B's on the top shelf in the store-room!
[AUNT ELLEN *enters left. She comes in rather quickly; her
expression is gracious; but she is astonished to find* AMES *on his
knees before* FLORENCE. *She halts sharply, speaks quickly; and*

at once turns to go out indignantly by the way she has come.]

AUNT ELLEN. *Excuse* me! [*Turns back left.*]

AMES. Oh— [*He would rise, but* FLORENCE *checks him.*]

FLORENCE. My other *slipper!*

AMES [*hastily*]. But I— [*He sees* ISABEL *through open door left.*] Oh, gracious! [*Rising.* ISABEL *enters, left.*]

ISABEL [*smilingly and smoothly—as she enters*]. Ellen, dear, I've been looking for you; to meet Mr. Ames. [*Laughing commiseratingly, she comes to them.*] Poor Florence, is she having trouble with her new slippers again? [ISABEL *points to tennis shoe* AMES *has under his arm; he immediately throws it on sofa.*] I'm afraid you'll think we're terrible people to make *use* of our visitors, Mr. Ames.

AMES [*who has risen*]. Oh, no, not at all, not at all, indeed!

ISABEL [*has crossed to right of him,* ELLEN *is left center*]. I'm afraid we do, though. You'll make up your mind never to come here again! [*With a gesture indicating* ELLEN.] I think I told you I wanted you to meet my other—ah— [*She is speaking with inconsequent cheerfulness—and tapers the sound off as he turns toward* ELLEN. ISABEL, *smilingly nodding toward* ELLEN.] Ellen, dear, this is Mr. Ames.

AMES. Ah, ah— [*He bows.*]

AUNT ELLEN [*non-committal*]. How do you do?

ISABEL. Mr. Ames, Ellen is my other niece.

AMES. Your other—how do you do! [*With a blank expression. He makes an inarticulate sound and stands in an instantaneously arrested attitude.*]

ISABEL [*easily*]. Now you know my whole family; my niece and my great-niece. They're both the greatest comfort to me.

AMES [*hastily*]. Oh, yes. Thank you!

ISABEL [*lightly turning from him*]. And, Florence, if you've finished with the—the footwear— [ELLEN *sits by the table, left center.*]

AMES. Oh, yes, we've finished.

ISABEL [*sunnily including* JOHNNIE *and speaking as if she were trying to think of something entertaining for them*]. Then wouldn't—wouldn't you three like to—wouldn't you three like to dance or something?

AMES. What?

ISABEL [*crossing to* ELLEN *near the table, left center*]. You must all go right on entertaining yourselves just as if we weren't here. We *love* to look on, don't we, Ellen?

AUNT ELLEN [*with a glance toward* FLORENCE'S *feet*]. Yes, when they behave. [*Sits left of table—*ISABEL *sits right of table.*]

ISABEL [*laughing to* ELLEN *on this, then at once speaking to the other group*]. Can't you think of *anything* to amuse yourselves? [*Then as with a quick afterthought, not seriously said, yet perhaps meant.*] You don't mind our being here, do you?

FLORENCE [*jumping up*]. Of course not! Turn on that record!

ISABEL. Yes. Music, Johnnie! [JOHNNIE *goes up.*]

AUNT ELLEN [*grimly, to* ISABEL, *who is taking her seat by the table*]. But they don't dance; they only waggle. It's fearful! [JOHNNIE *pauses.*]

ISABEL. Oh, but they love it so; they mustn't be disappointed. [*To the others.*] She doesn't really mind; you can dance. [*She sits, taking up her " work."*]

FLORENCE. Attaboy! [*She seizes* AMES' *hand.*]

AMES [*nervously*]. *I* don't know these new dances!

ISABEL. She'll teach you. Music, Johnnie! [JOHNNIE *turns on the record.*]

FLORENCE [*forcing* AMES *to dance*]. C'm on! I never *heard* of a man that couldn't dance with *me!* Ouch! [*She hops, her foot slightly injured, but keeps on dancing.*]

AMES [*as she cries out*]. Murder!

ISABEL [*under cover to him; he is close to her*]. Walk. Just walk. That's all you need to do. [*He does better upon this.*] That's it; just walk.

FLORENCE [*to* AMES]. Isn't it divine? [HENRY *enters up right.*]

ISABEL [*indulgently, to* AUNT ELLEN]. Isn't it delightful to see them so happy? [HENRY *comes down to* ISABEL. *He has a folded telegraph blank in his hand. She observes him.*] It isn't time for Mr. Ames' train, Henry?

HENRY. No'm. [*He shows the blank.*]

ISABEL. Oh! Something for me? [*She rises and extends her hand for the blank.*]

FLORENCE [*seeing this*]. *Oh,* murder! [*Under her breath. They stop dancing, left center.*]

ISABEL [*as* HENRY *hands her the blank*]. What is it?

HENRY [*as* ISABEL *examines the blank*]. I don't rightly know, ma'am. I was told about it in such a hurry. [*He glances nervously at* FLORENCE.] I may not 'a' got my instructions just exactly.

ISABEL [*puzzled*]. Your "instructions"? Oh, this isn't really a telegram. No; there's no envelope and date, and it's written in such a bad backhand I can hardly—oh! [*She speaks as though with a sudden revelation, comprehending, and glances quickly at* FLORENCE.] Oh, I see. [*Rises.*] I don't think it's for me, Henry. [*Hands telegram to* HENRY.]

FLORENCE. Here, let *me!* [*She comes to the rescue, seizes the blank, hands it swiftly to* AMES, *who stands dismayed.*] You see, Mr. Ames wired his partners from here and so this must be from them. Of—*course* it's a telegram; isn't it, Mr. Ames?

ISABEL [*gently insistent*]. Is it, Mr. Ames?

AMES [*desperately*]. *I* can't read it!

ISABEL. It is a difficult handwriting. [*She knows it is* FLORENCE'S *hand, though somewhat disguised.*]

FLORENCE [*taking the blank hastily*]. *I* can read most *any* hand. Why, yes, it's *perfectly* plain. It says: "No business in the office to-day. If you wish to remain where you are no reason whatever for returning to New York. Signed Witherspoon and Ames." He told me himself he had a partner named Witherspoon. [*Goes back of table.* JOHNNIE *stops phonograph.*]

ISABEL [*to* AMES]. Oh, then it is a real telegram? [*She knows, of course, it isn't.*]

AMES [*as* FLORENCE *turns quickly toward him*]. Why, it—ah—seems to be.

ISABEL. Oh, then you'll—you'll stay? [*If he stays it appears that he stays upon* FLORENCE'S *urgence.*]

AMES. Why—I—I—

ISABEL [*covering her real feeling*]. Mr. Ames won't be going to the station, Henry. [HENRY *exits up left.* FLORENCE *has carelessly set the blank upon the table, after reading it, her fingers resting upon it, but* AUNT ELLEN *draws it away to look at it,* FLORENCE *turning as if to reclaim it.*]

AUNT ELLEN [*rather excitedly*]. But there isn't even an *envelope;* it isn't a real *telegram;* the writing's queer but it *looks* exactly like *Flor—* [*She finishes the word, but* ISABEL *cuts her off loudly on "Flor."*]

ISABEL [*pushing the bell-button, on left wall*]. Music, Johnnie! Isn't it lovely? *Now* you can dance all day! [*She turns to center as she speaks, and limps suddenly. And says "Oh, oh!" as if in pain.* JOHNNIE *has started the vocalion at her first word. It plays softly.* FLORENCE *has seized* AMES' *hand with a jubilant "Hooray!" as the music starts. But they pause as* AUNT ELLEN *speaks.*]

AUNT ELLEN. What's the matter with you?

ISABEL. Nothing—oh! [*She limps again.*]

JOHNNIE [*coming down anxiously*]. What *is* the matter, Miss Stuart?

ISABEL. Nothing. I'm afraid I sat a little too long on a baggage truck in a cold wind last night, that's all. It's nothing.

FLORENCE. Oh, rheumatism; that's nothing! [FLORENCE *retains* AMES' *hand; moves as if to begin dancing.* MATTIE *enters, left, her right hand behind her.*]

AMES [*plaintively, to* FLORENCE]. Just a— [*He means "Just a moment," but breaks away from* FLORENCE *and crosses to center to speak to* ISABEL.] I *hope* it's nothing very—

ISABEL. No—no—it isn't—it's just a—just a *touch.* You *mustn't* stop dancing. [FLORENCE *crosses to center, takes* AMES *up center to dance.*]

JOHNNIE [*taking her arm decisively*]. Here! *I'll* look after *you,* Miss Stuart; I'd *prefer* to. [*He gives* FLORENCE *a bitter look.*]

ISABEL. Thank you, Johnnie. [*To* MATTIE.] Did you find them, Mattie?

MATTIE [*hurriedly*]. Ya don't want to put 'em on *here,* do you?

ISABEL [*quiet pathos.*] No, I'll— [*As if to go out left.*]

JOHNNIE. Put what on?

ISABEL. Nothing.

MATTIE [*bringing her hand from behind her, showing an old pair of rather large, flat black slippers. Not displaying*

them pointedly to audience]. Them. I don't mind lendin'
'em to you, but—

ISABEL [*quickly, checking her*]. I thought perhaps they
might help me, but not—not— [*"Not now and here," she
means; the scene is hurried.*]

JOHNNIE [*taking the slippers, speaks quickly and emphatically*]. *Why* not? Why, certainly! You let me put—
'em on for you, Miss Stuart. I'd *prefer* to! I'd very *much*
prefer to! Here! You better lie down. [*He is conducting
her to the sofa, her limp increasing a little.*]

ISABEL [*trustfully*]. Do you think I'd better lie down,
Johnnie?

JOHNNIE [*severely, to* MATTIE]. Whyn't you fix those
pillows for her? [ISABEL *lies down.* MATTIE *hastily obeys
the suggestion.*] She's all tired out. And I guess she's had
enough to make *anybody* tired! [*He takes off her slippers.*]

AMES. What *is* the matter, Miss Stuart?

JOHNNIE [*quickly, sharply*]. Why, she's been made awful
tired and she's got rheumatism and *every*thing!

ISABEL. Oh, no; not quite!

JOHNNIE [*to* MATTIE]. Put that wrap over her.

AMES [*starting to stoop to fix her slippers*]. Won't you let
me—

ISABEL [*stopping him*]. Oh, *no!* You must go on on
dancing.

AMES. But I— [AMES *stares all the time incredulously
at* ISABEL. So *does* AUNT ELLEN, *across left.*]

ISABEL. I'm so much trouble, Johnnie— [*Pointing to the
slippers.*] Aren't they awful!

JOHNNIE [*as he puts them on*]. No'm, they're not. I
prefer 'em myself! I very *much* prefer 'em! [*He puts her
other slippers defiantly under his arms.*] You just lie back and
rest, Miss Stuart. I'll look after you.

ISABEL. Thank you, Johnnie. [*She lies on sofa, head at
right of sofa, facing center.*]

FLORENCE. Louder, Mattie! [MATTIE *opens vocalion to
its loudest.* FLORENCE *seizes* AMES, *and they dance.*]

JOHNNIE. If you can rest with all this going on? [AMES
and FLORENCE *dance over to left front of table, go around table
and come to center.*]

ISABEL. That's right! That's right! [*Referring to the*

dance.] Isn't it lovely to see the young people so happy? [AMES *and* FLORENCE *start to whirl around in center,* AMES *looking at* ISABEL. ISABEL, *as if beating time, saying "One, two, one, two."*]

[CURTAIN.]

NOTE.—This final scene will have to be worked out carefully in rehearsal, beginning slowly; and the sequence, as shown here, may need altering when it is worked out. The effect is to bring the curtain down not on a "curtain line" but upon a scene of movement and sound conveying the "situation." Johnnie is only earnest and indignantly sympathetic with Isabel here, but the appearance of things *is:* both gentlemen are anxious about Isabel and that Florence is amazed.

ACT III

SCENE

The scene is the same interior shown in the Second Act, the time is late in the afternoon—toward evening—of the same day. The outdoor light, seen through the sun-room windows, has a rosier amber than in the Second Act. A fore-running of the approaching sunset; but the stage is still bright with light.

DISCOVERED

AUNT ELLEN, *as in Act II, sits by the fireplace, which sends out a warm glow; she is crocheting.* MATTIE, *on hands and knees, is facing the cabinet up right. The doors of the cabinet are partly open, revealing shelves of old boxes; old ornaments of various kinds, small vases, silver porringers, etc.; two or three old pistols; rolled papers—old and tied with red ribbon; some old books.* MATTIE *is pawing carefully among these, apparently puzzled.*
Scene to be played quietly and inconsequently; rather quickly.

[MATTIE *discovered rubbing the inside of the left door of the cabinet.* AUNT ELLEN *comes down, center.*]

MATTIE. It certainly ain't here, Miss Ellen.

AUNT ELLEN. But *that's* where it ought to be. Did she tell you to scrape that date off?

MATTIE. I wasn't to say, Miss Ellen. Anyway, it's only half the date was to be scraped off.

AUNT ELLEN. It's very singular! But the rest of it is more singular. [ISABEL *enters, left.*] Did you ask Aunt Isabel?

ISABEL. Did she ask me what, Ellen? [*She limps to center.*]

AUNT ELLEN. Oh, the poor thing. She's limping worse. It's very singular!

ISABEL. What is?

AUNT ELLEN. It's very singular, the Family Bible's missing.

ISABEL. Oh, is that all! [ISABEL *limps to sofa.*]

AUNT ELLEN. Is that *" all "*? Do you realize the date of my *birth* is written in that Bible?

ISABEL [*sits on sofa, lightly*]. Oh, yes; yours is there, too, isn't it? I've always thought fathers were an inconsiderate class of men. When they have a baby they only think of themselves; they go and write down the date in a Bible, even when the baby's a girl. They don't stop to *think*.

AUNT ELLEN [*looking at her with an approach to suspicion*]. What *is* the matter with you?

ISABEL. Do you think something *does* seem the matter with me? Do you *really?* [*She is pleased with the idea that " something " may really be the matter with her.*]

AUNT ELLEN. You haven't got upset this way for quite a long while now; but it certainly isn't the first time, is it, Mattie? [ISABEL *has her lace with her and begins to work.* AUNT ELLEN *doesn't turn her head to make this inquiry, but continues her crocheting.*]

MATTIE [*quickly and casually*]. No'm; it happens every time she has a shooter. Last one was that Philadelphy manwidower; she half-killed him horseback ridin'; and before him that awful youngish one from Buffalo; and then that *old* one—

ISABEL [*quickly, to check* MATTIE'S *list of suitors*]. Never mind the old one. Ellen, there's another Bible upstairs.

AUNT ELLEN. But I'm used to reading my daily chapter from this one.

ISABEL. Don't you suppose you'd find much the same ideas in both of 'em?

AUNT ELLEN [*sharply*]. Aunt Isabel!

ISABEL. Yes, Ellen?

AUNT ELLEN. I suppose you treat me like a child because I'm only your niece!

ISABEL [*reproachfully*]. Ellen, have I ever taken advantage of my position as your aunt?

AUNT ELLEN [*querulous*]. A great many people have very little respect for nieces; and as I'm only your half-niece—

ISABEL [*taking her up indulgently*]. As you're only my

half-niece you have only half as much respect for me as you ought to have?

AUNT ELLEN [*severely going on*]. I don't pretend to fathom your *purpose* in concealing the *Bible* from me—

ISABEL [*shaking her head*]. Oh, I'm not sure that nieces ought to be allowed to look at all the pictures in *any* old Family Bible. . . . But of course I don't admit I did *hide* it.

AUNT ELLEN [*incensed, becoming stately as she goes left*]. I decline to be treated like a child! [*Exits left.*]

MATTIE. She's on! [*Coming down center.*]

ISABEL. She's what?

MATTIE. She knows the Good Book never walked out o' there by itself.

ISABEL [*turning eagerly in her chair*]. Did you do just what I told you to?

MATTIE [*with a gesture to a chair, left center. She tells it quickly without " acting "*]. Yes'm. I waited till he was settin' in here alone a bit ago—so I come in and begun to look around, and I says to myself like, the way you told me, " Well, that's funny," I says, talkin' to myself. " It's funny where sech a thing as that could get to. A great big old Family Bible! " I says. *" What'd* you say was missin'? " he says. So I says, " Excuse me. It's nothin' . . . Only the Family Bible; we always keep it in here." [*With a gesture to the cabinet.*] " So I know it must be around somewheres," I says. Well, he jumped right up. " My goodness! " he says. " Let me help you look for it! " he says.

ISABEL. Yes, Mattie? Did he look all over the room?

MATTIE [*calmly*]. He pretty near took up the floor. Then he went out in the hall and looked under the stairs and under everything else. " Maybe somebody's usin' it fer jest a *while*," he says, " and they'll bring it back here where they got it." " Well," I says—I put this in myself; you didn't tell me to—" well," I says, " they might bring it back here, yes; or somebody might of put it up in the attic." " In the attic? " he says. " I hardly got time to go up there, though," I says. " I do take a terrible interest in Bibles," he says. " Do you think there's any objection to my goin' up in the attic to see? " he says. " Oh, no, sir," I says, " none at all." " Somebody might 'a' put it there, as you *say*," he says. " They often do," he says, " and if you think Miss Stuart wouldn't mind . . ." "Oh, no," I says, "I know she wouldn't. You just go ahead," I says.

ISABEL. Mattie! And he *did?*

MATTIE. Yes'm. I reckon he's still up there.

ISABEL. On the whole, he seems quite excited about it, then?

MATTIE. Well, I never see a man show so much energy tryin' to find the Good Book.

ISABEL. We all ought to be glad this has happened, Mattie.

MATTIE. Why ought we?

ISABEL. We ought to be glad to have such a religious man in the house.

MATTIE [*dryly, going left*]. Yes'm. [*Reflectively.*] I must say I don't blame you fer hidin' it—with all your ages—and the family scandal wrote out in it!

ISABEL. What "scandal"?

MATTIE. About your poor father, ma'am.

ISABEL. Good gracious, Mattie, it isn't a scandal for a man to marry a second time!

MATTIE. Yes'm. At his *terrible age,* it was.

ISABEL. Well, I never reproached him for it, because I shouldn't have been born if he hadn't! Have you seen my other case of needles, Mattie? [*Rises.*]

MATTIE. No'm. What I don't understand's why you wanted him to *know* it was missin'. [*She hopes to be told.*]

ISABEL. No, that's very true. You don't understand that, Mattie. [*Crosses left.*]

MATTIE [*opening the door to go out*]. No'm. [*Blankly.*]

ISABEL. When he comes down—oh, *there's* that case of needles! [*She sees it on the table, left center, and steps toward it.*]

MATTIE [*warningly*]. Sh! He *is* down!

ISABEL. Down *where?* [*She abandons her intention of getting the needles, though she is near them. She turns and goes quickly back, with almost no lameness—to the sofa and resumes her work. MATTIE stares, astonished.*]

MATTIE. I thought you was limpin' this afternoon.

ISABEL [*whispering across to her*]. Sh! I am! It comes and goes. Is he there?

MATTIE [*peering out of the door and looking back, whispering*]. He's lookin' under the hall sofy again! [*She coughs, steps back, and* AMES *enters, left.* AMES *comes in quickly, with the frown of a person intent on a serious search; his eye is on the cabinet, and he has come into the room to go there. He checks himself at sight of* ISABEL *by the fire.* MATTIE *observes them both with interest.*]

AMES [*center*]. Oh! Oh! How do you do?

ISABEL [*working*]. How do you do?

AMES. I hope you're—better? [*He glances at the cabinet.*]

ISABEL. Oh, yes; it comes and goes; *you* know. [*Touches her knee.*]

AMES [*in a sympathetic tone*]. No, I don't; I've never had it, so *far*.

ISABEL [*rising and looking about*]. Not " so far."

AMES [*rather eagerly*]. Are you *looking* for something?

ISABEL. Yes, I *had* it a little while ago, too; it's stupid of me! [*Rises.*]

AMES [*eagerly, quickly, hoping she means the Bible*]. Can't you remember where you put it? Did you have it in *here?*

ISABEL. Yes. [*She moves slowly and her lameness is now somewhat more apparent.* MATTIE, *kept by her curiosity, at the door, observes her with enlarging eyes and an opening mouth.* ISABEL *goes on.*] Yes, I'm sure I had it in here—if I could only think where I put it. [*Crosses left.*]

AMES [*eagerly*]. Let *me* look. You really shouldn't move about much, I'm afraid. [*He is already looking about.*]

ISABEL [*plaintively*]. You're so kind! It *is* a little bothersome, at times. [*There is a faint sound like a choke from* MATTIE, *not mirth, but a moral amazement.* ISABEL *turns toward her, at this.*] That's all, Mattie. I shan't want you for anything more.

MATTIE. Yes'm. [*Exits left.*]

ISABEL [*concentrating*]. If I could only think—it *seems* to me I left it *somewhere* over on this side of the room. [*The left side.*]

AMES [*dubiously*]. I hardly think so. [*He glances behind a large wall chair.*] I already *have* looked all over this— [*Crosses to left to lower end of table.*]

ISABEL [*with a little triumphant emphasis*]. Why, there it is! On the table all the time!!

AMES [*blankly*]. On the table?

ISABEL [*pointing to the little case of needles*]. Yes. Just where I left it, of course! [*He picks it up.*]

AMES [*blankly*]. This? Is this what you mean?

ISABEL [*laughing at him*]. Yes! My needles. What did you think I meant?

AMES. I? I didn't know exactly.

ISABEL. Then what were you looking for?

AMES [*quickly*]. I was looking for your needles, too. I didn't know they were what you wanted, I mean to say, but I wanted to find them if *you* were looking for them.

ISABEL. I see. You didn't know you were looking for them, but you were. I'll take them, please.

AMES. Oh, yes. [*He hands them to her. They are about center, down.*]

ISABEL. Thank you. [*She has stretched out her arm to take the needles, looking at him gravely. Something in her look arrests him and he unconsciously retains his grasp of the little red case; so that for a moment or two their fingers are almost in contact upon it. Their eyes meet, and her expression for that moment becomes one of an almost revealed mockery. He starts slightly; the mockery deepens, and she laughs.*]

AMES [*nervously*]. What are you laughing at?

ISABEL [*turning to go back to sofa*]. It was so peculiar, your looking for something without knowing what you were looking for! [*She changes to a sudden little gasp.*] Oh!

AMES. Are you in considerable pain? [*Comes to her.*]

ISABEL. It just comes and goes. [*She laughs again, gasps again, laughs once more as she goes to the chair.*]

AMES [*nervously*]. Won't you lean on me?

ISABEL [*as before*]. No, no!

AMES [*anxiously*]. Can't I get you something?

ISABEL [*sinking into sofa*]. No; there isn't any in the house.

AMES [*coming toward her*]. I'm so sorry.

ISABEL [*smiling*]. It's gone now. It comes and goes. That is, it comes but it does *go;* you know—like most other things in the world! [*Looking up at him charmingly, wistfully for a moment.*]

AMES. I *must* say—your eyes—

ISABEL. Yes? My eyes? I think I remember your speaking of them this morning.

AMES. Your eyes—

ISABEL [*looking back at her work, speaks with a change to a matter-of-fact tone*]. Ah, what were you going to say about them?

AMES [*set aback*]. I was going to say— [*He assumes a solicitous tone.*] I was going to *say,* don't you think you ought to get *advice* about using them for such fine work?

ISABEL. They've held out so well. I think now they'll last my time. Do you have any trouble with yours? [*Casually.*]

AMES. I? Oh, no. I use glasses some*times* for very fine print.

ISABEL. I'm so sorry.

AMES [*laughing nervously*]. Oh, it isn't because of my a— ["*Age,*" *he means to say, but cuts it off.*] I mean it just *happened.*

ISABEL [*consolingly*]. I know. Even *very* young people get these little astigmatisms. *They* don't mean anything.

AMES. There's something I haven't had a chance to explain to you—

ISABEL. Please don't explain anything—especially if it's about a telegram.

AMES. But that telegram *wasn't*—

ISABEL [*declining to listen*]. No, no! Poor man, you *had* to stay, didn't you? [*Affirmative.*]

AMES [*seriously*]. I wanted to!

ISABEL [*with light indulgence*]. Of course. [AMES *turns to center.*] What have you been doing for the last hour or so?

AMES. I? [*He unconsciously looks upward, thinking of the attic.*] I've just been looking about. [*He goes to the cabinet up right.* MATTIE *has left one of the doors ajar.*] You have so many interesting things. [*He quickly and surreptitiously opens the door wider as he speaks and takes a hurried survey of that half of the shelves revealed by the open door.* ISABEL *turns her head only a little, and applies herself to her work. She knows what he is doing without looking directly at him.*]

ISABEL [*as if absently*]. Florence was with you?

AMES [*absently*]. No; she went fishing in your brook with young Mr. White. [*He wishes to open the other door of the cabinet.*]

ISABEL. Fishing? [*She turns her head; and he moves*

down, away from the cabinet, with apparent carelessness.]
Did she wear her rubber boots?

AMES [*absently repeating*]. "Her rubber boots"? [*Then
with a sudden start, comes down right.*] I don't know! I
don't know *what* her "foot-wear" was; I'm *really* not in the
boot-and-shoe business: I'm a lawyer!

ISABEL [*consolingly, as she rises*]. She won't be gone *long.*
[*She goes toward up left as she speaks.*] I'm so glad you
changed your mind about them.

AMES. About *them?* [*Front of sofa.*]

ISABEL [*nearing the door up left*]. Yes, about the new
generation: the "brazen little hussies"! You frightened me
last night about them!

AMES. Why, how'd I frighten you?

ISABEL. Why, I was afraid you mightn't like my great-
niece. Under the *circumstances,* you see—well, that would
have been too bad, wouldn't it? [*She gives him a glance of
quick smiling mockery over her shoulder, and passes out of the
door up left. He stares after her, perplexed; passes his hand
hurriedly over his brow; then goes to the cabinet; opens its
other door and stoops to look within; ISABEL reënters down
left, having gone out only to see if he would go to the cabinet.
She sees him there as she comes in.*]

ISABEL [*apologetically*]. I'm afraid— [AMES *turns to
her.*] I'm afraid I left my work here. [*She comes down toward right.*]

AMES [*embarrassed, moving hastily away from the cabinet*].
Ah—I was—your work? Let me find it for you. [*In his
nervousness he goes to the table, left center, to look for it.*]

ISABEL. Oh, no. Don't bother. I think I left it on the
sofa. [*She reaches the chair.*] Yes. [*She sits on sofa.*] I
think I'll stay here, after all, if you're sure I won't be interrupting you.

AMES. Interrupting me! Why, *I'm not* doing anything.
What in the world do you mean?

ISABEL. You spoke of our having interesting things. I
didn't want to interrupt your looking at them.

AMES. Oh! [*A puzzled "Oh, that's-what-you-meant" is
what he expresses.*]

ISABEL [*placidly*]. I noticed you were interested in that
cabinet.

AMES [*somewhat relieved*]. Yes; so I was. [*He goes to it and completes his investigation.*] Yes, indeed. [*He sees that the Bible is not there, and adds, in a blank tone:*] Yes, it's a very interesting old piece.

ISABEL. Do you think so?

AMES. I'm not an expert—on periods, but I'd call it a very fine, quaint old piece.

ISABEL [*with a little too much serenity*]. Yes, they had it made for a present to me on my fifteenth birthday.

AMES. Oh, oh! I see, it's a reproduction. It was made for you—your fifteenth birthday?

ISABEL. Yes; it had an inscription with the date on it.

AMES [*trying to conceal his sudden great interest*]. It had? An *inscription* with the . . . where? [*He looks quickly over the top and sides of the cabinet as he speaks.*] Where's there any da—*where's* there any inscription? I don't see an inscription.

ISABEL. I think it's inside the door on the left.

AMES [*swinging the door open instantly and putting on his glasses*]. On the left. Yes. It says: "To Isabel Stuart. On her sixteenth birthday, June thirteenth." [*He begins the reading rapidly but slows up and looks more and more closely at the inscription, which is in small gilt letters; and the concluding words are slow with bafflement. He repeats:*] "Fifteenth birthday. June thirteenth." That's all it says. The rest seems to have been—uh—scraped off.

ISABEL [*lightly*]. Oh, that was only the year they gave it to me. I suppose the figures have been worn off—with time. Do you think it's an interesting piece of cabinet making?

AMES [*blankly, giving up the figures*]. Yes, very. A very interesting piece indeed, I should say!

ISABEL [*as if a little absently*]. Have you ever noticed how disappointing most fine quaint old pieces are when you come to look inside of 'em?

AMES. Yes, that's true; they often are. [*Glances at cabinet.*]

ISABEL. We try to do better with that one; we keep relics in it; daguerreotypes, all sorts of things—the Family Bible and— [*Then, as by a casual thought.*] Oh—Mattie tells me it's *missing*—by the way. She said you were so kind about it.

AMES [*flustered*]. She did? She said— [*Comes to center.*]

ISABEL [*smiling gratefully*]. She said you helped her look for it.

AMES. Oh, that was nothing. Nothing at all!

ISABEL. She said you were *so* kind.

AMES. Oh, no! Not at all!

ISABEL [*with benevolent appreciation*]. It's a little thing, of course, to stop and help a servant like that, but it's the little things that show our characters. We learn that in Sunday-school, don't we? It was so thoughtful of you to stop and help poor Mattie like that!

AMES [*hurriedly*]. Oh, no; you mustn't praise me for it. It was nothing at all.

ISABEL [*smiling wistfully and observing him as if rather wondering*]. Do you think you seem a little different to-day, from last night?

AMES. Oh, no. Not at all.

ISABEL. Don't *you* notice it?

AMES. Why, no, of course not. Not at all.

ISABEL. Last night you were—well, you were quite— fluent! But all day you've hardly said anything except " Oh, no, not at all, of course not " or " *Nothing,* oh, nothing at all."

AMES. Oh, no, not at—that is to say, I—

ISABEL [*rises—sympathetically*]. Is it because you can't *think* of anything else to say?

AMES. Oh, no, not at—no! No, it isn't because of that; not at—not a *bit!*

ISABEL [*solicitously*]. You do seem to be *thinking.* I can see you're doing *that;* but why don't *you tell* me *what* you're thinking?

AMES. Because I'm really not.

ISABEL. You're not thinking?

AMES. No. Not *about* anything, I mean.

ISABEL. Is it something you won't tell me, or something you *can't* tell me?

AMES. It's nothing. It's nothing at—nothing *whatever!* Nothing *whatever!*

ISABEL [*sympathetically*]. Can't you think of *anything* else to say?

AMES [*desperately, yet feebly*]. Why, yes, of course. Of

course I can. Anything at all; anything. [*Goes around table and crosses to left center.*]

ISABEL. You don't think *I've* changed since last night, do you? You aren't *disappointed* in me, are you?

AMES. Why, of course I'm not. Not at—certainly not. Why, no; not—

ISABEL. "Not at all!" "Certainly not!" And *you* haven't changed, have you?

AMES. Why, no—not at—

ISABEL [*going nearer to him, reproachfully*]. Not at all! Why, of course not! Not at *all!* Nothing whatever! [*She turns up.*]

AMES [*flustered*]. What on earth do you mean?

ISABEL. Why, that's what you were going to say, wasn't it? You haven't changed, have you? [*Finishing with quick reproach.*]

AMES. Why, of course not. Not at—no! I wouldn't!

ISABEL [*approvingly*]. That's all I meant! You wouldn't! When you've done a thing, you're the sort of man that stands by it, no matter what!

AMES [*astounded, breaking out*]. My soul! I believe you're making fun of me!

ISABEL. Why, of *course* I'm not! Not at all!

AMES [*with plaintive vehemence*]. But you say one thing and you seem to mean something else, and you seem to mean one thing and you say another! No *wonder* I can't say anything but "Not at all" and "Nothing at all"! [*Crosses right.*]

ISABEL. But, don't you see, I'm just trying to get us better acquainted with each other! I think we *ought* to be, don't you?

AMES [*subsiding to feebleness*]. I should think it would be a good thing, yes, indeed.

ISABEL. Let me see. I've told you why I never married. Isn't there something in particular—isn't there *some*thing else you'd like to know? Can't you think of anything at all? [*At each one of these interrogatories he seems about to speak; then checks himself and dumbly shakes his head. She insists.*] You're sure there isn't *anything*? [*She comes down closer, facing him. He shakes his head again.*] And you feel profoundly happy?

AMES [*with a manful effort*].   Yes, indeed!

ISABEL [*with a culmination of bitterness but not in a bitter tone*].   I believe that's the noblest *effort* I ever heard any man make!   [*Emotion chokes her a very little bit.*]

AMES.   Effort?

ISABEL [*covering her emotion by speaking quickly, but her voice shakes a little. She goes up center*].   Yes! It *was!* But don't be afraid! Mr. Ames! I *really* didn't expect you to be different from other men; you've done your best and you shall have your reward!

AMES.   *What* " reward "?

ISABEL [*a little chokingly, as she looks off up right*].   I think Johnnie White's bringing it. I think it's a message. [*She turns aside with some pathos.*]

AMES.   What " message "?   [JOHNNIE *enters gloomily up right. He wears an old knickerbocker suit, rough, muddy shoes, and he leaves an old rod and basket near the door. He comes down center and looks coldly at* AMES.]

JOHNNIE [*with a movement of his head to up right, speaks to* AMES *deliberately*].   She's—uh—she's sittin' out on a limb of a willow tree that sticks out over the water and she wants you to come and look at her.

AMES [*frowning*].   *Who's* sitting on a limb and wants me to come and look at her?

JOHNNIE.   Her.

AMES.   " Her "?

JOHNNIE [*coldly*].   I expect you know I mean Florence by this time, Mr. Ames.

AMES [*incredulous*].   She *sent* you for me?

JOHNNIE [*with the same even gloom*].   She got herself out on this limb and she looked over and took a look at herself in the water. Then she said, " Well, I do look right cunning out here, don't I? "   " Are we goin' to do any fishin'? " I asked her. Then she said, " I wish Mr. Ames was here. "   " What for? To look at you on that limb? " I asked her.   " I'll go get him for you. "   " Don't let him know I *sent* for him, " she told me. " No, I won't, " I told her. " He wouldn't even guess when he comes out and *looks* at you that you want him to! Oh, no; he wouldn't! "   That limb she's sittin' on, it's pretty old, and it might not hold her up *too* long, so don't you guess you'd better go, Mr. Ames?

AMES. I?

ISABEL [*gently*]. Yes, please do.

AMES [*a little sharply, to* JOHNNIE]. I think it would be much better if you'd go back and get her down from that limb and go ahead with your fishing, Mr. White. [*Turns away to right.*]

JOHNNIE [*still in gloom*]. Fishin'? *She* never meant *that kind.* I think you better go, because—from what I know of her she'll sit there either till you come and see how cunning she looks or else falls in the water.

ISABEL. Won't you please go and bring her in?

AMES [*doggedly*]. Oh, certainly, if you ask me. [*He goes abruptly up right.*]

ISABEL [*hurriedly, graciously*]. Of course I don't mean for you to hurry *back* with her. [*To piano.*]

AMES [*with some coldness*]. Thank you! [*Exits up right.* ISABEL *looks after him rather pathetically.*]

JOHNNIE. She's—she's goin' to get him, Miss Stuart. [*Up center.*]

ISABEL [*turning down blankly. Sits right of table left.* JOHNNIE *comes down center*]. What?

JOHNNIE. She's made up her mind, and there's just one thing my life's taught me and that is when a girl like her really starts after an older man—well, you know she's goin' to make him lift her down from that tree.

ISABEL [*quietly*]. Oh, yes, certainly.

JOHNNIE [*with a sudden change, coming to her solemnly*]. Miss Stuart; I'd like to see a great deal more of *you* in the—in the future—as—it—were—than we have in the—in the *past* as—it—were.

ISABEL [*quiet wonder*]. Why, what are you talking about, Johnnie?

JOHNNIE. What I've been thinkin', why, you take a person's *character,* especially you take a *woman's* character, and no matter what's the difference between her age and some younger man that thinks a lot of her character age, because she's settled down and quit her foolishness the way you have, Miss Stuart, well, it's the difference between a character like that and one that's got to make a collection of every old man she *sees,* no matter what his age is, so what I mean; why, this bein' used just for a messenger boy, I better *cure* myself and get over it, and the best way'd be to find some character I could look up to and get a sacred feeling about.

ISABEL [*incredulous*]. Do you mean *me,* Johnnie?

JOHNNIE. Yes'm; that's why I'd like to see more of you in the *future*—as—it—were. Will you?

ISABEL. Johnnie White, what *are* you up to?

JOHNNIE. Well, you've read *Henry Esmond*—or have you?

ISABEL. Yes.

JOHNNIE. Well, *he* had that sacred feeling the way a younger man does about a woman some older than he was, wasn't he, didn't he? [*Affirmative.*]

ISABEL [*she jumps up*]. You funny, *funny boy!* You think you'll make Florence jealous!

JOHNNIE [*earnestly*]. No'm; I don't care much whether she is or not, not much. I *mean* it!

ISABEL [*laughing*]. You mean you're a little cross with her for a few minutes, till she brings you around.

JOHNNIE. No'm, I *mean* it! I expect it would do her good— D'you see the way she looked at me when I said I *preferred* to, this morning? But what I mean is, about *you,* why, I *mean* it!

ISABEL [*still amused*]. You don't mean you've got a sacred feeling about me, Johnnie—White!

JOHNNIE. Well, there aren't many people'd understand but I'd *like* to think I've got a kind o' sacred feeling about you, instead of just a messenger boy, because I look up to you, because you're so *different* from her. Won't you let me?

ISABEL [*laughing, but rather touched*]. What nonsense!

JOHNNIE [*pathetically in earnest*]. Yes, but won't you? You know how she acts. *Won't* you let me?

ISABEL [*with amused indulgence, putting her arm lightly, affectionately, round his shoulders*]. Why, yes, if you *want* to, you dear thing! [FLORENCE *enters briskly up right just on the moment, but halts abruptly. She wears a " fishing costume" of a most effective kind.*]

JOHNNIE [*fervently*]. I *do* want to! [*He takes her other hand.*]

FLORENCE [*laughing rather loudly, with some disquiet of mind*]. Well; of all the foolish *sights*—what are you two *doing?*

JOHNNIE [*giving her a very short glance over his shoulder, speaks very gently and solemnly to* ISABEL]. Let's sit over there. [*He means the sofa, across the room. They are left center. He leads her.* ISABEL *is controlling amusement, but is rather tenderly pleased and touched by* JOHNNIE'S *absurdity.*]

ISABEL [*as they move toward right*]. Where is Mr. Ames?

FLORENCE. He's bringin' my fishin' traps. [*Then sharply.*] What *is* the—?

JOHNNIE. Lean on me. I *prefer* it!

FLORENCE. Is Aunt Isabel's rheumatism worse?

ISABEL. Oh, no! [*Emphatically on " oh."*]

JOHNNIE [*quietly*]. No. It isn't lameness. [*He looks continually at* ISABEL.]

FLORENCE. Then what is it?

ISABEL [*as they reach the sofa*]. Did you want me to sit here with you, Johnnie?

JOHNNIE [*solemnly*]. Yes. Let's sit here. This is the place I meant. [*They sit.*]

FLORENCE. Well, of all the foolish looking people I ever saw— [*She is moving up center as if to go out, but stops as* JOHNNIE *speaks. Then goes down right to chair below fireplace.*]

JOHNNIE. She couldn't understand. It's the difference in your character. She couldn't *ever* understand. [ISABEL *covers her mouth with her hand and clenched kerchief.*]

FLORENCE [*puzzled and beginning to be annoyed*]. What *are* you two—it really *was* a little queer, Aunt Isabel!

ISABEL. What was queer, dear?

FLORENCE [*laughing rather uncomfortably*]. Why, to walk in here and find you *locked* in an embrace with Johnnie White!

ISABEL [*choking down her amusement*]. Oh, dear! Did you *see* that, Florence?

FLORENCE [*still laughing thinly*]. And after last *night*— well, I guess the less said about *that* the better!

ISABEL. Yes, indeed, dear!

FLORENCE [*getting sharper*]. It seems to me your conduct is certainly open to interpretation.

ISABEL. Yes, Florence, I'm afraid I'm a wild thing!

FLORENCE. Why, you've got poor Mr. Ames so upset he isn't *normal*.

ISABEL. Isn't he? [*With more serious eagerness.*]

FLORENCE. I happened to be on the branch of a tree and he just said to "come down and go in the house, you were worrying about me." [*She imitates a brisk, rather peremptory, tone.*]

ISABEL [*quickly*]. Did he?

FLORENCE [*not "ugly" but reproachful*]. I don't believe you want *any*body to be nice to me; you just want to flirt with every man in the world, yourself! [*Starts up right.*]

ISABEL. But I don't *know* 'em all!

JOHNNIE. She couldn't understand!

FLORENCE [*very sharply, as this repetition goads her*]. I couldn't understand *what?* [*Comes back down right.*]

JOHNNIE [*to her coldly*]. Did you ever read *Henry Esmond?*

FLORENCE. No, I didn't! [*Sits on arm of armchair.*]

JOHNNIE. I expect not. You *aren't* intellectual particularly, Florence. It's by William Makepeace Thackeray.

FLORENCE. Well, what o' that?

JOHNNIE. Oh, nothing. Only he was kind o' carried away with a light weight for a while.

FLORENCE. This William Makepeace was?

JOHNNIE [*serenely*]. No. Henry Esmond was. It didn't last very long. Some novels are a good deal like life. [*To* ISABEL.] *She* couldn't understand.

FLORENCE [*raising her voice incredulously*]. Are you in earnest?

JOHNNIE [*ignoring her*]. If she lived to be a hundred she couldn't understand, could she?

ISABEL [*whimsically, gently, to him*]. I don't believe she could! [AMES *enters up right, carrying* FLORENCE'S *rods and basket.*]

FLORENCE [*stung*]. No! Well, if I *do* live to be a hundred I hope I'll understand how to behave at that age! [AMES *turns to go out again, right, as if to avoid a family scene, saying, "I beg your pardon."*]

ISABEL [*seeing him*]. Oh, don't go, Mr. Ames. [AMES *comes down center.*] It's nothing. [*She is gently cheerful.*]

JOHNNIE [*to* FLORENCE]. Aren't you ashamed *any?*

FLORENCE. Me? For saying if *I* live to be a hundred I hope I'll know better than to let mere adolescents talk mush to me! Golly, no!

ISABEL [*to* AMES]. I'm afraid she means her great-aunt.

FLORENCE. I should say I do!! [*Crosses center.*] Why, last month there was a three-times widower hangin' round here; he wasn't four *minutes* under eighty, and a week before it was a child about nineteen. Last night it was Mr. Ames and *now* it's Johnnie White; and they *began* with a fond *embrace!* I *saw* it!

ISABEL [*to* AMES]. Yes, she did!

FLORENCE. Sometimes she doesn't act more'n sixteen! [*Crosses right, back of sofa.*]

ISABEL [*rises*]. There, Mr. Ames, you have me!

AMES. I beg your pardon!

ISABEL. My portrait! Drawn by my *great*-niece! I flirt with three-times widowers and with children of nineteen and with you and with Johnnie White, and Johnnie and I began with a fond embrace. To finish it! I'm a hundred years old and I'm sixteen years old! So there, my friend, you *know* me! [*She curtsies to him, and moves rather quickly toward the door, left, limping a little.*]

JOHNNIE [*quickly, with a movement toward her*]. Won't you come back and sit here some more?

ISABEL [*checking him, smiling*]. No; not now. But you can run home and change your clothes and come back to dinner.

JOHNNIE [*solemnly eager*]. Can I?

ISABEL. Yes, you can; and I'll be *waiting* for you, Johnnie White! [*She gives* AMES *a little sudden bob of a nod, which seems to daze him, and exits quickly, left.* AMES *sits blankly— right of table left.*]

FLORENCE [*right*]. Well, of all the darn conduct I ever in my life—

JOHNNIE [*center. Coldly*]. Of course it's mysterious to *you;* you couldn't even be *expected* to understand. [*Goes up center.*]

FLORENCE [*coming a step toward him, irritated, speaking all in a breath*]. What *is* the matter with you? [*Follows* JOHNNIE *up center.*]

JOHNNIE. Nothing you'd be able to under—

FLORENCE [*almost shouting*]. Stop it! If you say that to me *again*—

JOHNNIE. I want to say just one last thing to you!

FLORENCE. Oh, you do, do you?

JOHNNIE. It's simply just only this: Hark! A man really does like to have somebody to look up to!

FLORENCE. Well, you don't haf to be *silly* about everybody you look up to, do you?

JOHNNIE [*with a pleasant thought about it and the manner assuming that this thought is beyond her*]. Well, I don't know. I might. Why, yes. Yes—I think a man might feel a good deal that way.

FLORENCE [*incredulously*]. What?

JOHNNIE [*easily, having put her in her place*]. Excuse me, I think that's about all I care to say for the time being. [*He goes up and gets his rods and basket.*]

FLORENCE. Why, you darned little—

JOHNNIE [*with easy superior carelessness, but not smiling*]. I *may* see you later in the evening for a moment or so, if I have time. [*Near door up right.*]

FLORENCE [*quickly, sharply*]. Why, you just told her you're coming back to—

JOHNNIE [*in the same tone as his last speech*]. To dinner— yes—yes. I *said* I may see you across the table or somewhere, prob'ly; thanking you for your kind attention, I beg to remain, et cetera, et cetera. [*Exits up right without smiling. Start to dim outside lights.*]

FLORENCE. Why, you— [*Then turns indignantly to* AMES. *Comes down center.*] Did you ever know any other girl that had an aunt like *my* aunt?

AMES [*shaking his head seriously*]. No—no—I never did!

FLORENCE [*gesturing to the door of* JOHNNIE'S *exit*]. Why, even that poor little *child*—it's terrible! What do *you* think *about* her?

AMES. "What do I"—I don't know; I don't know! I don't know anything *about* her! Not a single thing! [*The scene is rather quick.*]

FLORENCE [*viciously*]. Well, I think I know *one* thing about her.

AMES. You're her niece and you *think* you know *one* thing about her!

FLORENCE. I believe she's been a coquette from the day she was born!

AMES [*repeating*]. "From the day she was—" [*He jumps up sharply.*] Have *you* happened to see the Family Bible?

FLORENCE. *What* Family Bible?

AMES. Your family's. The one they keep in here!

FLORENCE. Well, for heaven's sake, what would I be doin' with it?

AMES. I don't know.

FLORENCE. What do you want it for?

AMES. What do I *want* it for! [*He recovers himself.*] I wanted to see if it's a first edition! I collect first editions!

FLORENCE. You collect first editions of the *Bible?*

AMES. Why, no.

FLORENCE. I thought not. [*Sits on sofa.*] Mr. Ames, do you believe an older man's feeling for a younger woman is deeper than a younger woman's feeling for an older man?

AMES. I don't know.

FLORENCE. Won't you sit here?

AMES. Very well. [*Sits on sofa, left of* FLORENCE.]

FLORENCE. Before I settle down or anything, I think I ought to have the experience of a serious affair with some older man. [*Start to dim the stage lights here, very slowly.*]

AMES. Oh!

FLORENCE [*giving him a lovely smile*]. Oh, dear. I wish I had my slippers on instead of these. [*She holds up her booted feet plaintively.*]

AMES [*rising nervously*]. Oh, I think you look *very* well in boots!

FLORENCE [*frowning*]. They're so heavy. I *do* wish I had my— [*She is interrupted by the opening of the door, left.* MATTIE *enters there, bringing a pair of pretty patent leather slippers.* FLORENCE, *staring.*] Well, for heaven's sake; *just* as I was sayin' I wanted 'em. [AMES *sees the slippers in* MATTIE'S *hand, turns and strides hurriedly up to the sunroom.* FLORENCE *goes on.*] How in the— [*She checks herself and at a thought speaks decisively.*] Mattie! That's no mere *coincidence!*

MATTIE [*bringing the slippers and setting them on the floor before* FLORENCE]. No'm. Your Aunt Isabel told me to listen at the door—

FLORENCE. What? [AMES *turns sharply and stares at* MATTIE.]

MATTIE [*going on casually*]. Your Aunt Isabel told me to

listen at the door till I heard you begin talkin' about changin' your *footwear* and then to bring 'em in for you.

FLORENCE. She told you to listen at the—

MATTIE [*casually*]. Yes'm; she says to be perfeckly honorable and pay no attention till I heard the word "slippers," and she says the rest of the conversation wouldn't be worth my while, anyway. [*Exits left.*]

FLORENCE [*frowning, puzzled. Stares thoughtfully at the closing door, then turns front*]. Well, if that isn't queer! [*Emphatically.*]

AMES. No! It's no queerer than anything else! [*Coming down right.*]

FLORENCE. Well, after all, now that my slippers *are* here—

AMES [*nervously*]. I don't think I'd—I don't think I'd better!

FLORENCE [*rising, concentrating disapprovingly*]. Well, what *do* you think?

AMES [*with vehemence*]. Nothing! [*He goes up to the sun-room. The light outside has grown rosier and inside it is a little darker. The glow from the fireplace brightens.* AUNT ELLEN *enters, left. She has changed her dress for a dark silk, which has a suggestion of state about it.*]

AUNT ELLEN [*left*]. Florence, do you consider that an appropriate costume for the drawing-room?

FLORENCE [*right. Peevishly*]. It ain't one!

AUNT ELLEN. "Ain't"? "Ain't"?

FLORENCE. No, it ain't! It ain't a drawing-room; it's a living-room! If people can't be young again, anyhow they *can* be modern!

AUNT ELLEN [*turning to go out again, left*]. I will withdraw from the room until you—

FLORENCE [*picking up her slippers*]. Murder! Don't go— I apologize, gosh—I apologize without the gosh—I'm going— Oh, murder, I'm tired!

AUNT ELLEN. Tired! Why, you haven't been doing anything compared to your Aunt Isabel.

FLORENCE [*going slowly and wearily up left with a gloomy sigh*]. It seems to me as if I just spent my life dressing! It's all so savorless! [*Suddenly she begins to sing brightly, breaks into a skip, calls back sweetly:*] "See you later, William!" [*Exits up left, skipping and singing.* AMES *is surprised.*

[AUNT ELLEN *looks after* FLORENCE, *disapprovingly, very slightly shaking her head.*]

AUNT ELLEN. You must overlook it, William. Good gracious! I mean— [*She corrects herself hastily.*] Mr. Ames!

AMES. Oh, don't bother.

AUNT ELLEN [*left center*]. She belongs to a very different generation from the one you and I grew up with.

AMES [*right center. Set aback by her " you and I "*]. Ah —yes. Yes, indeed!

AUNT ELLEN [*going slowly toward right*]. You and I were taught a very different behavior toward our elders.

AMES [*gloomily*]. Yes, the—the previous—ah—generations had a very different training, though this one certainly has charm, too. I wonder how many of—uh—*us,* though, can remember just what we were like in our own youth.

AUNT ELLEN [*somewhat surprised*]. Why, I recall my own, perfectly.

AMES [*brightening*]. That's remarkab-ully— [*He changes the word to " remarkably " with a slight vocal struggle in the midst of it.*] Pleasant. Your—ah—aunt, Miss Stuart does, too, and about public events she remembers wonderfully; we were reminiscing this morning; all about Hayes—and— Wheeler and Samuel J. Tilden. Do you happen to remember that campaign?

AUNT ELLEN [*looking at him over her shoulder; she is touching some music sheets on the piano*]. Why, of course.

AMES [*rather dismayed*]. Well, she said *she* thought it was a terrible thing, Hayes—and—Wheeler's not getting elected,

AUNT ELLEN [*with spirit*]. They *were* elected. Anybody that says they weren't is a—a despicable Democrat!

AMES [*hastily*]. Oh, I think they were myself. [*Feebly hopeful.*] I only wondered—I wasn't just able to recall what *year* that campaign was— [*He puts a rising, plaintive interrogative upon this.*]

AUNT ELLEN. It was in 1876, the same year as the Philadelphia Exposition.

AMES. In 1876—oh, yes; it was—ah—a *historical* reference—I see.

AUNT ELLEN. Historical? I went to that exposition myself.

AMES [*he looks at his watch with another feeble murmur of plaintive laughter*]. I'm afraid I—I suppose I'd better be— yes—ah, I suppose I'd better— [*He goes awkwardly left and glances upward, thinking of going to his room upstairs.*] I'd better—ah—I suppose I'd better make—ah— [*At the door.*] Well, I—

AUNT ELLEN [*inquiring rather shortly*]. Yes?

AMES [*wiping his forehead hurriedly*]. Well—thank you. Uh— [*Exit, dazedly, left.* AUNT ELLEN *sits at the piano and begins to play rather softly; she has a fine " touch" and plays with feeling. The light outdoors is the final rosiness of sunset; the firelight sends forth a broad rosy glow; but the rest of the scene is darkened as she plays through an old-fashioned melody. She has played about a dozen bars when a figure enters up left in the sun-room. It is* ISABEL, *but she is not distinctly seen. The glow up, beyond the sun-room windows, is behind her, and it is not until she reaches the table, left center, that the firelight falls upon l.er. She has changed her dress for another suggesting a gayer "smartness" than that previously worn in the act. She still suggests the slight lameness. She is carrying a large and heavy old book. When she reaches the table, the firelight falls on her and we should get a gleam of jewels. She opens the Bible upon the table, and lets it remain open.*]

AUNT ELLEN [*as* ISABEL *reaches the table*]. Is that you, Isabel? [*She does not turn her head.*]

ISABEL. Yes, go on playing, dear. [*She crosses to the fireplace, using her cane, and sits, gazing into the fire. There is a pause, the piano continuing, and then their talk goes on through the playing.*]

AUNT ELLEN. My old tunes are better than Florence's, aren't they? I think music was best of all in my day.

ISABEL [*gently*]. No. It was best in *my* day. [*Crosses right.*]

AUNT ELLEN. No; I think it *began* to fall off by the time *you* came along. Music was best when— *My* day was the best.

ISABEL [*sits in armchair at fireplace*]. Florence will say that some day. Music is best in each one's " day." What a pleasant thing that is; that we all of us see, afterward, that our first youth was best !

AUNT ELLEN. It isn't pleasant to see *anything afterward*.

ISABEL. Well, then, we can always look forward to— something—can't we?

AUNT ELLEN [*struck by this*]. Oh! [*Her hands pause on the keys and she glances round for a moment at* ISABEL.] Oh, I understand what you mean. He was in here a while ago trying to find *out*. *You* know what *I* mean.

ISABEL [*serenely*]. He didn't ask you, though.

AUNT ELLEN. No. You can see he'd be *nice* under any circumstances.

ISABEL [*with a little regret*]. "Nice"? Why, he's the bravest man I've ever seen. He's too plucky to withdraw— some remarks he made to me last night!

AUNT ELLEN [*plays a bar or two; then gravely*]. I wonder if I oughtn't to stop calling you "Aunt" Isabel.

ISABEL. Why? I *am* your aunt.

AUNT ELLEN. My *half*-aunt.

ISABEL. Isn't that plenty?

AUNT ELLEN. I've always liked calling you "Aunt Isabel" for *one* reason; nobody'd think I'm too old to be alive while I've still got an aunt. But it mightn't be consistent now.

ISABEL. Why mightn't it?

AUNT ELLEN [*very seriously, not playing for the moment*]. Well, if anything should *happen*—I really shouldn't *know* how to begin calling Mr. Ames "Uncle William."

ISABEL. Never mind, dear. It *won't* happen.

AUNT ELLEN [*stops playing and turns*]. I *never* could call Mr. Ames "Uncle." [*She is very serious.*]

ISABEL [*thoughtfully*]. You *might* call him "Nephew." [*Rises.*]

AUNT ELLEN. Pooh! [*She plays softly.*]

ISABEL. Why not? Isn't Florence what all men want? Think of father; mother was only nineteen or so when he married her, and he was sixty-five.

AUNT ELLEN. Poor grandfather's weakness in marrying a girl as your mother was oughtn't to be. [*She plays again.*]

ISABEL [*sits on sofa*]. Yes; but there it is. We're like Portia's caskets, we women, and the men come to choose without knowing what they'll find. Silver-and-gold, that's first youth, and it ought to have been written of that silver-and-gold casket: "Who chooses me shall choose what *every* man desires "! But if any man comes to choose *me*—well, a woman past twenty-eight is a thousand—I'll show him only lead!

AUNT ELLEN. I never heard before of a woman that *teased* a man to make him think she was *older* than she was. And if it isn't to make him feel better when he finds *out*—

ISABEL. No, I've just told you why.

AUNT ELLEN. Oh, you can give all the pretty reasons you want to, but I know. You thought you'd test him, and you've been punishing him for even daring to wonder how old you are. [ISABEL *rises to protest, saying, " Oh, I—"*] And he's beginning to suspect. Think how pretty dancing was in my day. [*She begins to play an old waltz.*]

ISABEL. They *were* pretty, the old waltzes.

AUNT ELLEN [*her memory of the music faltering*]. How did that go there? [*She tries to remember by singing it.*] La, la, la—

ISABEL [*rising*]. No, it's this. [*She hums it and beats time, moving a few waltz steps but keeping to a hint of her lameness.*] Yes. That's it. [*She hums and begins to waltz slowly in the same manner as before. ISABEL falls a little and a little more into the spirit of the waltz, never wholly abandoning the hint of lameness; the waltz-time is rather slow but quickens a little and almost imperceptibly. ISABEL moves in and out of the firelight glow as she dances and her scarf floats, following her. JOHNNIE WHITE enters, at the door, left, and stands looking on without surprise. ISABEL sees him, but only nods and continues. He wears a dinner coat.*]

JOHNNIE. Don't you want a partner?

ISABEL [*coming toward him*]. Johnnie White, do you know the *old* waltz?

JOHNNIE. Yes'm. [*Without losing her step she lets her left hand fall lightly upon his shoulder; he catches her step and they dance. The waltz-time is now a little quicker, and AUNT ELLEN plays it with great pleasure. ISABEL dances with a greater abandon until she has almost forgotten the hint of lameness. The sun-room is so dark that the opening of the door up left is unperceived. AMES, who has changed to a dinner coat, enters there, and stands dumbfounded. FLORENCE enters just behind him and comes forward.*]

FLORENCE [*exclaiming loudly. Crosses to up right above*

fireplace]. Well, for heaven's *sake!* What are you doin' *now?*

ISABEL [*startled as she sees* AMES]. Oh! [*She at once remembers her lameness. They stop dancing down right.* ISABEL *goes to center.* JOHNNIE *stays down right, below fireplace.*]

ISABEL. I—I'm afraid I forgot myself for the moment— I—you oughtn't to have tempted me, Johnnie. It might be— dangerous—

AMES [*striding down to her*]. Will you dance with *me— Isabel?*

ISABEL [*a little breathless*]. What?

AMES. Will you dance with me—*Isabel?* [ISABEL *looks at him incredulously.*]

ISABEL. Dance with *you,* Mr. Ames?

AMES. Yes. I *remember* the *old* waltzes.

ISABEL. But perhaps—you don't realize how old they are— or how lame I am?

AMES. I don't care. Won't you dance with me?

ISABEL. Yes. [*She puts her left arm on his shoulder, as she did with* JOHNNIE, *and with a much more pronounced lameness than before, and in very slow time, they begin to waltz,* AUNT ELLEN *playing softly. As they dance.*] So you and I are in the fashion again. They say everybody dances all the time nowadays.

AMES [*with profound earnestness*]. I don't know anything except when I saw you dancing I wanted to dance with you. I do.

ISABEL. Do you? No matter how slowly?

AMES [*crossly*]. Yes, I do!

ISABEL. But *Florence* would like to dance with you again.

AMES. What nonsense!

ISABEL [*suddenly radiant*]. Can't you play any faster than *that,* Ellen? Why don't you turn the lights up, Florence? [AUNT ELLEN *plays suddenly with greater spirit.* FLORENCE *snaps on the lights and is revealed to be laughing inextinguishably.*]

FLORENCE [*slapping* JOHNNIE'S *back with her other hand in her extreme jocosity*]. My! But those ole-fashioned dances are funny! Don't they look *crazy!*

ISABEL [*happily calling to her*]. Do we? [*She discards her lameness entirely during the next few measures. The two*

*dance like happy experts of eighteen. They look at each other
like lovers.* FLORENCE *ceases to laugh and becomes mystified.
So does* JOHNNIE. *They stare, with their mouths open.
Finally* FLORENCE *speaks with the emphasis of complete puz-
zlement.*]

FLORENCE. Well, just look at 'em lookin' at each other!

JOHNNIE [*grinning, but speaking indignantly to her*]. Ain't
you got *any* sense? [AUNT ELLEN *lifts her left hand from
the keys in a passionate gesture, not ceasing to play with her
right. As her back is obliquely to front and right her left
hand is toward* FLORENCE *and* JOHNNIE.]

FLORENCE [*inquiring poignantly the meaning of the gesture*]. What? [AUNT ELLEN *repeats the passionate gesture.*
FLORENCE *is more mystified and also somewhat petulant.*]
Well, I— [JOHNNIE *seizes her hand and drags her quickly
off up right.*]

ISABEL [*not stopping*]. I'm afraid we must stop.

AMES. No!

ISABEL. I mustn't wear you out. [*Upon this, without
looking at them,* AUNT ELLEN *abruptly stops playing in the
middle of a measure. She does not look at them at all, but
goes quickly up and straight off left without turning. They
are unconscious of her, and seem even unconscious that the
piano has stopped or that they have ceased to dance. They
have come to a halt directly up of the table left center and
close by it, looking at each other.*]

AMES [*speaking angrily the instant they and the music stop*].
I want to tell you just this: you've been mocking me every
second since we first met in that God-forsaken railroad station.

ISABEL. No!

AMES [*fiercely*]. You have! Every instant!

ISABEL. Never! Never once! Never! Never!

AMES. You were at it half the day yesterday and as much
of the night as you could stay awake and all day to-day! But
it won't do!

ISABEL. When did you decide I was mocking you?

AMES. I thought so all day, but I knew it when I saw
you dancing with that boy!

ISABEL. Do you mind my dancing with boys?

AMES. No! I'm not jealous. [*His tone is as angry as
before.*] But it came *over* me! You've just *mocked* me!

ISABEL. Can't you imagine a woman's being a little nervous about *one* man's knowing how often the earth's gone round the sun since she was born?

AMES [*with feeling*]. *Am* I the one man?

ISABEL. That's why women are afraid of *every*body's knowing; it might reach the one man. That's the reason a woman *cares* about her age; *he* might care! [*She touches the open Bible on the table.*] Look, Mr. Ames! I'll turn my back while you're looking. [*She walks away from him slowly. AMES puts one hand on Bible but keeps looking at ISABEL.*]

ISABEL [*as he does this, her voice tremulous*]. On the left hand page you'll find all of papa's descendants by his first wife. On the right-hand page you'll see where the poor old darling married again—such a *heathenish* time—afterward—

AMES. That's what I thought. That's why I was looking for your Bible.

ISABEL. Underneath is where you'll find me. [*Her voice trembles a little more.*] Have you found me?

AMES [*with great feeling under his laughter*]. Yes, I have! [*Closes Bible.*]

ISABEL [*weakly*]. Oh, you didn't look? [*AMES crosses to ISABEL, holds out his arms as if to embrace her.*]

AMES [*tenderly*]. Let's sit by the fire, shall we? [*Crosses right. He touches the switch key and the only light is the fire-light. She sits slowly on sofa, looking up at him, and he takes a chair near by. Then FLORENCE is heard laughing gaily off up left, and a moment later she is heard again.*]

FLORENCE [*affecting reproach, off up left*]. All right for *you*, Johnnie White. I'll tell your mother on you!

ISABEL [*softly*]. The fire's pleasant, even in April, isn't it?

AMES. Yes. Do you think you could say to me good night, dear, without the good night?

ISABEL. I think I could—if you're sure you don't mind anything you didn't see in the Bible, dear.

AMES. You infant!

ISABEL. Oh! [*AMES takes her hand, kisses it, and then lifts her hand to his cheek. ISABEL gives a little exclamation of delight.*]

[CURTAIN.]

SELECTED BIBLIOGRAPHY FOR THE STUDY OF DRAMA IN AMERICA

Charlton Andrews
  The Drama To-day, Philadelphia, 1913

William Archer
  A Talk with Mr. Brander Matthews, Pall Mall Budget,
  September 20, 1894, p. 7

George Pierce Baker
  Dramatic Technique, Boston, 1919
  Modern American Plays, New York, 1920:
      Augustus Thomas, *As a Man Thinks*
      David Belasco, *The Return of Peter Grimm*
      Edward Sheldon, *Romance*
      Louis Kaufman Anspacher, *The Unchastened Woman*
      Edward Massey, *Plots and Playwrights*

David Belasco
  The Theatre Through Its Stage Door, New York and
  London, 1919

T. Allston Brown
  A History of the New York Stage, New York, 1903, 3
  Vols.

Richard Burton
  The New American Drama, New York, 1913
  How to See a Play, New York, 1914

Sheldon Cheney
  The New Movement in the Theatre, New York, 1914
  *The Art Theatre; a discussion of its ideals, its organiza-
  tion and its promise as a corrective for present evils in
  the commercial theatre,* New York, 1917

Henry Austin Clapp
> *Reminiscences of a Dramatic Critic,* Boston and New York, 1902

Barrett H. Clark
> *The British and American Drama of To-day,* New York, 1915

Mary Caroline Crawford
> *The Romance of the American Theatre,* Boston, 1913.

Thomas H. Dickinson
> *The Case of American Drama,* Boston and New York, 1915
>
> *Chief Contemporary Dramatists,* First Series, Boston, 1915, contains the following American plays:
>> Clyde Fitch, *The Truth*
>> W. V. Moody, *The Great Divide*
>> Augustus Thomas, *The Witching Hour*
>> Percy MacKaye, *The Scarecrow*
>
> *Chief Contemporary Dramatists,* Second Series, Boston, 1921, contains the following American plays:
>> Eugene Walter, *The Easiest Way*
>> G. P. Peabody, *The Piper*
>> G. C. Hazleton and J. H. Benrimo, *The Yellow Jacket*

John Drew
> *My Years on the Stage,* New York, 1922. (In preparation.)

Walter Pritchard Eaton
> *The American Stage of To-day,* Boston, 1908
> *At the New Theatre and Others: The American Stage; Its Problems and Performances, 1908-1910,* Boston, 1910

Daniel Frohman
> *Memories of a Manager,* New York, 1911

Daniel Frohman and Isaac F. Marcosson
> *Charles Frohman: Manager and Man,* New York, 1916

Clayton Hamilton
>   *The Theory of the Theatre*, New York, 1910
>   *Studies in Stagecraft*, New York, 1914
>   *Problems of the Playwright*, New York, 1917
>   *Seen on the Stage*, New York, 1920

Norman Hapgood
>   *The Stage in America, 1897-1900*, New York, 1901

Archibald Henderson
>   *The Changing Drama*, New York, 1914

Arthur Hopkins
>   *How's Your Second Act*, New York, 1918

Laurence Hutton
>   *Plays and Players*, New York, 1875
>   *Curiosities of the American Stage*, New York, 1891

Arthur E. Krows
>   *Play Production in America*, New York, 1916

A. E. Lancaster
>   *Historical American Plays, The Chautauquan*, Volume
>   XXXI, Cleveland, 1900

Ludwig Lewisohn
>   *The Drama and the Stage*, New York, 1922

Kenneth Macgowan
>   *The Theatre of Tomorrow*, New York, 1921

Percy MacKaye
>   *The Playhouse and the Play*, New York, 1907
>   *The Civic Theatre*, New York, 1912
>   *Community Drama*, Boston, 1917

Burns Mantle
>   *The Best Plays of 1919-1920*, Boston, 1920
>   *The Best Plays of 1920-1921*, Boston, 1921

Brander Matthews
>   *The Historical Novel and Other Essays*, New York, 1901

The Development of the Drama, New York, 1903
Inquiries and Opinions, New York, 1907
A Study of the Drama, Boston, New York, and Chicago, 1910
A Book about the Theatre, New York, 1916
These Many Years, New York, 1917
The Principles of Playmaking, New York, 1919

Brander Matthews and Laurence Hutton
The Life and Art of Edwin Booth and His Contemporaries, Boston, 1907

Hiram K. Moderwell
The Theatre of To-day, London, 1914

Montrose J. Moses
Famous Actor-Families in America, New York, 1906
The American Dramatist, Boston, 1917
The Drama, 1860-1918, Chapter XVIII of Part II, *The Cambridge History of American Literature*, New York, 1921
Representative Plays by American Dramatists, New York, 1918-1921. Vol. I, 1765-1819:
    Thomas Godfrey, *The Prince of Parthia*
    Robert Rogers, *Ponteach; or, the Savages of America*
    Mrs. Mercy Warren, *The Group; A Farce*
    Hugh Henry Brackenridge, *The Battle of Bunker's Hill*
    John Leacock, *The Fall of British Tyranny; or, American Liberty*
    Samuel Low, *The Politician Out-witted*
    Royall Tyler, *The Contrast*
    William Dunlap, *André*
    J. N. Barker, *The Indian Princess; or, La Belle Sauvage*
    M. M. Noah, *She would be a Soldier; or, The Plains of Chippewah*
Vol. II, 1815-1858. (In preparation)
Vol. III, 1856-1917:
    Charles Burke, *Rip Van Winkle: A Legend of the Catskills*
    George Henry Boker, *Francesca da Rimini*

Oliver Bell Bunce, *Love in '76. An Incident of the Revolution*
Steele MacKaye, *Paul Kauvar; or, Anarchy*
Bronson Howard, *Shenandoah*
Augustus Thomas, *In Mizzoura*
Clyde Fitch, *The Moth and the Flame*
Langdon Mitchell, *The New York Idea*
Eugene Walter, *The Easiest Way*
David Belasco, *The Return of Peter Grimm*

A Study Course on the American Drama, Specially Prepared for the American Drama Year of the Drama League of America, 1916

George Jean Nathan
The Popular Theatre, New York, 1918
The Critic and the Drama, New York, 1922
Another Book on the Theatre, New York, 1915

William Lyon Phelps
The Twentieth Century Theatre, New York, 1918
Essays on Modern Dramatists, New York, 1921

John A. Pierce
The Masterpieces of Modern Drama. Abridged in Narrative with Dialogue of the Great Scenes; prefaced with a critical essay by Brander Matthews, New York, 1915. 2 Vols.

Channing Pollock
The Footlights Fore and Aft, Boston, 1911

Arthur Hobson Quinn
The Early Drama. 1756-1860, Chapter II of Part I, *The Cambridge History of American Literature,* New York, 1917
Representative American Plays, New York, 1917:
    Thomas Godfrey, *The Prince of Parthia*
    Royall Tyler, *The Contrast*
    William Dunlap, *André*
    James Nelson Barker, *Superstition*
    John Howard Payne } *Charles II*
    Washington Irving }

Richard Penn Smith, *The Triumph at Plattsburg*
George Washington Parke Custis, *Pocahontas; or, The Settlers of Virginia*
Robert Montgomery Bird, *The Broker of Bogota*
Nathaniel Parker Willis, *Tortesa the Usurer*
Anna Cora Mowatt Ritchie, *Fashion*
George Henry Boker, *Francesca da Rimini*
Dion Boucicault, *The Octaroon, or Life in Mississippi*
Joseph Jefferson, *Rip Van Winkle*
Steele MacKaye, *Hazel Kirke*
Bronson Howard, *Shenandoah*
William Gillette, *Secret Service*
David Belasco
John Luther Long } *Madame Butterfly*
Clyde Fitch, *Her Great Watch*
Langdon Mitchell, *The New York Idea*
Augustus Thomas, *The Witching Hour*
William Vaughn Moody, *The Faith Healer*
Percy MacKaye, *The Scarecrow*
Edward Sheldon, *The Boss*
Rachel Crothers, *He and She*

Oral Sumner Reed
    The Plays of Samuel Woodworth, The Sewanee Review, Sewanee, 1919, Vol. 27

P. I. Reed
    The Realistic Presentation of American Characters in Native American Plays Prior to Eighteen Seventy, Ohio State University Bulletin, Vol. XXII, May, 1919

Arthur Ruhl
    Second Nights, New York, 1914

Oliver Sayler
    The Real Eugene O'Neill, The Century, New York, 1922, Vol. 103, p. 351

E. H. Sothern
    The Melancholy Tale of "Me"; My Remembrances, New York, 1916

L. C. Strang
   Players and Plays of the Last Quarter Century, Boston, 1902. 2 Vols.

Augustus Thomas
   The Print of My Remembrance, New York, 1922. (In preparation)

J. Ranken Towse
   Sixty Years of the Theatre, New York and London, 1916

John A. Weaver
   Eugene O'Neill and Pollyannalysis, Vanity Fair, New York, 1921, Vol. 16, p. 43

William Winter
   Shadows of the Stage, New York, 1892-1895
   Other Days; Being Chronicles and Memories of the Stage, New York, 1908
   The Wallet of Time, Containing Personal, Biographical and Critical Reminiscences of the American Theatre, New York, 1913. 2 Vols.
   Vagrant Memories, New York, 1915

LIST OF AMERICAN PLAYS FOR SUPPLEMEN-
TARY READING

Mary Austin
The Arrow Maker

David Belasco
The Return of Peter Grimm

Alice Brown
Children of Earth

Walter Browne
Everywoman

Edward Childs Carpenter
The Cinderella-Man

Rachel Crothers
He and She

Olive Tilford Dargan
The Shepherd

Richard Harding Davis
The Galloper
The Dictator

William C. DeMille
Strongheart

Beulah Marie Dix and Evelyn G. Sutherland
A Rose o' Plymouth Town

Clyde Fitch
Captain Jinks of the Horse Marines
The Climbers
Barbara Frietchie
Nathan Hale
The Girls

James Forbes
The Famous Mrs. Fair

Zona Gale
Miss Lulu Bett

Eleanor Gates
The Poor Little Rich Girl

William Gillette
Held by the Enemy
Secret Service
Too Much Johnson

Robert Housum
The Gypsy Trail

Bronson Howard
Kate
Shenandoah
Saratoga

Charles Kenyon
Kindling

Charles Klein
The Lion and the Mouse

Edward Knoblock
Kismet
My Lady's Dress

Edward Knoblock and Arnold Bennett
Milestones

Percy MacKaye
A Thousand Years Ago
Jeanne D'Arc
The Scarecrow
Washington the Man who Made Us
Fenris the Wolf

Roi Cooper Megrue
Under Cover
It Pays to Advertise

Marguerite Merington
Captain Lettarblair

William Vaughn Moody
The Great Divide
The Faith Healer

Eugene O'Neill
Beyond the Horizon
The Emperor Jones

Josephine Preston Peabody
The Piper
The Wolf of Gubbio
Marlowe

Edward Sheldon
The Boss
Romance

Harry James Smith
The Little Teacher
A Tailor-Made Man
Mrs. Bumpstead Leigh

Winchell Smith
The Boomerang

Booth Tarkington
Clarence
Poldekin

Booth Tarkington and Julian Street
The Country Cousin

Booth Tarkington and Harry Leon Wilson
The Man from Home
The Gibson Upright

Augustus Thomas
Oliver Goldsmith
As a Man Thinks
The Witching Hour

Alabama
Arizona
The Earl of Pawtucket
In Mizzoura
The Other Girl

A. E. Thomas and Clayton Hamilton
    The Big Idea

Mark Twain and Frank Mayo
    Pudd'n Head Wilson